/.3. 50

Management Information Systems

Management Information Systems

George K. Chacko
University of Southern California
The Systems Management Center

PBI
a petrocelli
book
new york / princeton

Copyright © 1979 Petrocelli Books, Inc. :

Printed in the United States.
1 2 3 4 5 6 7 8 9 10

Dedicated affectionately to our daughter
  ASHIA
who, at fifteen, is keen on
developing her own personal information system
of people, places, and perspectives
to compare, contrast, and calibrate
the miracles of her international inheritance

Library of Congress Cataloging in Publication Data
  Chacko, George Kuttickal, 1930-
    Management information systems.

    Bibliography: p.
    Includes index.
    1. Management information systems. I. Title.
  T58.6.C38   658.4'03   79–15763
  ISBN 0–89433–095–0

Contents

2. ADP Systems in Products, Service, and Research

3. Context E-Context T Combination Index of Decision-Making Situations

PART II MIS (IIS) SEQUENCE

4. MIS (IIS) Sequence 1: Raw Data

5. MIS (IIS) Sequence 2: Pre-Information

6. MIS (IIS) Sequence 3: Information

PART III: MIS (IIS) TYPES

7. M-Zero MIS (IIS)

8. M-Negative MIS (IIS)

9. M-Positive MIS (IIS)

PART IV: MIS (IIS) DEVELOPMENT

10. MIS (IIS) Sequence 1: From Staff Position to Dry Run

11. MIS (IIS) Sequence 2: Computer Considerations

Preface

This work presents a unified treatment of the use of data to influence, by design, prespecified outcomes in the behavior of entities in the public sector as well as in the private sector. It eschews the indiscriminate automating of data processing in the name of "information," and insists on evaluating the use by management of the insights generated, instead of being awed by the number and variety of computer printouts generated.

Yesterday's data can affect today's decision-making to change tomorrow's outcome when the past data are used to project future behavior, making *forecasting for control* the indispensable characteristic of Management Information System (MIS): not completeness, timeliness, or accuracy, none of which can be achieved in an absolute sense when the latest data are yesterday's, the earliest decision is today's, and the earliest outcome is tomorrow's. This *incompleteness* is underscored in the suggested new phrase Incomplete Information System (IIS), a phrase which should caution the user against the impossibility of completeness of any information system. Parenthetically, if everything that needs to be known about the decision situation is "completely" tabulated and manipulated in multiple copies of a computer printout, that ensures the *uselessness* of the user's "decision-making."

Part I discusses MIS (IIS) dimensions. Every decision-maker needs to be simultaneously at the three levels of decision-making: (1) that affecting the operation, activity, or relationship as a *whole* (organismic); (2) that affecting the operation, activity, or relationship of significant *parts* of the whole (strategic); and (3) that affecting the operation, activity, or relationship of *components* of significant parts of the whole (tactical). No MIS (IIS) can satisfy equally well the requirements for data at each of the three levels which are inherently at conflict with each other—which conflict is recognized in the Context of Concurrent Conflict, or Context C. In addition to Context C, the decision-maker has to reckon with Context T (how products and/or services perform) and Context E (how well the customers are satisfied by the performance).

To aid the decision-maker, the MIS (IIS) has to transform data into information. A sequence of three steps for this transformation is identified in Part II: (1) Raw Data, (2) Pre-information, and (3) Information.

When the production technology is stable and the decision-making is nearly routine, the number of units inspected as a fraction of the total number of units produced is less than 100 percent, or 1. If this inspection ratio is designated 10^M, when the inspection ratio is less than 1, M is negative, e.g., $M = -2$, $10^M = 10^{-2} = 1/10^2 = 1/100$, or 1 percent. In Part III, M is used as the index of the decision-making situations: (1) M-Zero for quasistable Context T and risky Context E; (2) M-Negative for stable Context T and reduced risk Context E; and (3) M-Positive for unstable Context T and uncertain Context E.

In the concluding Part IV, computer considerations of MIS (IIS) development are discussed in step by practical step. Throughout the 9 large-scale applications of MIS (IIS) to decision-making, the accent of the 1,134 combinations of data and decisions is upon use: *Who* utilizes the MIS? (the PDM); *What* does he use? (forecasts); *How* are the forecasts made? (by data decoding); and *When* does the PDM use the forecasts? (in terms of the Δt separating the raw data origination, and the influencing of the organismic behavior).

Management information systems is written at the graduate (and advanced undergraduate) level for students with backgrounds varying from philosophy and sociology to engineering and physics. It is problem oriented, and applies the effective concepts of management information systems (MIS), really IIS, to problems in the public sector and the private sector, making it a "must" for practitioners of management as well as their advisors.

To make the book useful to both the audiences, each chapter is prefaced with a Technical Overview and an Executive Summary. Questions at the end of chapters are worked out at the end of the book identifying the important elements useful as points of departure, so that the book may be used as a text or supplementary text, making it possible for the student to compare his methods with those of the text. This feature also facilitates self-study by the student or the practitioner.

Management information specialists will be particularly interested in the careful development of MIS (IIS) matrix with 1,134 combinations of data and decisions, representing the context and content of decision-making, on the one hand, and the sequence of transformation of raw data into information on the other.

Corporate program managers will be especially interested in the problem-oriented approach to management information systems. Real-life and near-to-life situations are discussed in clear, *practical* detail with respect to the *information* needs of the principal decision-maker and other decision-makers. Not only the technical aspects of the products and/or services but also the market aspects are incorporated in deriving the needs for information for decision-making.

Policy makers and their advisors will be interested in the treatment of decision-making situations, specifically, the real-life situations in which there is little or no prior applicable experience and in which there is partial applicable experience in both public and private sectors: ranging from unemployment research by the Department of Labor to the commercial development of a new jet engine by General Electric for the French Government; and from the delivery of hospital care to the utilization of company patents.

Computer systems application specialists will be particularly interested in the comprehensive classification of MIS (IIS) utilization matrix of 729 elements which provide a *practical* profile of what a decision-maker *uses* by way of information in widely varying decision situations. The MIS (IIS) sequence discusses the three major elements in the sequence: (1) raw data, (2) pre-information, and (3) information. Three major types of MIS (IIS) are identified: (1) M-Zero, (2) M-Negative, and (3) M-Positive, each of which uses the inspection ratio of total units inspected to the total units produced to calibrate the demand for and supply of products and/or services. Step by practical step, the sequence of MIS (IIS) development is lucidly developed including the organizational location of the MIS (IIS) activity, as well as the computer system services (CSS) activity.

Systems analysts will be most interested in the systems thinking which pervades the volume, particularly in the development of *information* needs to meet system and subsystem needs. The four principal elements of systems analysis, context, cost, effectiveness—absolute, and effectiveness —relative, are applied to real-life problems to arrive at the types of data required for decision-making.

Part I
MIS (IIS) Dimensions

1
Decision Demands upon MIS (IIS)*

TECHNICAL OVERVIEW / Datum is *what is*. Data become information only when they affect behavior; or information is *what does*. The statement "It is 42°F in Paris now" is a description of what is; it is a datum. The statement "It is 42°F in your town now" is also a description of what is. But it is more, because unlike the first datum about a far away event, the second is closer to home and *induces action*—to wear or not wear winter clothes. Even if the decision is *not* to wear winter clothes, the datum still affects one's behavior insofar as one considers the datum to plan behavior.

The datum affects the behavior, *not* on the basis of the present temperature, but rather on the basis of what the *future* temperature will be, whether it be in the next hour or several hours later when one will be exposed to the particular temperature in one's hometown. In other words, there is an inevitable time lag between the time of the raw data input, and the time at which the behavior is affected. It takes time to process the raw data to yield a forecast of the state of affairs in the future, based on which forecast, a decision is made to influence the outcome in the future. In other words, the latest data are *yesterday's*, the earliest decision is *today's*, and the earliest outcome is *tomorrow's*.

Under these circumstances, it is clear that information for

* MIS and IIS are used interchangeably throughout the book.

decision-making will be *incomplete*. It will be incomplete, both with reference to time (in the sense that the data are *past* data), and with reference to content (in the sense that the raw data will not cover *every* characteristic of the phenomenon, but only some). In other words, the information will be incomplete, generating *Incomplete Information Systems (IIS)*.

If the information cannot be "timely" or "complete" in an absolute sense, and if the relative measures of both timeliness and completeness correctly depend upon the decision processes which may use, or choose not to use, the information provided, then what makes or breaks the information system as an aid to decision-making?

One is that datum, i.e., *what is*, should become information, i.e., *what does*. In other words, the data have to be converted into information. What the principal decision-maker (PDM) requires is the projected performance. We may refer to this as forecasting (*fore:* front; *casting:* throw). The intent of the forecasting is to help exercise control: the influencing of the behavior of an entity in a prespecified manner by means of elements within or without the entity.

A formal definition of Management Information System (MIS), really IIS, is developed on the basis of the notions of management, information, and system.

The term "organism" is used to indicate the fact that wherever human beings are involved, as in the case of a corporation, the whole is rarely equal to the sum of its parts. Owing to the interactions among the human members of the organism, the output will be more than or less than, but rarely equal to, what the individual units individually represent. Information must have an organismic context. Without such a context, projections made of individual pieces of data would at best be of limited value. This "total" or "macro" context must be prespecified. To suggest that we could put together first a marketing information system, and then a production information system, and then put the two together to form a "total information system" is as meaningless as saying that we could build a basement washroom, part of an attic and a living room, and connect all the three by a corridor to give a total house. When the architect does not plan the total house to begin with, you simply will not get one.

Turning to management, it should be recognized as more than the sum of a few functions—even if these functions are what management does, such as planning, allocating, coordinating, etc. When we mentioned control as the essence of management decision-making, it already transcended the mere functions of planning, allocating, and coordinating. Using the analogy of the conductor of a symphony orchestra, we find that the conductor *interprets*—what the composer has in mind, what the orchestra is presenting, etc. He manages, i.e., creates, music out of the inputs of musical notes produced by the various elements of the orchestra, without himself playing a single note.

Management is the *process* of creative *utilization* of scarce resources to satisfy departmental goals consistent with *organizational objectives* without necessarily contributing materially to the output.

Management Information Systems (MIS), or IIS, is an aid to decision-making for the *organism as a whole*. The past data are forecast into the future, so that control may be exercised by the decision-maker. In other words, MIS (IIS) has two primary characteristics: forecasting and control.

EXECUTIVE SUMMARY / What the decision-maker is interested in is what affects his behavior, not what the state of affairs is. The statement "It is 42°F in Paris now" is a piece of datum: *what is*. The statement "It is 42°F in your town now" is also a datum. But it is more, because the second datum *induces* action—whether or not to wear winter clothes. The datum becomes *information* when it affects behavior, whether or not a specific action is taken—the decision *not* to wear winter clothes is also acceptable behavior because it takes into account the datum of hometown temperature.

More than the immediate temperature, what matters is the temperature at the time when one ventures out into the open, i.e., it is the *future* temperature that affects the behavior. The latest data are *yesterday's*; the earliest decision is *today's*; and the earliest outcome is *tomorrow's*.

In other words, with respect to the decision, the data will be behind. Even though the small time segment, Δt, can be made as small as possible, it nevertheless exists. Further, the data can hardly be complete in any absolute sense, because completeness is with reference to the characteristics of the phenomenon, with reference to the particular characteristics which are of most significance to the decision-making. There is no guarantee that the data on *all* characteristics will be known, or are even desirable. In short, information which affects behavior is based upon *incomplete* data, generating *Incomplete Information Systems (IIS)*.

It is not the past data that the decision-maker is interested in, but the earliest data which his decisions can hope to influence. Therefore, what will be the *future* outcome if things were to continue at the present rate is the most important question with regard to the available data of the decision-maker who seeks to influence tomorrow's outcome.

What makes a Management Information System (MIS), really IIS, is a question discussed in terms of the basic ideas of management, information, and system.

The word system somehow connotes many well-connected parts all running in perfect harmony. This does not happen when human beings are part of the whole. Because human beings interact with each other, the output of a group will be more than or less than, but rarely equal to, what the individual units each represent by themselves. The word "organism" suggests the working together of many parts, but in such a way that a human body is more than the sum of its parts, such as head, heart, hands, feet, etc.

Management is often represented in terms of the various functions, such as planning, organizing, coordinating; however, if management were merely these functions put together, then the functions can be performed by different individuals, as indeed they are—without the need for an additional activity called management. To underscore what management does, the analogy of a symphony orchestra conductor is used. The members of the orchestra are experts, each able to play his part quite competently; however, what makes the music is the interpretation by the conductor of what the composer intended and what the orchestra is performing. He tells the musicians where to come in, how to modulate the performance of each musical section, so that the result would be integrated music, instead of a number of individual, though beautiful, notes. Notice that the conductor himself plays no musical notes. He produces *no thing* (not nothing).

Management is the *process* of creating utilization of scarce resources to satisfy departmental goals consistent with *organizational objectives* without necessarily contributing materially to the output. Management Information Systems (MIS) (IIS) is an aid to decision-making for the organism as a whole. MIS (IIS) provides forecasts to exercise control.

One of the stories about two gods in the Indian Pantheon throws an interesting light on the true source of authority which comes from something surpassing mere knowledge.

Authority in Abstraction

In the days of the native rulers of kingdoms, the courts were also patrons of the arts. Several poets would be in residence, and they would compose poems with religious themes or secular praise. Tests of intellectual strength were performed under well-prescribed rules. One of the tests of strength came in the form of completing the fourth line of a stanza of which the first three were given. The completed stanza should not only tell a coherent story, but also strictly conform to the metric and rhyming style. The poet who first completed the stanza correctly would of course be the winner. The more skillful among the poets were able to complete the stanza no sooner than the three lines were uttered.

The gods also have favorites among the poets. In one of the stories, a god and goddess argue who is the better of two poets. To settle the argument, they decide to take on human form as man and wife, and perform a test on both the poets in succession. The test is to complete a stanza; to add to the motivation, the couple tells each poet that their child is dead, but that they have been given a blessing which guarantees that the child will live again if the stanza is completed correctly.

So the couple waits with their "dead" child along a path traversed by both poets at an appointed hour. The first poet completes the stanza just as soon as he is given the three lines. Nothing happens. The child lies still. The distraught couple asks the poet what they could do. He says, "There is another poet coming behind me; try him."

So the couple presents the three lines of the stanza to the second poet, requesting him to complete it so that their child may live again. He, too, completes the stanza just as soon as he is given the three lines. Furthermore, he completes it in exactly the same way as did the first poet. Again, nothing happens. The child lies still. The distraught parents ask why their child has not come to life. The poet replies, "Your child is not dead; if he were, he would have certainly come to life." The god and goddess decide that the second poet is the superior one.

Both the poets are equal in their capability and performance, because both completed the stanza virtually instantaneously and in the same fashion. The objective of both the poets is the same, viz., resurrect the "dead" child. The means that they employ is *information*. Each provides the information which he thinks will solve the problem. The information that each provides is something *abstract*. It is abstract because the fourth stanza has to match the original idea. Not only the content, but also the form must conform to the original. More than the abstractness of the expression itself is the stipulation that the 25 percent that the poet contributes must form a piece with the other 75 percent; which means, someone else's idea is what the poet has to build upon. According to the rules of the game, what the poet conceives to be the abstract ideal in the mind of the originator with respect to the entire stanza has to be so well replicated in his own contribution that the completed stanza would be indistinguishable from the original.

Here is a clear case of bias and prejudice on the part of the decision-maker who receives the information. It is as though the originator says: "Tell me what I want to hear, and your guess better be right!" We find that the first poet in fact guesses correctly, but doubts his own capability to have guessed the mind of the decision-maker correctly. Therefore, when challenged by the capricious decision-maker (in the form of the unfulfilled blessing of life for the child), the first poet backs down from his own assessment of the information he provides. What distinguishes the second poet from the first is his assurance that his information is *authoritative*. Therefore, he can tell the decision maker: "Take it or leave it; there is no other information that is appropriate to this situation."

In the case of the second poet, what provides him with his authority as to the appropriateness of his information? His authority springs from both knowing the relevant alternative forms in which the stanza could be completed, and from knowing that he selected the best from among them. He recognizes that the form and content could not be improved upon by any other way of completing the stanza. To be able to make this assertion, he should (1) know the rules of the stanza completion; (2) know the alternative forms of completion; (3) evaluate all relevant alternative forms of completion, to do which he must; (4) establish criteria which are applicable to any form of stanza completion; and (5) know the margin of error in his application of the criteria to the composition(s).

It should be noticed that none of the five essentials directly refer to the prejudices or preconceptions of the originator of the stanza, who is the decision-maker dealing with life and death presumably on the basis of the 25 percent information. As a matter of fact, the second poet is able to challenge the decision-maker on the basis of his requirement of the information. If the best stanza completion is what is required, then there is no other. The poet is not saying that the decision-maker is right or wrong in his exercise of his prerogative of granting or withholding life. All he is saying is that if the decision-maker is granting life on the basis of the best stanza (best information), then by the rules of the information generation, the decision-maker is bound to accept the completed stanza.

The Inevitable Time Lag

In this illustration, time does *not* enter explicitly as it does in real life. Whatever be the prejudices of the decision-maker, he uses or sets aside the information *today* for his decisions affecting *tomorrow*. What is the latest information that he can use or choose not to use in making decisions today? It is *yesterday's* information.

The inherent time lag between the input of information for the output of decisions and the input of decisions for the output of results can be stated more precisely and universally in terms of $t + \Delta t$. The Δt is a relative quantity. It can be an hour, a day, a week. In the case of the spacecraft trajectory Δt would be a thousandth or a millionth of a second, while in the case of the age of the moon, it could be thousands or millions of years. As a matter of fact, the current estimate of the age of the moon is 3.19 billion years, give or take 60 million years. With respect to a decision-making framework, we can say that the decisions made in time t generate results in $t + \Delta t$. The information that can be used, or chosen not to be used, in the decisions at time t pertain to $t - \Delta t$.

$$\text{Information} \rightarrow \text{Decision} \rightarrow \text{Results}$$
$$t - \Delta t \qquad\qquad t \qquad\qquad t + \Delta t$$

"Timeliness" of information

Given the inevitable time lag between the generation of information and its utilization, the shouts for "timely" information are at best relative, and at worst, meaningless. The most "timely" information is still yesterday's information, which is not timely, but behind in time with respect to the point of utilization. The Greek mathematician Zeno argued that Achilles could never catch up with the slowest tortoise, provided the tortoise had a head start. His reasoning was that when Achilles was at point A, the tortoise was at point B; when Achilles was at B, the tortoise was at C, and so on. Zeno's implied premise was the Greek belief that the whole has more terms than the part. Therefore, to overtake the tortoise, Achilles would have to be in more places than the tortoise, which, if granted, would validate his reasoning. "But we saw that he must, in any period, be in exactly as many places as the tortoise. . . . As the conclusion of Achilles having to be in more places than the tortoise is absurd, the axiom must be rejected."[1]

Decisions do have a head start over information. The distance between decision and information can be reduced (at a cost). But no matter how much the distance is reduced, the information at time t *cannot* be used for the decision at time t. The Δt separates the two; no matter how small the magnitude of Δt is, its existence itself is undeniable, unlike in the case of Zeno who can overtake the tortoise by converting his handicap of $-\Delta t$ to an advantage of $+\Delta t$. Therefore, if by "timely" information is meant information at time t for decision at time t, it is meaningless, for, it ignores Δt.

While rejecting "timeliness" as an absolute measure with respect to the location of the information on the time axis, it should be pointed out that "timeliness" does have an important meaning as a relative measure. In the case of a spacecraft trajectory, if decisions had to be made every millionth of a minute, and if information were available on the status of the trajectory only every thousandth of a minute, then that information would *not* be timely for the decisions that are based on it. However, if the decisions would not be affected significantly by changing the time unit of information from the millionth of a minute to the thousandth of a minute, then the latter would be "timely" with respect to the decisions.

In other words, the principal consideration pertaining to "timeliness" of information is *not* the clock time. Instead, it is the proportionate change in the decision consequences corresponding to the proportionate change in the time unit of information. If the decision is not sensitive to the information on a weekly basis, then it behooves us to try utilizing monthly information

---

[1] Bertrand Russell, "Mathematics and the Metaphysicians," in *The World of Mathematics*, ed. James R. Newman (New York: Simon & Schuster, 1956), pp. 1586–7.

instead. Again, if the monthly information does not seem to make too much difference to the decisions that are made, change the time unit of information from 1 month to 2 months, or to 6 months, or even to 12 months.

"Completeness" of information

The inherent time lag between the decision point and the information point also knocks out any argument for "complete" information. The completeness of the information presupposes the completeness of characteristics that pertain to any given situation. For, how would one know if the information were complete, unless one had *previously established* a complete list of all the characteristics that are germane to the situation? To arrive at such a complete enumeration, it is helpful, if not necessary, to prespecify the perspective of the situation. Depending upon the perspective, the "completeness" varies. Thus, "complete" census data would require the verification of the age, occupation, and sex of every member in the household. For the age, an entry in an age group (yes or no) would suffice, if the exact age in years and months were not available. The age characteristic may have 8 or 9 age groups which together comprise "complete" enumeration of that characteristic. Again, the "complete" enumeration of sex is accomplished by 2 entries: male and female. With respect to occupation, either an individual description or a check in a prespecified list of occupations would provide "complete" enumeration.

These entries, which are "complete" with respect to the census requirements, are totally *incomplete* for decision-making by, say, one's personal physician. He would want one's age, sex, and occupation, but he needs much more. For instance, he needs a medical history, which can vary from cursory and short to elaborate and long. He needs present measurements, which again, can vary from nominal and few to detailed and many. The "complete" information that the physician requires will have to be checked against a set of characteristics entirely different from that which constitutes the "complete" set for census purposes.

In other words, there can be no *absolute* set of characteristics in terms of which information can be "complete" for any situation. It is the decision(s) which specifies the characteristics in terms of which the information has to be furnished. When the decisions change, the perspective of "completeness" of information changes. Therefore, the cry "Give me all the information that you have so that I can make my decision" signals a fishing expedition with little knowledge of either the water or the fish.

Even if it were possible to collect "complete" information on any situation, chances are that a good part of it would be thrown away by the decision-maker. Without selectivity, the decision-maker becomes a garbage collector. If he pores over all pieces of information on any given situation, he will be in a worse position than a physician who pores over X-rays from the top of the patient's head to the tip of his toe in search of the ailment. He is in a worse position because the physician at least has the assurance that the X-rays disclose the accurate, instantaneous state of the patient, but the nonphysician decision-maker has no such assurance that the massive information he is pursuing has any resemblance to what is germane to the situation.

A decision-maker has to *reject* information, probably more often than he accepts it. His rejection denotes the *inapplicability* of some particular information to the particular decision. If he can reject well, he can accept well, i.e., with discrimination. Even if his acceptance ratio is high, the decision-maker would reject about 1 or 2 pieces of information for every 1 that he accepts. Since the raison d'être of information is use in decision-making, the fact that 50 to 75 percent of the information submitted is going to be rejected by the decision-maker should give pause to those who would cry: "Give me *all* the information!"

Data and Information

So far, we have used the word "information" in the everyday sense of the term. The dictionary definition is "knowledge communicated or received concerning some *fact* or circumstance. . . . Information applies to *facts* told, read, communicated, which may be unorganized and even unrelated" (italics supplied). In both statements, "fact" is a common word. Fact is defined as "what has really happened or is the case."

The words "information" and "data" are used interchangeably in everyday use. With good reason, because the dictionary definition puts "fact" as the centerpiece in both data and information. Data is the plural of datum: "any *fact* assumed to be a matter of direct observation" (italics supplied).

For our purposes, careful distinction should be made between "data" and "information." Datum is *what is*. Data become information only when they affect behavior; or information is *what does*.

Consider the statement "It is 42°F in Paris now." It is a description of *what is*; it is a datum.

Consider another statement: "It is 42°F in your town now." It is also a description of *what is*. But it is more, because unlike the first datum about a distant entity, the second datum *induces* action. You have to decide what to wear. Should you decide *not* to wear winter clothes, the datum still *affects your behavior* insofar as you considered the datum to plan your behavior. Notice that before the datum can affect one's behavior, the datum had to be *processed with reference to the decision*. It is this processing which converts data into information. We can now modify the earlier schematic from

Information→Decision→Results
$t - \Delta t$ t $t + \Delta t$

to

Data→Information→Decision→Results
$t - 2\Delta t$ $t - \Delta t$ t $t + \Delta t$

The displacement by $2\Delta t$ of the data and by Δt of the information is only illustrative. It emphasizes that the data and information cannot have an identical index. The time index of information is $t - \Delta t$ because the time index of decision is t. The *earliest* time index of data is $t - 2\Delta t$, because the data must be processed before they can become information, and the processing takes at least Δt time.

Characteristics of Information for Decision-Making

If the information can never be "timely" or "complete" in an absolute sense, and if the relative measures of both timeliness and completeness directly depend upon the decision processes which may use, or choose not to use, the information provided, then what are the elements that make or break information as an aid in decision-making?

Control

The relevance of any aid to decision-making really depends upon the decision process and its context. The purpose of decision-making is to exercise *control: which is the influencing of the behavior of an entity in a prespecified manner by means of elements within or without the entity*. An automobile in motion is controlled by elements within the entity, such as the accelerator, the brake. Its motion can also be controlled by an element outside the entity, such as a tree. To know whether the accelerator or the brake should be used, the driver needs information.

A careful distinction should be made between data and information. What is registered on the speedometer is data. Let us say that it reads 30 miles. That *datum becomes information only when it affects the behavior of the driver*. How can the data become information? There must be a criterion, which is the "ought" proposition that governs the objectives of the entity. In the case of the driver, he finds the criterion of the community expressed in the form of a standard, which is the measure(s) which calibrates the observance of the criterion. The community's objectives of health and safety are reflected in the criterion(a) governing the traffic in the streets, this criterion(a) being translated into standards of performance, e.g., speed limit.

The datum that the automobile is traveling at 30 miles an hour becomes information only when it affects the behavior of the driver. Let us say that the posted speed limit is 35 miles an hour. The control exercised by the driver, the decision-maker in this instance, may be to speed up, using the accelerator, to 35 miles and no more. He may elect to continue at 30 miles an hour, without changing the pressure on the accelerator. In both instances, control is exercised using data to calibrate compliance with a preestablished standard derived from a set of criteria.

Without criteria—more precisely, without standards—there can be no control. If there is no control, there is no management, because the end product of management is the achievement of objectives of the entity, whether it be a person, a corporation, a nation. The selection of the objectives is the principal concern of the top level management. The objectives are the source from which the criteria of performance are derived. From the criteria the standards are developed; and the performance at any time is measured against the standards it was designed to comply with or exceed. Thus, when a salesman is reprimanded for fulfilling only 85 percent of his quota, the quota figure expressed in units or dollars constitutes the standard. Notice that the standard is *prespecified*. How is the quota figure arrived at? That comes from the criterion, which says that the particular salesman "ought" to sell so many dollars worth of goods. That figure may have been arrived at by a careful study of the potentials of the market, or it may have been a seat-of-the-pants figure. The fact that the sales performance is used as the criterion really reflects the objectives of the organization as of that time, viz., sell as much of the products as possible.

Top management may well choose another criterion: *total profit*, not the total sales. The two are by no means interchangeable. In any group of products, there will be some which are more profitable than others. The emphasis on profit would lead to the establishment of quotas which are different from the total quantity of products or total dollar volume of products assigned to each salesman. For instance, the quotas would be not in terms of total dollars or total units, but in terms of total units or dollars *by* products and product groups.

Yet a third objective of the corporation could be that of *net return on investment*. In this case, the standards would be probably quite different, because the criteria are necessarily different. Instead of the total profit, *net profit* becomes the criterion. The net profit figure itself is modified by the financial transactions. Net *loss* may well be incurred by some divisions of the company while increasing the net return on investment. Taxation obviously becomes the crux of the matter in choosing between maximum net profits and maximum return on investment. If there is a net loss, which permits a significant write-off, it would probably permit the company to retain more of its profits than if it had no losses at all, depending upon the particular tax situation.

The upshot of the foregoing is that control is the essence of management, and control cannot be exercised without comparing what is with what ought to be. Even the decision not to change the present course of action becomes an instance in which the *what is*, the data, have influenced the *what does,* the behavior of the entity, and in so doing have been converted from data into information.

Forecasting for management control

The representations of *what is* (data) have to be processed in a particular way before they can become *what does* (information). What is the essence of this requirement?

"Timeliness" was rejected as meaningless in an information context in any *absolute* sense. The inevitable time lag sets aside any notion of usefulness in instantaneity. Nothing can be done at the instant when "what is" is recorded. It was shown that the decision to control cannot be made before time t, and cannot be implemented before time $t + \Delta t$. Since it will be $t + \Delta t$ before the results of the decisions made will be felt, events have bypassed the decision-maker whose best data relate to $t - 2\Delta t$.

Insofar as the corrective measure relates to the future, it is indispensable that the data in time $t - 2\Delta t$ are somehow utilized to indicate what is ahead at time $t + \Delta t$. Notice that the description of what will be has to apply *not* to time t when the decision is made, but to time $t + \Delta t$ when the decision is implemented. In other words, the data at time $t - 2\Delta t$ should be projected or forecast to time $t + \Delta t$. Fore means front, and casting is throwing. What is it that is being thrown to the front? It is the *past,* or data at time $t - 2\Delta t$.

The advantage of forecasting is that it really makes no revolutionary assumptions. It says that tomorrow will be like yesterday, or different from yesterday. In either case, one does not stray far from the known world of past data. This may be perfectly satisfactory in many kinds of decisions. In the case of the automobile, the speed is really a statement of the form: *at this rate.* When the speedometer registers 60 miles, it neither says that the automobile has traveled 60 miles during the past hour nor will travel 60 miles in the future hour. It simply states that *if the future is as the past was,* the automobile will travel 60 miles in the future hour. The requirement that the future be a replica of the past demands that every element of the situation remain absolutely unchanged. It includes the nature of the road, environmental conditions such as wind and rain and snow, speed limits, the desire of the driver to watch the scenery, evenness of the pressure on the accelerator, absence of impedances such as traffic accidents, etc.

In most instances, where human beings are involved in producing a product or providing a service, such assumptions of replicating the past in the future may be hard to justify. The production rate of assembly line workers will obviously reflect the element of fatigue in the latter part of the day, contrasted with the element of vigor in midmorning. The providing of services will also reflect changing rates of output, and quality of output, from day to day and from hour to hour. Furthermore, any functions involving human beings will reflect a learning curve. Usually, new skills are acquired and applied, leading to an increase in the average output after an initial learning period. It may also reflect a waning of interest once the task has become too familiar, probably contributing to a decline in the average rate of output.

Forecasting, therefore, may be *inadequate* in situations involving outputs of products or services primarily by human beings. Serious modification may be essential to the mere throwing to the front of the past. Nevertheless, forecasting itself would be a useful first step.

Whether it is forecasting, or preferably prediction, that is employed, the object is to answer the question: Given data in time $t - 2\Delta t$, what will be the data in time $t + \Delta t$? Since the essence of management is control, and since control cannot be exercised without data being transformed into information and since the control refers to a future time period, the data have to be forecast, if not predicted, to be useful for management decision-making. To say that the current temperature in Paris is 72°F is a piece of datum. It may never become information to someone living in Washington, D.C. On the other hand, the statement that the current temperature in Washington, D.C. is 48°F is also a piece of datum which will never become information unless someone decides to take a coat (or not to take a coat) on the basis of that datum. What is the standard that one is comparing the datum with? It is the standard of comfort when exposed to 48°F. He may want to check additional data, such as wind velocity, and choose or not choose to wear a coat if the wind is no more than 3 miles an hour. It should be noted that even to someone living in Washington, D.C., the *present* temperature of 48°F is *not* what affects behavior; on the contrary, it is the *future temperature* when he has to face that temperature condition. If he goes from his garage to the basement garage in the office in the morning and comes back in the evening, without ever leaving the protection of indoors, then the 48°F remains a datum, and never information.

Definition of forecasting

We can now modify the concept of forecasting, which has so far been only used in the sense of literally throwing (casting) the past to the front (fore), i.e., future. Such a throwing to the front would be to say that, at this rate, product number 23 is likely to sell between 400,000 units and 410,000 units in the next month. Such a projection can affect the decision-making of the marketing manager and the production manager, because they can each compare the figure with some standard of performance. Thus, if the projected figure is below the marketing standard of, say, 500,000 units, or the production standard of 450,000 units, which would provide the break-even point for economical production, the two managers together may try to stimulate the sales performance to be closer to 450,000–475,000 units in the next month.

However, such a view of forecasting does *not* help the *creative interpretation* of the principal decision-maker (PDM).* His concern is with the effective use of resources to further the accomplishment of the organismic objective of survival and growth. To him, the question is: Are there new and/or related needs of customers which I can satisfy with my present resources, and/or with added resources? That requires knowledge of the differentiated customer needs. It is not everyone who would want or will be able to pay for a modified or totally new product. Further, the customers' needs would be responsive to the activities for which the product is an input. Thus, if the product in question is steel, and the new demand by the customer is for a different grade steel or even aluminum, for manufacturing automobile bodies, that new demand itself will depend upon a customer's estimate of the market that he can satisfy. From the point of view of the PDM of the organism manufacturing steel, "new business opportunities" are disclosed by the management information system in the form of trends in the sale of steel to the automobile industry, and in the form of customer willingness to pay for different steel or different metal.

Before the "new opportunities" can be utilized, the principal decision-maker must carefully assess the strengths and weaknesses of his own resources to meet the needs of customer demands. Therefore, forecasting should yield not only the future demand, but also the future supply: the future demand of the customer, and the future supply of resources of the principal decision-maker. However, forecasting is not to displace management itself; on the contrary, it is to supplement management. Furthermore, for repeated use, forecasting must be less individualized than management itself; if it is highly individualized, it will be nonrepeatable by others. On the other hand, if the forecasting can be repeated, it will have to be a *procedure,* instead of a process:

Forecasting is the *procedure* for inducing *management action* by utilizing yesterday's and today's data as they pertain to tomorrow's events and relationships, while maintaining a balance between *external* events and relations and *internal* capabilities.

This definition of forecasting still fits in with the concepts of infor-

* Defined in chapter 3, p. 52.

mation systems developed earlier. It says that an information system is an aid to decision-making for the organism* as a whole, projecting past data on the performance characteristics of the components of the organism. This "projecting" of past data has to influence the behavior of the organism to accomplish the organismic objective. The "projecting" is by the forecasting; therefore, it can be in a limited sense of throwing the past to the future, which would assist the marketing and production managers; or it can be in the extended sense of assisting the principal decision-maker to recognize "new business opportunities." In either case, the word "projecting" is quite consonant with the extended definition of forecasting.

What Is a Management Information System?

Norbert Wiener says ". . . any organism is held together by the possession of means for the acquisition, use, retention and transmission of information."[2] From the point of view of management information systems, the key word is *use*. Use is the emphasis in our discussion of forecasting for control. It is again the emphasis when data are transformed into information.

Definition of system

Turning first to the notion of system, its historical evolution goes back to the 1950s when the notion of the weapon had to be modified by the advent of technology to that of "weapon system." A rifle could be considered a weapon; its operation could be stated adequately in terms of the soldier, the rifle, the target, and the means to hit the target, viz., the bullet. However, when unmanned missiles emerged as a new operational concept in the 1950s, it was found inadequate to talk about the intercontinental ballistic missile as merely a weapon. The performance of the missile requires several major functions, each of which itself depends on a large number of component elements. Thus, for the acquisition of target, in the case of the soldier it is the sighting of the enemy and bringing him into the line of sight of his rifle. However, in the case of the intercontinental ballistic missile, the target(s) is several thousand miles away, the journey to which has to be most carefully planned and executed. Components of the target acquisition include target detection and evaluation, calculation of the trajectory, etc. Even at the initial stage of the use of the weapon, the decision to launch presupposes a number of prelaunch checkouts and postlaunch calculations to ensure that the chosen target will in fact be hit.

The complexity of the missile system operations led to the establishment

* See section on Organismic Context of Information (p. 19).
[2] Norbert Wiener, *Cybernetics* (New York: John Wiley, 1948), p. 18.

of a term which recognizes (1) the large number of separate parts of the missile, (2) the large number of interactions between the numerous parts, and (3) the necessity of all the components to function *as one* to achieve the objective. The most significant element of the system is the *interactions*. It is also the most intractable. Successful performance of the missile thus includes the components of the propulsion unit working together, the components of the guidance mechanism working together, the components of the control mechanisms working together, to mention a few. Reflecting the necessity for the simultaneous performance of the component elements, we may define a system as follows:

A system is an entity (behavior, event, and/or relationship) the component elements of which perform within specifiable limits both individually and collectively, functions which further the objective(s) of the system as a whole.

Definition of information

An information system will have as its elements information of different types. Since information is transformed data, an information system will have as its elements data of different types. What is it that will make the data into an information system? Clearly, data per se are not an information system; something has to be done to them. That something is forecasting, if not prediction. Since the forecasting is to satisfy the decision-making requirements in different functions of the organism, it is inevitable that the demand for the forecast would vary both in nature and magnitude. Thus, in the case of a space trajectory, the future position of the spacecraft will have to be specified with reference to a number of characteristics, such as the altitude, attitude, etc. The forecasting of data on the astronaut in the spacecraft would be with reference to entirely different sets of characteristics, such as blood pressure, pulse, etc. The demands of forecasts would vary from time to time. For instance, the demands for forecasts of the physical condition of the astronaut would be a minimum when he is asleep, and perhaps a maximum when he is performing extra-vehicular activities (EVA) on the moon or in space.

On the terrestrial level the demand for forecasts of the sales of a company would also vary from the demand for forecasts of its production lines. The frequency of the latter may be daily or hourly, for if the quality control of the units that are produced is not tolerable, then it is mandatory that corrective action be taken the next day, or preferably the next hour. To this end, it is necessary not only to collect data which express the performance of the production line with respect to the performance characteristics on the basis of which quality control can be measured, but also to *forecast* them to indicate what will be the status of quality control on the basis of the

18

production data. In the case of salesman performance, the frequency may be weekly, or monthly, or even quarterly. The common requirement is that the data be collected in terms of the *measurable performance characteristics* and that they be forecast for use in decision-making.

Information is the future projected data on the performance characteristics of the system and/or subsystems which affect behavior.

Organismic context of information

Projection of the *data* can only relate to the performance characteristics *of the components* in terms of which it is collected, such as quality control of the production line, meeting of quotas by salesmen. However, such projections do *not* become an information system until the *interrelationship* of the forecast of the performance characteristics of the components are also identified within the context of the decision-making, not by the production department or the sales department by itself, but by the company as a whole. For instance, what good does it do to have excellent control in the production department if there is no parallel control in the sales department? Products of excellent quality will then be on the shelves, gathering dust and reducing the return on investment. On the other hand, if there is excellent control in the sales department, but no such control in the production department, there will be an accumulation of unfilled orders and unsatisfied customers who are unhappy with the quantity and/or quality of the products promised them by the sales department.

It is therefore meaningless, if not counterproductive altogether, to talk of "total production information," or "total sales information." The word total can be applied correctly only in one context—the context of the *organism* as a whole.

The term "organism" is used to indicate the fact that wherever human beings are involved, as in a corporation, the whole is rarely equal to the sum of its parts. Owing to the interactions among the human members of the organism, the output will be more than or less than, but rarely equal to, what the individual units individually represent. To recognize this synergistic effect, the term "organism" is useful. It suggests interacting parts, which yield more than the sum of its parts: a human being is clearly more than the sum of the parts, such as head, heart, limbs, etc. Insofar as the elements have no existence outside the human body, the case for synergy is made even more strongly. If a group is formed of 10 people, they can be identified as engineers, scientists, psychologists, etc., in terms of the training they have had. They could just as well be described in terms of their work experience. No matter how they are described, the output of the group will have to be *more* than the sum of what each would have contributed individually to a given problem. If a problem is given to the group, and if the solution is no different from what each one could have produced by himself, it is a waste of time and effort to constitute that group: the synergy is zero, if not negative. It may well be that to begin with, the synergy may be negative; but as the members of the group interact with each other, the perspective of each background brought to bear upon the same problem should lead to a perspective of the group as a whole which is different from the sum of the individual perspectives.

Information must have an organismic context. Without such a context, projections made of individual pieces of data would be at best of limited value. This "total" context must be prespecified. To suggest that you could put together first a marketing information system, and then a production information system, and then put the two together to form a "total information system" is as meaningless as saying that you could build a basement washroom, part of an attic and a living room, and connect all the three by a corridor to give you the total house. If the architect does not plan the total house to begin with, you simply will not get one. Even if the architect were to plan a total house, there is no guarantee that the working drawings will have translated the architect's drawings into the necessary details; and even if both the architectural and engineering drawings were excellent, there is no guarantee that the builders will carry out the specifications. *With* an architectural plan, you have a well-specified standard of the total house, against which the performance at any time can be compared and controls exercised to achieve the organismic objective of the total house. *Without* such a total concept, there can be no standard with which to compare the performance of the data, elements, the transformation of the data into information; and therefore no means of control to move the disparate elements of data files into an information system.

Management as more than some functions

Turning now to the idea of management, the emphasis has to be *operational*. It should represent what management is, irrespective of the context of its operation. We have discussed control as the essence of management decision-making and have also mentioned the responsibility of the top-level management to set the organismic objectives.

To identify what management does, several of its functions, such as planning, allocating, coordinating, can be identified. However, it will not do justice to the essence of management, simply because there must be more to management than merely the sum of these functions. When we mentioned control as the essence of management decision-making, it already transcended the mere functions of planning, allocating, and coordinating. If the functions could effectively represent management, then management could be split into those functions, thus meaning that there is nothing more to management than these three elements. However, if there is more to management, then it has to be recognized as such.

It is true that management involves men, materials, machines, and money. It is also true that planning, allocating, and coordinating are performed by management. Is there any characteristic which is unique to management? If there is, recognition of it would be indispensable to developing an information system to serve that particular characteristic over and above all the other functions and attributes. In other words, a management information system should provide forecasts facilitating the exercise of control by management of men, materials, machines, and money. It should, in addition, provide continuing support for that which makes management what it is.

A MANAGEMENT ANALOGY

In a symphony orchestra, every one of the members is an expert; he knows precisely what he should play, and how, and when. If everyone knows what to do, why then is a conductor needed? The reason is that, left to themselves, the large group of orchestra members would each produce beautiful tones. Together, they would produce a collection of beautiful tones. But it would hardly be music. Each one, while performing his part with great competence, cannot by any means perceive the *total effect* of the different parts of the orchestra. Each one may be able to listen to his neighbors, but will be unable to listen carefully to the majority of the orchestra membership and to perceive the total impression created by the orchestra as a whole.

What the individual members are unable to provide are two essential ingredients: (1) data on the *collective input* in terms of the overall effect, and (2) *feedback* to the individual parts of the orchestra as to what they should do in order to truly reflect the intent of the symphony as written by the composer, and as interpreted by the conductor.

It should be noted that the conductor may not play a single note. While he does not play, he is the highest paid member of the orchestra. This may appear paradoxical. What he is being paid for is for creating music out of what would otherwise be a cacophony, not symphony, of individual notes of music played with competence. To make the transformation from individual notes into music, the conductor needs to know (1) every single note of every part at every moment, (2) the dynamics that the composer has indicated, (3) the musical intent of the composer for the piece as a whole, and for the segments of the piece, and (4) the capabilities of the particular musical group to carry out the intent of the composer. In short, the symphony orchestra conductor manages: he *controls* the output of music by (1) receiving the data inputs from the members of the symphony, (2) forecasting where the data are heading, (3) comparing the forecast with the

21

standards of performance, and (4) indicating corrective actions where appropriate. He may ask one section to play louder, another to play softer, a third section to accent a phrase, etc. In all of this, the conductor contributes nothing physically to the output in that he does not play a single note. However, it is he who makes music out of the notes of others. He produces *no thing* (not nothing).

In managing the symphony orchestra, the conductor does use men, machines, materials, and money; he does plan, allocate, and coordinate. But he does something more which transcends the mere sum of these elements he uses or the functions he performs. He has to continually *interpret*. He first interprets what the composer has in mind. It is not every composer who explicates what he has in mind. When the conductor interprets the intent of the composer, he is only part of the way. He also has to *interpret* the capabilities of his own organization. He may decide that for a particular performance the soprano section is not up to its usual strength; therefore, to maintain the overall balance, he may ask the bass section to take it easy, lest they smother the performance of the sopranos. In other words, his interpretation of the capabilities of his resources to meet the objectives of the performance is what sets his plan of attack. In the performance itself, he again has to interpret: this time, the inputs of musical notes as compared with the intended output of the music as a whole. This continuing function of interpretation may be generalized as that of comparing what *ought to be* with *what is*. This comparison clearly transcends all of the functions that one can name.

Definition of management

What makes a good manager? It is the interpretation, the assessment of the capabilities of the group, and the evaluation of the input compared with the intended output. The manager has to creatively utilize resources which are *scarce*. The scarcity comes from the fact that there are *alternative* ways of employing the resources; the employment in one use makes it unavailable to every other possible way of employment. It is futile to look at the number of times an orchestra conductor shakes his head or flashes his baton to judge what constitutes the creative utilization of scarce resources. These are the external expressions which are void of meaning without the *communication* of the *content* that has been made by the conductor to the chorus or orchestra.

Because of its intangible but significant performance characteristic of interpretation, which varies with the individual and from individual to individual, management cannot be subject to the same performance measures as applied to the production of physical products. The percent of acceptable quality products issuing from a production line is a good measure of performance, because the production is a repetitive process which varies only within very small limits which can be specified. But it is utterly meaningless to suggest to a conductor to mimic another conductor, because mere imitation of the physical characteristic totally fails to appreciate the *process* of communication that underlies the physical characteristic.

A working definition of management is:

The *process* of creative *utilization* of scarce resources to satisfy departmental goals consistent with *organizational objective(s)* without necessarily contributing materially to the output.

Management rejection of (rational) data

As a process, management is *transrational*. Therefore, the strict limitations of the aids that management information systems can provide management must be recognized. If we recognize that management is a continuous process of interpretation, then the focus clearly is the future. All that the forecast can do is to give the manager something to look at. He should have the conviction of his interpretation to accept, modify, or override whatever is presented to him as a forecast or prediction. If he is only acting in obedience to the forecast, then he is no manager. What he does can be done more easily and accurately and less expensively by a computer program which can automatically compare the forecasts with a specified standard, the successive values of which can be repeatedly computed.

Therefore, management is something which deals with control of a special kind. It is *not* the *mechanical* comparison of one set of numbers with another, but the *creative interpretation* of the *what is* with the *what ought to be*. It is this aspect of management which makes it endurable. No matter how sophisticated computer programs become, they can only reproduce the discriminatory capabilities that can be preplanned. To the extent that the conceivable alternatives can all be preplanned, there is no need for management: mechanical interpretation will do nicely. However, to interpret the present input and future forecast in light of what the organism can achieve, personal knowledge of *intangibles,* such as morale, motivation and market, has to be utilized. And that is where the manager earns his keep.

It has been mentioned repeatedly that the data may be used, or chosen not to be used, in performing the management function of decision-making. The data collected and presented, probably in a modified form, are expensive. Therefore, investment in data acquisition and dissemination is presumably guided by good business sense. Within limits, let us assume that the data are accurate. Why would the decision-maker throw away most of the data which are accurate, and which have been collected, processed, and presented at not inconsiderable expense?

The reason is that management is a *transrational process*. To use the medical analogy, much more than the precision of the test (the precise data on which can at most relate to a specific segment of the anatomy at a small segment of time), it is the "hunches" of the physician that lead to the pinpointing of the disease. In other words, the medical diagnosis is a judgmental process, the success of which depends upon the physician's capability to transcend the instantaneous and the precise to gauge the living organism as a whole. So also, the decision-maker, whether in industry, government, military, or institutional environments, has to look beyond the precision of the data on segments of the activity; he must accept selectively and reject firmly a sizeable portion of the data because of his perspective which goes beyond the past and the present. It is almost a vision of what (his organization) can be.

Definition of management information system

We can now put together the elements of a Management Information System:

A *Management Information System* is an aid, mechanical, manual, or both, to *decision-making* for the organism as a whole, *projecting* the past data on the performance characteristics of the components of the organism, both individually and collectively, so that the *influencing* of the behavior of the organism as a whole toward the accomplishment of the organismic objective may be furthered, if not accomplished.

Incomplete information system (IIS)

In the section on data and information, the *in*completeness of the information for decision-making was emphasized. The definition of MIS is really the definition of IIS which further emphasizes the inherent *in*completeness of information systems. We shall use IIS interchangeably with MIS which has greater currency of use, but would mean an *in*complete system whenever MIS is used.

QUESTIONS

Chapters 1, 2, and 3 deal with the decision demands made upon information systems. In chapter 1 the characteristics of information for decision-making were developed, as well as the context of decision-making. The purpose of the following questions is to develop an appreciation for the constituent elements of the information systems for management decision-making.

A. DATA AND INFORMATION

1. Distinguish between data and information.
2. What are the two indispensable characteristics of information for decision-making?

B. INFORMATION SYSTEM

3. Why would management want to reject data in decision-making?
4. What is management?
5. What is a system?
6. Why would the information system be incomplete?
7. Define forecasting to incorporate the role of management in decision-making.

2
ADP Systems in Products, Service, and Research

TECHNICAL OVERVIEW / MIS is distinguished from statistics: forecasting and control are central to MIS, while establishment of relationships and interrelationships are central to statistics. Statistical methodology is used in different MIS operations in developing pre-information from raw data; in empirically fitting statistical functions to raw data; in separating the information elements into the more relevant and the less relevant groups, etc. However, none of these elevates statistical manipulations to MIS.

In this chapter, eight automated data processing (ADP) systems are examined. They are found to be not MIS, but data update systems and status reports relating to products, service, and/or research, because none of them performs forecasting and control.

Two *data update systems* are considered: American Airlines' SABRE System on seat availability, and the "speed tally" system of John Plain Company on the total sales tally of any item at any time.

Two *service status reports* are discussed: stock market tape, and hospital operations. The stock market tape reports the status of stock transactions. The hospital operations reports also concentrate upon the accounting reports on the patients. The emphasis upon the accounting applications is understandable because they represent some 25 percent of the operating costs of the hospital. An account update is not an MIS (IIS).

Two *product status reports* are covered, both belonging to IBM. The Advanced Administrative Systems (AAS) deals with some 450 transactions which fall under the category of product status report, because the system is initiated by an order for a product—a very large product—and the prime objective is that of processing the order both formally (entering the order into the accounting system) and substantially (expanding the order into system components for manufacture) and monitoring the status from order entry through the computer installation. The AAS deals primarily with the customer, while the Common Manufacturing Information System (CMIS) follows customer orders through plant operations. The change from the individual, and often incompatible, record-keeping operations of the 13 different plants on the different elements of the computer to a *common* manufacturing information system has been instrumental in reducing the time required for a change in the production order from 15 weeks to 3 weeks. However, neither AAS nor CMIS make any forecasts.

Research status reports, similar to the product and service status reports, are also updates, with little forecasting for control purposes. In an examination of the 35 *Selected Federal Computer-Based Information Systems* from the various agencies of the U.S. Government, Library of Congress, National Aeronautics and Space Administration, Smithsonian Institution, it is found that all are data files. Similarly, the National Technical Information Service (NTIS) provides abstracts of current research reports, the NTIS information now exceeding 680,000 titles with more than 100,000 documents in current stock.

The upshot of the discussion of the data update or status report systems is that all that is automated is not MIS. While none of the data updates and status reports perform the two critical functions of an MIS (IIS), namely, forecasting and control, they do provide excellent starting points for MIS (IIS). To give practical orientation to the function of forecasting identified with MIS (IIS), we turn to two surveys, in 1963 and 1969, of companies, ranging from heavy manufacturing to retail distribution both in the United States and abroad, using computers in data processing.

The success of the 9 companies out of the 27 reported in the McKinsey Survey in 1963 is traced to the fact that the executive management spends time integrating "computer systems with critical management process." Six years later John Diebold, reporting on a survey of more than 2,500 executives, said that the present investment criteria "utilizing return on investment evaluations are generally not satisfactory for evaluating ADP-Based Management Information Systems." He points out that the preoccupation with cost displacement savings ignores the "value of the new information which, when properly used, opens new business opportunities and allows operating economies."

EXECUTIVE SUMMARY / All that is automated is not MIS. We will examine in this chapter a number of automated data processing systems to ascertain if they qualify as MIS (IIS).

Two *data update systems* are considered. Although utilizing ADP, American Airlines' SABRE Reservation System merely updates the seat availability, just as the "speed tally" system of John Plain Company of Chicago does with respect to the total sales tally of any item at any time.

Unlike a number of seats or units of sale, the stock market tape is a *service status report* which presents the latest status of stocks traded, their volume, and price. Another service status report is that of hospital operations. The emphasis is upon the accounting reports which take up some 25 percent of the operating cost of the hospital.

From service status reports, we turn to two *product status reports*. Both are from IBM. The Advanced Administrative Systems (AAS) deals with the accounting entries and customer relations initiated by the order for a large product, such as the IBM 370 machine of a particular model type. The filling of the order requires coordination among several, if not all, of the 13 different plants of IBM which manufacture the various parts of the computer. One of the purposes of Common Manufacturing Information Systems (CMIS) is to speedily effect changes in customer orders at the model type level down through the parts, subparts, down through the small transistors. Both systems, in spite of their enormous ADP usage, still are not MIS because they do not forecast for control purposes.

Turning to *research status reports*, we find that none of the 35 Selected Federal Computer-Based Information Systems qualifies as MIS (IIS). Similarly, the National Technical Information Service, which deals in specialty information, provides abstract reports on ongoing research and has no forecasting functions.

While none of the data update and status reports perform the two critical functions of MIS (IIS), i.e., forecasting and control, they do provide excellent starting points for MIS (IIS). To give practical orientation to the function of forecasting identified with MIS, we turn to two surveys, in 1963 and 1969, of companies, ranging from heavy manufacturing to retail distribution both in the United States and abroad, using computers in data processing.

The important fact that emerges is that success with ADP in management can be directly traced to the integrating of the computer systems with the critical management process. However, even in early 1970, the criteria for evaluating the worth of the ADP System tend to run in terms of return on investment. Typically, the cost displacement savings, i.e., the number of clerks displaced by the computer, happens to be the basis of the evaluation. John Diebold makes the point that emphasis should be placed upon the "value of the new information which, when properly used, opens new business opportunities and allows operating economy." To appreciate the "new business opportunities," it is necessary to know both external demands and internal capabilities as recognized in our definition of forecasting:

> Forecasting is the *procedure* for inducing *management action* by utilizing yesterday's and today's data as they pertain to tomorrow's events and relationships, while maintaining a balance between *external* events and relations and *internal* capabilities.

If data were information, the earliest management information system (MIS) (really IIS) would be that of Kautilya, a king in East India, who in his *Arthásāstra* (*arthá:* wealth; *sāstra:* principles), dated around 350 BC, refers to a considerable collection of data by the government. However, it is not clear if any forecasting in the sense of chapter 1 was made. What he had would at best be a data file, not an MIS (IIS).

MIS (IIS) Distinguished from Statistics

Some 2000 years later, an Englishman, John Graunt, published another book which also referred to data collection. However, he went further; he tried to interpret mass biological phenomena from crude figures of births and deaths. His 1662 book won him the coveted original Fellowship of the Royal Society, F.R.S. His efforts to interpret numerical data are evident from his book:

> It may now be asked to what purpose tends all this laborious buzzling and groping? To know,
>
> 1. The number of the People? . . .
> 5. How many of every *Septenary*, or *Decad* of years in age? . . .
> 9. What proportion die of each general and perticular *Casualties?* . . .
> 13. Why the Burials in *London* exceed the *Christnings*, when the contrary is visible in the Country?
>
> To this I might answer in general by saying that those, who cannot apprehend the reason of these Enquiries, are unfit to trouble themselves to ask them.[1]

Insofar as Graunt sought to interpret data, and not merely collect it, Graunt becomes a statistician. But statistics is not management information systems as would be apparent in the comparison of the two definitions:

> A *Management Information System* is an aid, mechanical, manual, or both, to *decision-making* for the organism as a whole, projecting the past

---

[1] John Graunt, "Foundations of Vital Statistics," in *The World of Mathematics*, ed. James R. Newman (New York: Simon and Schuster, 1956), p. 1433.

data on the performance characteristics of the components of the organism, both individually and collectively, so that the *influencing* of the behavior of the organism as a whole toward the accomplishment of the organismic objective may be furthered, if not accomplished.

Statistics is the scientific study of the relationships and interrelationships of quantifiable instances of data, present and/or potential, established on the basis of rules of evidence, applied equally to all instances of data irrespective of their intrinsic characteristics.[2]

The principal difference between MIS(IIS) and statistics is in forecasting and control. The competent establishment of relationships and interrelationships fulfills the purpose of statistics, while in MIS (IIS) relationships only take the data to the *pre-information* stage. To convert them into information, the context and content of decision-making have to be identified, neither of which is necessary for statistics.

Statistical methodology may well be employed in developing preinformation output from raw data input. It may be employed in empirically fitting statistical functions to raw data; it may be applied to separating the information elements into the more relevant and the less relevant groups. However, none of these processes elevates the statistical manipulations into MIS, simply because the inherent requirements in MIS of forecasting and control are not mandatory in the case of statistics.

MIS (IIS) Distinguished from Data Update

ADP system (1): SABRE reservation system

One of the earliest large-scale data manipulations was that of American Airlines' SABRE System. Developed in the late 1950s and early 1960s, the system permits the allocation of seats in airplanes throughout the American Airlines.[3] Considering the fact that there are 76,000 seats a day sold through 1,008 reservations and sales desks, requiring access to as many as 600,000 passenger records stored simultaneously for 27,000 flight segments,[4] the enormity of the data handling emerges clearly. However, conceptually, SABRE is a "simple" data update system. The question that has to be answered is simply yes or no. Is there a seat available on this particular

---

[2] George K. Chacko, *Applied Statistics in Decision-Making* (New York: American Elsevier, 1971), p. 10.

[3] M. U. Perry and W. R. Plugge, "American Airlines SABRE Electronic Reservation System," *AFIPS Conference Proceedings* (Western Joint Computer Conference, May 1961), pp. 593–601.

[4] C. C. Gotlieb and A. Barodin, *Social Issues in Computing* (New York: Academic Press, 1973), p. 50.

flight at this particular time? To provide the answer, the flight and the type of seat desired (first class or tourist) have to be specified. If the total number of seats available is known, and if the total number of seats allocated up to the present time is known, the question can be immediately answered as to whether or not any seat(s) is available at the present time.

There is no forecasting associated with the SABRE System. It does not answer the question of the type: Given the present rate of reservations, *at this rate* when will the flight have no more room left? Neither is there any control in the sense of influencing the behavior of the entity, in the sense of bringing about, or avoiding, a specified outcome. In an indirect fashion, one may say that control is exercised in not issuing more tickets than space available. However, there is no influencing of the behavior of the entity, viz., the assignment of space in the flight in this case, by any deliberate mechanism as in the case of steering, braking, or accelerating an automobile on the road.

ADP system (2): "speed tally" system

Another data update system which went into operation in 1953 was that of the John Plain Company of Chicago. It comprised a centrally located magnetic drum processor to which 10 keyboard units were connected. As sales progressed, catalogue numbers and order quantity were typed in by human operators. Each keyboard could be queried to ascertain the totals of selected items or the total for the entire store. During the Christmas rush, the "speed tally" system maintained some 39,000 daily totals.

Here again, emphasis is upon the *data update*. To make it comparable to the American Airlines' SABRE System, the additional data of total number of items available in each category would also have to be kept on record. From such totals, the sales up to the moment could be subtracted to provide the answer to the question: Is there another unit of the item available? In the "speed tally" system, the operators could read out the total sales of any item at any time which could be interpreted by the operators in conjunction with additional data on the total availability of the unit.

MIS (IIS) Distinguished from Service Status Report

ADP system (3): stock market tape

A variant of the data update system is the data status report. Stock market quotations are an example. The evening news commentary that "the tape was running late" during the stock market day underscores the fact that time is of the essence in the data status of stock transactions. Here the question is not as much whether the stocks are available as at what price. In other words, there are two variables: the price, and the number of stocks, of which the first is more important. The latest "bid/asked" data updates the previous input on the subject, but the ceiling that constrains the SABRE System does not directly apply to the stock market. Further, price, which does not enter into the SABRE System to guide the allocation of seats, does play the principal role in the stock market data systems.

ADP system (4): hospital operations

Another example of the status report is that of health operations. In hospitals, there are a limited number of facilities such as medical staff, and technical facilities such as X-rays. The scheduling of the facilities to meet demands which are variable becomes highly significant as the cost of operation of man and machine increases sharply. One of the prime concerns of Congress has been with the rising cost of health operations, and as the Presidential Commission on Health Manpower pointed out in 1968, we could put more money and more manpower into the health services, but would receive *less* care—unless systems approach is employed to ensure that the supply of resources meets the demand for them.[5]

In the period of rising costs, the demand for services also has increased, an increase encouraged by the recognition of health as a constitutional right. To schedule the human and machine resources to meet this rising demand effectively, it is important to have data updates on the status of the service facilities in the hospital. Pressed by the increasing demand for health services on the one hand, and the nonincreasing supply of man and machine on the other, the need for a much better status reporting system has made its presence felt. It has led to the mechanization of record processing in many hospitals.

Smaller hospitals which feel the most pressure for economy and efficiency are precisely the ones which can least afford the initial investment cost in machinery for status reports. However, there are two recent developments which hold promise: minicomputers and computer utility.

The idea of a computer utility goes back to the utilities in the communications industry (telephone, telegraph), gas, electric power, etc. Electric power utility makes the electric current available at a given operational level which may be put to use by anyone located anywhere within the reaches of the system. Similarly, the idea of a computer utility is to make available the entire spectrum of services to anyone who can reach the system. In the case of the electric utility, the user places his demand upon the utility by pressing a switch; in the case of the computer utility, the

---

[5] U.S. Department of Health, Education, and Welfare, *Report of The President's Commission on Health Manpower* (Washington D.C.: Government Printing Office, 1968), vols. I, II.

user places his demand upon the system by typing his user code at a terminal which may be in his home, office, or some other facility.

The advantage of a computer utility for small hospitals which are faced with the problem of automating the records of hospital operations is that the large number of users makes it possible to bring the computer utility within their reach. On computer utility network in health care, Aronofsky said in his paper:

> Headquartered in Dallas, University Computing Company [UCC] provides a full range of computing services, including design, development, implementation, operation, and management of part or all of a customer's data processing facilities. UCC has offices in 44 cities throughout the United States and 11 foreign countries. The company employs more than 1,700 computer professional and operations personnel and operates 19 computer centers and satellite centers located in [select] cities throughout the United States. The centers are equipped with systems of various sizes and manufacture. There are hundreds of terminals on the communications lines. The company serves the computing needs of over 5,000 customers.... The company's three-year-old subsidiary, Data Transmission Company (Datran), is developing a network of microwave towers, switching centers, and local distribution systems which will link 35 large U.S. cities by 1974.[6]

What the UCC utility network offers to the small hospital is the economies of scale. Emphasis is on data processing, as indicated by the concentration in Phase I of the Hospital-Oriented Programmed Environment (HOPE) system upon patient accounting programs. In Phase II also the activities are designed to provide status reports of patients and hospital man/machine facilities. Even in Phase III, which is billed as the medical applications phase, the activity is essentially status reporting which will permit the monitoring of patients and scheduling of ancillary services. In phases IV and V, the services are extended from the City of Hope, which is a medical center in Duarte, California, to areawide locations, and in Phase V, HOPE develops into a nationwide Health Data Net.

According to Aronofsky, "our studies indicate that [when the five phases of the system will be operational], it is feasible to plan for it to cost not over 4 percent of patient day costs."[7] If achieved, it will be no mean accomplishment, because it will reduce by some 84 percent the present operating cost of a hospital which will relate to business functions such as bookkeeping, billing, ordering, etc., which today accounts for 25 percent of the operating cost of a hospital.

---

[6] Douglass M. Parnell, Julius Aronofsky, and Thomas G. Paterson, "Role of Computer Utility Networks in Health Care" (paper presented at AAAS National Meeting, Washington, D.C., December 29, 1972), pp. 6–7.

[7] Ibid., p. 17.

In spite of the significant reduction in cost promised by the computer utility in the hospital system, the fact remains that it is a service status report.

MIS (IIS) Distinguished from Product Status Report

ADP system (5): IBM's AAS

The stock market tape and the computer utility network service both refer to the status of *services*. Similarly, there are other reports which give status of *products*.

We find that IBM has had to use a very large administrative system to meet the ever-increasing options that customers have in the orders they can place for the various configurations of System 360. In spite of the enormous size of the operations, what the administrative system accomplishes is not dissimilar to that of the computer utility network in the HOPE System.

The motivation for the large-scale administrative system came in 1964 when IBM was anticipating the introduction of IBM 360. As Wimbrow puts it:

> The anticipated introduction of the System 360 would increase almost exponentially the number of possible configurations available for ordering, and hence magnifying the complexity of the order-entry process. Projections indicated that system complexity coupled with a growing volume of orders were likely to stretch the existing order-processing systems almost to the breaking point. Added personnel and equipment to bolster the existing systems would ultimately have become inefficient.[8]

To cope with order processing, the starting point is an order. Since a computer may have some 10–15,000 different parts with a number of elements in each part, it is necessary to translate the order in terms of the parts and their component elements. Further, not all parts are made at the same location. Therefore, it becomes necessary to assign the production of the different parts and the component elements to the various production facilities of IBM located throughout the country.

Production is only one part of the problem; installation and assembly of the product is another. The many components of the IBM computer are shipped directly by the different plants to the customer location, where they are put together for the first time. To ensure that the installation is a success, the specifications communicated to the different manufacturing installations throughout the country have to be most specific.

[8] J. H. Wimbrow, "A Large-Scale Interactive Administrative System," *IBM Systems Journal* (New York, 1971), p. 261.

Between the entry of an order and the installation of a computer, there is a whole spectrum of activities which occupy six to twelve months. During this period, monitoring of the production progress of all components, their capability to dovetail one into the other, and their overall fulfillment of the schedule in such a way that the installation commitment would be kept, required continuous status reports. These status reports are of interest, not only to the manufacturing department, but also to the sales and to the inventory management departments. The type of operation required in the Advanced Administrative System (AAS) is indicated by Wimbrow:

> To achieve the prime objectives of faster, more accurate order processing and the related internal operations of inventory control and accounts receivable, a certain system capability is required. That system, however, could handle a greater data processing load than was initially planned, and the number of transactions was incrementally increased until there are now about [four hundred and fifty]. Indicative of the branch office operations that the administrative system performs are the following applications:
>
>   Order entry
>   Delivery scheduling
>   Territory assignment
>   Payroll
>   Commission accounting
>   Configuration validation
>   Accounts receivable cash application
>   Customer master record
>   Installed machines in inventory
>   Billing
>   Customer student enrollment
>   System user training (CAI)[9]
>   [CAI—computer-assisted instruction]

The 450 transactions still fall under the product status report variety because the system is initiated by the order for a product—a very large product—and the prime objective is that of processing the order both formally (entering it into the accounting system) and substantively (expanding the order into system components for manufacturing) and monitoring the status from order entry through installation. The physical size is enormous—more than 20 million records, 27 million index records which require 2.5 billion bytes of data and 0.5 bytes of indexes; System 360 Model 85 with 2 million bytes of high-speed core; some 10,000 application programs. Its capability to perform over 20 major business functions by sharing a single large and varied data base is remarkable. However,

[9] Ibid., pp. 262–263.

forecasting in the sense of chapter 1 is absent, and so is control. True, control is exercised in the sense of meeting the installation date, to accomplish which the production schedules of the various plants will have to be modified from time to time. However, that does not come from the Advanced Administrative System (AAS) directly, but indirectly from the different levels of management which work toward the assigned target dates.

ADP system (6): IBM's CMIS

The manufacturing side of the AAS is the Common Manufacturing Information System (CMIS), which IBM has found to be successful in its operation since its inception in 1968.

The motivation for CMIS came from an overstock of a million dollars worth of inventory of a particular group of parts for a computer manufactured in one of the 13 IBM plants. This was a result of the independence of the 13 plants in their functional organization. They utilized different methods and set up independent records, files, and programs.

One of the consequences of the independent record-keeping activity was the large amount of time required to put through even a moderate change in the customer's specifications. This delay in updating the order files, coupled with the "increase almost exponentially [of] the number of possible configurations available for ordering," led to increasing delays in transmitting the changes in the customer order, and resulted in the alarming situation of a million dollars worth of overstock.

To remedy the situation, a "common" manufacturing data system was developed, the word "common" emphasizing the uniform record-keeping system. This system now provides data services with reference to product schedules, customer orders, stock lists of parts, stock lists of subassemblies, and stock lists of surplus units.

One of the indices of the improvement brought about by uniformity in the production reporting system is the rapidity with which changes can now be incorporated. According to Peter Norden,[10] it now takes three weeks for what it previously took 15 weeks. The rapidity of the change in the product schedule comes from the common data base that can now be accessed by the plants throughout the country. The "Requirements Planning" is what Winbrow referred to as the expansion of the order into system components for manufacturing. In other words, what is the requirement imposed upon plan number 7 because of the new order or a change in order?

Again, the magnitude of operations of CMIS is impressive. Its facility for interaction between the plants via on-line terminals and access to a

[10] Peter V. Norden, "CMIS," paper presented at *ORSA Meeting*, November 8, 1972.

common data base is impressive. Nevertheless, CMIS does *not* perform any forecasting in the sense of chapter 1, nor does it perform control. True, control is exercised in the sense of meeting a given installation date. But in that sense, control is exercised by the SABRE airlines reservation system which does not issue tickets beyond available space. The reason why CMIS is considered not to be exercising forecasting and control is that it does not relate to *external* environment in arriving at the internal capabilities which can serve best to meet the external environment. For CMIS, the external environment is frozen; the only "forecasting" referred to by Norden resides in the somewhat mysterious "headquarters."[11]

Only when forecasting, which is now a "given" of CMIS, becomes an output of CMIS will it have taken the next step toward becoming an MIS (IIS).

MIS (IIS) Distinguished from Research Status Report

ADP system (7): COSATI selections

In late 1960, TRW, a diversified company, announced that in the next decade, approximately two-thirds of its revenue would come from products which were not even on the drawing board at the time of writing.[12] In other words, the profits in 10 years hence would come from what is now only a gleam in the eye of the scientist and/or engineer.

This primary emphasis upon new ways of manufacturing a product and marketing it underscores the necessity of the organism to keep up with the latest developments in *research* which offers the promise of new products and/or services. In fact, if the organism fails in this, it is quite likely that the initiative shall have passed to some organism which does. The reason is that the rapidity of technological advances has shortened the lead time in which a particular organism can enjoy exclusive rights to the novel idea or process that it has successfully converted into a profitable venture. Once a new product(s) becomes a business venture, competition will be sure to follow, the only question being how close.

Talking on a national scale, the United States enjoyed monopoly over the atomic bomb for 18 years; however, its monopoly over the hydrogen bomb was only 6 years. Should another weapon of startling significance be invented by the United States, the lead time will be even shorter, other nations being sure to catch up in even shorter time than it took the Soviet Union to catch up with the United States in the production of the hydrogen bomb.

---

[11] Ibid.
[12] TRW Annual Report, One Space Park, Redondo Beach, 1967.

On the industrial scene, the keenness of competition is even stronger, the number of products and/or services that each organism tries to offer to the public being considerably larger than the few types of major weapons that the superpowers compete with each other in producing first and maintaining the monopoly in producing. With an extremely large number of products, the 300,000 establishments in the United States literally make it or break it on the competitive edge that each is able to secure over its competitors by using advantageously the technical results of research.

The results of research, when embodied in products and/or services, are already too late for appropriation by the competing organism. It should know the *research status* well before it has been converted into a competing product and/or service. Since the results of research are not generally available in terms of a marketable product, the research status will have to be ascertained, not in the sense of market research, but rather in the sense of a theoretical technical paper in probably a basic area of scientific inquiry. In that fundamental state, the impact—eventual impact—upon the products and/or services is far from discernible. Any company president who could have foreseen in Einstein's Theory of Relativity the promise of color television, would indeed have been way ahead of his times; and if he also had a prescience of the market, he could indeed have made a fortune.

The *research status* is therefore a critically necessary, but primarily elusive, piece of data which by no means assures an early or easy determination as to potential profitability of product and/or service. The *Selected Federal Computer-Based Information Systems*, published in 1972, presents 35 "information systems." The 1972 volume was prepared in cooperation with the Panel on Operational Techniques and Systems of the Committee on Scientific and Technical Information (COSATI). The support of COSATI underscores its emphasis on scientific and technical information. The intent of the publication is to provide a bibliography of the more important sources of scientific and technical reports and data.

A study of the 35 systems reported shows that they are primarily of the *research status* variety. For instance, "Information Systems" 1 and 2 are, respectively, Cataloging and Indexing System (CAIN) and Current Research Information System (CRIS) of the U.S. Department of Agriculture.[13] The CAIN data base "contains literature pertaining to agriculture and associated subjects, gathered on a worldwide basis." As an index of literature, there is no forecasting and no applicable notion of control to achieve or further the organismic objective.

The second system, CRIS, is also an automated system for the storage and retrieval of "information regarding the research activities of the USDA,

[13] Saul Herner and Mathew J. Vellucci (eds.), *Selected Federal Computer-Based Information Systems* (Washington, D.C.: Information Resources Press, 1972).

the state agricultural experiment stations, and other cooperating institutions."[14]

Similarly, the remaining 33 information systems indicated in parenthesis included in the volume from the different agencies are all *data systems*: U.S. Department of Commerce (8), U.S. Department of Defense (1), U.S. Department of the Air Force (1), U.S. Department of the Army (3), U.S. Department of the Navy (2), U.S. Department of Health, Education, and Welfare (2), U.S. Department of the Interior (5), U.S. Department of Transportation (4), U.S. Atomic Energy Commission (2), The Library of Congress (1), National Aeronautics and Space Administration (1), and Smithsonian Institution (3). They contain large files of data on a number of things, but there is no evidence that any of the data affect any behavior of any organization (the data collection activity itself does not qualify as a decision-making process).

An element of forecasting enters into the National Environmental Satellite Service (NESS). The general system description states that NESS collects environmental data and develops techniques for the application of "such data to atmospheric, solar, oceanographic, and other geophysical problems. Basic information collected is used in forewarning of hazardous or significant storms, hurricane eyes, snowcover, floods, cloud area, temperature conditions, etc., and also in the quantitative analysis and modeling of geophysical processes."[15] Similarly, the National Meteorological Center (NMC) "analyzes the (weather) data and predicts weather conditions."[16]

The hint of utilization is contained in the general system description of Marine Corps Automated Readiness Evaluation System (MARES) when forecasting is indicated: "The ... MARES was established in 1968 to provide timely and detailed information on the current and projected capabilities of the Fleet Marine Forces to execute contingency and other plans."[17]

The only other claims to use are made for an inventory file and a financial file. The Marine Corps Unified Material Management System (MUMMS) which began in May 1967 is "an integrated system of centralized supply management designed to satisfy all internal and external Marine Corps requirements by utilizing modern management and automatic data processing techniques at a single Inventory Control Point (ICP) and several Remote Storage Activities (RSA's)."[18]

The Transportation Research Activities Information Service (TRAIS),

[14] Ibid.
[15] Ibid.
[16] Ibid.
[17] Ibid.
[18] Ibid.

initiated in 1969, is also a storage and retrieval service, but its objectives include becoming a management information system: "TRAIS is a management information system with the primary purpose of providing data needed for planning, controlling, assessing, and reporting DOT R&D programs. TRAIS captures, stores, and selectively retrieves details and summary data on DOT research and development plans, budgets, and work in progress.[19]

What we have in the 35 systems is 35 data files. They contain data which, with very minor exceptions, are never converted into information. The data never reflect any organism's behavior. If they do, that has to be established by querying the customer as to what he does with the data that have been provided by the "information systems." Without such evidence, the reported "information systems" must be classified as computerized data files.

ADP system (8): NTIS

In mid-1973, the automation of 300,000 government research reports covering all federally sponsored research projects completed since 1964 was made available to provide virtually instant access to the technical reports on U.S. Government research through the new on-line NTISearch (pronounced en-tee-search). In the words of NTIS Director Knox:

Now you can have a direct pipeline to the computer file of the nation's central source of business and technical reports produced by hundreds of Government agencies...

Your customized NTISearch Report gives you the abstracts of reports related to your current research problems. You also receive bibliographic information such as order numbers, price, personal and corporate authors, and dates of publication....[20]

The National Technical Information Service is a central source for the public sale of Government-sponsored research reports and other analyses prepared by Federal agencies, their contractors, or grantees. It fills 5,000 new orders a day and it is one of the world's leading processors of specialty information, supplying the public with more than two and one half million documents and microfilms annually. The NTIS information collection exceeds 680,000 titles with more than 100,000 documents in current stock. All are available for sale and a wide interest bulletin and best seller lists emphasize those most in demand.

The agency is directed by statute to recover its cost and has become

[19] Ibid.
[20] William T. Knox, "*National Technical Information Service*" (Washington, D.C.: U.S. Department of Commerce, May 1973), pp. 1–2.

largely self-sustaining with less than 20 percent of its financing from direct appropriations.[21]

All That Is Automated Is not MIS (IIS)

The upshot of the preceding discussion has been that there is more to MIS (IIS) than machines or automation. A number of well-known and highly useful data systems which use a computer have been identified and discussed in some detail. It is found that these systems, selected because of their representative nature, fall into two categories: data update and status report. The distinction between data update and status report is in the level of subclassification. In the case of the SABRE airline reservation system and the "speed tally" system, the subclassifications are limited to a few: first class or coach; Item 1 or Item 359. In the case of the HOPE System on hospital operations, a much larger level of subclassification is available, ranging from diets ordered and multitest screening, to general ledger accounting and scheduling of ancillary services.

When we turn from the status reports on *services* to that on *products*, the nature and magnitude of the subclassifications increase enormously. The AAS of IBM handles some 450 transactions, utilizing more than 20 million data records pertaining to manufacture and sales. So also, the CMIS which deals with as many as 20,000 elements that go into the making of a computer.

Still dealing with status reports, but of the *research* type, we continue to find an enormously large subclassification scheme in the COSATI selections of the federal technical data systems, as well as in the NTIS of data collection of more than 2.5 million documents.

While none of these data updates and status reports perform the two critical functions of an MIS (IIS), they do provide excellent starting points for MIS (IIS). To give practical orientation to the function of forecasting identified with MIS (IIS), we turned to two surveys, in 1963 and 1969, of companies using computers in data processing.

Computer Usage in Corporations

Several surveys have been conducted from time to time on the use of management information systems, particularly when they are automated. The significant expenses associated with the installation and operation of a

---

[21] National Technical Information Service, "A New On-Line Interactive Information Retrieval System NTISearch" (U.S. Department of Commerce, 1973), Panel 6.

computerized management information system invariably raises the question: Are we getting our money's worth?

McKinsey survey, 1963

McKinsey and Company, Inc., undertook a survey in 1963 of 27 companies in 13 different industries, ranging from heavy manufacturing to retail distribution. A principal of the company, John T. Garrity, reports on the survey:

> Based on a survey of business computers installed in 1958, we estimate that these companies account for 15 percent of industry experience with computers for four and more years. . . . The companies are extensive computer users, spending in aggregate over $100 million a year on 300 major installations, not counting those used for engineering and process control. . . .
>
> In the 27 companies surveyed, we (1) measured the dollars and cents return earned from the computer systems investment [for every dollar currently laid out for computer systems, the typical lead company's annual return is in the neighborhood of $1.30]; (2) assessed the intangible (i.e., longer term, indirect) benefits; and (3) considered the range and scope of applications currently installed on the computer.[22]

Accounting for the unmistakable success in 9 companies, and contrasting them with the remaining 18 with at best marginal results, Garrity points out that in every lead company, executive management devotes time to the computer systems program, *not* on the technical problems, but on the management problems "involved in integrating computer systems with the critical management process of the business."[23] He also points out that in every lead company and in two-thirds of the average companies, the computer executive is no more than two levels below the chief executive.

In our terminology, the responsibility for management information systems in the successful companies is vested in the tactical level of the management hierarchy, the organismic level being that of the principal decision-maker. Further, our emphasis on the management information system as an aid to decision-making has been fully underscored when Garrity points out that the executive management spends time in integrating "computer systems with the critical management process."

What the survey does not point out is the nature of the management process itself. Admittedly, management will be understood here as what management does. Garrity states that "predominantly, these are large

---

[22] John T. Garrity, "Top Management and Computer Profits," *Harvard Business Review, Computer Management Series*, Part I, 1967, p. 71.
[23] Ibid., p. 73

companies, outstanding in their respective industries, with a record of being well managed."[24] In other words, for the purposes of the survey, the mere fact of the involvement by the executive management was adequate. Since the management was "good or excellent management," when they take personal interest in integrating the computer systems with "critical management process," it would be assumed to be *creative interpretation* in the sense of our earlier discussion. It should be borne in mind that the intent of the survey, undertaken in the early part of the first decade of computer usage in business (IBM brought out IBM 650 designed for business use in 1958), was to find out how the computers were being used, and not what constituted management.

Diebold survey, 1969

Six years later, John Diebold, President and Board Chairman of The Diebold Group, Inc., concerned with computer users and computer technology, reported on a survey of more than 2,500 executives undertaken on behalf of 140 United States and overseas companies sponsoring the Diebold Research Program. It should be remembered that the time of the survey is at the end of the first decade of the introduction of computers to business. He finds some disquieting tendencies in the attitude of management toward computers, leading to misuse:

> The survey indicates that *technicians*, not management, are setting the goal for computers. This is one of the prime reasons why companies often fail to realize the true potential from their data processing investment. Communications between top management and senior ADP executives is obviously far from adequate. . . .

> The average company which responded reports spending just under $1,000,000 per year on ADP activities: 4.3% spent over $5,000,000 and 17% under $100,000 per year.[25]

The major deficiency in the approach to computers by management lies in the lack of communication between technicians and management, which leads to the piles of computer printouts languishing in managers' offices. Diebold points out that cost displacement, i.e., savings in data processing costs because of reductions in the clerical work force and other changes, "is rarely the sole or even the major benefit from the new ADP systems":

> Present investment criteria utilizing return on investment evaluations are not generally satisfactory for evaluating ADP-based management

[24] Ibid., p. 71

[25] John Diebold, "Bad Decisions on Computer Use," *Harvard Business Review Computer Management Series*, Part II, 1969, p. 31.

information systems because they typically include only cost displacement savings and ignore the value of the new information which, when properly used, opens new business opportunities and allows operating economies.[26]

Diebold's reference to "new information" must be interpreted as data which affect decision-making and, as such, must incorporate forecasting, if not prediction. What is more important is that the "new information" must open "new business opportunities." The new business opportunities are clearly *outside* the organism. Peter Drucker has said: "Neither results nor resources exist inside the business. Both exist outside."[27]

Therefore, "new business opportunities" really means the *creative interpretation* by the manager of what can be. His attunement to the potentials of demand for his goods and services should be stimulated by the information generated by his management information system. The mere addition of the number of units or number of dollars sold would do little to provide such stimulation. Instead, the management information system should provide a forecast of customer needs and product satiability (the capability of the goods and services to satisfy customer needs). Instead of the number of units of a particular product that have been sold in the last reporting time period, it is the type of needs that are satisfied and the type of customers who are satisfied that will provide the principal decision-maker (PDM) with a stimulus to perceive new business opportunities.

QUESTIONS

Chapters 1, 2, and 3 deal with the dimensions of decision demands made upon information systems. In chapter 2 a number of automated data processing (ADP) systems were examined. They were found not to be management information systems, or in the terminology of the book, incomplete information systems. The purpose of the following questions is to develop an appreciation for the distinction between automated systems and information systems.

A. DATA UPDATE SYSTEMS

1. What type of data are updated in the American Airlines passenger seat reservation system?
2. If an airline passenger seat reservation system were to become an incomplete information system, what differences will be made in the decisions?
3. What type of modifications are required if the "speed tally" were to be made an information system?

[26] Ibid., p. 33.
[27] Peter F. Drucker, *Management by Results* (New York: Harper & Row, 1964), p. 5.

B. SERVICE STATUS REPORTS

4. What is the order of magnitude of the cost of business functions of a hospital in relation to total operating cost?

5. Outline the role of computer utility networks in service update reports.

C. PRODUCT STATUS REPORTS

6. Compare the Advanced Administrative System (AAS) and Common Manufacturing Information System (CMIS) of IBM.

7. How is forecasting incorporated into CMIS?

D. RESEARCH STATUS REPORTS

8. Compare TRAIS and MARES as research status reports.

9. What is offered by National Technical Information Service?

E. COMPUTER USAGE SURVEYS

10. What was the measure of outcome used by McKinsey to evaluate the investment in computer systems?

11. What does Diebold consider to be the reason for lack of utilization of computers?

3
Context E-Context T Combination Index of Decision-Making Situations

TECHNICAL OVERVIEW / In this chapter we shall explore at some length the contexts of decision-making in order to arrive at a generally valid classification scheme which will permit us to characterize decision-making situations in terms of their demands upon MIS (IIS).

We begin by developing the triad of objectives in the objectives hierarchy. The concept is flexible: top-level management generally being associated with the *organismic level*; middle-level management with the *strategic level*; and lower levels of management with the *tactical level*. However, these three levels can be used in a *relative sense,* the same level of management being at the organismic level with respect to those who are at two levels below; at the strategic level with reference to those at one level above; and at the tactical level with reference to those who are two levels above. The successive triads of the organismic hierarchy are as follows:

	Triad 1	*Triad 2*	*Triad 3*
Organismic Level	President	Vice-President	Director
Strategic Level	Vice-President	Director	Manager
Tactical Level	Director	Manager	Supervisor

The logic of the objectives hierarchy makes it possible to identify people at different administrative levels, who are nevertheless at the same organismic level. It is quite conceivable that two people at the same tactical level with respect to the objectives hierarchy can communicate with each other only by going through the channels up, across, and down—up to the vice-president for production, across to the vice-president for marketing, and down to the tactical level at the marketing operations in order to communicate what the tactical level at the production operations wants to get across to his colleague in the objectives hierarchy. The bigger the organization, the larger the chain of command in the administrative hierarchy and, therefore, the slower the communication. It almost invites end-running the administrative hierarchy in the interests of fulfilling the higher concerns of the objectives hierarchy.

To make matters worse, most decision-makers have to operate at not one but all the three levels of the organismic objectives hierarchy. In the presentation above, the director is at the organismic level in Triad 3, at the strategic level in Triad 2, and at the tactical level in Triad 1. It should be remembered that he is *simultaneously* at all the three levels, requiring him to think long term, intermediate term, and short term all at once, giving rise to the concurrent conflict of context—Context C.

The Context C of the decision-maker governs his effort in balancing the external demands with internal capabilities. The external demands are represented by Context E—environmental status of fulfillment characteristics; and the internal capabilities are governed by Context T—technological status of performance characteristics.

If the principal decision-maker (PDM) were to think of "new business opportunities" as suggested by Diebold, he cannot do it without considering at least two types of variables and their interactions: environment e_i $(i = 1,2, \ldots, m)$, and technology t_j $(j = 1,2, \ldots, n)$.

Stable technology is a situation in which the process of production of products and/or service is so well known that their performance characteristics can be well assured. The decision-making also correspondingly operates in a better defined manner, utilizing applicable probability distributions. In other words, we can state with a good deal of confidence the number of hours of life of light bulbs (*stable* technology performance); and we can state with a good deal of confidence how many of what kind of bulbs would be sold (*reduced risk* environment of fulfillment characteristics).

Less stable technologies can be identified: *unstable* and *quasistable*; so also less certain decision-making environments: uncertain, risky. The risk environment is one in which the applicable probability distribution is known, but not the parameters.

We can use the *inspection* ratio—the total number of units inspected as a percentage of the total number of units produced—as an index of decision-making situations. When the technology is stable, the ratio can be much less than 1, or much less than 100 percent, say 1 percent. On the other hand, when the technology is unstable, as in the case of the manufacture of experimental spacecrafts, each unit has to be inspected over and over again, the inspection ratio being well beyond 1, or beyond 100 percent. When M is negative as in $M = -2$, $10^M = 10^{-2} = 1/10^2 = .01$, or 1 percent. When M is positive, the inspection ratio will be greater than 1. The three types of decision-situations are thus: M-Zero, M-Negative, and M-Positive.

To aid the PDM in decision-making, the MIS (IIS) has to transform data into information. A sequence of three steps is identified: raw data, pre-information, and information.

Internal and external sources of raw data are discussed with reference to the three major factors of demand, supply, and profit. Raw data processing is divided into data management and data analysis. The former relates to how the computer manages data; the latter relates to how the problems can be categorized in terms of their content for analytical purposes.

Data analysis only provides pre-information. To convert it into information, both the Context C and the PDM and the content of his decision-making have to be reckoned with. The *content* of the PDM's decision-making must, of course, observe the boundaries of the problem as perceived by the decision-maker: the *context*. In other words, context represents the best specification of the nature of the environment by the decision-maker.

Next to context, *cost* is the major consideration. Cost in the sense of opportunity foregone is readily recognized; but not so cost in the sense of *opportunity acquired,* e.g., the capability to perform manned space explorations which was not available heretofore.

The object of the supply of products and/or services is to meet the demands of the environment. How well does the organism meet the demands placed upon it? What "ought" to be the performance of the organism, and what is it in fact? *Effectiveness* is a measure of the actual in terms of the ideal.

The measure of performance must take into account the *changes* in the performance corresponding to the changes in the system resources, i.e., the *relative* effectiveness.

EXECUTIVE SUMMARY / We shall examine at some length the contexts of decision-making to develop an operational classification of MIS (IIS).

Context C refers to the concurrent conflict which the decision-maker faces because he is simultaneously required to think in the long term, in the intermediate term, and in the short term. He has to think at all the three levels because of his roles in the objectives hierarchy of the organism. Roughly speaking, top-level management is at the *organismic level*;

middle-level management at the *strategic level*; and the lower levels of management are at the *tactical level*. These three levels are not absolute; they can be relative as seen from the three triads:

	Triad 1	Triad 2	Triad 3
Organismic Level	President	Vice-President	Director
Strategic Level	Vice-President	Director	Manager
Tactical Level	Director	Manager	Supervisor

The difference between the objectives hierarchy and the administrative hierarchy stems from the fact that the former is abstract, while the latter is concrete. Because of the established lines of communications in the administrative hierarchy, two people at the same tactical level cannot communicate with each other unless they go up through their chain of command, say, to the vice-president for marketing, who will communicate to his colleague, the vice-president for production, and who, in turn, will communicate down the channels to the individual in his department for whom his counterpart in marketing has a message. Often, the administrative hierarchy may well have to be end-run in the larger interests of the objectives hierarchy.

The necessity to end-run the administrative hierarchy becomes even more acute when the same individual is at different levels of the objectives hierarchy as the director is in the three triads shown above. The Context C of concurrent conflict governs the decision-maker's efforts to balance external demands with internal capabilities, i.e., with market demand for the products and/or services with the capabilities of the organism to meet the demand.

The external demand can be designated by Environment; and the internal capabilities by Technology. The combinations of the two give rise to the characterization of decision-making situations.

Consider the production of light bulbs. The technology is *stable* because the methods of manufacture are well known. So also, the demand for light bulbs is well established. The demand for a particular brand at a particular time is not known; however, prior applicable experience can be invoked. Thus, not only can the number of hours of life of the light bulbs be specified within narrow limits (technological performance characteristics), but also the demand for the particular brand of bulbs over a period of time (environmental status of fulfillment characteristics) can be specified within narrow limits.

When the technology is stable, the consumer can assure himself that the product fulfills his requirements by inspecting only a small fraction, say, 1 percent, of the products he purchases. To ensure consumer acceptance, the producer also inspects the products. The total number of units inspected by both the producer *and* the consumer as a fraction of the total number of units produced can be used as an index of the decision-making situation, combining both Context E and Context T. If we designate the inspection ratio by 10^M, when $M = 0$, $10^M = 10^0 = 1$ or 100 percent. When M is negative, as in $M = -2$, $10^M = 10^{-2} = 1/10^2 = .01 = 1$ percent. As the stability of technology becomes less, so does knowledge of the market, raising the value of M. When M is positive as in $M = 2$, we have $10^M = 10^2 = 100$ or 10,000 percent for the inspection ratio. The three types of decision situations are thus: M-Zero, M-Negative, and M-Positive.

In his capacity at the top management of his unit, the PDM is at the *organismic* level, having to think of the organism as a whole which is a *long-term* point of view. However, when he reports to a vice-president, the PDM is at the *strategic* level, taking an *intermediate-term* point of view. Simultaneously, the PDM reports to the president of the corporation, in which capacity he takes a *short-term* point of view, because he is at the *tactical* level with respect to the president.

No MIS (IIS) can be equally effective in the short term, intermediate term, and the long term all at once. The MIS (IIS) should therefore be so designed as to best suit the decision needs of the PDM, giving more emphasis to one of the three viewpoints. We refer to the inevitable conflict of the three roles of the decision-maker as the Context of Concurrent Conflict, or Context C.

If the production technology is stable, then only a small portion of the total number of products and/or services, say, 1 percent, needs to be inspected to assure satisfactory performance. If we designate the inspection ratio of the total number of units inspected to the total number of units produced by 10^M, when $M = 0$, $10^M = 10^0 = 1$ or 100 percent. When production technology is stable M is negative, e.g., $M = -2$, $10^M = 10^{-2} = 1/10^2 = 1$ percent. We can use M as the index of decision-making situations: (1) M-Negative for stable Context T and reduced risk Context E, (2) M-Zero for quasistable Context T and risky Context E, and (3) M-Positive for unstable Context T and uncertain Context E.

From the decision-making situations, we turn to the transformation of data into information. A sequence of three steps is identified: raw data, pre-information, and information. Raw data can be obtained from internal or external sources. They relate to demand factors, supply factors, and profit factors. These data are processed according to the type of problems facing the decision-maker, and the alternative capabilities of the computer to manage the data.

Four major elements of a systematic approach to the problems of the decision-maker are developed: context, cost, effectiveness—absolute, and effectiveness—relative.

In chapter 2 eight ADP systems in products, service, and research were examined with respect to their adequacy as MIS (IIS). In light of the decision demands placed upon MIS (IIS) as developed in chapter 1, the eight systems turned out to be data update systems pertaining to the status of the products, service and/or research—but *not* MIS (IIS).

We shall now explore at some length the decision demands made by the decision-maker upon MIS (IIS) to arrive at a generally valid classification scheme which will permit us to characterize decision-making situations in terms of their demands upon MIS (IIS).

Principal Decision-Maker (PDM)

Given any level of management, a higher and a lower level can always be specified. Therefore, management has to be viewed in the hierarchical context. A minimum view of management hierarchy will thus have three related levels: the higher, the in-between, and the lower—which have been called organismic, strategic, and tactical.

To provide perspective on the hierarchy, the notion of a *principal decision-maker (PDM)* is in order. He is the one who is at the top of the administrative hierarchy and whose actions affect the given unit more potently than anyone else. Thus, the PDM can be the president of the United States, the president of a corporation, the secretary of state, the division manager of a products division, the owner of a gas station, and so on. The identifying characteristics are that the PDM *commands a unit of significant administrative responsibility with resources and authority, which is charged with an identifiable objective.*

Diverse PDM roles

If a higher and a lower level of management can always be specified, then the notion of PDM is not an absolute one, but a *relative* one. The relative nature of PDM underscores the need to recognize the different hats worn by the same decision-maker *simultaneously*. The recognition of these simultaneous demands is made when we identify the congressional decision-maker as not only (1) a national lawmaker, but also (2) the member of a national political party, who nevertheless has been sent to Congress as (3) protector of the interests of his own congressional district. While to his district voters he may often appear to be at the organismic level, he is at the strategic level in piloting legislation of special interest to his district through his party, and at the tactical level with respect to national legislative issues.

Since the decision-maker cannot be all things to all people at all times, he has to choose, by design or by default, those roles which he shall emphasize at any given time to the deemphasis, if not exclusion, of others.

Thus, if the congressional decision-maker leaves the appropriations hearings in progress to listen to less important problems of the police chief of his congressional district and if the congressional decision-maker finds on return to the hearings room that $10,000,000 have been appropriated while he was away, it shows that the PDM role of protector of district interests was emphasized to the exclusion of his role as national lawmaker. The $10,000,000 is not an exaggeration when it is considered that the Appropriations Subcommittee appropriated $5 billion for NASA in five days. On a 10-hour day, the hourly rate of appropriation was ($10^9/10 = $) 10^8; a 6-minute call, or 10^{-1} hour, represented ($10^8 \times 10^{-1} = $) 10^7, or $10,000,000.

The reversion to the organismic role as national lawmaker on his return to the appropriations hearings from his PDM role with respect to his district which is at the tactical level (with respect to his national lawmaker role) shows the successive nature of his roles. The PDM roles are simultaneous and successive. To fix ideas, let us first consider PDM levels and how the same decision-maker becomes sub-PDM, and sub-sub-PDM:

Organismic	PDM
Strategic	sub-PDM
Tactical	sub-sub-PDM

Triad of Objectives

In the foregoing text we identified the three elements of the objective hierarchy. The three levels—organismic, strategic, and tactical—constitute a hierarchy because there is a clear succession or rank, the organismic objective being higher than the strategic, and the strategic being higher than the tactical—implying that the higher objective can overrule the lower objective.

More than a hierarchy, it is a *triad*. A triad is a group of three persons, things, etc., but it implies more interrelatedness than that of a mere collection of three entities. It is used here in the sense of three interrelated objectives in which each has a specified relation with each other. In that sense, the musical use of the word triad is more applicable—a musical chord of three tones, especially one consisting of a root tone and its third and fifth: a triad with a major third and perfect fifth is called a *major triad*; a triad with a minor third and perfect fifth is called a *minor triad*.

It should be pointed out that the triad of objectives is a flexible concept which can be applied to different levels of the same organism. We can talk about the president/vice-president/director. If we go one step down the hierarchy and include the manager, the manager will be at the tactical level, raising the director to the strategic level, thereby placing the vice-president at the organismic level. If another lower level is added, viz, that of the

53

supervisor, then the supervisor will be at the tactical level with the manager at the strategic level, and the director at the organismic level. The *successive triads* of the objectives hierarchy are as follows:

	Triad 1	*Triad 2*	*Triad 3*
Organismic Level	President	Vice-President	Director
Strategic Level	Vice-President	Director	Manager
Tactical Level	Director	Manager	Supervisor

Inherent Conflict Between Objectives Hierarchy and Administrative Hierarchy

We have tacitly made the objectives hierarchy correspond to the administrative hierarchy in our triads.

The administrative hierarchy specifies the chain of command. It also specifies the chain of communication. Consider the Supervisor 1111 who wants to communicate with Supervisor X. The administrative hierarchy would require:

Upward line of communication	Supervisor	1 1 1 1	to go to his superior
	Manager	1 1 1	who should go to his superior
	Director	1 1	who should go to his superior
	Vice-President	1	who should go to his superior
	President		

Let us say that the President says "yes." Then that communication goes down as follows:

Downward line of communication	President		instructs his inferior
	Vice-President	1	who instructs his inferior
	Director	1 1	who instructs his inferior
	Manager	1 1 1	who instructs his inferior
	Supervisor	1 1 1 1	

Now Supervisor 1111 has permission to communicate with Supervisor X. They discuss and come up with some agreement. Now the four upward and downward communications and the two lateral communications are:

1. Agreement between Supervisor 1111 and Supervisor X.
2. From Supervisor 1111 to President through proper channels.
3. From President to Supervisor 1111 through proper channels.
4. From Supervisor X to President through proper channels.
5. From President to Supervisor X through proper channels.
6. From Supervisor 1111 to Supervisor X.

Let us say that Supervisor 1111 is assigned to Warehouse 32 to keep track of the status of the warehouse. To fulfill the task, he must keep track of the total capability of the warehouse, and the capacity that has been taken up by the different products that are stored at any given time.

To exercise control, Supervisor 1111 must have a prespecified outcome, which must differ from that of merely not exceeding the capacity of the warehouse. The forecasting that has to be employed will tell the supervisor something more than the cumulative use of space. The mere cumulative total does not contribute to the performance of the function of control; it is only an accounting tally. To exercise control, he needs a forecast. The minimum forecast would be one which says: *At this rate,* Warehouse 32 will be filled to capacity at such and such a time. With this forecast, if he wants to exercise control, he must have the authority to say: Do *not* send any more of Product 329 or Product 455 to Warehouse 32 beyond such and such a time. To do this, he must have the capability to distinguish between products 329 and 455. If he asks the *production department,* it may choose Product 329; if he asks the *marketing department,* it may choose Product 455. The choice between the two must be made at the vice-presidential level, above both the competing departments. The upward and downward communications may be impractical: the supervisor may have to cut across the administrative hierarchy to fulfill the objectives hierarchy.

Context C— Concurrent Context of Conflict

At higher levels of management, the decision-maker wears more than one hat with reference to the objectives hierarchy. Thus, the vice-president is at the strategic level with reference to the president of the corporation, but he is *simultaneously* at the *organismic level* with reference to the manager. Looked at in another way, any decision-maker who has two levels of superiors above him, and two levels of inferiors below him in the administrative hierarchy wears simultaneously the triple crown of responsibility: he is *simultaneously* at the organismic, strategic, and tactical levels of the organism.

There is a direct and present conflict which arises from the wearing of the triple crown. At the organismic level, the objective is *long term*

—survival in the long run, and growth in the long run. However, at the strategic level the point of view is that of the intermediate term—meeting the market demands *tomorrow,* but not the day after tomorrow; the accent is upon meeting the markets that are recognized and established, instead of worrying about potential markets for potential products. At the tactical level, concern is with the short term—meeting the orders that have been placed *today,* with no thought of meeting the demands tomorrow, let alone the day after; and certainly not potential markets for present products or potential markets for potential products.

The conflict arises from the fact that the decision-maker has to keep in mind all three perspectives *concurrently.* True, not all three perspectives will be simultaneously demanded all the time. However, the decision-maker does have to assume the responsibility to actively participate in all three levels at any time, and also to change from one level to the other. We refer to the conflict due to this triple responsibility as Context C (for conflict).

There is an important implication for the MIS (IIS) to meet these concurrent conflicts of context. *No MIS (IIS) can simultaneously satisfy the long-term perspective, the intermediate-term perspective, and the short-term perspective, all at once, equally well.*

Context E—Environmental Status of Fulfillment Characteristics

The Context C of the decision-maker governs his efforts to balancing external demands with internal capabilities. What is perceived as the "external demand" therefore makes a major difference.

If there is no applicable experience which the PDM can draw upon to guide his assessment of external demand, then we have a situation of *uncertain* context. It means that there is no index of the environment which can be stated in terms of a desired value and its variations, the frequency with which the different values are obtained being undefinable. In other words, there is no guideline to suggest how often a given index of the environmental activity will occur, i.e., the probability distribution itself is unknown. If the shape of the curve, the probability distribution, is unknown, clearly the parameters which define the curve are also unknown.

At the other extreme is the behavior of the environment with respect to well-defined products, such as the light bulb. How the market responds to the need for light bulbs is fairly well established, because the product itself has been on the market for some time and both the nature and magnitude of product demand are well known. For instance, let us say that it could be stated fairly accurately that 100,000 light bulbs will be required in a month. In some months, more than 100,000 bulbs, and in some months less than 100,000 bulbs will be demanded. How often each quantity is demanded can

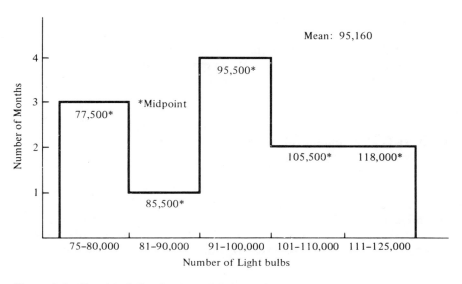

Figure 3.1: Empirical distribution of demand for light bulbs

be gathered from the experience of the organism, or it can be gauged from the experience of other organisms in the light bulb business. It becomes possible to predict accurately how many bulbs will be required how often, as shown in Figure 3.1. In other words, the *average* demand and the *variability* of that demand are rather precisely stated.

Such an empirical distribution of the demand can be used to derive an idealized distribution, which says how often and how much will be the demand for light bulbs, not just in one year, but in many years, if the experience is similar to the one in the previous paragraph. To construct such a distribution which states the relative frequency of the different magnitudes of demand, the measures of average and its variability would be adequate in most instances. What we shall derive is a probability distribution, which is the statement of the *probability that a random variable* (in this case, the demand for the light bulb) *will assume a value less than, equal to, or greater than a specified value* (say, 110,000). In this case, the probability distribution is known; so also its parameters (in this case, the average life of the bulb and its variability). When the probability distribution as well as the parameters of the distribution of the fulfillment characteristics are known, we have a situation of *reduced risk* context.

In between the situations of uncertain context and reduced risk context is the *risk* context. It is a context in which the probability distribution is known, but its parameters are not known. In other words, it could be said that some 100,000 light bulbs will be demanded in some months of the year; and in others, as low as 75,000 or as high as 125,000 bulbs will be demanded. However, we cannot say *how often* each of the different quantities will be demanded as we were able to say in the case of the reduced risk context, viz., 4 months, 3 months, etc., for different quantities.

The fulfillment characteristics of the environment of the organism can be classified into three contexts: uncertain, risk, and reduced risk. Since the reference is to the environment, we designate it as *Context E*.

Context T—Technological Status of Performance Characteristics

From Context E, we now turn to Context T—Technological Status of Performance Characteristics. The decision-making is designed to influence the projected course of phenomena—whether it is the production of a product(s), the sale of product(s), the control of process(es), the bringing about or the preventing of event(s), the fostering or the smothering of relationship(s).

State-of-the-art instability

PRODUCTION

In the 1960s, the state of the art with respect to semiconductors was quite unstable. The instability in production arose from the fact that the joining of metallic conductors in arsenic was a difficult process, known as "growing the crystal." There was considerable uncertainty in "growing" because the resulting product was unknown. It could give rise to a very effective diode, transistor, or rectifier; or it could give rise to a semiconductor which just did not perform.

USE

Given the instability in the state of the art, the decision-maker had to concern himself with the product that he introduced, not only in terms of the *physical* characteristics that it represented, but, more importantly, from the point of view of the *psychic* characteristics of the product in the mind of the would-be buyer. What the buyer required of the semiconductors would be unknown to the producer. If we further consider the fact that the buyer himself would not know what he would use the semiconductors for —whether in the manufacture of computers, or in the fabrication of spacecraft, or in the manufacture of a household appliance—then the instability of the state of the art emerges with alarming clarity.

It is clear that the MIS (IIS) which merely projected the number of semiconductors that would be manufactured by a certain date, or which listed semiconductors by characteristics at the time of manufacture, would be of little use to the decision-maker engaged in the production of semiconductors. The reason is that it is not the internal characteristics at the time of production that determine the value of the product to the customer, but rather the external requirements at the *time of use.* Since the computer and the spacecraft were novelties, the customer himself could not specify what particular performance characteristics had to be fulfilled at the time of use. Both the customer and the producer would *overspecify.*

Context E and Context T together conspire to produce a large area of excess performance characteristics which would necessarily go unused. It is like specifying that an automobile should be capable of doing 120 miles per hour, but the user never has had to go more than 55 miles per hour. Further, the customer specifies that the automobile should have the capability to accelerate from start to 85 miles per hour in half a second; but he has never had to accelerate beyond 30 miles per hour in three seconds. It should be noted that the customer would reject the product, the automobile, on the grounds of nonperformance in speed (120 miles) as well as in acceleration (0–85 miles in half a second), although neither of the specifications come anywhere near the actual requirement.

Stability of context T from the statistical point of view

The characterization of the Context E-Context T interaction—whether it be the performance characteristics of the semiconductors or the response of the human body to the treatment of cuts and bruises—subsumes in it a wide range of sequences and patterns. It is one thing to suggest that the nature of Context T is threefold: unstable, quasistable, and stable. It is quite another to suggest the measurement of its *magnitude.*

We can give precision to the notion of unstable, quasistable, and stable environments. The stable environment is one in which the state of statistical control is obtained. The production of light bulbs in a factory may be considered an instance of a *stable* environment. By that we mean that the characteristics of the bulbs will vary, but they will vary within limits which are acceptable to the consumer. Therefore, to satisfy the needs of the customer, the manufacturer can specify performance characteristics which will maximize the probability of acceptance of the entire batch of light bulbs that the manufacturer produces.

The *stability* of Context T can be measured directly in terms of the number of units inspected by the consumer and the producer together, or *total units inspected.* If the production process is in a state of statistical control, the producer will have reason to inspect less. If the supply process is in the state of statistical control, so that the customer can feel confident about the quality of products furnished by the different manufacturers, he will have reason to inspect less also, making the *total units inspected,* less. On the contrary, in the case of semiconductors, the total units inspected will be considerably greater because both the producer and the consumer are operating in unstable environments.

Classification of Decision-Making Situations

We can combine the differential inspection procedure with the total units inspected.

Inspection ratio

We will count every inspection of every unit every time as an inspection event. The ratio of the inspection events to the total production units, such as the ratio of 600,000 inspection events to the 60,000 units of the spacecraft, may be called the *inspection ratio*. Knowing that the inspection ratio is of the order of 10^{-3} for stable environments and of the order of 10^1 or 10^2 for unstable environments, the index of complexity of MIS (IIS) can be effectively expressed in terms of the inspection ratio:

Context \ Content	Unstable	Quasistable	Stable
Uncertain	10^M		
Risk		10^M	
Reduced Risk			10^M

M-zero, M-negative, and M-positive

In unstable-uncertain combinations of Context E-Context T, the value of the exponent M is more often positive, *M-Positive*, because the number of units inspected will be greater during the unstable state of the art than when stable. On the other hand, when the state of the art is stable, the inspection ratio decreases, giving rise to a value equal to 1, 10^0: *M-Zero*. When the value is less than 10^0, it will be 10 raised to a negative power. We can designate this by *M-Negative*.

Context E is directly related to the role of the decision-maker: the uncertain context is associated with the PDM, the risk context is associated with the sub-PDM, and the reduced risk context is associated with the sub-sub-PDM. In the PDM role, if the context is uncertain and the state of the art is unstable, the inspection ratio is likely to be greater than 1, making the M in 10^M positive: M-Positive.

Characterization of MIS (IIS) comprises the following elements:

Context E	Uncertain	Risk	Reduced Risk
Context T	Unstable	Quasistable	Stable
Inspection Ratio	M-Positive	M-Zero	M-Negative
PDM Roles	PDM	Sub-PDM	Sub-sub-PDM

We have suggested implicitly a parallel of constructs, associating the PDM role with the uncertain context and the unstable technology. However, a PDM can work with quasistable or even stable Context T. If he is selling chocolates, Context T is stable insofar as the state of the art of manufacturing is well established. However, as the PDM, he has still to face the uncertainty of the market, making the PDM role stable Context T, but uncertain Context E. The production foreman also has a PDM role as far as production itself is concerned. However, the foreman has little uncertainty in Context E: he is given a specific assignment, viz., produce X number of chocolates, so his Context E is reduced risk:

Context T Stable / Context E	PDM Roles	
Uncertain	President	PDM
Risk	Vice-President	Sub-PDM
Reduced Risk	Foreman	Sub-sub-PDM

Outline of This Work

The triple contexts of decision-making provide the setting for the development of MIS (IIS) in the sequence comprising the three elements of raw data, pre-information and information.

The two primary characteristics of information are *forecasting* and *control.* In providing the projections of the present into the future in such a way that the decision-maker can assess the progress *at this rate*, the major consideration is that of using the data that have been gathered. Each piece of data can be given the same weight as every other piece; or some pieces of data can be given more importance than others. There are methods to give equal or *unequal* importance to the different pieces of data. The choice between the two methods, or rather the classes of methods, depends upon the understanding that one has of the phenomenon in question. What the computer can handle is the rapid, repeatable, and reliable performance of the operations; but management has to provide its understanding of the phenomenon on a continuing basis.

MIS (IIS) sequence 1: raw data

Whether the forecasting is based on equal or unequal weighting of data, the validity of the controls exercised by management depends upon the validity of the data upon which the forecasting methods are applied. The sources of data can be internal or external. In both instances, the data can be classified into demand, supply, and profit. By supply is meant the products and/or services that the organism can offer or render. The demand for these products and/or services comes from outside the organism. How well the demand and supply are brought into equilibrium is reflected in the profit that accrues to the organism.

Raw data processing may be divided into (1) data management and (2) data analysis, as shown in Figure 3.2. Data management refers to the way in which the computer conducts its operations. For instance, the *executive routine* schedules the work in such a way that the operations are performed with minimum delay and maximum efficiency. It would include the procedures to observe priorities that are specified and logical precedents that are implied. The *processing programs* perform housekeeping chores. The efficiency of both the executive routines and the processing programs is greatly enhanced by the capability to move the data files.

MIS (IIS) sequence 2: pre-information

With respect to *data analysis*, all problems can be divided into three types: (1) solution oriented, (2) structure oriented, and (3) structural solution oriented. In solution-oriented problems, primary concern is with the value of the variable(s) that yields the best solution under the given circumstances (e.g., the number of units of product X which will maximize profit). However, in many instances the emphasis is *not* upon a particular number, but upon the relationship between a number of variables which are critical to the solution of the problem (e.g., the relationship between the man and machine variables in landing a man on the moon). If the manner in which the variables are related to each other is known, alternative values can be assigned and the consequences explored.

MIS (IIS) sequence 3: information

The raw data input is acted upon by the facilities of data management and the capabilities of data analysis. As a result, the raw data yield *pre-information* as shown in Figure 3.2. The reason why the output is pre-information and not information itself is because the solution or the structure that emerges from the data analysis is only a modified input into the decision-making. Given this input, two principal elements are essential to transform the pre-information into information. They are (1) the context of decision-making, and (2) the content of information for decision-making.

The raw data from both internal and external sources that have been acquired and subjected to data management and data analysis can now become information. The four elements of analysis should each be identified by the stage of growth of the life cycle. If, for instance, the demand for a product is in the declining stage, the absolute figures may well be similar to the figures in the rapid growth stage. The major difference is that in successive periods the value of the sales increases in the latter case, and decreases in the former. Therefore, it is essential to recognize whether the information relates to a rapid growth stage, a maturation stage, or declining stage, before action can be recommended.

With the information on hand, what should the decision-maker do? His own objective is twofold: survival and growth of his organism. The survival is not in a mere physical sense: it is more in the form of preservation of capabilities of the resources on hand to perform the technological operations that are required of the organism at the present or in the future. To assess what his organism can do, the decision-maker has to keep tabs on internal and external variables on a continuing basis. He has to specify what the outcome of the activity of his organism should be: not only in the present, but also in the future. The analysis for decision-making in the four categories can then be used to make decisions with respect to the resources at his command in an adaptive fashion, so that the prospects of meeting the demands of the external environment with his internal capabilities in a profitable manner are enhanced in the long run.

Four elements of decision-making

From the point of view of management decision-making, the *content* of the analysis for decision-making should comprise four major elements: context, cost, effectiveness—absolute, and effectiveness—relative.

CONTEXT

The *context* of decision-making is the boundaries of the problem as perceived by the decision-maker. In other words, it represents the best specifications of the nature of the environment by the decision-maker. It may be one in which prior experience with similar endeavors has been available; or it may be one in which no such prior experience is applicable. In between the two types of decision-making situations is a third one, viz., one in which some prior experience is applicable.

COST

Next to the context, the deciding influence upon the nature and magnitude of the MIS is the *cost* of the undertaking. By cost is meant the cost in dollars and cents in the traditional sense which is found from the accounting data. But, far more important is the cost in the sense of *opportunity acquired*, viz., the capability to perform manned space explorations which was not available heretofore. In other words, from the point of view of the decision-maker, what is important is the capabilities that are represented by the combination of resources that are available to the organism. In fulfilling the demands for the products and/or services that are offered by the organism, the most important element is not what has

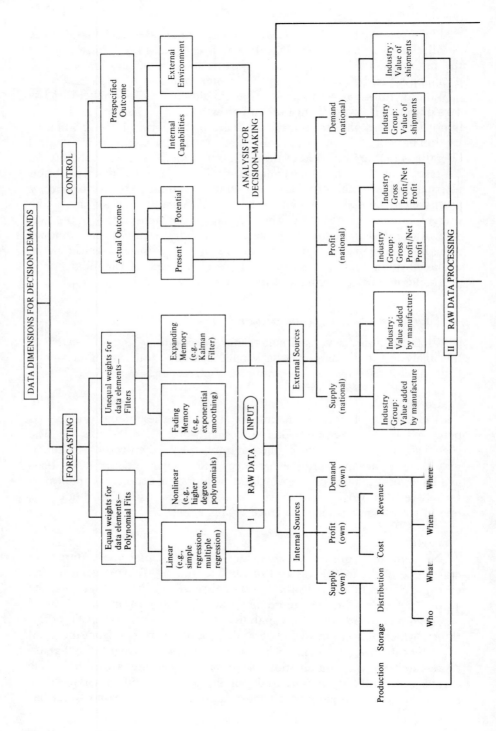

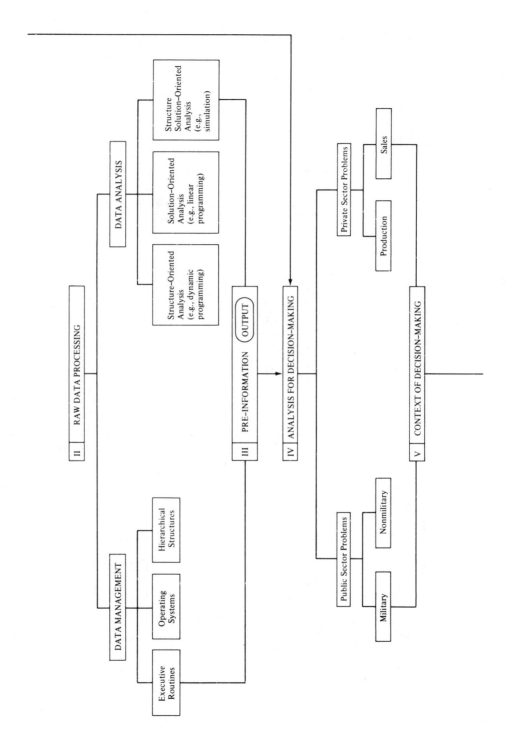

65

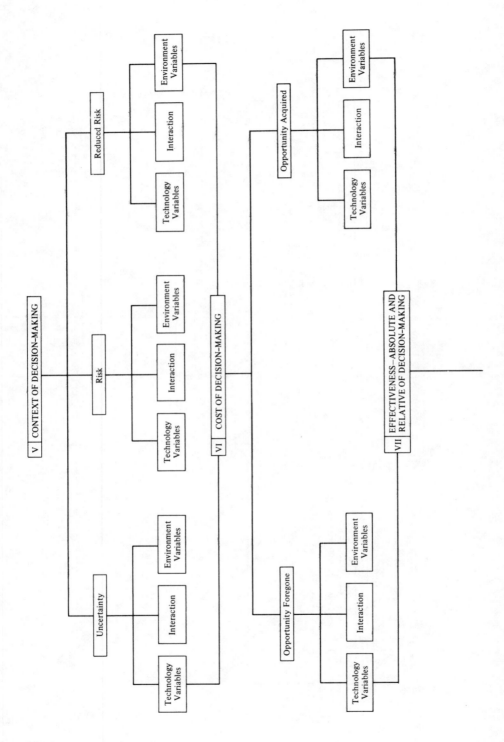

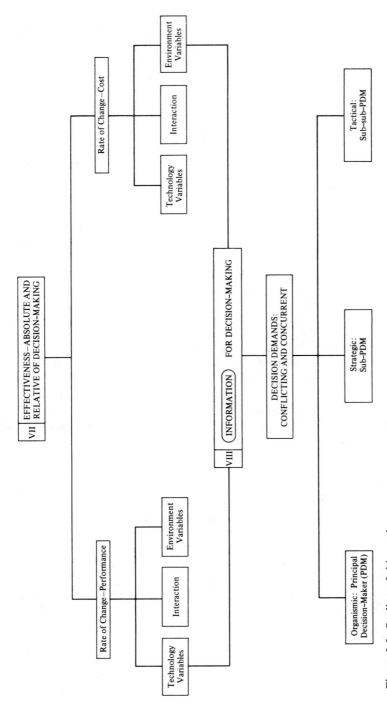

Figure 3.2: Outline of this work

been accomplished, but what *can* be accomplished by the same combination of resources, meeting the demands of the new environment with new skills.

EFFECTIVENESS—ABSOLUTE

The object of the supply of products and/or services is to meet the demands of the environment. How well does the organism meet the demands that are placed upon it? The MIS (IIS), which aids the decision-making, must therefore have a prespecified outcome. This must be measurable, qualitatively or quantitatively, so that the outcome may be measured in light of the specified outcome. Effectiveness is a measure of the actual performance in terms of the ideal performance.

EFFECTIVENESS—RELATIVE

Not only is the ideal performance necessary to calibrate system performance, but also equally, if not more, important is the capability to calibrate the *changes* in performance corresponding to the changes in system resources. If a small change is made in the resources, what will be the corresponding change in the output? Does the change in the output justify the changes in the input? This *sensitivity* of output to input provides management with a significant aid in decision-making.

All of the four elements can be discussed in terms of variables and interactions. It may be possible to describe the phenomenon in terms of a few variables or several variables; it may be possible to ignore all interactions, or some interactions; it may be possible to incrementally introduce variables and/or interactions as knowledge about the system is gained so that the MIS (IIS) can respond to the gain in the understanding of the phenomenon appropriate to the decision-making.

Problem-oriented exposition of MIS (IIS)

This work deals with the *information* aspects of decision-making. The demands for data are derived from the design for decision-making, instead of first designing a system and then looking for decisions.

In Figure 3.2, the MIS (IIS) sequence from raw data to pre-information and from pre-information to information is set forth. The reasoning is developed with reference to real-life problems, showing the relevance of the particular types of data to the needs of decision-making in both the public and private sectors.

In Figure 3.3, the problem orientation is shown in greater detail. The interaction of the environment, E, of operation of the organism with the technological capabilities, T, of the organism gives rise to the *simultaneous* consideration of the internal capabilities of the organism *and* the external demands for the capabilities of the organism in the form of products and/or

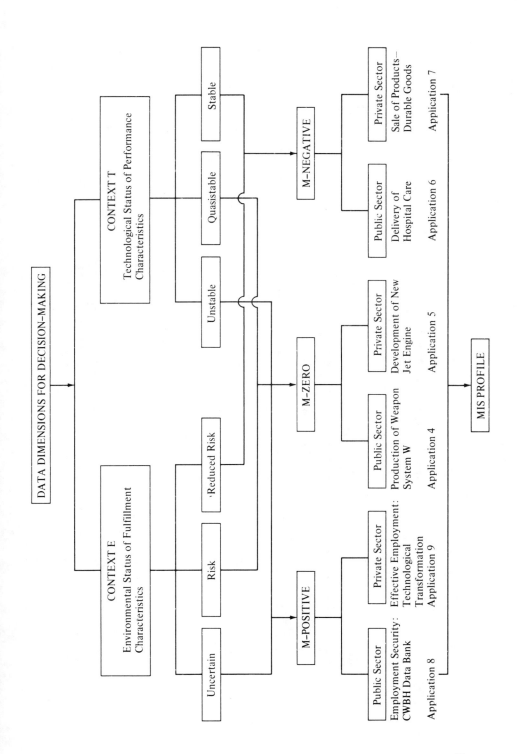

69

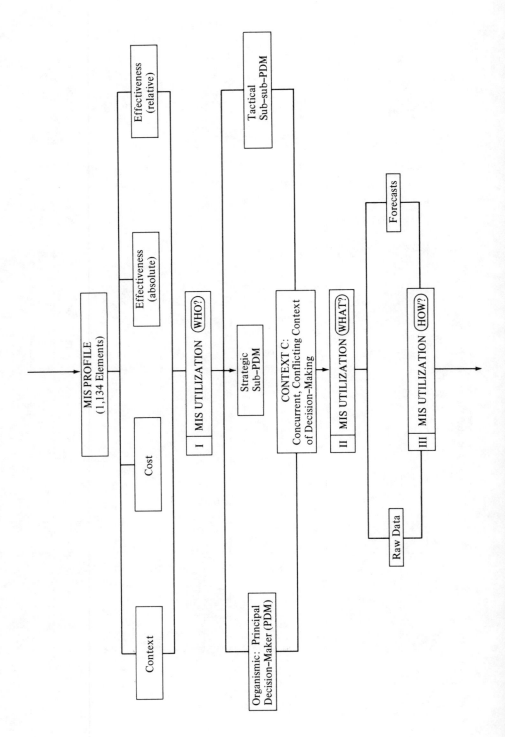

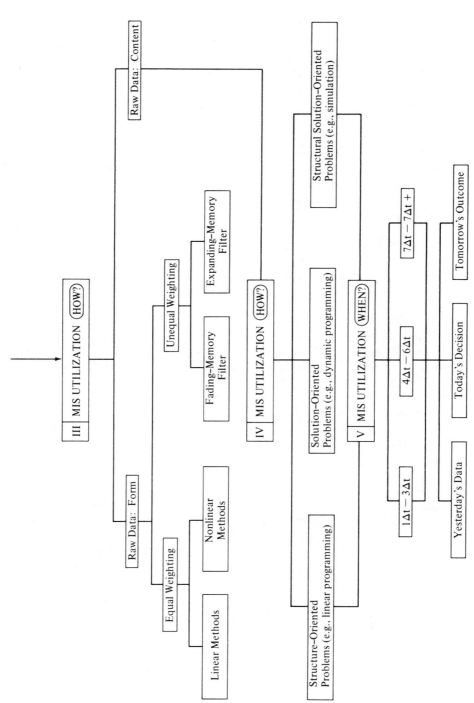

Figure 3.3: Applications by sector

71

services. It is most important to recognize both contexts: environment (E) and technology (T). Too often the former is ignored because it is more difficult to calibrate. The undue preoccupation with only the latter leads to myopic decision-making which, in its concentration upon the woods, loses sight of the forest of the environment which circumscribes the very existence of the organism.

Context E is divided into three components: uncertain, risk, and reduced risk, based upon the degree of prior applicable experience relative to the capability of the organism to fulfill external demands, or *fulfillment characteristics*. Context T is also divided into three contexts: unstable, quasistable, and stable, based upon the degree of specifiability within limits, large to small, of the performance of the products and/or services, or *performance characteristics*. The 9 combinations that are possible among the elements of Context E and of Context T can be grouped into three situations: M-Zero, M-Negative, and M-Positive.

The detailed discussion of real-life problems in both the public sector and the private sector emphasizes the requirements for forecasts by the different roles of the principal decision-maker (PDM). The types of raw data are determined by the types of forecasts that are to be made; and the conversion of the raw data into pre-information is carried out with respect to form and content of the raw data.

An MIS (IIS) profile is developed in chapter 6 to characterize every one of the 1,134 combinations of data and decisions, representing the context and content of decision-making on the one hand, and the sequence of transformation of raw data into information on the other. The accent is upon use: *Who* utilizes the MIS (IIS)? (the PDM); *What* does he use? (forecasts); *How* are forecasts made? (by data decoding); and *When* does the PDM use the forecasts? (in terms of the Δt separating the raw data origination, and the influencing of the organismic behavior).

Problems are the prime mover in the exposition of the methodology of MIS (IIS). How can the principal decision-maker in the public and private sectors use MIS (IIS) is the question, *not* how the increasing speed of automatic data processing can multiply manyfold the status reports based upon internal raw data. By making the problems of the decision-maker the principal focus, the elegance of computations is subjected to the relevance to the problems.

QUESTIONS

Chapters 1, 2, and 3 deal with the dimensions of decision demands made upon information systems. In chapter 3 a classification was made of the decision-making situations, so that the demands upon the information systems can be identified within a general framework. The purpose of the following questions is to develop an appreciation for the three contexts of decision-making.

A. OBJECTIVES AND ADMINISTRATIVE HIERARCHIES

1. Identify the triad of objectives of an organism.
2. Distinguish between the objectives hierarchy and the administrative hierarchy.
3. Why would there be conflicts between the objectives hierarchy and the administrative hierarchy with respect to communication?

B. CONTEXT C

4. What is the inherent conflict in any decision-making role in an organism?
5. What is the implication of Context C for MIS (IIS)?

C. CONTEXT E

6. Why is it important to recognize Context E?
7. Distinguish between the different classifications of Context E.

D. CONTEXT T

8. Distinguish Context T from Context E.
9. Illustrate the interaction between Context E and Context T.

E. THREE TYPES OF MIS (IIS)

10. How can the three types of Context E and Context T be measured in terms of physical units?
11. Identify the three types of MIS (IIS).

F. DECISION CONTEXT

12. Why has MIS gotten such a bad name?
13. How would the needs of the customer be incorporated into the information system for management decision-making?
14. Indicate the nature of conflict inherent in every decision-making situation which places peculiar demands upon the information system.

G. MIS (IIS) SEQUENCE

15. Identify the type of raw data inputs to MIS (IIS).
16. Distinguish between data management and data analysis.
17. What are the four elements of the content of decision-making?
18. Discuss the combination of fulfillment characteristics and performance characteristics to arrive at a classification of MIS (IIS).

Part II
MIS (IIS) Sequence

4
MIS (IIS) Sequence 1: Raw Data

TECHNICAL OVERVIEW / In chapter 3 the three MIS (IIS) elements of raw data, pre-information, and information, were identified to characterize the transformation of yesterday's data into tomorrow's forecasts. In this chapter, we look at the first of the three elements, raw data.

The principal elements of *internal* raw data are (1) demand factors, (2) supply factors, and (3) profit factors. The raw data on demand factors comprise the data on customers, products and/or services, prices, quantity, demand locations in space, and demand locations in time. The raw data input on supply factors deals with the production of products and/or services by the combination of men, machinery, materials, and money. The raw data on profit factors are the profit and loss statement items and the balance sheet items.

Since demand is external to the organism, external sources of raw data should be identified. Internal raw data on customers refer only to the customers of the organism. It would be instructive to compare notes on customers of similar organisms. Similarly, it is instructive to compare the financial data, such as return on investment, with other companies who are part of the larger group of manufacturers of the same group of products and/or services.

Under U.S. Code Title 13, every establishment is required to file reports demanded of it by the Census of Manufactures. The establishment is "an economic unit which produces goods or services, for example, a farm, a mine, a factory, a store. In most instances, the establishment is at a single physical location: and it is engaged in only one, or predominantly one type of activity for which an industry code is applicable." Every establishment is included in the Standard Industrial Classification (SIC) in its hierarchy, comprising Division (single letter), Major Group (two digits), Industry Group (three digits), Industry (four digits), Product Group (five digits), and Products (seven digits).

In Application 1, the SIC data norms are applied to a *present* product, mattresses and bedsprings, as distinguished from the *potential* product discussed with reference to the utilization of patents in Application 2. It shows the application of shipment data, key financial data, and other data relating to both the particular product and to the product group to which mattresses and bedsprings belong.

How the raw data from both the internal and external sources can be put together is a question explored in Application 2. Raw data input forms from two of the six departments—(1) patents and licenses—corporate headquarters, (2) patents and licenses—research facility headquarters, (3) sales analysis, (4) product management, (5) marketing, and (6) new enterprises—are developed in detail. Each input form is preceded by a one-page statement signed by the departmental representative, identifying the inputs, outputs, and estimated frequency of use of the information system by each department. In the input forms, the data items are identified by serial number. Space is provided for appropriate codes associated with each serial number of the data. For instance, the SIC code corresponding to any item can be designated in the report form.

Consideration is given to the raw data input for *nonprofit* organisms as well. The word "service" is developed as the surrogate for "profit." The three sets of factors relevant to public sector operations would be: (1) demand factors, (2) supply factors, and (3) service factors. Three specific measures are developed as an index of the American Way of Life with particular reference to survival, as well as to quality of life. The PDM is the president of the United States. His priority goals (objectives) must include the *expected* survival of the American Way of Life as reflected in the measures of: (1) the percent of U.S. population earning income under the poverty level, (2) the percent of U.S. population unable to pursue its own choices because of lack of health, and (3) the percent of U.S. population unable to pursue its choices for lack of opportunity. The raw data input should correspond with the forecasts on each of the three measures, so that the "service" rendered by the public sector can be maintained within desirable limits.

EXECUTIVE SUMMARY / For the decision-maker to make decisions, yesterday's data have to be converted into forecasts of tomorrow's outcome. This conversion requires a sequence of three elements: raw data, pre-information, and information; the first is the subject of this chapter.

The principal elements of *internal* raw data are (1) demand factors, (2) supply factors, and (3) profit factors. The raw data on demand factors comprise six elements: (1) who, (2) what, (3) how much, (4) how many, (5) where, and (6) when. The raw data on supply factors deal with the production of products and/or services by the combination of men, machinery, materials, and money. The raw data on profit factors are the profit and loss statement items and the balance sheet items.

In addition to these internal raw data sources, the organism must look to *external* sources of raw data as well. How well is this organism doing in comparison with peer organisms? Under U.S. Code Title 13, every establishment is required to file reports demanded of it by the Census of Manufactures. Establishment is a term which includes the corner tobacco store as well as multibillion dollar corporations. The data that have been reported are keyed to the Standard Industrial Classification (SIC) code in which an industry is represented by four digits and a product by seven digits.

In Application 1, the SIC data norms are applied to a *present* product, mattresses and bedsprings, as distinguished from the potential products discussed in connection with the utilization of patents in Application 2. Among the different types of data are the shipment of mattresses and bedsprings by area; the gross sales volume of both in succeeding years; the number of employees; the total wage payroll, etc. How profitable is the business? Direct data are not available on mattresses and bedsprings, but they are available for furniture and fixtures of which mattresses and bedsprings are a part.

Application 2 explores how the raw data from external and internal sources may be put together in raw data input forms. Raw data input forms from *two* of the six departments—(1) patents and licenses—corporate headquarters, (2) patents and licenses—research facility headquarters, (3) sales analysis, (4) product management, (5) marketing, and (6) new enterprises—are developed in detail. The representative of each department has indicated his agreement by his signature on a one-page statement which includes the specific inputs, outputs, and estimated frequency of use of the information by each department. The SIC code is associated with as many data items in the input forms as can be meaningfully related to SIC.

In turning from profit-making corporations in the private sector to the public sector, the major change is the absence of the profit motive. A substitute measure in the form of "service" is developed for use to calibrate performance of public sector agencies.

In chapter 3 the triple context of decision-making was developed, which provides the setting for the development of MIS (IIS) in the sequence comprising three elements: raw data, pre-information, and information. In this chapter we discuss the first of the three elements, raw data.

Insofar as the stimulus to the activities of the organism and the response comes from *outside* the organism, the principal elements of data which are internal to the organism should also reflect the external orientation. It is this recognition that is reflected in Context E which classifies the fulfillment characteristics of the activities of the organism. The components of Context E are uncertain, risk, and reduced risk. The internal inputs of raw data will be a disservice to MIS (IIS) unless these differences in Context E are recognized. This recognition will enable the intelligent collection of raw data inputs, discussed in this chapter, as well as their processing to generate information, which will be discussed in chapter 6.

Principal Elements of Internal Data

Demand factors

The first, and most important, raw data pertain to the customer (*who*).

CUSTOMERS

The customer could be past, present, or potential. If the customer is a past or present one, the internal documents should indicate past or present transactions. The present data on the customer will probably be primarily available from the marketing department, and the past data will be accessible through the accounting records. If he is a potential customer, the *who* data would come from market intelligence.

PRODUCTS AND/OR SERVICES

The next raw data factor is the nature of the customer's demand (*what*). The type of products and/or services that the customer has asked for in the past and in the present provide invaluable guides to the assessment of the capabilities of the products and/or services of the organism to satisfy customer demands. The record of past demands for particular products and/or services also provides a clue to changing preferences and tastes. These are particularly helpful in assessing potential customer acceptance of new products and/or services which the organism may offer in the future.

PRICES

Next is the price of the products accepted by the customer in the past and the present (*how much*). When a product or service is offered by a number of competing manufacturers, price may be a heavily determining factor, other things being equal. In instances of unstable technology and uncertain environment, pricing becomes an enormous gamble. If the organism seeks to cushion itself against the variabilities in the cost due to the uncertainty of the environment and instability of technology, it may find that it is pricing itself out of the market. On the other hand, if its price is too conservative it may find that either it cannot deliver the product(s) and/or service(s) as promised, or that it may have to sustain a heavy loss. It could, of course, be possible that the organism wants to enter the market ("buy in") by bidding low—a practice not uncommon in organizations providing intellectual services, such as technical studies. In order to enter a particular area of activity, such organizations may well underbid, considering the loss sustained in one or two initial products or services to be well worth the experience of penetrating a new segment of activity. In short, there is more to price than mere columns of numbers.

QUANTITY

The practice of underbidding brings up the consideration of the quantity of products and/or services required by the customer (*how many*). No company can survive for long by selling below cost all the products and/or services that it manufactures and/or sells. The underbidding, if practiced, has to be selective: incur losses in some of the products and/or services some of the time. A low return, as distinguished from a loss, may be acceptable from the point of view of providing the organism with enough demand to keep its resources employed. In other words, it would be to the advantage of the organism to accept low profits if there is large volume. Therefore, the quantity of products and/or services demanded by the customer is a factor in the pricing. The discount for quantity volume buying represents a reimbursement back to the customer by the organism of the economies of scale in producing in quantities. In general, a larger order is preferable to a smaller order, because the set-up costs are fixed for a production lot.

DEMAND LOCATION IN SPACE

The customer demand is for a specific number of products, at a specific price, to be delivered at a specific place (*where*) and time (*when*). Unless the customer receives the product right at the source of production, transportation costs will have to be incurred to move the products from the production location to the customer location.

DEMAND LOCATION IN TIME

Depending upon the number of products, the frequency and magnitude of their demands, and the importance of *time* as an element, the organism may find it necessary to use warehouses (its own or those of others) to store the products en route to the customer. When so stored, storage and handling costs will enter the cost of distributing the product.

These six elements are the principal elements of raw data *internal* to the organism. They are the basic building blocks upon which the MIS (IIS) should be founded. Orientation to the customer and his needs must provide the primary focus of the MIS (IIS) designed to aid in decision-making. Without demand, supply suffers. If there is demand, present and/or potential, then there is justification for the supply of the products and/or services by the organism.

Supply factors

By supply is meant the providing of products and/or services by the organism to the customer. In chapter 1 we referred to the creating of capabilities out of the physical assets of men, machinery, material, and money as *technology*. These four elements are the principal elements of the raw data on supply for which internal inputs are directly available.

MEN

By *men* is meant the skills, training, and experience that are represented in the human component of the organism. Without this component there can be no supply of products and/or services by the organism. As the technology becomes stable, the machine component is likely to increase in its contribution to the supply of products and/or services by the organism. At the other end of the spectrum, when the technology is unstable and the environment is uncertain, the human component will be far more important and predominant. In either case, for the supply of products and/or services, the human component is indispensable, the only question being the magnitude of its contribution.

What should be the raw data input on men? Clearly, the time card data of hours spent in one activity or another or the weekly reports of time distribution by salaried employees constitute an elementary input, which permits the allocation of cost to the human component in the supply of products and/or services by the organism. Except in the case of stable technology and reduced risk environment of decision-making, such raw data inputs are of limited value. They indicate the actual effort expended, not the creative output that comes from *alternative* deployment of the skills, training, and experience of the human component. If there is any element of instability in technology and of risk or uncertainty in the decision-making environment, the critical difference will be made by the human component. As the technological pace of production increases, the training that is received in schools and universities tend to be subject to rapid obsolescence. The raw data input of the organism must reflect this degree of obsolescence, and the necessity to compensate for it. It is customary to report on the depreciation of machinery; it is equally, if not more, important to report on the depreciation of the human component of the organism. The internal raw data inputs must provide for the depreciation of the capital investment represented in the human component, so that remedial measures can be instituted in time. Of course, the depreciation of the capabilities of the human component must be stated in terms of the *function* that they are required to perform in the supply of products and/or services by the organism. In other words, it is necessary to determine what combination of skills, training, and experience it takes to generate the products and/or services.

MACHINERY

The raw data input on *machinery* are reasonably standardized; however, the standardized procedures, again, are applicable to reduced risk environment and stable technology. In the uncertain environment of decision-making and of unstable technology, the machinery has to be referred to in terms of performance characteristics of products which may yet be on the drawing board: which makes the guesses about the yet-to-be-produced product and/or service the critical factor in reporting machine performance. It is as though the replacement for a piece of machinery that has not yet been fabricated to produce a product and/or service which is not yet performed is already being considered in earnest. Furthermore, provision has to be made to acquire the new replacement: the cost of the replacement machinery has to be calculated while the original piece of machinery itself has not been installed as yet. Under these circumstances, the machinery component also becomes less tractable.

MATERIALS

The *materials* input is also subject to technological uncertainties. Here again, the raw data input on materials is straightforward when it comes to stable technology and reduced risk environment of decision-making. However, the performance characteristics that are desired from experimental materials in the future make the specification of the materials a hazardous venture. Consider, for instance, the choice of titanium by the United States as the metal for the supersonic transport plane to withstand extremes of temperatures, while the British-French Concorde Supersonic Transport settled for aluminum alloy, which could only perform under more limited thermal conditions. Since the Supersonic Transport (SST) program has already been cancelled by the United States, whenever it is reopened the input of raw data from the Boeing Co. will be a product of uncertain environment and unstable technology because it has to take into account the yet-to-be-proven performance characteristics of titanium as the material for the hull of the SST plane.

MONEY

The *money* component of the raw data input is more than the cash available to the organism to enable it to supply products and/or services. In

83

the context of unstable technology and uncertain environment of decision-making, money represents the powers of persuasion on the part of the organism to infuse confidence in the bankers in what may look like a pipe dream. If the venture fails completely, what will that mean to the organism? Will it go under, or will it be able to write off the failure as a tax loss? The interest of the banks is in the return of the capital with interest; therefore, the raw data input on money must provide for the estimate of the bank's trust in the performance of the organism in the different combinations of Context E and Context T. Of course, the standard book-keeping procedures which keep track of the dollars and cents received and paid out are applicable to the raw data input on money in all the Context E-Context T combinations.

Profit factors*

It should be noted that unlike demand and supply factors, profit factors are *derived data*. They are derived from the *direct data* on demand and supply. The derivation of profit factors is an *internal* operation to assess the organism's capability to respond to external demand.

The principal elements of raw data input on profit are (1) profit and loss statement items, and (2) balance sheet items.

The profit and loss sheet items reflect the efficiency with which external demands are met by internal capabilities of the organism. Given the same external demand, management of the physical assets can make the difference in the excess of income over expenditures in a nonprofit corporation, and in the profits in a profit-making corporation.

A number of ratios is computed on the basis of the balance sheet items, as well as the profit and loss statement items. The intent of these ratios is to reflect the strength and weakness of the operations of the organism. The principal orientation is toward the *net return on investment*. It shows the net return per investment dollar; however, if considerable reserves are held for depreciation, for distribution to stockholders at a subsequent period, and for other contingencies, then the net return will be understated to that extent.

A number of other ratios is computed to assess the financial strength and operational strength of the company. Several ratios are based on net sales, such as the ratio of net profit to net sales, inventories to net sales, and so on.

With reference to the Context E-Context T combination, all of these ratios have different significance. In the unstable technology and uncertain environment of decision-making, the cost to generate business is likely to be higher than that for other combinations of Context E-Context T. So also,

* For specific categories, see section on Key Financial Data in this chapter.

the cost of providing products and/or services could also be higher than in other combinations of Context E-T. In other words, the indices of profit and profitability must be categorized by the particular combination of Context E-Context T in order to appreciate the reality of the physical phenomena underlying the profit figures.

Raw Data Input—External Sources

A wide variety of useful data on the performance of the *industry* of which the particular organism is a part, as well as on the performance of the product(s) which are manufactured and/or sold by the organism, are available from the Census of Manufactures. The first census was taken in 1810. Under 1964 legislation the census will be held in the years ending in 2 and 7.

Corporate data on demand, supply, profit

The data include all the three principal categories of raw data input developed in previous sections. Thus, data are available on the demand, supply, and profit factors. The wealth of data made available through the Census of Manufactures and its update is extraordinary in coverage in both width and depth. Under U.S. Code Title 13, every establishment is required to file reports demanded of it by the Census of Manufactures:

An "establishment" is an economic unit which produces goods or services, for example, a farm, a mine, a factory, a store. In most instances, the establishment is at a single physical location; and it is engaged in one, or predominantly one, type of economic activity for which an industry code is applicable.[1]

The results of the Census of Manufactures now carried out are made available in three principal volumes: Volume I: Summary and Subject Statistics, Volume II: Industry Statistics, and Volume III: Area Statistics. In Volume I the manufacturing establishments are reported in terms of: (1) size of establishments; (2) type of organization; (3) manufacturers' inventories; (4) expenditures for new plant and new equipment; (5) materials consumed; and (6) water used in manufacturing. In Volume II, the industrial statistics are reported for major groups 19–39, and in Volume III, the data are shown by states, Standard Metropolitan Statistical Areas (SMSA), counties, selected cities, industry groups, and industry. In Table 4.1, the general statistics are shown from Volume I for major groups 24–27.

---

[1] Executive Office of the President, Bureau of the Budget, *Standard Industrial Classification Manual*, (Washington, D.C.: U.S. Government Printing Office, 1957), p. 3.

Table 4.1: General Statistics for Establishments by Industry Groups and Industries (1967)

		1967		
			Establishments*	
		Companies*	Total	With 20 employees or more
Code	Industry group and industry	(number)	(number)	(number)
24	Lumber and wood products	35 573	36 795	5 803
2411	Logging camps, logging contractors	16 265	16 334	598
242	Sawmills and planing mills	11 058	11 461	2 355
2421	Sawmills and planing mills, general	10 016	10 271	1 916
2426	Hardwood dimension and flooring	613	665	331
2429	Special product sawmills, nec**	454	525	108
243	Millwork, Plywood, related prod	4 308	4 558	1 496
2431	Millwork	3 292	3 342	767
2432	Veneer and Plywood	516	667	515
2433	Prefabricated wood structures	519	549	214
244	Wooden containers	829	905	304
2441	Nailed wooden boxes and shook	567	596	182
2442	Wirebound boxes and crates	118	134	63
2443	Veneer and Plywood containers	81	84	39
2445	Cooperage	67	91	20
249	Miscellaneous wood products	3 319	3 537	1 050
2491	Wood preserving	278	375	177
2499	Wood products, nec**	3 044	3 162	873
25	Furniture and fixtures	9 518	10 008	3 449
251	Household furniture	5 948	6 306	2 366
2511	Wood household furniture	2 934	3 084	1 011
2512	Upholstered household furniture	1 582	1 644	727
2514	Metal household furniture	464	486	251
2515	Mattresses and bedsprings	939	1 013	341
2519	Household furniture, nec**	75	79	36
252	Office furniture	334	365	189
2521	Wood office furniture	172	178	69
2522	Metal office furniture	166	187	120
2531	Public Building furniture	428	438	188

All employees		Production workers			Value	
Number	Payroll	Number	Man-hours	Wages	added by manufacture	Value of shipments
(1,000)	(million dollars)	(1,000)	(millions)	(million dollars)	(million dollars)	(million dollars)
554.0	2 798.9	495.7	977.0	2 290.6	4 973.4	11 205.7
70.6	338.8	67.5	125.9	306.8	695.1	1 476.3
215.5	1 028.3	196.5	385.0	874.5	1 783.9	3 997.8
180.5	884.6	164.7	322.7	754.8	1 556.4	3 506.4
27.9	115.1	25.2	51.5	94.4	176.8	373.5
7.1	28.5	6.7	10.9	25.4	50.7	117.9
154.0	896.3	132.0	268.8	697.3	1 505.4	3 653.2
64.8	373.0	53.9	106.6	274.1	636.4	1 472.4
72.9	420.6	66.2	138.4	361.9	678.1	1 687.2
16.3	102.6	11.9	23.8	61.2	190.9	493.7
31.3	134.5	28.3	55.6	109.5	238.6	529.5
15.9	70.9	14.4	27.8	56.9	123.0	273.8
9.4	36.5	8.5	17.2	29.8	71.1	144.9
3.3	11.6	3.0	5.9	9.8	18.4	32.0
2.7	15.5	2.4	4.7	13.0	26.1	78.8
82.6	401.2	71.3	141.6	302.5	750.3	1 548.8
12.2	61.9	10.3	21.7	47.1	135.6	344.2
70.4	339.3	61.0	119.9	255.4	614.8	1 204.6
425.3	2 258.3	357.5	715.7	1 653.7	4 169.5	7 749.8
297.8	1 456.1	257.3	513.1	1 101.0	2 649.5	5 111.0
157.4	738.1	139.7	283.9	582.8	1 322.0	2 438.9
75.2	376.2	64.8	125.9	287.0	670.3	1 266.4
31.0	155.5	25.8	50.3	109.6	291.3	605.3
31.2	171.5	24.4	47.8	110.7	335.5	745.1
3.0	14.8	2.6	5.2	10.9	30.4	55.3
35.2	225.0	28.0	57.2	160.9	478.1	781.2
8.2	46.4	6.9	14.3	35.6	88.8	158.3
27.0	178.5	21.1	42.9	125.3	389.3	622.9
22.6	132.2	17.5	36.3	89.2	233.6	421.2

Table 4.1 (continued)

		1967		
			Establishments*	
		Companies*	Total	With 20 employees or more
Code	Industry group and industry	(number)	(number)	(number)
254	Partitions and fixtures	1 947	1 970	526
2541	Wood partitions and fixtures	1 463	1 470	338
2542	Metal partitions and fixtures	491	500	188
259	Misc. Furniture and fixtures	898	929	180
2591	Venetian blinds and shades	581	605	61
2599	Furniture and fixtures, nec**	317	324	119
26	Paper and allied products	3 913	5 890	3 813
2611	Pulpmills	45	61	43
2621	Papermills, except building paper	203	354	313
2631	Paperboard mills	148	283	264
264	Misc. Converted paper products	2 030	2 492	1 284
2641	Paper coating and glazing	334	397	202
2642	Envelopes	172	228	163
2643	Bags, except textile bags	466	557	310
2644	Wallpaper	74	77	31
2645	Die-cut paper and board	368	440	189
2646	Pressed and molded pulp goods	43	58	45
2647	Sanitary paper products	91	125	86
2649	Converted paper products nec**	566	610	258
265	Paperboard containers and boxes	1 681	2 606	1 835
2651	Folding paperboard boxes	476	569	393
2652	Setup paperboard boxes	418	454	295
2653	Corrugated and solid fiber boxes	568	1 071	803
2654	Sanitary food containers	144	244	184
2655	Fiber cans, drums, related material	165	268	160
2661	Building paper and board mills	43	94	74
27	Printing and publishing	36 431	37 989	8 035
2711	Newspapers	7 589	8 094	2 029
2721	Periodicals	2 430	2 510	454

All employees		Production workers			Value added by manufacture	Value of shipments
Number	Payroll	Number	Man-hours	Wages		
(1,000)	(million dollars)	(1,000)	(millions)	(million dollars)	(million dollars)	(million dollars)
48.0	323.6	37.6	76.0	220.1	587.0	1 010.7
25.3	170.7	20.7	40.9	124.1	284.6	498.6
22.7	152.9	17.0	35.1	96.0	302.5	512.0
21.6	121.4	17.0	33.0	82.5	221.2	425.7
11.6	62.1	8.6	15.9	37.7	122.3	246.8
10.1	59.4	8.4	17.2	44.8	98.9	179.0
638.9	4 436.2	507.7	1 071.2	3 205.5	9 756.3	20 969.9
15.1	125.6	12.2	25.4	96.0	333.7	730.5
140.0	1 120.7	112.3	249.2	849.2	2 356.3	4 844.0
67.0	533.5	53.8	118.2	405.9	1 508.8	2 907.0
186.6	1 187.4	146.8	298.8	819.1	2 833.3	6 210.1
37.1	260.8	27.0	56.4	165.6	728.0	1 566.5
22.5	141.9	18.1	37.6	98.0	253.1	470.3
46.3	278.3	37.1	75.6	197.4	563.7	1 375.6
2.3	14.6	1.8	3.6	9.9	27.0	48.6
18.6	117.3	14.7	29.4	79.9	247.3	577.5
6.7	44.8	5.4	11.4	33.0	97.8	145.9
22.0	154.2	18.3	37.6	119.2	540.2	1 293.4
31.1	175.5	24.4	47.2	116.2	376.1	732.2
218.6	1 386.5	172.6	358.2	967.9	2 540.5	5 937.3
49.3	322.6	39.5	82.1	228.8	563.2	1 216.2
21.1	100.4	18.3	35.4	73.3	160.2	282.4
97.1	656.0	73.0	152.5	435.0	1 130.0	2 959.6
35.3	213.8	28.5	60.2	157.8	506.1	1 093.9
15.7	93.7	13.3	27.9	72.9	181.1	385.2
11.7	82.5	10.0	21.5	67.4	183.7	341.1
1 031.0	7 151.5	631.6	1 196.1	4 011.3	14 355.1	21 738.4
335.9	2 223.7	169.2	302.0	1 121.5	4 184.7	5 757.1
79.1	633.7	14.5	25.2	80.5	1 868.7	3 095.9

Table 4.1 (continued)

		1967		
			Establishments*	
		Companies*	Total	With 20 employees or more
Code	Industry group and industry	(number)	(number)	(number)
273	Books	1 673	1 766	603
2731	Book publishing	963	1 022	287
2732	Book printing	720	744	316
2741	Miscellaneous publishing	1 433	1 493	204
275	Commercial printing	19 162	19 497	3 216
2751	Commercial printing, exc. litho	11 955	12 098	1 439
2752	Commercial printing, lithographic	6 718	6 822	1 648
2753	Engraving and plate printing	569	577	129
2761	Manifold business forms	454	542	295
2771	Greeting card publishing	203	222	92
278	Blankbooks and bookbinding	1 409	1 462	527
2782	Blankbooks and looseleaf binders	402	444	193
2789	Bookbinding and related work	1 008	1 018	334
279	Printing trade services	2 366	2 403	615
2791	Typesetting	1 518	1 535	365
2793	Photoengraving	732	735	193
2794	Electrotyping and stereotyping	124	133	57

* An establishment is a single physical location at which business is conducted. An establishment is not necessarily identical with the "company" or "enterprises" which may consist of one or more establishments.
** Not elsewhere classified.

Annual survey of manufactures

One of the sources to update data by SMSA is the Annual Survey of Manufactures, initiated in 1949 and conducted for years not covered by the Census of Manufactures. It provides data on employment, payroll, man-hours, value added by manufacturers for geographic divisions, states, and SMSAs:

The survey currently covers approximately 65,000 plants out of a total of about 300,000. Included in the sample are all large manufacturing plants, which account for more than two-thirds of total employment of

All employees		Production workers			Value	
Number	Payroll	Number	Man-hours	Wages	added by manufacture	Value of shipments
(1,000)	(million dollars)	(1,000)	(millions)	(million dollars)	(million dollars)	(million dollars)
96.5	688.0	49.9	98.1	304.5	1 967.4	2 922.1
51.8	390.1	13.2	24.7	76.6	1 456.5	2 134.7
44.7	297.9	36.7	73.4	227.9	510.9	787.4
31.1	197.4	15.0	25.6	79.7	417.5	605.3
330.6	2 357.9	261.8	511.1	1 689.3	3 944.4	6 532.8
175.1	1 186.0	142.3	273.2	880.1	1 947.9	3 255.5
146.5	1 113.2	112.2	223.3	766.5	1 897.7	3 139.4
9.0	58.7	7.3	14.6	42.7	98.8	137.9
34.4	240.2	25.3	51.4	158.9	550.5	932.3
27.6	150.6	16.4	31.3	75.0	372.3	517.9
53.5	294.2	46.6	88.7	225.6	506.0	721.9
23.2	130.3	19.4	38.4	94.5	245.4	381.3
30.3	163.9	27.2	50.3	131.0	260.6	340.6
42.2	365.8	32.9	62.7	276.4	543.7	653.1
25.5	208.3	20.9	40.2	164.1	304.3	356.7
13.2	126.2	9.4	17.5	89.8	191.7	234.3
3.6	31.3	2.6	5.0	22.5	47.7	62.0

all manufacturing establishments in the United States, and a sample of the more numerous medium- and small-sized establishments.[2]

Key plant data

There are about 300,000 plants in the United States, and insofar as the sales of products depend upon their manufacture in these plants, it would be most valuable to business interests to know the plants by SIC classification. The publishers of *Sales Management*, who publish data by SMSAs, also publish the identity of the plants, their address, and their respective number of employees by SIC code in *Market Statistics: Key Plants*, in which, as early as 1970, data on 41,000 "key plants" with 100 or more employees was available.

[2] Bureau of Census, *Catalogue 1971, Part I: Publications* (Washington, D.C.: U.S. Department of Commerce, 1971), p. 65.

91

APPLICATION 1
SIC DATA NORMS FOR RAW DATA INPUT

One of the industries which appears in Table 4.1 is Industry 2515: Mattresses and Bedsprings.

Key company data

From Table 4.1 it is seen that there were 939 companies in the industry in 1967 with 31,200 employees and a payroll of $171.5 million. The value of the shipments by the industry is $745.1 million. As one of the 939 companies, are you performing as well as could be expected? Knowing nothing else, one could take a stab at what one's shipment "ought" to be by simply dividing $745.1 million into 939, giving approximately $793,400. However, averages imply above average and below average. Therefore, the mere fact that your shipment is, say, $800,000 does not give much cause for comfort.

On the other hand, suppose that the share of the market of some of the 939 companies were known. That would provide a yardstick with which to compare your own performance. For instance, is your performance closer to the highest or lowest or middle group of companies in your industry? If not in the highest group, should you try to be, and if so, how?

Fortunately, such a yardstick is indeed available. It is published in the Bureau of the Census publication, *Concentration Ratios in Manufacturing:*

> Information on the shipments of approximately 1,200 classes of products and the proportion accounted for by the 4, 8, 20, and 50 largest companies manufacturing each class of product. Data are given for 1967 with comparative statistics for 1963, 1958, and 1954.[3]

A page out of the *Concentration Ratios* is reproduced as Table 4.2. It is found that in the mattresses and bedsprings industry, the 4 largest companies accounted for 26 percent of the 1967 shipments, i.e., an average of 6.5 percent each; the remaining 935 shared 74 percent of the shipments. The 8 largest companies accounted for 34 percent of the shipments. Or, the 5th, 6th, 7th, and 8th largest companies together shipped (34 − 26 =) 8 percent, each shipping an average of 2.0 percent of the industry shipments, less than a third of the 1st, 2nd, 3rd, and 4th largest companies. The next 12 largest companies, viz., 9th through 20th, each averaged 0.83 percent. The average share of the next 30 largest companies, viz., 21st through 50th, is even smaller at 0.47 percent.

---

[3] Bureau of the Census, 1971 Census of Manufactures, *Concentration Ratios in Manufacturing,* Part II: Product Class Concentration Ratios (Washington, D.C.: U.S. Department of Commerce, 1971), pp. 61–62.

On the basis of these concentration ratios, if one were in the group of 21st to the 50th largest companies, the yardstick would be the average share of the shipment, viz., 0.47 percent of $745.1 million or $3.5 million. Of course, the $3.5 million is an average figure. Therefore, the higher ranking companies in the lowest group of 21st through 50th may be closer to the average of the 9th through 20th largest companies, or 0.83 percent representing $6.2 million.

Key financial data

It is one thing to arrive at a yardstick to compare one's own performance in shipment (sales) with that of one's industry; it is quite another *to know how profitable* the performance is.

If sales figures are closely held by the companies, profit figures are even more so. However, corporations are required to file U.S. Corporation Income Tax Form 1120. The Federal Trade Commission and the Securities and Exchange Commission have published *Quarterly Financial Report for Manufacturing Corporations* since 1947 based on a sample representing about 88 percent of a composite frame. The component parts of the sample frame are the Internal Revenue Service Form 1120 returns and the Social Security Administration applications for Employer Identification Number. The sample covers the companies accounting for the bulk of corporate assets—the 9,500–10,500 manufacturing companies included in the quarterly sample accounting for approximately 88 percent. In the second quarter in 1971, the 9,665 manufacturing companies included in the sample had corporate assets of $584,253,000,000.

The *Quarterly Financial Report for Manufacturing Corporations* publishes 10 tables. They are:

Table 1: Rates of Change in Sales and Profits by Industry
Table 2: Profits per Dollar by Sales by Industry
Table 3: Profits per Dollar by Asset Size and Industry Group
Table 4: Annual Rates of Profit on Stockholder's Equity by Industry
Table 5: Annual Rates of Profit on Stockholder's Equity by Industry Asset Size and Industry Group
Table 6: Financial Statements in Ratio Form by Industry
Table 7: Financial Statements in Ratio Form by Asset Size and Industry Group
Table 8: Financial Statements in Dollar Amounts by Industry
Table 9: Financial Statements in Dollar Amounts by Asset Size and Industry Group
Table 10: Composition of the Sample by Total Assets

Table 4.2: Percent of Selected Statistics Accounted for by the 4, 8, 20 and 50 Largest

Item	Number of		Value of shipments	All employees	
	Com-panies	Estab-lishments		Number	Payroll
	(a)	(b)	(c)	(d)	(e)
Industry 2515—Mattresses and bedsprings					
Total (columns c, e, g, h to m in millions d and f in thousands)	939	1,013	$745.1	31.2	$171.5
Percent of above totals accounted for by					
4 largest companies	(x)	3	26	26	28
8 largest companies	(x)	5	34	33	36
20 largest companies	(x)	8	44	44	47
50 largest companies	(x)	12	58	55	58
Industry 2519—Household furniture, N.E.C.					
Total (columns c, e, g, h to m in millions d and f in thousands)	75	79	$55.3	3.0	$14.8
Percent of above totals accounted for by					
4 largest companies	(x)	8	36	26	29
8 largest companies	(x)	13	53	47	49
20 largest companies	(x)	29	82	74	75
50 largest companies	(x)	68	98	98	98
Industry 2521—Wood office furniture					
Total (columns c, e, g, h to m in millions d and f in thousands)	172	178	$158.3	8.2	$46.4
Percent of above totals accounted for by					
4 largest companies	(x)	4	29	23	24
8 largest companies	(x)	8	48	42	44
20 largest companies	(x)	15	71	68	68
50 largest companies	(x)	32	88	87	87

Companies Ranked on Value of Shipments in Each Industry (1967)

Production workers			Value added by manufacture	Capital expenditures, new			Cost of materials
Number	Man-hours	Wages		Total	Structures and additions to plant	Machinery and equipment	
(f)	(g)	(h)	(i)	(j)	(k)	(l)	(m)
Industry 2515 — Mattresses and bedsprings							
24.4	47.8	$110.7	$335.5	$10.3	$4.3	$6.0	$408.8
26	25	31	30	22	21	23	23
32	32	39	37	29	24	31	30
43	44	48	47	43	40	45	42
53	54	58	60	58	58	59	55
Industry 2519—Household furniture, N.E.C.							
2.6	5.2	$10.9	$30.4	$1.3	$0.7	$0.6	$24.7
25	28	29	35	10	(D)	(D)	36
46	48	48	51	81	(D)	(D)	54
74	75	75	80	94	(D)	(D)	83
97	98	98	98	99-	99-	99-	98
Industry 2521—Wood office furniture							
6.9	14.3	$35.6	$88.8	$5.7	$2.8	$2.9	$71.7
23	24	23	26	45	46	46	33
41	42	42	46	70	68	72	52
68	69	67	68	89	93	85	74
86	87	87	88	94	95	94	90

Table 4.2 continued

Item	Number of		Value of shipments	All employees	
	Com-panies	Estab-lishments		Number	Payroll
	(a)	(b)	(c)	(d)	(e)

Industry 2522—Metal office furniture

Item	(a)	(b)	(c)	(d)	(e)
Total (columns c, e, g, h to m in millions d and f in thousands)	166	187	$622.9	27.0	$178.5
Percent of above totals accounted for by					
4 largest companies	(x)	7	38	31	37
8 largest companies	(x)	11	52	47	52
20 largest companies	(x)	20	75	71	75
50 largest companies	(x)	38	92	88	91

Industry 2531—Public building furniture

Item	(a)	(b)	(c)	(d)	(e)
Total (columns c, e, g, h to m in millions d and f in thousands)	428	438	$421.2	22.6	$132.2
Percent of above totals accounted for by					
4 largest companies	(x)	1	23	21	27
8 largest companies	(x)	3	36	31	37
20 largest companies	(x)	7	54	49	54
50 largest companies	(x)	14	72	67	70

Industry 2541—Wood partitions and fixtures

Item	(a)	(b)	(c)	(d)	(e)
Total (columns c, e, g, h to m in millions d and f in thousands)	1,463	1,470	$498.6	25.3	$170.7
Percent of above totals accounted for by					
4 largest companies	(x)	(Z)	6	4	5
8 largest companies	(x)	1	10	8	9
20 largest companies	(x)	2	20	16	17
50 largest companies	(x)	4	36	31	33

(Z) Less than half of 1 percent
— Represents zero
(D) Withheld to avoid disclosing figures of individual companies
(x) Not applicable
r Revised
N.E.C. Not Elsewhere Classified
N.S.K. Not Specified by Kind

Production workers			Value added by manu- facture	Capital expenditures, new [1]			
Number	Man- hours	Wages		Total	Structures and addi- tions to plant	Machinery and equip- ment	Cost of materials
(f)	(g)	(h)	(i)	(j)	(k)	(l)	(m)

Industry 2522—Metal office furniture

21.1	42.9	$125.3	$389.3	$31.5	$15.9	$15.6	$239.5
31	31	37	37	26	28	25	38
47	48	54	53	74	79	69	51
70	71	75	76	84	85	83	73
88	88	91	93	94	94	94	91

Industry 2531—Public building furniture

17.5	36.3	$89.2	$233.6	$10.0	$4.4	$5.6	$194.7
17	18	25	26	18	13	22	21
27	28	34	38	29	28	30	34
46	47	52	56	48	43	53	53
64	66	68	73	68	65	69	72

Industry 2541—Wood partitions and fixtures

20.7	40.9	$124.1	$284.6	$8.1	$3.8	$4.3	$214.8
4	4	6	7	8	11	5	5
8	8	9	10	(D)	(D)	(D)	10
15	15	17	20	28	37	21	20
31	32	32	35	51	61	43	37

(1) Includes expenditures for plants in operation and for plants under construction but not yet in operation

Table 4.3: Financial Statements in Ratio Form for All Manufacturing Corporations by Industry

	Furniture and Fixtures				
	2Q 1970	3Q 1970	4Q 1970	1Q 1971	2Q 1971
INCOME	(percent of sales)				
Sales (net of returns, allowances, and discounts)	100.0	100.0	100.0	100.0	100.0
Deduct: Costs and expenses (net of purchase discounts)	95.1	94.5	95.0	96.0	93.8
Net profit from operations	4.9	5.5	5.0	4.0	6.2
Add: Other income or deductions (net)	−0.1	−0.2	−0.1	0.0	−0.1
Net profit before Federal income taxes	4.9	5.3	4.9	3.9	6.1
Deduct: Provision for Federal income taxes	2.5	2.4	2.5	2.2	2.7
Net profit after taxes	2.4	2.9	2.4	1.7	3.3
Depreciation and depletion included above, including accelerated amortization of emergency facilities	1.8	1.7	1.8	1.9	1.8
ASSETS	(percent of total assets)				
Cash on hand and in bank	5.7	6.3	6.7	6.4	6.4
U.S. Government securities, including Treasury savings notes	1.7	1.5	1.8	1.7	1.2
Total cash and U.S. Government securities	7.4	7.8	8.5	8.0	7.6
Receivables from U.S. Government, excluding tax credits	0.4	0.2	0.1	0.2	0.1
Other notes and accounts receivable (net)	24.9	26.1	25.4	24.6	24.2
Total receivables	25.2	26.3	25.5	24 8	24.3
Inventories	31.9	30.3	29.2	29.6	29.4
Other current assets	3.0	3.1	3.0	3.4	3.3
Total current assets	67.5	67.4	66.2	65.9	64.7
Property, plant and equipment	50.6	50.9	51.7	52.9	53.1
Deduct: Reserve for depreciation and depletion	23.6	23.8	23.7	24.5	24.3
Total property, plant and equipment (net)	26.9	27.0	28.0	28.4	28.9
Other noncurrent assets	5.6	5.5	5.8	5.7	6.5
Total assets	100.0	100.0	100.0	100.0	100.0

Lumber and Wood Products, Except Furniture					Instruments and Related Products					Miscellaneous Manufacturing, and Ordnance				
2Q 1970	3Q 1970	4Q 1970	1Q 1971	2Q 1971	2Q 1970	3Q 1970	4Q 1970	1Q 1971	2Q 1971	2Q 1970	3Q 1970	4Q 1970	1Q 1971	2Q 1971
(percent of sales)					(percent of sales)					(percent of sales)				
100.0	100.0	100.0	100.0	100.0	100.0	100.0	100.0	100.0	100.0	100.0	100.0	100.0	100.0	100.0
94.8	94.9	96.4	94.8	92.7	85.9	85.2	86.1	88.4	85.9	93.5	93.4	92.8	93.7	92.4
5.2	5.1	3.6	5.2	7.3	14.1	14.8	13.9	11.6	14.1	6.5	6.6	7.2	6.3	7.6
−0.3	−0.2	−0.2	−0.3	0.0	−0.3	−0.6	−0.5	−0.5	−0.4	0.0	−0.3	−0.2	0.0	−0.5
4.9	4.9	3.4	4.8	7.3	13.8	14.2	13.4	11.1	13.6	6.5	6.3	6.9	6.2	7.1
2.1	2.1	1.6	1.8	2.6	6.6	6.6	5.8	5.4	6.2	3.0	2.8	3.1	2.9	3.3
2.9	2.8	1.8	3.0	4.7	7.2	7.6	7.6	5.7	7.4	3.5	3.6	3.8	3.3	3.3
4.3	4.2	4.5	4.6	4.5	4.5	4.4	4.9	5.6	5.3	2.0	2.0	2.1	2.3	2.3
(percent of total assets)					(percent of total assets)					(percent of total assets)				
4.0	4.0	4.1	4.0	4.2	4.2	4.7	5.2	5.4	4.4	5.3	5.7	6.5	5.5	5.9
9.3	0.4	0.4	0.3	0.2	1.8	1.8	2.1	1.7	1.6	0.4	0.2	0.4	0.3	0.3
4.3	4.4	4.5	4.3	4.4	6.0	6.4	7.3	7.1	6.0	5.8	5.9	6.8	5.8	5.2
0.0	0.0	0.0	0.0	0.0	1.3	0.9	1.1	1.3	1.3	0.3	0.3	0.4	0.4	0.3
14.0	13.9	12.7	13.8	13.8	20.1	20.9	19.4	18.4	19.1	27.1	28.8	27.7	25.9	26.3
14.0	13.9	12.7	13.9	13.8	21.3	21.8	20.5	19.7	20.4	27.4	29.1	28.1	28.3	26.3
19.5	19.5	19.2	19.1	18.6	26.4	25.7	24.2	24.0	24.2	30.4	29.3	28.9	30.5	30.4
3.1	3.2	2.9	3.4	4.3	5.8	5.8	5.8	6.2	5.6	2.7	2.6	2.5	2.6	2.9
41.0	41.0	39.3	40.7	41.0	59.6	59.8	57.8	57.0	56.2	66.4	66.9	66.3	65.1	66.9
79.7	79.2	81.6	80.2	79.7	61.5	61.6	65.3	66.9	68.2	45.1	44.8	46.8	47.1	46.7
30.2	29.8	30.5	30.4	30.5	27.0	27.2	29.0	30.0	30.8	21.0	21.2	21.9	22.5	22.2
49.5	49.4	51.2	49.8	49.2	34.5	34.4	36.2	36.9	37.4	24.0	23.6	24.4	24.5	24.6
9.5	9.6	9.6	9.4	9.7	5.9	5.8	6.0	6.1	6.4	9.6	9.6	9.2	10.2	9.1
100.0	100.0	100.0	100.0	100.0	100.0	100.0	100.0	100.0	100.0	100.0	100.0	100.0	100.0	100.0

Table 4.3 continued

	Furniture and Fixtures				
	2Q 1970	*3Q 1970*	*4Q 1970*	*1Q 1971*	*2Q 1971*
LIABILITIES AND STOCKHOLDERS' EQUITY					
Short-term loans from banks (original maturity of 1 year or less)	5.7	5.5	5.2	5.1	4.4
Advances and prepayments by U.S. Government	0.0	0.0	0.0	0.0	0.0
Trade accounts and notes payable	10.5	10.7	10.0	9.4	9.4
Federal income taxes accrued	1.5	1.7	1.6	1.6	1.1
Installments, due in 1 year or less, on long-term debt					
(a) Loans from banks	1.2	1.0	0.7	0.8	0.8
(b) Other long-term debt	1.1	1.0	1.0	1.1	1.1
Other current liabilities	5.9	6.0	6.0	6.0	5.9
Total current liabilities	25.9	26.0	24.6	23.9	22.8
Long-term debt due in more than 1 year (a) Loans from banks	3.5	3.4	3.1	3.1	3.8
(b) Other long-term debt	8.7	8.5	8.9	9.4	9.2
Other noncurrent liabilities	1.0	1.1	0.9	0.9	1.0
Total liabilities	39.1	39.1	37.5	37.3	36.8
Reserves not reflected elsewhere	–	–	–	–	–
Capital stock, capital surplus, and minority interest	18.4	18.4	19.0	18.8	19.1
Earned surplus and surplus reserves	42.4	42.5	43.5	43.9	44.0
Total stockholders' equity	60.9	60.9	62.4	62.7	63.1
Total liabilities and stockholders' equity	100.0	100.0	100.0	100.0	100.0
OPERATING RATIOS	(percent)				
Annual rate of profit on stockholders' equity at end of period –					
Before Federal income taxes	15.4	17.0	15.8	11.4	19.1
After taxes	7.6	9.2	7.8	4.9	10.5
	(times)				
Current assets to current liabilities	2.60	2.59	2.69	2.76	2.84
Total cash and U.S. Government securities to total current liabilities	.28	.30	.34	.34	.34
Total stockholders' equity to debt	3.02	3.12	3.30	3.22	3.25

Lumber and Wood Products, Except Furniture					Instruments and Related Products					Miscellaneous Manufacturing, and Ordnance				
2Q 1970	3Q 1970	4Q 1970	1Q 1971	2Q 1971	2Q 1970	3Q 1970	4Q 1970	1Q 1971	2Q 1971	2Q 1970	3Q 1970	4Q 1970	1Q 1971	2Q 1971
4.8	4.5	3.7	3.7	3.4	5.7	5.5	5.2	5.2	5.3	11.1	12.3	10.5	9.2	11.0
0.0	0.0	0.0	0.1	0.1	0.6	0.5	0.4	0.4	0.4	0.0	0.0	0.0	0.0	0.0
6.7	7.1	6.5	6.3	6.3	5.3	5.6	6.0	5.5	5.4	10.3	10.4	10.7	9.5	9.1
1.2	1.1	1.1	1.1	1.0	3.5	3.7	3.3	4.0	3.2	1.9	2.2	2.5	2.7	2.2
1.5	1.4	1.6	1.5	1.6	0.6	0.6	0.6	0.7	0.6	0.6	0.5	0.6	0.6	0.5
1.4	1.4	1.5	1.3	1.3	0.6	0.5	0.9	1.0	1.0	1.2	1.2	1.4	1.4	1.2
5.8	6.5	5.2	6.2	6.1	8.0	8.2	8.6	8.0	8.0	6.3	6.1	6.4	6.9	6.4
21.5	22.1	19.6	20.2	19.8	24.3	24.6	25.1	24.7	24.0	31.4	32.5	32.1	30.3	30.5
6.4	6.2	6.2	7.2	7.0	3.4	3.5	2.0	1.7	2.3	2.3	2.1	2.9	3.2	3.6
19.7	19.3	21.9	20.6	21.9	8.5	8.5	11.2	10.9	10.2	12.1	12.2	12.2	11.9	11.9
2.5	2.5	2.6	2.1	2.2	2.9	3.0	3.2	3.4	3.3	1.7	1.9	1.8	1.8	2.3
50.1	50.2	50.3	50.1	51.0	39.1	39.5	41.6	40.8	39.9	47.6	48.8	49.0	47.1	48.3
—	—	—	—	—	—	—	—	—	—	—	—	—	—	—
20.6	20.2	20.8	21.6	20.9	20.8	19.8	19.6	20.0	20.2	18.3	18.2	18.6	18.7	18.2
29.3	29.6	28.9	28.3	28.2	40.1	40.7	38.8	39.2	39.9	34.1	32.9	32.4	34.1	33.5
49.9	49.8	49.7	49.9	49.0	60.9	60.5	58.4	59.2	60.2	52.4	51.2	51.0	52.9	51.7
100.0	100.0	100.0	100.0	100.0	100.0	100.0	100.0	100.0	100.0	100.0	100.0	100.0	100.0	100.0
(percent)					(percent)					(percent)				
12.3	12.2	8.1	10.8	19.3	26.5	27.5	27.4	19.9	26.0	19.3	18.8	21.3	16.2	19.7
7.1	7.1	4.3	6.7	12.4	13.9	14.8	15.5	10.2	14.2	10.3	10.7	11.7	8.6	10.6
(times)					(times)					(times)				
1.90	1.85	2.01	2.02	2.08	2.45	2.43	2.30	2.31	2.34	2.11	2.05	2.07	2.15	2.17
.20	.20	.23	.21	.22	.25	.26	.29	.29	.25	.18	.18	.21	.19	.20
1.48	1.52	1.43	1.45	1.39	3.24	3.28	2.92	3.05	3.09	1.91	1.81	1.85	2.01	1.83

A portion of one of the tables is reproduced as Table 4.3. The first column gives the data for furniture and fixtures. Industry 2515: mattresses and bedsprings whose shipments were discussed in the previous section is part of the major industry group 25: furniture and fixtures. Its breakdown, as shown in Table 4.1, is as follows:

		Value of Shipments (millions)
25	FURNITURE AND FIXTURES	$7,749.8
251	Household Furniture	5,111.0
2511	Wood household furniture	2,438.9
2512	Upholstered household furniture	1,266.4
2514	Metal household furniture	605.3
2515	Mattresses and bedsprings	745.1
2519	Household furniture, nec (not elsewhere classified	55.3
252	Office Furniture	781.2
2521	Wood office furniture	158.3
2522	Metal office furniture	622.9
2531	Public building furniture	421.2
254	Partitions and Fixtures	1,010.7
2541	Wood partitions and fixtures	498.6
2542	Metal partitions and fixtures	512.0
259	Misc. Furniture and Fixtures	425.7
2591	Venetian blinds and shades	246.8
2599	Furniture and fixtures, nec	179.0

In Table 4.3, financial statements in ratio form for major industry group 25: furniture and fixtures is shown. In other words, the figures relate to an industry group with 1967 shipments of $7,749.8 million, of which mattresses and bedsprings shipments account for 9.5 percent at $745.1 million.

It is seen that the net profit after taxes increased from 2.4 percent of sales in the 2nd quarter of 1970 to 3.3 percent in the corresponding quarter of 1971. The 2nd quarter figure is even more impressive when compared with the preceding one—a figure of 1.7—almost double!

In using these figures as a yardstick for the profits in mattresses and bedsprings, it bears repetition that this industry is only 9.5 percent of the major industry group whose net profit figures are published.

If one were contemplating investment in the most profitable industry group, instruments and related products is clearly the choice from among the four groups in Table 4.3.

Shipment data

SINGLE PRODUCT COMPANY

The reason why the national data do not readily lend themselves to the development of a company organismic index of performance is that if it were a single-product company, say, mattresses and bedsprings, it is only one among 939 companies engaged in the shipment of that product, as seen from Table 4.1. The key company data on shipment would be a point of departure for the potentials of the particular company under discussion. However, the data on the 939 companies cannot be readily or directly applied to the single company in question.

MULTIPRODUCT COMPANY

More often than not, the company is likely to be multiproduct rather than single product. Even if mattresses and bedsprings were treated as a single product, the associated products which the company deals in would probably include it in the furniture and fixtures group, which is the major industry group 25 of which the mattresses and bedsprings industry is a component. It would mean that the industry figure of 2.4 percent in the second quarter of 1970, rising to 3.3 percent in the second quarter of 1971, must be even more seriously qualified for use as a company yardstick. Nevertheless, if the company activity justifies including it within the furniture and fixtures group, the net profit after taxes for the 9,518 companies would be a useful starting point.

Area data

More than the gross shipment figures for the nation as a whole, the specific shipments to particular areas of the country would be useful for a given company. Improvement in the shipment(s) to the country as a whole is made up of improvements in shipments to various segments of the country.

At this level, the national data tend to become less reliable. The reason is that the shipment data are no longer for the entire line of mattresses and bedsprings treated as a unit, but for different kinds of mattresses and bedsprings. In terms of the SIC numbers, the level of detail increases from 4 to 7 digits—from 2515 to 2515115—which introduces errors in reporting. It is not that the figures at the 4-digit level are more accurate, but simply that the classificatory errors at the lowest level are less significant to the overall figures at the gross level than at the finer detail. Thus, the distinction between orthopedic, regular, heavy duty, and firm mattresses would be most significant at the 7-digit level if each of the products does, in fact, have a single product "line." But, the errors in reporting at this level do not affect the usefulness of the 4-digit figure for mattresses and bedsprings as a whole.

APPLICATION 2
RAW DATA INPUT FORMS

Having identified the external sources of data as well as the types of internal data, we can now proceed to the development of input forms for the raw data.

The combining of two or more pieces of data to develop *more* than the sum of the individual data inputs could be referred to as information.* Figuratively speaking, the retrieval of data elements contributed by different departments (e.g., the number of units of a particular product sold to a particular customer at a particular time) and similar data on another product can be represented as $2 + 2 = 4$. All that has been put in has been retrieved: no more, and no less.

On the other hand, if in examining the data on sales to one customer of a particular SIC industry and of another customer in a different SIC industry, the organism finds that it is able to detect a pattern of preference in the demand for the products of the organism, say, an increase in the demand by one customer industry and a simultaneous decrease in the demand by another customer industry, then it will require action on the part of the organism either to counteract the decrease in demand in the one instance, and/or to foster the increase in the demand in the other instance. In this case, by the bringing together of two pieces of data, *more* than their respective intrinsic content has been obtained, or figuratively, $2 + 2 = 5$.

In the case of the utilization of the data on the technological edge of a corporation, i.e., patents, the discovery of a potential user of the patent yields more than information: it yields *intelligence*. There is a qualitative difference between intelligence and information. Both affect the behavior of the organism. Both represent additions to the sum of the separate data elements that comprise it. However, in the case of intelligence, a different kind of prognostication is involved; it is based on less reliable data than the input for information, and its conclusions are more far reaching. We may signify this by figuratively stating that in the case of *intelligence* $2 + 2 = 9$. The system is one in which data are the input, but intelligence is the output. We may say that it is an Intelligence Retrieval System (which includes both information retrieval and data retrieval). Since intelligence retrieval pertains to the highest level of organismic operations, we may refer to it as central, and the system as Central Intelligence Retrieval System (CIRS) (See Figure 4.1).

* In chapter 1, projected data were called information. The projection here is in *space*, as distinguished from the projection in *time* in chapter 1.

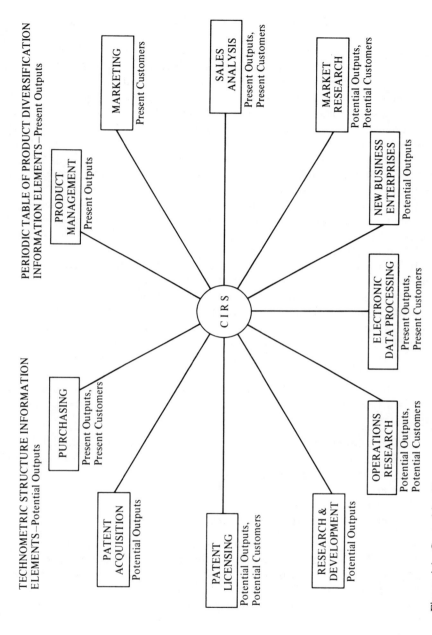

Figure 4.1: Central intelligence retrieval system

105

CIRS Data Input Forms

For every department, a CIRS input form needs to be developed in consultation with the particular department. Each department has to be assured that it can get back what it puts in (data retrieval). Further, it is most important that each department be able to get back something more. If such a quid pro quo is not established, chances are slim that the departments would cooperate in a fruitful manner. The liaison with CIRS requires investment of additional time and resources. As an inducement to the additional investment, the department must see some results for itself. Only if such a return is envisaged, will the department assign somebody with reasonable authority to perform the liaison. If the liaison is left to the lowest clerical level possible, as it would be unless the department sees in it sufficient advantages, then the entire basis of raw data input would be suspect. The resulting damages are not merely to the individual inputs, but to the entire CIRS.

It is a welcome feature indeed if the outputs from CIRS for the department are identified at the outset. Further, it is important to know the estimated frequency of use of CIRS by the department. It indicates that the department has given adequate thought as to how it will utilize the CIRS, what it would contribute to and receive from CIRS, and how often. The latter element, summarized in Table 4.4, permits a reasonable estimate of the time that the ADP installation has to reserve for the particular department.

Tables 4.5 and 4.6 and figures 4.2 through 4.4 set forth the *illustrative* raw data input forms from three of the following departments concerned with patent utilization:

> Department 1: Patents and Licenses—corporate headquarters
> Department 2: Patents and Licenses—research facility headquarters
> Department 3: Sales Analysis
> Department 4: Product Management
> Department 5: Marketing
> Department 6: New Enterprises

Each table is preceded by the inputs, outputs, and estimated frequency of use of CIRS by the department. In the input forms, the data items are identified by serial number. Space is provided for appropriate codes associated with each serial number of the data. The SIC code, for instance, corresponding to any item can be designated in the report form.

Raw Data Input for Nonprofit Organisms

Unlike the private sector, where profit is a clear and present motivating fact, in the public sector there is no profit which can be used as a gauge of customer acceptance of the organism's efforts to balance external demands with internal capabilities.

In the absence of a profit concept, it has become necessary to devise a substitute which will reflect the services in meeting external demand by internal capabilities. It has been suggested that the allocation of the federal budget is the result of the public mandate given by the people to the government to employ their resources to achieve public welfare. However, even in the concept of participative democracy as in the Swiss form of government, the relationship between public preferences and the allocation of public funds is far from established. How much more remote is the possibility of meaningfully asserting that in the protracted negotiations between the executive and the legislative there is any direct bearing of popular preferences upon the federal budget. For instance, it will be very hard to establish that in 1961, there was a clear and present expression of popular preference for the exploration of outer space, when President Kennedy asked for a national commitment to the lunar landing goal to be achieved before the end of the decade. Similarly, the abrupt deemphasis upon space exploration which the Nixon administration put into force right after the successful lunar landing will also be indeed a tenuous "popular preference" proposition to establish. If it is not by any means easy to identify the expression of popular preference in first going into space and second in getting out of space, how much less is the possibility of finding in the line items of the federal budget an index of popular preferences?

The word "service" may be used as the surrogate for profit in the public sector. It has the advantage of emphasizing the absence of product(s) in the provisions of services by the different cabinet departments. For instance, the service of "national security" is provided principally by the Department of Defense. However, other agencies such as the Atomic Energy Commission, also contribute to the service of national security; so does the Department of State. Similarly, the Department of Health, Education, and Welfare provides the service of "health." However, other agencies such as the Environmental Protection Agency also contribute to the service of health.

The value of a "service" measure of the public sector lies in its ability to rise beyond the administrative lines of each cabinet department and government agency, and to emphasize the combined output of several agencies to the same "service" measure. On this basis, $1.00 spent for "national security" has to compete with $1.00 spent for "health." Other competitive bids include the competition of $1.00 spent in "national security" with $1.00 spent in "transportation," "education," and so on. Within each of the "service" measures is the intra-agency competition for the federal dollar.

Before meaningful comparisons can be made between the dollar spent on security, education, health, transportation, and the like, it is essential to

Table 4.4: CIRS Output Format and Estimate Frequencies

Primary Topic	Data/Information Retrieval		Intelligence Retrieval	
Company	Marketing practices, known plans, etc., of specific competitors	(2)*	Relationships with specific other companies	(1)
	Rapid current intelligence	(5)	General relationships with specific other companies	(2)
			Market position of specific other companies	(2)
			Competitor marketing strategy	(4)
			Competitor development strategy	(8)
Total—24		(7)		(17)
Product	Product performance	(3)	Company's market position with respect to individual products	(3)
			Industry review and forecast ⎫ Equivalent to	(4)
			Product review and forecast ⎭	
			Quarterly achievements	—
Total—10		(3)		(7)
Patent	Retrieval of patent document	(2)	Potential patent listing by specific companies	(1)
			Patent listing by field	(1)
			Status and outlook	(5)
Total—9		(2)		(7)
License			Potential license listing	(5)
			Infringement searches	(¼)
Total—5				(5)
Invention	Company technology listing	(5)	Performance of inventions	(3)
	Invention and/or patent information	(3)	Company research vis-a-vis industry	(2)
	Invention idea performance	(1)		
Total—14		(9)		(5)
TOTAL—62		(21)		(41)

*Estimated frequency of use on *weekly basis* unless otherwise specified.

Table 4.5: Liaison with CIRS: Departments 1, 2

1. *Department:* Patents and Licenses—Corporate Headquarters
   Patents and Licenses—Research Facility Headquarters
2. *Liaison:* Mr. ABC
   Mr. DEF
3. *Departmental Contribution of Data:*

   The department will abstract on CIRS forms No. 1 and No. 2:

   a) Data relating to the elemental and structural details covered by patents issued to the organism pertaining to compounds, processes and apparatus.
   b) Patent utility.
   c) Licensing disposition.
   d) Status of know-how and disposition.
   e) Classification of prospective companies in terms of licensing potentials.
   f) Inquiries by mail, phone, personal contact, etc., about licensing of patent properties and/or know-how owned by the organism.

4. *CIRS Intelligence for Department:*

   1) Retrieval of patentable assets identified by (a) patent memorandum numbers, (b) docket numbers, (c) serial number and (d) U.S. patent number at any stage of development, easily and with minimum of error.
   2) Given any patent, a listing of the potential licensees in the order of desirability from the organism's point of view.
   3) Given any company and a technological field, a listing of the organism's patents, inventions under patent prosecution, and know-how of interest to the particular company.
   4) Given a technological field, a listing of all patents and inventions in the process of being patented that are owned by the organism and related to the field.

5. *Estimated Frequency of Use of CIRS by the Department:*

   The frequency will vary from time to time, but will generally be in the neighborhood of the following estimates:

1) Retrieval of patent document	2 times a week
2) Potential licensee listing	5 times a week
3) Potential patent listing by specific company	1 time a week
4) Patent listing by field	1 time a week
5) Infringement searches	¼ time a week

6. *Signature of Cognizant Authority:* Mr. ABC _____
   Mr. DEF _____

Figure 4.2: Raw Data Input for CIRS: Department 1

Date of Information:	ANALYTIC RECORDER:

Year Month Day

Year	Month	Day
75	01	11
76	02	22
77	03	33
78	04	44
79	05	55
80	06	66
81	07	77
82	08	88
83	09	99
84	10	00
85	11	
86	12	

FULL TITLE OF PATENT:

IDENTIFICATION

1. U.S. Patent No.   2. Date of Issue

4. Filing Date   5. Division & Docket No.

7. Inventor(s)   8. Originating Laboratory

10.   Foreign Filing: Yes ___ No _____
          Countries:

Information:
Source & Type

UTILIZATION

12. Functions and End-Uses

Reliability Index:

13. Availability Status:

#R.I.	#R.I.	#R.I.
01	02	03
04	05	06
07	08	09
10	11	12
13	14	15
16	17	18
19	20	21
22	23	24
25	26	27
28	29	30

Current Organism Use	Organism Not Using Now
Joint Development	Availability
Cross-licensing	Year of review
Royalty-bearing	
Royalty-free	
Exclusive	
Non-exclusive	
how many (_____)	

15. Raw Materials, Availability   16. Facilities

Notes:

ELEMENTAL ANALYSIS

Date of Statistics:

17. Atomic Structure   18. Skeletal Structure

Year	Month	Day
75	01	11
76	02	22
77	03	33
78	04	44
79	05	55
80	06	66
81	07	77
82	08	88
83	09	99
84	10	00
85	11	
86	12	

19. Reactive Groups   20. Market Information

PATENT POTENTIALS

21. Type of Claims & Number

22. Know-How Status: Bench-scale research, Bench-scale development, Pilot-scale, Eng. specifications, Marketing Efforts/Know-How

23. Disposition of Know-How: Licensing—
          Available & Year of Review   ; Trade; Sale
          Not Available & Year of Review

24. Comments

			CODES			
	#	Role	SIC	CSA	End-Use	Idiot

3. U.S. Serial No.

6. PM Number

9. Patent Attorney

11. Name of Product(s)

14. Size of Enterprise:

Quantity

1-49
50-4,999
5,000-99,999
100,000-4,999,999
5,000,000-19,999,999
20,000,000-99,999,999

Dollars

1-49
50-4,999
5,000-99,999
100,000-4,999,999
5,000,000-19,999,999
20,000,000-99,999,999

Figure 4.3: Raw Data Input for CIRS: Department 2

Date of Information:				
Year	Month	Day		
75	01	11	ANALYTIC RECORDER:	
76	02	22		
77	03	33	NAME OF COMPANY:	
78	04	44		
79	05	55	CALLER:	DEPT:
80	06	66		
81	07	77		
82	08	88	WRITER:	DEPT:
83	09	99		
84	10	00	Company Code: Not Applicable/Applicable	
85	11			
86	12			

TYPE OF LICENSING PROSPECT

Information:
Source & Type

1. Current Licensee: Yes _____ No _____

    2. Patents Applicable

Reliability Index:

#R.I.	#R.I.	#R.I.
01	02	03
04	05	06
07	08	09
10	11	12
13	14	15
16	17	18
19	20	21
22	23	24
25	26	27
28	29	30

3. Licensing Agent

4. Research Facility

5. Direct Inquirer

6. General Listing

LICENSING INTEREST

Notes:

7. Yes _____ No _____

8. Areas

Date of Statistics:

Year	Month	Day
75	01	11
76	02	22
77	03	33
78	04	44
79	05	55
80	06	66
81	07	77
82	08	88
83	09	99
84	10	00
85	11	
86	12	

COMPANY OFFERINGS

9. U.S. Patent Number(s)

DIVISION AND LOCATION:

TITLE:

TITLE:

Code:

CODES

#	Role	SIC	CSA	End-Use	Idiot

Figure 4.4: Raw data input for CIRS: Department 3

NAME AND LOCATION OF COMPANY:

Company Code: Not Applicable/Applicable; Code

Date of Information:

Year	Month	Date
75	01 07	11
76	02 08	22
77	03 09	33
78	04 10	44
79	05 11	55
80	06 12	66
81		77
82		88
83		99
84		00
85		
86		

Company Total Sales $	1979 Total $	1978 Total $	1977 Total $	Rate of Growth	1979/78	1978/77
100,000,000				−50% and below		
20,000,000 – 99,999,999				−49% to −6%		
5,000,000 – 19,999,999				−5% to 0%		
100,000 – 4,999,999				0% to 5%		
5,000 – 99,999				6% to 14%		
50 – 4,999				15% to 49%		
1 – 49						

Pounds (LBS)	1979 lbs. Potential	Actual	1978 lbs. Potential	Actual	1977 lbs. Potential	Actual	Dollars ($)
Product Code & Name 100,000,000							100,000,000
20,000,000 – 99,999,999							20,000,000 – 99,999,999
5,000,000 – 19,999,999							5,000,000 – 19,999,999
100,000 – 4,999,999							100,000 – 4,999,999
5,000 – 99,999							5,000 – 99,999
50 – 4,999							50 – 4,999
1 – 49							1 – 49
Product Code & Name 100,000,000							100,000,000
20,000,000 – 99,999,999							20,000,000 – 99,999,999
5,000,000 – 19,999,999							5,000,000 – 19,999,999
100,000 – 4,999,999							100,000 – 4,999,999
5,000 – 99,999							5,000 – 99,999
50 – 4,999							50 – 4,999
1 – 49							1 – 49
Product Code & Name 100,000,000							100,000,000
20,000,000 – 99,999,999							20,000,000 – 99,999,999
5,000,000 – 19,999,999							5,000,000 – 19,999,999
100,000 – 4,999,999							100,000 – 4,999,999
5,000 – 99,999							5,000 – 99,999
50 – 4,999							50 – 4,999
1 – 49							1 – 49
Product Code & Name 100,000,000							100,000,000
20,000,000 – 99,999,999							20,000,000 – 99,999,999
5,000,000 – 19,999,999							5,000,000 – 19,999,999
100,000 – 4,999,999							100,000 – 4,999,999
5,000 – 99,999							5,000 – 99,999
50 – 4,999							50 – 4,999
1 – 49							1 – 49

Figure 4.4: Raw data input for CIRS: Department 3

CREDIT TERMS:

Rate of Growth	1979/78	1978/77
50% to 99%		
100% to 199%		
200% to 999%		
1000% and above		

1979 $		1978 $		1977 $					1979/78 $ %	1978/77 $ %
Potential	Actual	Potential	Actual	Potential	Actual					
						Industry Code		−50% and below		
						SIC Number		−49% to −6%		
						End-Use No.		−5% to 5%		
						End-Use %		6% to 14%		
						Contract		15% to 49%		
								50% and above		
						Industry Code		−50% and below		
						SIC Number		−49% to −6%		
						End-Use No.		−5% to 5%		
						End-Use %		6% to 14%		
						Contract		15% to 49%		
								50% and above		
						Industry Code		−50% and below		
						SIC Number		−49% to −6%		
						End-Use No.		−5% to 5%		
						End-Use %		6% to 14%		
						Contract		15% to 49%		
								50% and above		
						Industry Code		−50% and below		
						SIC Number		−49% to −6%		
						End-Use No.		−5% to 5%		
						End-Use %		6% to 14%		
						Contract		15% to 49%		
								50% and above		

Table 4.6: Liaison with CIRS: Department 3

1. *Department:* Sales Analysis

2. *Liaison:* Mr. GHI

3. *Departmental Contribution of Information:*

The Department will abstract on CIRS forms No. 3 and No. 4:

a) Total dollar sales by the organism to other companies by year.
b) Organism's potential sales of individual products—quantity and dollars.
c) Organism's actual sales of individual products—quantity and dollars.
d) Industry code of organism's customers and prospects.
e) End-user code of organism's customers.

These data are available from organism's records. They can be manually transcribed on CIRS forms No. 3 and No. 4 from the customer and product reports available.

4. *CIRS Intelligence for Department:*

1) Trade by company.
2) Trade by industry.
3) Prospective analysis of company position in the market place vis-a-vis product relationships including those of: (a) manufacturer; (b) end-user; (c) processor of special facility for manufacturing; (d) purchaser of organism's products as raw materials for their own manufacture, etc.
4) Growth profile of organism's sales in dollars by customers in successive years.
5) End-user analysis of organism's customers by product.
6) Performance of organism's products vis-a-vis the Standard Industrial Classification System of the U.S. Government.

---

define service to *whom, when* (over what period of time), and *where* (it is rendered). This will lead to the necessity to define what is meant by health, by transportation, by education, and so on. None of these profound questions bothers the private sector; it can simply look to a physical, identifiable measure, such as the difference between what was taken in and what was given out in terms of dollars and cents.

The implications for the raw data input of the necessity to define *operational* measures of "service" are that the principal elements of raw data input for public agencies, as well as for private sector organisms who do business with the public sector agencies (private contractors), will be demand factors, supply factors, and service factors.

Table 4.6 continued

5. *Estimated Frequency of Use of CIRS by the Department:*

The frequency will vary from time to time, but will generally be in the neighborhood of the following estimates:

1) Trade—Customer- Patent Licensing Manager	2 times a week
Marketing Manager	1 time a week
2) Trade—Industry—Marketing Manager	1 time a week
3) Prospective Analysis—Research & Development	2 times a week
Marketing Manager	2 times a week
Market Research	2 times a week
Product Managers	2 times a week
Marketing Management	2 times a week
4) Growth Analysis—Technology Managers	2 times a week
Marketing Managers	2 times a week
5) End-user Analysis—Product Managers	2 times a week

6. *Signature of Cognizant Authority:* Mr. GHI

The 1971 reorganization of the Office of Management and Budget reflects the importance of identifying "service" measures. One could paraphrase the April 1973 announcement by Roy Ash to suggest the division of services with which the federal government is concerned into human resources development and physical resources development. There are four program areas headed by associate directors:

> National Security and International Affairs
> Economics and Government
> National Resources, Energy, and Science
> Human and Community Affairs

The federal agencies that seek approval for their allocations in the federal budget, as well as private contractors who seek to do business with these agencies, will do well to recognize the orientation of the Office of Management and Budget, and calibrate the contributions—present and potential—that they will provide in furthering the achievement of the organismic objective of public welfare.

Calibration of Fulfillment Characteristics in the Public Sector

In previous sections the raw data input for the profit-making organism was developed to achieve the fulfillment characteristics of the activities of the organism, viz., *profit*, however defined. This section will develop operational

117

concepts which will calibrate the surrogate for profit in the public sector, viz., *service*, however defined.

To calibrate the fulfillment characteristics in the public sector, it is necessary to identify the objectives of the system. Development of the proper objectives of the organism, whether in the public or the private sector, is a sizable undertaking and is properly the domain of systems analysis, not management information systems. The distinction between the activity known as operations research/systems analysis (OR/SA) and MIS (IIS) is the focus upon *information*. Since the raison d'être of management is control, and control is exercised by influencing the behavior of the organism, MIS (IIS) is an aid in exercising control by projecting the data on the components of the system in such a way that decisions can be made to alter or leave alone the projected performance profile. On the other hand, OR/SA is the systematic approach to problem-solving in terms of its two basic characteristics: (1) conceptualization of the problem as a whole, or *diagnosis*; and (2) development of prescriptive solutions, or *prescription*. MIS (IIS) can be an aid in both diagnosis and prescription; however, MIS (IIS) is not OR/SA, or management, even as X-rays, electrocardiograms, and so on, do *not* constitute diagnosis or prescription.

In the case of the private sector, we could proceed directly to the discussion of the raw data elements because the fulfillment characteristics are well understood. Profit, irrespective of the particular type of measurement, still serves as a valid statement of the measure of fulfillment of the performance characteristics. In the public sector, a surrogate for profit is service. To calibrate service, it is necessary to briefly perform the definition of system objectives, which is properly the domain of OR/SA.

The development of the objectives for the public sector is presented elsewhere.[4] We shall merely present the essence of the argument here for the identification of the operational measure of service.

In chapters 1 and 3, the two basic objectives of the principal decision-maker (PDM) were identified as those of survival and growth. If one role is to be sacrificed, it would be growth, because without survival there simply can be no growth. The first requirement for OR/SA is to define operationally what *survival* means to the given organism.

What does survival mean as an overall national objective? Certainly the physical survival of the 50 states is included in the notion of survival. Not only does survival refer to the existence in the same physical form, but also the continuance of the capability to perform equivalent functions, i.e., yielding the means for food, shelter, and other necessities of life to the population of the 50 states.

[4] George K. Chacko, *Systems Approach to Public and Private Sector Problems* (Amsterdam: North-Holland, 1976), chapter 5.

Equally, if not more important, is the survival of what is loosely described as the American Way of Life. It includes more than physical survival; it includes the concept of "quality of life." If survival means *existence,* quality of life would mean *enjoyment.* Enjoyment itself comprises health and happiness. Both can be defined in a number of different ways. One operational way of defining health would be: *The physical and mental capability to pursue one's own choices.* If health means the capability to pursue one's choices, *happiness is the opportunity to pursue one's choices.*

The emphasis upon the presidential priority in terms of survival was underscored by Office Management and Budget (OMB) Director Roy L. Ash:

> We have to set specific targets. Every agency has hundreds of goals and objectives. Some of them are of importance to the President; most are not. The President may have a hundred things he wants to accomplish in the year. We're going to help the President do it by focusing the agency's attention on his priority goals.[5]

The President's priority goals (objectives) must include the *expected survival of the American Way of Life as reflected in the measures of* (1) percent of U.S. population earning income under the poverty level; (2) percent of U.S. population unable to pursue its own choices because of lack of health; and (3) percent of U.S. population unable to pursue its choices for lack of opportunity.

What are the implications of the operational measures of the object of national survival to the MIS (IIS)? The MIS should provide forecasts which will permit the exercise of control in fulfilling the objective of national survival. Clearly, no single, colossal MIS will be meaningful or helpful. Several MIS, each serving a PDM, will be required; exactly how many are required will depend upon the number of PDMs who may be recognized as constituting meaningful components of national decision-making for survival. As a rule of thumb, in a large corporation or organism a PDM is one who has the responsibility for some 2,000 employees and/or $500,000 in annual operations. Of course, the single owner/operator of the corner gas station, is a PDM as long as he (1) exercises significant responsibility to achieve organismic objectives; (2) wields appropriate authority; and (3) commands requisite resources. He would need an MIS, but not of the same nature and magnitude as that for the PDM with greater responsibility.

Emphasis upon the objectives hierarchy gives clear direction to the MIS: provide forecast(s) to the PDM to enable him to exercise control. The input of data at the OMB level, the department level, and the subdepart-

---

[5] David S. Broder, "OMB Reorganized by Ash," *The Washington Post,* April 26, 1973, p. A4.

ment levels must be oriented toward answering the question of the President: *At this rate,* what will be the expected survival of the American Way of Life?

Summary

This chapter discussed the first of the three elements that constitute the MIS (IIS) sequence, raw data.

Three sets of factors were identified in the *internal* inputs of raw data: (1) demand factors, (2) supply factors, and (3) contribution factors. In the case of a profit-making organism, the contribution is profit; in the case of a nonprofit-making organism, the contribution is service.

In addition to the internal inputs, there are *external* sources for raw data input. Every economic activity in the United States, whether of the public or the private sector, is included in the Standard Industrial Classification (SIC). Every establishment, which includes every organism upwards of 1-person operations, is required under the law to file returns at least once every five years for the Census of Manufactures. In between, the census is updated by an annual survey which covers 65,000 plants out of a total of about 300,000, accounting for more than two-thirds of the total employment of all manufacturing establishments in the United States.

The internal and the external sources of raw data were considered in two applications: (1) potential utilization of patents, and (2) SIC data norms for raw data input for mattresses and bedsprings manufacturers. In Application 1, the predominant influence of technology upon the products and/or services of organisms was emphasized, the technological context being *unstable.* In Application 2, however, the technological context was *stable* and the methods of manufacturing mattresses and bedsprings were well known and well established.

Detailed raw data input forms were developed for a Central Intelligence Retrieval System (CIRS). A coding scheme based on SIC was developed to facilitate the input of data from external and internal sources, to maximize the expected total profit in the long run. The implications of a surrogate for profit in the nonprofit-making organisms were explored.

QUESTIONS

Chapters 4, 5, and 6 deal with the MIS (IIS) sequence from raw data to information. Chapter 4 discussed the principal elements of the first part of the sequence, i.e., raw data, and its application to 2 real-life and real-to-life problems. The purpose of the following questions is to develop an appreciation for the data collection and data utilization problems from the point of view of incomplete information systems for management decision-making.

A. RAW DATA INPUT

1. Identify the principal elements of demand factors.
2. Identify the principal elements of supply factors.
3. Distinguish between the evaluation of the organism's performance in the profit-making and nonprofit-making contexts.

B. APPLICATION 1

4. What type of decisions are made with respect to patents, once they are in the possession of the organism?
5. Why are interdepartmental inputs of raw data essential for question 4?

C. APPLICATION 2

6. What types of data are available from national sources to provide a comparison of an individual establishment's performance?
7. Would you purchase the *Market Statistics: Key Plants?* How much would you pay for it?
8. Indicate the modifications you have to make of the available national data to use them as a measure of comparative performance: (a) sales, (b) profits.

D. CIRS

9. How would you utilize various pieces of data to determine whether or not your company should retain the patent(s) for its own use—present or potential?
10. Distinguish between information and intelligence.
11. What are the data implications of potential products distinguished from present products?
12. Why is quid pro quo essential to departmental contributions to CIRS?
13. Develop tables parallel to tables 4.4–4.6 for you own activity, paying special attention to Item 4.
14. If your activity is nonprofit-making, devise a measure(s) of contribution as a surrogate for profit.

121

5
MIS (IIS) Sequence 2: Pre-Information

TECHNICAL OVERVIEW / The second of the MIS (IIS) sequence of three elements—pre-information—is the subject of this chapter.

The discussion has two parts: *data management*, as carried out in the computer; and *data analysis*—both with reference to the form and the content of raw data.

Data management within the computer is one of control programs, which, with the processing programs, comprise the operating system. Control programs are concerned with the operation of the computer and the operation of the job, which require task management, job management, and data management. Job management provides a logical interface between task management and a job, or between task management and the system.

Data management in the computer minimizes access time. The same set of data can be manipulated in a number of different ways; therefore, the capability to organize and reorganize data according to different needs would be most welcome. At MIT, McIntosh and Griffel have developed a representation language which "will make it possible to associate together categories of information from several files into a new file" installed in a computer. Their system, ADMIN (administrative system) has the principal advantage that what usually requires special programming now only requires simple instructions. Relations can be established initially between categories on the basis of relation norms. New relations can then be developed out of those already existing; the new relations are named, and they yield a new relation norm. The value of the ADMINS language lies in its capability to perceive this new norm and use it as an instruction.

Application 3 discusses the use of the ADMINS system in Israeli logistics. In the demonstration problem, the ADMIN system was able to furnish the answer in a matter of minutes to the question of the form: Where should tank XYZ be fabricated? Without ADMINS, the identification of the major components of the tank, the inventory of each part in different Israeli warehouses, the functional interchangeability of parts, the requirements for the technical skill to fabricate the different types of tanks, etc., would have taken an enormous amount of time and effort just for the data collection. Then the data would have had to be merged from different files, and the calculations performed. The capability of ADMINS to generate instructions empirically out of relation norms suggests the possibility of versatile handling of data basis in the computer.

While data management deals with the ordering of raw data in the computer, data analysis deals with the processing of the raw data itself. Either the *form* or *content* of the raw data can be the subject of data analysis. In emphasizing form, the raw data are treated simply as a set of numbers, the repeating pattern of which needs to be discovered, so that it can be applied to forecast the outcome in the future.

The data can be given equal, or unequal, weights. If we assume that, for instance, Gross Nationl Product (GNP) datum for every year beginning with the earliest has an equal role to play in arriving at the GNP for the present year, then the forecast has to be recomputed beginning with the first year, *every time* the datum for a new year is added. In giving equal weights to the different data points, we can use the same variables, or different variables, X_1, X_2, . . . X_n, and the different powers of each of the variables. A polynomial of degree 1 is the equation to the straight line: $Y = a + bX$, where the power degree of X is 1. When higher powers of X are included in the equation, we get a curve, whether the higher powers are those of one variable or of several variables.

When *unequal* weights are given to the different data points, we employ a *filter*. The purpose of the filter is to separate the phenomenon into two parts: wanted components and unwanted components. In telephone communication, the wanted component is a signal; the unwanted components are the noise. We know what we are looking for, because we know what the signal is like. However, in applying a filter to the data stream, we do *not* know precisely what the signal is. Should we consider last year's GNP, last two years', last ten years', or last twenty years'? The choice depends upon the underlying forces of the economic activity of the United States which exerts significant influence upon *next year's* GNP.

There are three principal classes of filters: (1) fixed-memory filter;

(2) expanding-memory filter; and (3) fading-memory filter. In the fading memory filter, remote data will get less weight, i.e., they fade away. Exponential smoothing is a fading memory filter. In the modification of the exponential smoothing developed, the data are divided into two sets: "recent," and "remote." This classification itself is flexible, because any data point can be used as the separator, making it possible to divide ten-year data into the first and the last nine; the first two and the last eight; the first three and the last seven, and so on.

The weight of α is attached to the "recent" data points, making the "remote" segment assume a weight of $(1 - \alpha)$. What would be an appropriate criterion to choose the α-value? It would be the closeness of correspondence of observed data with predicted data. For instance, the fourth data point as "recent," and the first, second, and third data points as "remote" can be used to predict the value of the fifth data point. The predicted value can be compared with the observed value, and the difference computed. If the difference is squared, it implies that a negative variation is as important as a positive variation. Since the efficiency of the forecasting method is what is in question, the prediction itself can be used as the basis to evaluate the differences between the actual and the ideal. That which gives consistently smaller deviations for all the different data points can be chosen as the appropriate α for the given set of data.

The forecast by itself may be misleading because the stage of growth in the life cycle of the phenomenon reflected in the data points could suggest decline, maturation, or rapid growth. If the α-values can be associated with different stages in the life cycle of the phenomenon under study, then the decision-maker has an important added asset in his arsenal: the different *empirically* determined α-values are identified with the different stages of growth of the phenomenon.

So far, consideration has been given only to the treatment of the data form as a repeating pattern. Now we turn to the *content* of the phenomenon.

Three categories of problems are identified: (1) solution oriented; (2) structure oriented; and (3) structural solution oriented. In solution-oriented problems, the objective is *the* particular *value(s)* of the variable(s) fulfilling the problem specification(s), which is called the solution(s). The variables are treated as independent of each other, and the interactions between them are ignored. In structure-oriented problems, the objective is a set of *stages* of decision-making fulfilling the problem specifications. The stages are so chosen that the knowledge of the structure of the problem, i.e., the knowledge of the interactions among the variables, gained from experience, is applied to *subsequent* decisions. Structural solution-oriented problems look for statistical representation of the behavior of the system based on the replication of how the system functions, utilizing the knowledge of the subsystems and the theory of how the subsystems are related to each other.

EXECUTIVE SUMMARY / To convert raw data into forecasts for decision-making, the MIS (IIS) sequence of three elements has been identified. Pre-information—the second element—is the subject of this chapter. There are two parts to the discussion: *data management*, as carried out in the computer; and *data analysis*—both with reference to the form and the content of raw data.

Control programs can be considered the mechanical managers within the computer. These programs are concerned with the operation of the computer and the operation of the job, which require task management, job management, and data management.

Data management in the computer seeks to reduce the time needed to get hold of the data to process it. If it is possible to make the computer establish relationships between categories of data and then to apply the relationships to other data files, then there will be considerable savings in the effort now required to write separate programs, because instructions will take the place of programming. At MIT, the ADMIN system (administrative system) is designed to provide such a capability. A demonstration problem is discussed as Application 3, where the question is: How best can Israel rebuild tanks out of parts from different types of tanks? A number of different data files can be visualized as relevant to the problem, such as the inventory of each part of the tank in the different warehouses, the technical interchangeability of parts, the requirements for the technical skill to fabricate the different types of tanks, etc. Even after locating the scores of data files, they will still have to be merged to find the answer to the question. The calculations which will otherwise take considerable effort and time could be answered by ADMINS in a matter of minutes!

Turning to data analysis, data can be treated as a sequence of a repeating pattern of numbers, with no reference to what they represent. In treating the data in terms of its *form*, the different data points can be given equal weight, or *unequal* weight. When they are given equal weight, every data point has to be used in every calculation, and with every new data point, a *new* calculation has to be made. If unequal weights are given the data points, then some of the data can be discarded, or given very low weight. Which should be included, and which should be discarded? The data on Gross National Product (GNP) would suggest that the GNP data for nineteenth-century years, or even early 1900s, would have far less significance to 1970 GNP than the data of the 1960s. What we do not know is how much weight should be given; therefore, it is advantageous to have a method which permits us to split the data into different segments, and to try different weights. We could, for instance, use the data for 1960–1965, and on that basis predict the 1966 GNP. We can compare the actual GNP with the predicted value, and repeat the operation for other years. The closest predictions would have the pragmatic appeal of being the most useful for the decision-maker who wants to know what the GNP in the *next* time period will be.

It is important to know the forecast for the next time period; it is equally important to know what stage of growth the particular product and/or service is in: declining stage, maturation stage, rapid growth stage, etc. Depending upon the particular stage, the same identical figure would have quite a different meaning. If the method used to forecast the next time period would also indicate the appropriate stage of growth of the phenomenon, then that would be an important added capability. This capability has been provided in the method of modified exponential smoothing.

So far, no consideration has been given to the *content* of the data. In regard to content, we can identify three major categories of problems facing the decision-maker. In the simplest case, he is looking for an answer of the form: produce so many units of such and such a product to maximize profit. The raw data for this type of problem are *constants*. In a second type of problem, the objective is not a particular answer, as much as how to split up the complex problem into manageable segments. In 1961, when the decision was made to go the moon, the problem was how to break up the journey from Earth to the moon so that the knowledge gained from experience in each segment could be applied to the *next* stage, i.e., the experience gained from suborbital flight applied to orbital flight; the experience gained from the earth orbital flight applied to the lunar orbital flight, and so on. In the third type of problem, partial knowledge is available in the form of statistical descriptions of subsystems; and the problem is that of determining the behavior of the whole system on the basis of partial knowledge through an actual replication of the whole system.

In chapter 1 the triple context of decision-making was developed; it provides the setting for the development of MIS (IIS) in the sequence comprising three elements. This chapter discusses the second of the three elements—pre-information—which comprises (1) data management, and (2) data analysis of raw data.

Library Analogy to Data Management

If raw data inputs are like the accession of books in a library, data management is like the arrangement of the books in the library to minimize the time between the origin of a request for material by the patron, and the time the request is fulfilled (turnaround time).

To minimize the turnaround time in the library, a number of elements has to be provided: (1) classification by subject, (2) classification by the author; (3) numbering of books employing a uniform numbering system, so that every book and/or reading material has one and only one call number; (4) catalogue of the reading material in the library from which the patron can identify the call number; (5) storage arrangement of the library shelves by subject matter; (6) storage arrangement within each library shelf by call number; (7) user index of reading material, by which all reading material can be located when it is not on the shelf; (8) user prioritization by which the demands for different types of reading material by different patrons at different times can be equitably met; (9) checkout procedures which permit the issuance of the reading material expeditiously; (10) accession procedures under which reading material is added to the shelves—whether the first time as new material, or the first or the nth time as patrons return the material; and (11) withdrawal procedure under which reading material is removed from the shelves—whether the first time, or the nth time as patrons take out the material.

Data management by the computer includes additional types of functions beyond those of the library. In a library, the reading material is taken out in exactly the same form it is put in (with the exception of adding the call numbers and other identifications of the transaction for the library records). The parallel activity of the computer would be *data retrieval*. This is by no means the only, or the principal, function of data management activity in the computer. It has to provide for the smooth and efficient *processing* of data by means of which the data are *transformed* from their input status to a different one of output.

Review of Computer Operations

To identify the nature and magnitude of data management, it would be useful to review the four elements of computer operations. They are: input, storage, processing, and output.

In chapter 1 datum was defined as *what is*: numerical, literary, symbolic, and/or logical representations of reality. Data do *not* become inputs until they are located in the computer storage (which is synonymous with computer memory). To locate data in the computer, the data first have to be codified. The rules for codifying vary, but the data are mostly codified using alphabets and numbers (alphanumerically). In order for the computer to accept the alphanumerical codes, they have to be punched on cards, or put on tape, or put into some other form which will permit the computer to convert them into electrical impulses. Just as in the library when the books arrive they have to have a particular location in which they can be stored temporarily and/or permanently, so also the computer must find a specific location for the new data. If the location is temporary, the data have to be transferred from the temporary to the permanent location subsequently.

Data become *inputs* which are codified data located in the storage (memory). The input must be so located in storage so as to permit retrieval without change in form or content (data retrieval). Even for data retrieval, the storage must have unique locations for each data element. This unique location is known as the *address* of the data element. The magnetic tape is a long thin strip of material which can be looked upon as being divided into grids which are the cells of a matrix, specifiable in terms of rows and columns. The address can be a *direct address* which says that grid number 34, 56 (row 34 and column 56) is where the particular datum is stored. It is like saying that a particular book is the fourth book on the fifth row of a specific shelf in the library. If every data element were to be given an individual grid location, and if every grid were to be assigned only a single data element, it can make the identification unique. By the same token, the bookkeeping would be quite extensive.

On the other hand, if a whole group of data elements can be stored in a sequence of many different grids, only the beginning and end grids need to be identified. It is like saying that to locate books on computer data management, look on the shelf under computer science, beginning with the 15th book through the 23rd book. Here, instead of individually specified locations 15, 16, 17, 18, 19, 20, 21, 22, and 23 (or nine individual direct addresses), it is possible to identify simply the 15th and the 23rd, or two direct addresses. Numerous subject matter classifications under computer science, such as data management, random access, virtual memory, etc., can be given a single *indirect* address which will say: For material on data management, random access, virtual memory—see "computer science." The storage of data items can be by means of direct or indirect addresses.

Not all the books and reading materials are in the central library. Books that are not frequently used are stored in remote locations. The archives are an example of a storage location far removed from the central library. When the books are stored away from the main library, there should be some kind of courier service between the distant location(s) and the main library where the patrons request and receive the reading material. In the computer, the parallel to the central library is the core of the computer; the parallel to the archives is the off-line storage in discs, tapes, etc., which are *not* under the control of the central processing unit.

Storage is the organized collection of inputs (coded data) located on-line or off-line, accessible through direct and/or indirect address.

Processing is the retrieval of inputs without change, as well as the modification of the inputs by performing operations on the inputs in accordance with an organized sequence of instructions, which together bring about the intended modification of the inputs. The sequence of instructions could be as simple as add, multiply, subtract, divide; or they could be as complex as the determination of the optimum trajectory of the spacecraft en route to Mars. To plot the space trajectory, it is necessary to compute the instantaneous values of an incredibly large number of variables, to compare them with what they should be to accomplish the mission, and to take corrective action when the actual values differ from the ideal values. To make matters more complicated, the values of one or more variables will probably affect other values of the variables, and the interaction of the different sets of variables has to be calibrated, in some instances for infinitesimally small increments of time. Part of the function of data management is to retrieve the inputs on the many different variables, and facilitate the performance of operations upon each of the variables the appropriate sequence of instructions, and to have the variables returned to the original locations in either the changed form and/or in the original form.

Like the input, the output is also an organized collection of coded data. The output could be unchanged from the input; or, it could be changed by means of the operations performed upon the data. The output could be presented on paper, cards, tape, visual displays, and so on. Unlike the processing which must be done on-line, the output can be on-line or off-line.

The role of data management is to facilitate the processing within the computer. However, to efficiently perform the processing, the data have to be retrieved and replaced fast. It means that the data have to be located fast, which requires not only unambiguous address, but also an efficient arrangement by which *collections* of related data can be accessed. This leads to the consideration of the particular collections of data elements. Which specific collection is preferable? Given two alternative collections, the preferred one is that which accesses faster the data that are used more often. In other words, data management calls for intelligent allocation of space in the computer which requires an appreciation of the nature and magnitude of the uses to which the coded collections of data would be put. Or, the storage itself requires substantive knowledge of the uses of the data. Since the raison d'être of the MIS (IIS) is to provide forecasting, which aids the exercise of management control, storage allocation of activity data management has to reflect the needs of conversion of data into information, i.e., the nature of the particular management process itself.

Data Management as an Element of Operating Systems

A single job may require repetitive operations of the same kind performed on different parts of the data, and at different times. Assume that Job 1 requires the three operations of addition, division, and subtraction to be performed on some data. It may well be that additions have to be performed on some parts of the data, the results of which have then to be divided; the results of the division may have to be added again, and the addition may have to be followed by subtraction and another division, and so on.

If the various subunits could be grouped as part of a group of operations that can be performed sequentially, such as performing addition on Job 1, Job 23, Job 27, and Job 183, all of which require the performance of the operation called addition, then the delay that would have been otherwise necessary in performing on Job 1 *all* of the required operations (in the sequence of multiplication, addition, division, and subtraction) could be reduced.

Control programs and processing programs

The speed of processing could be related to operations, such as addition, multiplication, division, and subtraction, that have to be performed. But the data upon which the various operations have been performed may not be readily available. They may have to be brought in from different locations, either on-line or off-line. It is this bringing together of the data and the particular operation to be performed upon it that takes time: time during which the high-speed computing capabilities remain idle.

To avoid or to minimize the idle time on the computer, various programs which arrange the accession of data, the organizing of data according to the operations that have to be performed on it, the observing of the priorities in which the various jobs have to be performed, and so on, have been developed. The key to the minimization of delay between performing different operations is *multiprogramming* for internal management of computer resources:

A multiprogramming operating system is composed of two types of programs: (1) control programs and (2) processing programs. (1) *Control programs* are concerned with the operation of the computer and the operation of a job... (2) *Processing programs* operate under control of the control programs and exist as a unit of work to the system. Processing programs are conveniently divided into three categories: *language translators* (such as a FORTRAN Compiler), *service programs* (such as the linkage editor), and *user programs* (such as a payroll program)....

Data Management provides a software interface between processing programs and auxiliary storage. Functions performed by data management are:

1. assigning space on direct-access volumes,
2. maintaining a catalogue of data sets,
3. performing support processing for IO operations (i.e., open, close, etc.), and

4. processing IO operations (which includes IO supervision, access routines, data set sharing, etc.).[1]

Data management—a control program

As discussed earlier, the organization of data according to the manner in which they are used is an important element of data management. The data are stored in blocks with space (gaps) in between them. Each of the data blocks is controlled through a *data control block (DCB)*. The data set required in conjunction with a job is identified by a *data definition (DD)* statement. Thus, each data set used in a program is specified by a DD statement and a DCB.

A DCB applies to a collection of *data records*; a collection of data sets can be called a *data set*, each of which is a collection of related data items. The data sets, similar to the data units, are also under the control of a block: *data set control block (DSCB)*. The DSCBs of all the data sets on each direct-access storage device volume are included in the volume table of contents (VTOC).

Virtual memory

Data management uses the features of DSCB and VTOC. The principle is that of accessing data, not as individual units, but as collections of data, and collections of collections (data sets). How much more efficient will it be if even larger collections of data could be retrieved with the same instruction.

The physical locating of data is carried out in such a way that the access time to store or retrieve data is minimal. Data are recorded on disks, much like the way music is recorded on a phonograph record. Instead of the spiral tracks in the phonograph record, in the computer disk the tracks are concentric. The disk storage unit has two access arms per each disk, so that the access arms can move in and out on both sides of the disk when directed by the disk control mechanism. The access arms have read-write heads, all of which are located in the same vertical position, which enables access to a *cylinder* of information.

The importance of data management emerges when we consider the fact that the most important single delay element in computer processing is delay in accessing data for computation. The use of a cylinder of information reduces the access time; so does the use of virtual memory, which also economizes the use of the main core storage. The physical means

---

[1] Harry Katzan, Jr., *Operating Systems—A Pragmatic Approach* (New York: VanNostrand Reinhold, 1973), pp. 47, 107, 108, and 109.

of economizing will be counterproductive unless the organization of the data itself reflects the nature and magnitude of the use of different types of data in the programming activity for decision-making purposes of the organism.

MIT's ADMIN System

While the data management capability of the more modern computers permits the accessing of data with minimum delay, and facilitates the performance of computational operations on the data sets, there is still a significant limiting factor. This factor is the requirement that a new *program* be utilized virtually every time a new question is to be asked of the data for decision-making purposes. Programming is costly; as a matter of fact, programming costs are of the order of $180 per $100 of computer hardware.

The burgeoning investment in computers is more for *applications programming* use than for improvements in hardware. It shows that a number of interesting questions are increasingly being raised for decision-making purposes, which require that the data be manipulated in different forms to provide the answers. If for each manipulation a new program has to be written, that requires a considerable amount of investment of computer programmer time. In addition, it also requires the use of the main computer time.

This requirement of programming is *independent* of the efficiency of data management within the computer. Data management merely minimizes the access time of the computer to bring the data to the main computer where the calculations are performed (and to store the data either initially or subsequently); it has no reference to the requirements for the different sets of instructions themselves.

One of the consequences of increasing the speed of modern computers is that, in order for it to be economically viable, it must be utilized on as continuing a basis as possible. As the time required for a given job decreases with increasing speed, the need is even more pressing for a larger number of jobs, all of which require the use of the computer concurrently. If these users must each have access to his own particular data file, concurrently, the problem of data management becomes crucial.

To provide the capability to perform three classes of data management tasks upon a data base that is (1) built and (2) manipulated by several different people, (3) from many backgrounds, and (4) for wide-ranging reasons, McIntosh and Griffel have developed a representation language which "will make it possible to associate together categories of information from several files into a new file."[2]

---

[2] Stuart D. McIntosh and David M. Griffel, "Large Disparate Data Bases," in *Associative Information Techniques,* ed. E. L. Jacks (New York: Elsevier, 1971), p. 85.

The principal advantage of the ADMINS (administrative system) is that what used to require special programming would now only require simple instructions, representing savings in programming and reprogramming. Furthermore, the new data sets that are created as a result of manipulations will be available as new records, without prejudice to the initial records from which the new records are generated.

The onus is still upon the user to organize the different data sets in accordance with the nature and magnitude of the use that is to be made of the data sets. In fact, under ADMINS, user involvement is more explicit. It is the user who has to identify how the data files should be organized in accordance with his perception of the uses of the data files. What the ADMINS language offers is the facility to relate the contents of any one file with that of any other(s) across hierarchies. Thus, the data item in hierarchy 1 may be associated with data items in the 6th hierarchy in the second file, or vice versa:

> The object data records [(computer readable records)] would be stored on lower performance, random access storage (e.g., large disks) and on tape. . . . Classifying a category means being able to observe an object category and tag it, using a code from a classification code list. . . . Control of object category code lists is also needed for update and analysis purposes. . . .[3]

What the ADMINS language can do is to "perceive a derivation written in the calculus of relations as an instruction. This instruction is applied to the relational records; the applications yield a new relational record."[4] In other words, once the data are organized into object data, inventory categories and subject catalogues, relations can be established initially between categories on the basis of relation norms. New relations can be developed out of those already existing; the new relations are named, and they yield a new relation norm. The value of the ADMINS language lies in its capability to perceive this new norm and use it as an instruction.

It is this capability to perceive the creation of new norms as new instructions and to apply the new relations to new situations that makes possible an efficient and adaptive process of data management in the ADMIN system. The efficiency comes from the fact that no new programming is required as would have been the case otherwise. The process is *adaptive* because the logic of the new relational norms is already understood by the ADMIN system as an instruction, and it is applied to the *next* situation.

In short, what is done by a program is now replaced by an instruction, and the new instruction itself is perceived by the ADMIN system.

---

[3] Ibid., p. 81.
[4] Ibid., p. 91.

APPLICATION 3
USE OF ADMIN SYSTEM IN ISRAELI LOGISTICS

The management of logistics records involves the use of extensive data files. In the summer of 1972, Israel sent some military officers to MIT to inquire into the applicability of the ADMIN system to manage the logistics data base of the Israeli military system. One of the main functions of the logistics operations is to rebuild tanks out of usable parts of tanks of different makes. One could illustratively think in terms of the data management considerations pertaining to the rebuilding of tanks as follows:

1. Identification of the major components of the tank
2. Inventory of each of the parts in Israeli warehouses, including the type of parts, technical description, quantity, and location
3. Functional interchangeability of parts, which suggests that, say, part 345 of make 123 can be interchanged with part 567 of make 345
4. Requirements of technical skills to fabricate the different types of tanks
5. Availability of the different skills by location and quantity
6. Requirements of physical facilities to perform the fabrication
7. Availability of facilities to perform the fabrication
8. Requirements of transportation of major components from one location to another to perform the fabrication
9. Availability of resources to transport human and material resources from locations of availability to locations of fabrication (the cost of fabrication of one configuration against another)
10. Tradeoff of different configurations

Each file has to be able to answer extensive questions in terms of subcategories of resources requirements. Further, data elements at different hierarchy levels need to be associated with data elements in different hierarchy levels in other files. This would require special programming unless there is provision for such association, as there is in the ADMIN system itself. Further, if a new relation norm is established, say, permitting the use of a particular part of a particular make in a configuration, that relational norm will have to be written into a new program. Since the rebuilding of tanks is based upon a series of such interchangeabilities, and since each interchangeability would necessitate building that into a new program, the enormous cost of programming skills and computer utilization becomes apparent.

Similar considerations apply to the other important elements of data that have to be handled by individual programs, ranging from the summarization of requirements and availabilities of human skills, machine parts and transportation resources to alternate configurations of tank fabrication. Instead of individual programs, each newly developed to handle each of the elements of the configuration, ADMIN system makes it possible to make statements of the form: Warehouse 2,953 has parts 457Z and 23A. To make such a statement, a program has to merge three separate files: one on the warehouse lists, another on the stocks of parts, and yet another one on the stock of particular parts. When it is found that a particular part can be interchanged with another, the ADMIN system builds into its sets of instructions the new relational norm, obviating the necessity to write a new program incorporating the substitution of a given part of a particular make for another part and make. In a demonstration problem, the ADMIN system was able to furnish in a matter of *minutes* an answer to a question of the form: Where should Tank XYZ be fabricated?

A brief survey of the importance of data management to MIS (IIS) has highlighted the critical nature of the organization of the data according to the needs of the installation, grouping the data into data sets of shared features, and of access to the data with minimum delay. It has also been found that in spite of the efficiency with which data can be accessed in a modern computer, there still remains the problem of writing separate programs to answer segments of questions which are germane to decision-making purposes, a problem partly answered by the ADMIN system's capability to generate instructions empirically out of relation norms.

Raw Data: Form—Forecasting Methods

In preparing raw data for use in decision-making, the data have to be stored in the computer to allow the maximum facility in *accessing* the internal input in the computer. That is only a part of the problem; the other part is *analyzing* the raw data. In analyzing the data we can emphasize the *form* or the *content*. We shall first focus attention upon the *form* of the data, trying to forecast as best as we can without worrying about the underlying phenomena. In the next section we shall turn to the content.

Relative importance of different time periods

Time is of the essence in MIS. In chapter 1 attention was called to the inevitable time lag, which makes the latest information available for decision-making to be at least $2\Delta t$ time periods behind. The Δt therefore becomes an important measure in determining the role of time in a particular MIS.

How finely should the time periods be divided? It is *not* the rapidity with which the data can be generated that matters, but the rapidity with which the information can be used. In other words, if the maximum frequency with which decisions to make changes can be instituted is *monthly,* there is little purpose served by detailed data gathering and analysis on a daily basis. There may be some merit in collecting the data on a weekly basis, in case a month is too long a time period. If increasing the number of decisions made from 1 to 12 (by decreasing the time period from a year to a month) provides correspondingly increased benefits to the fulfillment of the organismic objective, then the additional expense to increase the number of decisions would be justified. To fix ideas, if 1100 percent is the increase in the number of decisions (arrived at by subtracting the original number of decisions (1) from the new number of decisions (12), i.e., 11, divided by the number of original decisions (1)), then the corresponding improvement in the achievement of the organismic objective, say profits, should also be significant. In other words, the criterion for the time period for decision-making is given by

$$\frac{\text{proportionate improvement in organismic objectives fulfillment}}{\text{proportionate increase in number of decisions}}$$

When the number of decisions is increased by 1100 percent, the profits may not increase by 1100 percent. If the profits do not increase at all, then there has to be substantial outside justification for incurring the extra expenditures to increase the frequency of decision-making.

Equal weighting of data

Irrespective of the time unit of the data collection, the methods of forecasting can be classified into (1) equal weights for all instances of data, and (2) unequal weights for all the different instances of data.

In giving equal weights, we are stating that the earliest instance is as important as the latest instance. If the subject is a new product or process, little may be known about its behavior; therefore, for a while all data inputs may have valuable insights to yield. If equal weight is given, then every time a new piece of data is added, there must be a *recomputation.* For instance, if we assume that the Gross National Product (GNP) datum for every year beginning with the earliest, say 1890, has an equal role to play in arriving at the GNP for the present year, then the forecast has to be recomputed beginning with the year 1890 every time the datum for a new year is added.

LINEAR AND NONLINEAR METHODS

In giving equal weights to all data points, we would use either linear or nonlinear methods. If we consider time to be the primary influence upon the values of the data observed, such as GNP, then we can establish a relationship between the successive years and the successive GNP values. The linear relationship between GNP and time can be expressed as: $Y = a + bX$, where Y is the GNP, and X is the time (in this case in years).

This equation states that for every unit increase in X, the value of GNP increases by a fraction b. Notice that *it makes little difference what the nature of the process is.* We could change the Y from GNP to some other activity, and the form of the relationship will still hold. It simply says when you increase the time period (X) by one unit (a year, a day, a month) the corresponding increase in *whatever Y stands for* is by a small multiple, b. The Y could be GNP, or the number of books in the library. The only requirement is that we assume that the phenomenon is one which can be identified in terms of time units.

The advantage in giving equal weight is that no datum is thrown away. The disadvantage is in the increasing amount of data for successive calculations; and what is more, the necessity to *recompute* every time a new piece of datum is added.

Unequal weighting of data

When *unequal* weights are given the different data points, we employ a *filter*. The purpose of the filter is to separate the phenomenon into two parts: wanted components and unwanted components. With respect to telephone communications, the wanted components would be the signal and the unwanted components would be the noise. Occasionally, in long distance telephone calls, the background noise is such that it drowns out the signal; in which case, the operator redials the number to get a better connection.

The same idea of a filter is applicable to the data stream. In the case of the telephone call, we know what the signal is because we know what human speech sounds like. However, consider that the call is an overseas call, say from Tokyo. If the person at one end speaks in Japanese, and if the listener at the other end does not know what Japanese sounds like, it is possible that the listener would not know if what he is receiving is signal or noise. In other words, in order to insure that what one receives is in fact signal, one has to know at least approximately what the signal sounds like.

In the case of the data on GNP, we do *not* know precisely what the signal is. Should we consider the last year's GNP, last two years', last ten years', or last twenty years'? The choice depends upon the underlying forces of the economic activity of the United States which exert significant influence in the *next year*. Since we do not know for sure the basic elements that determine the economic profile of a country, we can at best make guesses about what constitutes the important influences upon the data stream of GNP.

There are three principal classes of filters: (1) fixed-memory, (2) expanding-memory, and (3) fading-memory. These are identified by Morrison:

We will examine in detail three classes of smoothing procedures. The first will be the *Fixed-Memory Filters* in which the trajectory is always chosen on the basis of observations taken over a fixed-time interval into the past. The *Expanding-Memory Filters,* on the other hand, base their current estimates on all observations made up to the present, and as time moves forward, this is naturally an expanding set. Finally the *Fading-Memory Filters* perform their trajectory selection on the basis of all observations made up to the present, but a stress-factor is applied so that the older or staler an observation becomes, the less influence it exerts on the current estimate.[5]

In the case of the GNP data, it is clear that the expanding-memory filter is inapplicable. Neither can fixed-memory filter be applied, because we do not know that the observations taken over a fixed-time interval in the past, such as 7 years or 11 years or 23 years, would provide the best fit for the data. That leaves us with fading-memory filter in which the influence of older data on the current estimate decreases. In other words, it is as though the effect of the most remote years is reduced to practically nothing, the effect of the more recent years is given heavier weight, and the most recent years receive the highest weight.

EXPONENTIAL SMOOTHING
One of the methods which gives differential weights to the data stream is that of *exponential smoothing.* In presenting the method, R.G. Brown suggested that a function of the most recent observation be given a weight of α, and a function of all the preceding observations be given the residual weight of $(1 - \alpha)$. Thus, if the most recent observation, say the year 1972, is given a weight of 0.8, then the GNP data for all the years prior to 1972 would receive the weight of $(1 - 0.8 =)$ 0.2.

UNKNOWN PHENOMENON AND SUCCESSIVE VALUES OF α: Brown's suggestion that the new forecast can be modified in light of the difference between the observed and the expected values of the forecast of the present data point assumes that the most recent observation is in fact the pivotal observation. However, this may not be the case.

Not only must the unequal weights be given to particular data, but also there must be provision to divide the data into unequal periods. For instance, if data are available for eight successive periods, the datum of the ninth period needs to be given higher weight than the data for the 1 through 8 periods. Further, since it is not known whether the eighth and ninth data points should be given more weight than data points 1 through 7, or whether data points 7, 8, and 9 should be given greater weight than data

[5] Norman Morrision, *Introduction to Sequential Smoothing and Prediction* (New York: McGraw-Hill, 1969), p. 8.

points 1 through 6, it would be desirable to have a mechanism by which the data can be regrouped in any manner into two segments which can be given differential weights.

Consider the classifications "remote" and "recent." The word "recent" can include data point 9, or data points 8 and 9, or data points 7, 8, and 9, so on through data points 2 through 9. Correspondingly, the "remote" segment can include data points 1 through 8, data points 1 through 7, data points 1 through 6, and so on through data point 1.

How much weight should be given to the "recent" data as compared with "remote" data? We do not know why a particular α value must be chosen. Why not try them all? Thus, we may give a weight of 0.1, 0.2, 0.3, and so on until α is 0.9. Based on a weight of 0.7 for α for "recent," the corresponding weight for the "remote" period would be 0.3.

Instead of obtaining a single modification of the old forecast on the basis of the difference between the observed and the expected in the latest period, we can have a number of different forecasts, which are based on not only the latest period, but also different groups of latest periods. We have to determine two questions: (1) which α value is best, and (2) which grouping of "recent" is best?

χ^2 CRITERION FOR SELECTION OF α: A pragmatic criterion for the selection would be the correspondence between the observed and the expected value for the next time period.

What if the forecast is 96, and the observed value is 100? The difference between the observed and expected is $(100 - 96 =)$ 4; and the square of 4 is 16. Consider also a forecast of 1,000, with a corresponding observed value of 996. Here again, the difference is $(996 - 1,000 =) - 4$, the square of which is also 16. It is necessary to distinguish between the variations of the two different estimates. The logical basis is of course the fact that in the first case, the expected value is 96, and in the second case the expected value is 1,000. Since the expected value is the basis upon which the variability is measured, the square of the difference, 16, in the first case is $(16/96 =)$ 1/6 or 16.67 percent. In the case of the second forecast, the variation is $(16/1,000 =)$ 1.6 percent, i.e., only a tenth as much as the first. In assessing the significance of the forecast, we should take note of the variations between the observed and the expected expressed in terms of the respective expected values.

The quantity [(observed − expected)^2/ expected], when summed over all the different number of observations, is defined as χ^2. It stands to reason that if the χ^2 is smaller for the given number of observations, that method provides a better forecast in the sense of being closer to the actual, than another method which gives a larger χ^2.

The χ^2 Tables are constructed for different probabilities. In other words, the values in the Table could occur with different degrees of chance. For instance, a given value may occur by chance only 10 percent of the time;

another value may occur by chance 75 percent of the time. Two usual probabilities chosen are 95 percent and 99 percent. In other words, the values that are in the χ^2 Table could occur by chance 95 percent of the time, or 99 percent of the time. Therefore, when we conclude that the particular χ^2 value computed on the basis of our observations is less than the Table χ^2 value at 95 percent level, and therefore conclude that our method of forecast is a good one, we run the risk of $(100 - 95 =)$ 5 percent of being wrong. Or, our conclusion that the forecasting method is good could be wrong 1 in 20 times. If, on the other hand, we compare our computed values with the table value at 99 percent, our conclusion that the forecasting method is good could be wrong in $(100 - 99 =)$ 1 percent of the time, or 1 in 100 times. The same caveat applies to our conclusion whether the forecasting method is good or that it is bad.

Unequal weights—stages of growth

The equal and unequal methods of weighting the data focus attention upon the relationship between successive observations in time, with little reference to what generates the data points. In the discussion of exponential smoothing, we allowed for the possibility of the underlying forces by grouping the data points into "recent" and "remote." We now turn to an investigation of the entire span of *data points,* instead of in two segments.

LIFE CYCLE STAGES OF GROWTH BASED ON α-VALUES

In exponential smoothing, a particular smoothing constant, α , determines the weight given to the past data in arriving at the new estimate. Can α-values be used as a basis to identify stages of growth of products?

To answer the question, expected demand, the end product of exponential smoothing procedure, has to be expressed in terms of the new data added at any one point, and the previous data already in the system up to that point. In Table 5.1, this derivation is shown. Expected demand is expressed in terms of three factors: new demand, old average, and old trend. The coefficients of the three factors are expressed in terms of α. When the particular α-value that satisfies the empirical data most closely is determined empirically, if the *relative importance of new data and old* is established, this could be used as a basis to determine the *growth stage* of the particular product from its sales data.

We see from Table 5.2 that when $\alpha = 0.1$, the coefficient of the new demand is 0.19, the coefficient of old average is 0.81, and the coefficient of old trend is 8.1. How important is the new demand with respect to old average? We get the fraction 0.23. How important is the new demand with respect to old trend? We get 0.02. It means that the new demand does not really add very much to the information already contained in the system in the form of old average and old trend.

Table 5.1: Stages-of-Growth Identification by α-Values in Exponential Smoothing

Expected Demand

$\quad$ = New Average $\quad + \dfrac{1-\alpha}{\alpha}\quad$ New Trend

$\quad$ = α (New Demand) + $(1 - \alpha)$ (Old Average)

$$\frac{+\,1 - \alpha}{\alpha}\; [\alpha\,(\text{Current Trend}) + (1 - \alpha)\,\text{Old Trend}]$$

Current Trend $\quad$ = New Average $\qquad -\qquad\qquad\qquad$ Old Average

$\qquad\qquad\qquad$ = α (New Demand) + $(1 - \alpha)$ (Old Average) $\quad -\quad$ Old Average

$\qquad\qquad\qquad$ = α (New Demand) $-\ \alpha$ (Old Average)

$\dfrac{1 - \alpha}{\alpha} \cdot \alpha$ (Current Trend) $\quad = (1 - \alpha)\,[\alpha\,(\text{New Demand}) - \alpha\,(\text{Old Average})]$

$\qquad\qquad\qquad\qquad\qquad = (\alpha - \alpha^2)\,(\text{New Demand}) + (-\alpha + \alpha^2)\,(\text{Old Average})$

Expected Demand

= New Demand	Old Average	Old Trend
α	$1 - \alpha$	$(1 - \alpha)^2$
$\alpha - \alpha^2$	$-\alpha + \alpha^2$	$\overline{\alpha}$

$$= (2\alpha - \alpha^2)\ \text{New Demand} + [1 - (2\alpha - \alpha^2)]\ \text{Old Average} + \frac{(1 - \alpha)^2}{\alpha}\ \text{Old Trend}$$

Raw Data: Content—Problem Category

In making the forecasts, in previous sections the *form* of the data was taken into account; form, in the sense of successive values in time of the phenomenon—whether it is GNP, product sales, contract values, etc. Now attention will be paid to the *content* of the phenomenon which gives rise to the different values that have been observed.

Solution-oriented problems

The simplest statement about the *content* of the observed data is that it is a function of a single variable, e.g., $Y = a + bX$, where Y is the GNP, and X is the time. The values of a and b have to be determined on the basis of a number of values of Y and X; on the basis of which, the value of Y for a given value of X can be forecast.

Table 5.2: Importance of New Demand Relative to Prior Data Corresponding to Different α-Values

Growth Stage	(1) α-Value	(2) Coefficient of NEW DEMAND	(3) Coefficient of OLD AVERAGE	(4) (2)/(3)	(5) Coefficient of OLD TREND	(6) (2)/(5)
G₄	0.1	0.19	0.81	0.23	8.10	0.02
	0.2	0.36	0.64	0.56	3.20	0.11
	0.3	0.51	0.49	1.04	1.63	0.31
	0.4	0.64	0.36	1.78	0.90	0.71
G₃	0.5	0.75	0.25	3.00	0.50	1.50
	0.6	0.84	0.16	5.25	0.27	3.11
	0.7	0.91	0.09	10.11	0.13	7.00
G₂	0.8	0.96	0.04	24.00	0.05	19.20
	0.9	0.99	0.01	99.00	0.01	99.00

A different type of problem emerges when the objective is not simply to forecast the value of Y corresponding to the next value of X; instead, the question is to *maximize* the value of a variable: profit or service. The question is: How many units of each product or how many units of each type of service should be provided in order to *maximize* the total profit or the total public welfare? In finding the answer, not one, but several variables will be involved. The different products which an organism can manufacture, or the different kinds of services that the nonprofit organism can offer, compete with each other for the resources of the respective organism. For instance, a desk can be made out of steel, paint, and rubber; so also a chair. Since the steel that is used up in making the desk cannot at the same time be used in making the chair, the two products compete for the same resource. So also, the human skills, experience, and training that are devoted to the production of curative health services cannot simultaneously be used to create preventive medical care: the hospital cure and preventive care compete for the same sources.

To determine which of the products and/or services needs to be offered to maximize the total profit or service, it is necessary to know the profit or service that each product and/or activity can provide. Further, it is necessary to know the precise input of each of the resources, to produce one unit of output of the particular product or service. In addition, it is necessary to know the total quantity of each type of resource that is available. In other words, we need to know the *constants* of the problem to find the solution. The question is: Given the units of contribution of each product to the objective, and given the inputs necessary for the unit output of each product or service, what is the number of units of each product and/or service that should be produced in order to maximize the total product or service within the given quantity of resources? The solution-oriented problem can be defined as follows:

A solution-oriented problem is one in which the objective is *the particular value(s)* of the variable(s) fulfilling the problem specification(s), including the *ignoring* of *interactions* among the variables and the denying of any *learning curve* in either the performance characteristics of the variables or in the exercise of the decision-making process.

Structure-oriented problems

Not all problems facing the decision-maker can be expressed in the form of maximizing profits or service. Consider the commitment to land a man on the moon and to return him safely to Earth before the end of the 1960s. We were not interested in maximizing the distance traveled, or minimizing the time for the travel. Subject to the constraints of weight that would be carried into space, we could say that maximization of the utilization of unit resources could be advanced as an objective, but certainly not *the* objective: we would rather give up the efficiency of utilization of resources to the overriding consideration of a safe round trip to and from the moon.

The lunar landing problem is far more difficult than a profit-maximization problem because there is a large area of ignorance. In profit-maximization problems, we *know* how much each unit contributes to the objective and how much input of each unit goes into the output of each product or service. This is possible because we can state the problem in terms of variables and associated constants. In the lunar landing problem, however, new problems arise. Even if we knew exactly how each of the 20,000 parts of the spacecraft would function, we did *not* know how they would function *together*. Each part was manufactured separately, and the performance characteristics of each unit was specified by its respective manufacturer. What they could *not* specify was the *interaction* between the parts. Even if a small number of component parts could be put together into a subunit, and the performance of the subunit as a whole could be studied, that would be a far cry from the missile as a whole functioning as a unit. The only way the performance characteristics of the missile as a whole could be determined was in the actual execution of the flight.

Even if the interactions among parts of the *spacecraft* could be specified fully, what about the interactions among the component parts of the *human* organism? We know how a man functions, but not in space. We could generate conditions which may be encountered in space; but the difference between what takes place in space and what has been hypothesized could be considerable. Further, what about the interactions between man and machine?

It is the importance of these interactions which separates the lunar landing type problem from the profit-maximization type problem. Unlike the profit-maximization problem, the interest is not in finding a solution in terms of fixed constants. Instead, it is in finding a *structure,* which is the understanding of the interactions—which of the interactions are more important, and which are not? The mere enumeration of all the possible interactions would help little in making decisions about the space mission. What would help is the identification of the interactions in such a way that attention can be focussed upon the more important interactions to the exclusion of the less important. In chapter 1 management was envisaged as rejecting (rational) data. This rejection implies that management knows what it is looking for or which interactions are important. In structure-oriented problems, the *concepts* (of the important interactions) are what is significant; *not constants* (in the form of the number of units of each activity which will maximize total profit or total public welfare). The structure-oriented problem can be defined as follows:

A structure-oriented problem is one in which the objective is *a* set of *stages* of decision-making fulfilling the problem specifications, selected to maximize the *experiential* knowledge acquired in every *state* of the functioning of the problem or phenomenon, and applied to exercise control in the *subsequent* state(s).

Structural solution-oriented problems

The mission to land a man on the moon certainly needed constants (the parameters of the orbital trajectory and the landing site); but equally, if not more important, it needed concepts (the method of determining alternate landing sites). Were the method of alternate landing sites selection not available, the first manned lunar landing would have been perfect; but the spacecraft would have crashed on the "football field-sized crater littered with boulders from 10 to 15 feet in diameter where Eagle's computer program landing approach [was] aiming the craft."[6] The catastrophe was averted by Neil Armstrong switching to semiautomatic controls, and instructing the computer to fly Eagle over the danger area. The computer could not have done this if it had not been programmed to find alternate sites, given the unacceptability of the first landing site.

There are a number of important problems in which the features of both structure-oriented and solution-oriented aspects are simultaneously present. Such a problem was the impact of religious issue upon the 1960 national elections. Like the lunar landing, the Democratic candidacy of a Roman Catholic for the presidency was without parallel. However, unlike the lunar landing problem, the results of modifications of the course were not instantaneous and much less predictable.

---

[6] *The National Observer,* July 28, 1969. Quoted in *Congressional Record,* August 4, 1969, E 6579.

The basic question before the national campaign managers was not merely that of identifying the interactions which might be more important, i.e., the structure of the problem, but equally, if not more, important was the identification of the particular efforts to influence the outcome of the elections. In other words, the *constants* (the chance of victory) were important, but the *concepts* (the probable changes in the chance of victory due to events and strategy) were critical. Among the different sets of counsel available to the Democratic candidate for president was a computer simulation. Simulation is the replication of the functioning of one system by another in such a way that the results of the replication reflect sufficiently closely the original system for the purposes on hand.[7] The simulation by the Simulmatics Corporation showed that "The Democrats could hold the consequences of the religious issue to a minimum by facing it frankly rather than by attempting to soft-pedal it."[8]

The structural solution-oriented problem can be defined as follows:

A structural solution-oriented problem is one in which the objective is *a statistical representation* of the *entire* span of *outcome* of an entity (event, activity, and/or relationship), the knowledge of one or more of whose components, characterized by numbers specifiable within limits, is used to replicate sufficiently closely the *functioning* of the entity to use the results for *decision-making*.

We have seen that the problems facing the decision-maker can be divided into solution-oriented, structure-oriented, and structural solution-oriented problems. This classification takes into account the *content* of the data that are available, as distinguished from the emphasis upon the *form* of the data in the forecasting methods.

Summary

In this chapter, we have looked at the generic functions which transform raw data input into pre-information output. We first discussed the highlights of data management within the computer which assumes ever-increasing importance with the increasing complexity of modern computers. How the data are stored and how they are retrieved exert significant influence upon the speed and efficiency of computer processing of raw data.

In spite of efficient data management in the computer, the necessity to devise new programs to perform calculations imposes restrictions upon the usefulness of high-speed computers to assist in decision-making. A recent

[7] George K. Chacko, *Computer-Aided Decision-Making* (New York: Elsevier, 1972), p. 291.
[8] The Simulmatics Corporation, "Human Behavior and the Electronic Computer" (New York, 1962), p. 8.

development at MIT holds promise in alleviating this problem. The ADMIN system will, by means of *instructions* developed on an adaptive basis, perform functions which now require computer *programs*. In other words, a series of adaptive instructions generated in the ADMIN system's language will make it possible for extensive investigation of associative operations which cut across hierarchial levels of data.

QUESTIONS

Chapters 4, 5, and 6 deal with the MIS (IIS) sequence from raw data to information. In chapter 5 the principal elements of the second part of the sequence, i.e., pre-information, as well as an application to a real-life problem, were discussed. The purpose of the following questions is to develop an appreciation for data management as carried out in the computer, and data analysis to convert raw data into pre-information from the point of view of incomplete information systems for management decision-making.

A. COMPUTER OPERATIONS

1. How is data processing different from accession of books in a library?
2. When do data become inputs to the computer?
3. What are the principal elements of computer operation?

B. OPERATING SYSTEM

4. What constitutes OS (Operating System)?
5. What are the functions performed by data management in a computer?
6. What is virtual memory?

C. APPLICATION 3

7. What is the principal feature of Administrative System (ADMINS) that makes it attractive to applications programming?
8. What are the constituent parts of a data base in ADMINS?
9. Indicate the application of ADMINS to a large logistics problem.

D. DATA ANALYSIS

10. How would you determine the time period for raw data collection?
11. What is the basis for choosing between equal and unequal weighting of data points?
12. Discuss the principal filters employed in data analysis.
13. What is the advantage of being able to divide data into "recent" and "remote" segments in exponential smoothing?
14. Why are stages of growth important to data analysis?
15. How can the stages of growth be determined from raw data inputs?
16. Discuss the classification of problems by content from the point of view of decision-making.

6
MIS (IIS) Sequence 3: Information

TECHNICAL OVERVIEW / The third of the MIS sequence of three elements—information—is the subject of this chapter.

The profile of an MIS (IIS) matrix of 1,134 elements is developed as well as a utilization matrix of 729 elements—both of which provide a reasonably exhaustive specification of elements that comprise an MIS (IIS) and its use.

In chapter 3 decision-making situations were defined in terms of Context E-Context T interactions. In chapter 5 reference was made to the life cycle stage of growth of each product and/or service. The MIS (IIS) matrix is broken down into stages of life cycle growth, in which the Context E and Context T are held constant. There are seven stages of growth: (1) gestation, (2) birth, (3) infancy, (4) rapid growth, (5) maturation, (6) decline, and (7) death. In each of these stages, the combinations of Context E and Context T are held constant. For instance, uncertain Context E and unstable Context T would be one combination held constant through the seven stages of the life cycle, so that we have: (1) uncertain, unstable, gestation; (2) uncertain, unstable, birth; (3) uncertain, unstable, infancy; and so on until (7) uncertain, unstable, death.

In each of the tables by stage in the text, the changes are made in three elements: (1) cost, (2) effectiveness—absolute, and

(3) effectiveness—relative. These elements were discussed in chapter 1 as part of the *content* of decision-making. Cost is considered not only as opportunity foregone but also as opportunity acquired. Absolute effectiveness—is also subdivided: system performance, and subsystem performance; effectiveness itself is the ratio of observed performance over desired performance. Relative effectiveness is divided into (1) relative change in system performance, (2) relative change in cost, and (3) relative change in performance/cost.

There are 18 elements of the MIS (IIS) matrix in stage one, gestation, for the uncertain environment and the unstable technology. Since there are 7 stages, we have ($18 \times 7 =$) 126 elements for the uncertain, unstable combination. There are 9 such combinations of Context E and Context T, giving rise to a total of ($126 \times 9 =$) 1,134 elements for the MIS (IIS) matrix.

How important are the data on each of the 18 elements? The simplest assumption is that they are equal in importance. Similarly, which of the 7 stages is the most important? We can assume that all are equally important. Combining the two assumptions, we find that each data element has a weight of 0.008, or 0.8%, which can be used as a basis for comparison of the actual data in real life. For instance, an organism which is heavily technology oriented would probably register a much heavier weight than the 1.296% for gestation registered in column 1 of Table 6.6. By the same token, an organism with a large degree of obsolescence in its products will register a much larger quantity for rapid growth in column 4 than 1.296%, and so on.

We now turn to the utilization of the MIS (IIS) matrix. The utilization matrix is broken into frequency of use, in which the objectives hierarchy and PDM roles are held constant. There are three frequencies of use: infrequent, intermittent, and frequent. In each of these the combinations of objectives hierarchy and PDM roles are held constant. For instance, organismic level and PDM role would be one combination; organismic and sub-PDM combination would be another; organismic and sub-sub-PDM would be yet another combination, there being 9 such combinations.

In each of these tables by frequency of use, the changes are made in three elements: forecasting time period, data weighting, and problem category. The forecasting time period is divided into the (1) immediate (represented by $3\Delta t$), (2) intermediate (represented by $6\Delta t$), and (3) indefinite (represented by $9\Delta t$). The Δt refers to the smallest time interval, in terms of which the data in time $t - 2\Delta t$ have to be forecast for time $t + \Delta t$, i.e., at least three Δt time periods beyond.

The data can be weighted equally for the forecast by (1) linear methods, and (2) nonlinear methods; or *unequally* by (3) exponential (and other) methods.

The problem category is divided into solution oriented, structure oriented, and structural solution oriented. There are 27 elements of the MIS (IIS) utilization matrix in frequency one—infrequent—for the organismic level and PDM roles. Since there are 3 utilization frequencies of the organismic, PDM combination, there are a total of 81 elements. There are 9 combinations of hierarchy and PDM role, giving rise to $(81 \times 9 =) 729$ elements for the MIS (IIS) utilization matrix.

How important is the utilization represented by each of the 27 elements? We can assume that all the 27 elements are equal in importance; and also that each of the hierarchy level, decision role combinations is equally important. Combining the two assumptions, we find that each data element has a weight of 0.004, or 0.4%, which can be used as the basis for comparison of the actual data in real life. No matter how the split is made between the hierarchical levels and their components, there is no doubt that unless some use is made by at least some of the hierarchy levels, there is no justification for the development of the MIS (IIS) matrix. *Use makes the MIS (IIS).*

EXECUTIVE SUMMARY / The third of the MIS (IIS) sequence of three elements—information—is the subject of this chapter.

We said in chapter 1 that data become information only when they affect behavior. To affect the behavior of the organism, the decision-maker must use forecasts of the future outcomes of the organism which take into account not only the form of the data but also its content, i.e., the real-life basis of the phenomenon in question. Further, the decision-maker has to know where the particular product and/or service is in its own life cycle. In addition, he needs to know if changes can be made in the performance of the subsystems to affect system performance, at what cost, and with what probable changes.

While the individual needs of the organism vary significantly, the use of forecasts for decision-making purposes can be systematically identified. Such an identification is made, and we find that there are 1,134 elements of the MIS (IIS) matrix. These are arrived at by enumerating the elements of the MIS (IIS) matrix by lifecycle stage, one table for each of the 7 stages: (1) gestation, (2) birth, (3) infancy, (4) rapid growth, (5) maturation, (6) decline, and (7) death. In each of these stages, the combinations of Context E and Context T are held constant. For instance, uncertain Context E and unstable Context T would be one combination held constant through the 7 stages so that we have: (1) uncertain, unstable, gestation, (2) uncertain, unstable, birth, (3) uncertain, unstable, infancy; and so on until (7) uncertain, unstable, death.

In each of these tables by stage, the changes are made in three elements: cost, effectiveness—absolute, and effectiveness—relative. There are subcategories in each of the three elements, which together utilize the 18 elements of the MIS (IIS) matrix in one stage. Therefore, we have (18 × 7 =) 126 elements for the uncertain, unstable combination. There are 9 such combinations of Context E-Context T combination, giving rise to a total of (126 × 9 =) 1,134 elements of the MIS (IIS) matrix.

How important are the data on each of the 18 elements? We can assume that they are equal in importance. Similarly, we can assume that each of the 7 stages is equally important. Combining the two assumptions, we find that each data element has a weight of 0.008, or 0.8%, which can be used as a basis to compare the actual data in real life. The difference between the real-life weight for the data element, and the equal weight basis of the MIS (IIS) matrix identifies the particular profile of the given organism.

It is one thing to have an MIS (IIS) matrix; it is quite another to use it. We have pointed out that the use should be associated with the PDM roles. The frequency of use can be divided into (1) infrequent, (2) intermittent, and (3) frequent. In each of the frequencies, the combinations of objectives hierarchy and PDM roles are held constant. For instance, organismic level and PDM role would be one combination; organismic and sub-PDM combination would be another; organismic and sub-sub-PDM would be yet another combination, there being 9 such combinations.

For each of the 9 combinations, there are three tables by frequency of use. In each of these tables we vary the forecasting time period (immediate, intermediate, and indefinite); data weighting (equal, unequal); and problem category (solution oriented, structure oriented, structural solution oriented), giving rise to 27 elements per table. The three tables for 1 combination of organismic level and PDM role have (27 × 3 =) 81 elements; and the 9 combinations of organismic hierarchy and PDM roles give rise to (81 × 9 =) 729 elements for the MIS (IIS) utilization matrix.

How important is the utilization represented by each of the 27 elements? We can assume that all the 27 elements are equal in importance; and also that each of the hierarchy level, decision role combinations is equally important. Combining the two assumptions, we find that each data element has a weight of 0.004, or 0.4%, which can be used as the basis for comparison of the actual data in real life. No matter how the split is made between the hierarchical levels and their components, there is no doubt that unless some use is made by at least some of the hierarchy levels, there is no justification for the development of the MIS (IIS) matrix. *Use makes the MIS (IIS).*

In chapter 3 the triple context of decision-making was developed which provides the setting for the development of MIS (IIS) in the sequence comprising the elements of raw data, pre-information, and information. This chapter will discuss the third element.

Also in chapter 3, four major elements of decision-making were identified: (1) context E, (2) cost, (3) effectiveness—absolute, and (4) effectiveness—relative.

Context E-T Profile

Context E-Context T interactions

In chapter 3 the interactions between the external environment, as perceived by the decision-maker, Context E (uncertain, risk, and reduced risk) and the internal capabilities as reflected in the technological context, Context T, (unstable, quasistable, and stable) were identified. The Context E-Context T interactions shown in Table 6.1 are:

1. uncertain, unstable
2. uncertain, quasistable
3. uncertain, stable
4. risk, unstable
5. risk, quasistable
6. risk, stable
7. reduced risk, unstable
8. reduced risk, quasistable
9. reduced risk, stable

In constructing a profile of MIS (IIS), provision must be made to identify each of these interactions.

The use of the terms Context E and Context T are generic. If an organism is engaged in manufacturing, say, 10 different products, chances are that the technology of some of them would be different from that of the others. Therefore, the Context E-Context T should be specified with reference to each product and/or service offered by the organism. What the MIS (IIS) should permit is the listing of all products and/or services by the Context E-Context T interaction.

Table 6.1: Context E by Context T

Context E \ Context T	Unstable	Quasi-stable	Stable
Uncertain	(11) first	12	13
Risk	21	22	23
Reduced Risk	31	32	(33) last

153

From the point of view of decision-making, an additional consideration is that of the stage of growth of the product and/or process. There are 7 stages in the life cycle: (1) gestation, (2) birth, (3) infancy, (4) rapid growth, (5) maturation, (6) decline, and (7) death. The product and/or process must not only be identified in terms of the interaction between Context E and Context T, but also the particular stage of growth to which the product and/or process belongs.

When the stage of growth is added to Context E and Context T to specify decision-making, we get the matrix in Table 6.2. The rows are the combinations of Context E-Context T:

Row 11   uncertain, unstable
Row 12   uncertain, quasistable
.   .
.   .
.   .
Row 33   reduced risk, stable

Now the life cycle stage has to be associated with each cell. We are using the third dimension, which cannot be represented directly in a two-dimensional matrix. We shall therefore use the third digit to signify the stage of growth as follows:

Row 11 uncertain, unstable:
111 uncertain, unstable, gestation
112 uncertain, unstable, birth
113 uncertain, unstable, infancy
114 uncertain, unstable, rapid growth
115 uncertain, unstable, maturation
116 uncertain, unstable, decline
117 uncertain, unstable, death

The three variables can be subscripted, respectively, by i, j, and k: Context E becoming E_i, Context T becoming T_j, and life cycle stage S becoming S_k.

Cost Content Profile

Context E deals with the environmental status of fulfillment characteristics (the success of the organism in fulfilling external demands) while Context T deals with the technological status of performance characteristics (the capability of the resources of the organism to perform). No consideration has been given to the cost that has to be incurred. We now turn to the cost content of an MIS (IIS).

Table 6.2: Context E-T by Stage of Growth

Context E-T	Stage of Growth						
	Gesta-tion	Birth	Infancy	Rapid Growth	Matu-ration	Decline	Death
Uncertain, Unstable (11)	(first) 111	112	113	114	115	116	117
Uncertain, Quasistable (12)	121	122	123	124	125	126	127
Uncertain, Stable (13)	131	132	133	134	135	136	137
Risk, Unstable (21)	211	212	213	214	215	216	217
Risk, Quasistable (22)	221	222	223	224	225	226	227
Risk, Stable (23)	231	232	233	234	235	236	237
Reduced Risk, Unstable (31)	311	312	313	314	315	316	317
Reduced Risk, Quasistable (32)	321	322	323	324	325	326	327
Reduced Risk, Stable (33)	331	332	333	334	335	336	337 (last)

Cost as opportunity foregone

Underlying the discussions of cost are two major concepts of economics: utility, and marginalism.

Why do people acquire goods and services, or why do they spend money to acquire goods and services? People spend money because they expect to gain satisfaction. Utility is *potential satisfaction* associated with goods and/or services. The *potential* nature should be fully recognized, because the commitment of resources are made at time t, and the satisfaction or dissatisfaction from the consumption of the goods and/or services cannot be registered before time $t + \Delta t$, i.e., in the future with reference to the spending of the money itself. Therefore, even if the cup of coffee for which

15 cents is paid turns out to be undrinkable, the utility, being *potential* satisfaction, remains unchanged.

If utility governs the expenditure of money, how do people distribute their expenditures? The homo economicus is, by definition, rational. The test of rationality is that he seeks to maximize his utility. Therefore, he will allocate his resources among products and/or services in such a way that the potential satisfaction from an additional dollar will be the same from every product and/or service. The increase (decrease) in the potential satisfaction corresponding to a small increase in the resource (money) spent on a product or service is its *marginal utility*.

Marginal utility basis underlies most cost considerations. In a project, the allocation of money (the resources it represents) really reflects the utility of the particular segment of the project (changes in the marginal utilities of the various segments of the project). The same principle holds at the level of the national budget. If human resources are allocated $85 billion and defense efforts are allocated $80 billion, the potential satisfaction out of the investment in human resources is considered to be 85/80 = 1.06, or, human resources are considered 6% more important than defense efforts. It should also be remembered that a similar evaluation exists with respect to all the other competing uses of the federal dollar, the federal budget reflecting the national utility expressed through the necessarily imperfect medium of popular representation in Congress and the vesting of executive authority in the executive branch of the government.

Cost as opportunity acquired

Despite the apparent precision which accompanies the allocation of federal dollars in such a way that $1 spent in education is equal in its utility to the $1 spent in defense, transportation, or medical research, there are a number of serious problems of measurement. For instance, how is the utility of education, defense, or medical research for a voter represented by a representative who is chosen by that voter and 500,000 other voters? Even if the utilities of both the individual voter and the representative coincide, the representative's influence in bringing to bear upon the national budget the utilities of his constituency may be distant and remote, unless the representative is a member of the U.S. House Appropriations Committee, preferably chairman of one of the subcommittees. The particular form of the budgetary allocation reflects a considerable amount of horse trading among competing legislative interests, and among competing legislative and executive interests. Therefore, the application of marginalism is more an abstract theory than an act of practice.

Recall that marginalism is founded upon the incremental unit of the *same kind*. In any instant of technological uncertainty, the new product or process is anything but "of the same kind." The modified product is not the same as the previous product; therefore, the marginal utility concept is *inapplicable*. As the technological uncertainty increases, so does the difficulty of finding in the new product an additional unit "of the same kind." By no stretch of the imagination could the principal decision-maker of an aircraft company in the early 1950s talk about the first missile as a marginal unit of the aircrafts. For him to say that a missile, if and when developed, will be equal to 3.2 aircrafts would be an exercise in imagination. He would be hard put to convince any board of directors that they should allocate 3.2 times the money for an aircraft for the unknown missile. On the contrary, the really basic investment criteria that the principal decision-maker can offer are precisely the *opportunities acquired,* or rather, *potential* opportunities acquired. To convince the board of directors, he would in fact have to show that if the potential opportunity acquired were not seized upon by the organism, it would seriously jeopardize the survival and growth of the organism, because when missile technology becomes the major technological fact of the day, the skills and capabilities to manufacture only aircrafts would leave the organism way behind. Notice that this is a direct application of the extended definition of forecasting developed in chapter 1.

To distinguish between the two types of costs that are associated with each project and/or service, we have to go to the 4th digit, the first three having been devoted to Context E, Context T, and stage of growth. To make a two-dimensional presentation, we present three digits in the row: Context E, Context T, stage of growth, and make the column entries represent the two types of costs as in Table 6.3. We have:

    1111 uncertain, unstable, gestation, foregone
    1112 uncertain, unstable, gestation, acquired
    1121 uncertain, unstable, birth, foregone
    1122 uncertain, unstable, birth, acquired
    1131 uncertain, unstable, infancy, foregone
    1132 uncertain, unstable, infancy, acquired
    1141 uncertain, unstable, rapid growth, foregone
    1142 uncertain, unstable, rapid growth, acquired
    1151 uncertain, unstable, maturation, foregone
    1152 uncertain, unstable, maturation, acquired
    1161 uncertain, unstable, decline, foregone
    1162 uncertain, unstable, decline, acquired
    1171 uncertain, unstable, death, foregone
    1172 uncertain, unstable, death, acquired

The four variables can be subscripted, respectively, by i, j, k, and m: Context E becoming E_i, Context T becoming T_j, life cycle stage S becoming S_k, and cost C becoming C_m.

Table 6.3: Context E-T, Stage of Growth by Cost

Context E-T, Stage of Growth	Cost	
	Opportunity Foregone	*Opportunity Acquired*
Uncertain, Unstable Gestation (111)	1111 (first)	1112
Uncertain, Unstable Birth (112)	1121	1122
Uncertain, Unstable Infancy (113)	1131	1132
Uncertain, Unstable Rapid Growth (114)	1141	1142
Uncertain, Unstable Maturation (115)	1151	1152
Uncertain, Unstable Decline (116)	1161	1162
Uncertain, Unstable Death (117)	1171	1172
Reduced Risk, Stable Gestation (331)	3311	3312
Reduced Risk, Stable Birth (332)	3321	3322
Reduced Risk, Stable Infancy (333)	3331	3332
Reduced Risk, Stable Rapid Growth (334)	3341	3342
Reduced Risk, Stable Maturation (335)	3351	3352
Reduced Risk, Stable Decline (336)	3361	3362
Reduced Risk, Stable Death (337)	3371	3372 (last)

Effectiveness—Absolute—Profile

The principal step in transforming an uncertain problem into a risky one is the specification of appropriate performance characteristics, measures of whose performance have to be devised. The performance measures gauge the extent to which the performance characteristics are realized in practice. In other words, a measure of performance is required. The performance measure must reflect the most important performance characteristics considered essential to the effective functioning of the organism. It is rare that a single performance characteristic would adequately represent all, or most, of the significant characteristics of the organism. Therefore, not only must the appropriate performance measures be established, but they should also be combined to yield a composite measure of effectiveness for the organism as a whole.

To arrive at a composite measure of effectiveness on the basis of the known experience of the performance characteristics of particular segments of the organism, it will be necessary to expose the transplanted individual members to the erratic occurrence of "high resistance" and "low rejection" in an equally likely manner. Only by exposing the individuals to such vagaries of the performance characteristics can meaningful statements be made about the composite effectiveness measure.

Effectiveness is the ratio of observed performance over desired performance.

The desired performance can be stated in terms of either the parts or of the organism as a whole. With respect to large systems, it will frequently be necessary to specify the performances of the parts, and not that of the organism as a whole. In the case of a large system, such as a spacecraft, it is logical to recognize three kinds of performances: (1) system performance, (2) subsystem performance, and (3) sub-subsystem performance. We can incorporate these three types of performance into the profile of MIS matrix as shown in Table 6.4:

> 11 uncertain, unstable
> > 11111 uncertain, unstable, gestation, foregone, system
> > 11112 uncertain, unstable, gestation, foregone, subsystem
> > 11113 uncertain, unstable, gestation, foregone, sub-subsystem
> > 11121 uncertain, unstable, gestation, acquired, system
> > 11122 uncertain, unstable, gestation, acquired, subsystem
> > 11123 uncertain, unstable, gestation, acquired, sub-subsystem
> > 11211 uncertain, unstable, birth, foregone, system
> > 11212 uncertain, unstable, birth, foregone, subsystem
> > 11213 uncertain, unstable, birth, foregone, sub-subsystem
> > 11221 uncertain, unstable, birth, acquired, system
> > 11222 uncertain, unstable, birth, acquired, subsystem
> > 11223 uncertain, unstable, birth, acquired, sub-subsystem
> > . . . .
> > 11723 uncertain, unstable death, acquired, sub-subsystem

The five variables can be subscripted, respectively, by $i, j, k, m,$ and n:

Context E becoming E_i, Context T becoming T_j, life cycle stage S becoming S_k, cost C becoming C_m, and effectiveness—absolute, F, becoming F_n.

Table 6.4: Context E-T, Stage of Growth, Cost by Effectiveness—Absolute

Context E-T, Stage of Growth, Cost	Effectiveness–absolute		
	System Performance	Subsystem Performance	Sub-Subsystem Performance
Uncertain, Unstable, Gestation, Foregone (1111)	11111 (first)	11112	11113
Uncertain, Unstable, Gestation, Acquired (1112)	11121	11122	11123
Uncertain, Unstable, Birth, Foregone (1121)	11211	11212	11213
Uncertain, Unstable, Birth, Acquired (1122)	11221	11222	11223
Uncertain, Unstable, Infancy, Foregone (1131)	11311	11312	11313
Uncertain, Unstable, Infancy, Acquired (1132)	11321	11322	11323
Uncertain, Unstable, Rapid Growth, Foregone (1141)	11411	11412	11413
Uncertain, Unstable, Rapid Growth, Acquired (1142)	11421	11422	11423
Uncertain, Unstable, Maturation, Foregone (1151)	11511	11512	11513
Uncertain, Unstable, Maturation, Acquired (1152)	11521	11522	11523
Uncertain, Unstable, Decline, Foregone (1161)	11611	11612	11613
Uncertain, Unstable, Decline, Acquired (1162)	11621	11622	11623
Uncertain, Unstable, Death, Foregone (1171)	11711	11712	11713
Uncertain, Unstable, Death, Acquired (1172)	11721	11722	11723
Reduced Risk, Stable, Death, Acquired (3372)	33721	33722	33723 (last)

Effectiveness—Relative—Profile

We have defined effectiveness as the ratio of observed performance over desired performance. The desired performance itself has to be stated in terms of the performance characteristics of the technological and/or environmental variables.

To management, absolute values of performance are important: however, relative values are likely to be equally, if not more, important. The reason for the importance stems from the fact that the relative changes that can be brought about in the performance characteristics suggest to the decision-maker the value of the effort that may be invested in bringing about the changes. For instance, to achieve a small increment in the value of the performance characteristics, say, speed of the aircraft, beyond certain plateaus, it may require an enormously large investment. Thus, for an increase in speed of 10 miles per hour at 1100 miles, the cost may be double that of a speed increase of 10 miles per hour at 600 miles an hour. The question that management must decide is: Is the increase from 1100 to 1110 worth twice the effort in raising the speed from 600 to 610 miles per hour?

To accomplish the small change in the performance characteristics of the system as a whole, it is generally a *sub*system performance characteristic that has to be affected. The important question then is: By how much will *system* performance be improved by the specific improvement in subsystem performance? Often, the functional relationship between system performance and subsystem performance is not well defined. Further, the difference in the performance of one subsystem may well affect the performance of other subsystems, and thus system performance as a whole. In other words, when we talk about system performance as influenced by *a* subsystem performance, we are in fact recognizing explicitly or implicitly the interactions that may be set in motion by the change in subsystem performance.

The decision to invest in the improvement of the subsystem performance has, however, to be made ahead of any precise determination of the functional relationship between the subsystem and the system. While the precise relationship itself may be unknown, it can be represented by probability distributions, the parameters of which can be estimated. That would still leave the interactions between the subsystems a largely indeterminate area. Therefore, the management investment decision has to take into account the technological uncertainties of subsystem interactions in arriving at a decision to commit resources to the promise of the improvement in the system performance.

An example of such prior commitment of resources is found in the decision by Great Britain in 1937 to commit virtually the entire defense of the island to the promises of radar which was only in the experimental stages. In Churchill's words: "The plans for the air defence of Great Britain

161

had, as early as the autumn of 1937, been rewritten around the assumption that the promises made by our scientists for the still unproven radar would be kept."[1]

While the reference is to the performance of the system as a whole, it is quite likely that there were a number of subsystems in which investment of resources was required. Both in his capacity as a member of the Air Defence Committee, and later as Prime Minister, Churchill depended upon the advice of Professor Lindemann. It would be Lindemann who would have to decide the improvement in the system performance, i.e., radar detection, that would probably result from an improvement in the subsystem performance of one or more of the subsystems. In this case, it could be said that money was no object. Therefore, the proportionate change in system performance corresponding to a proportionate change in subsystem performance could well be considered in terms of the performance alone.

In most instances, however, cost may in fact be an important consideration. The numerator would still be the proportionate change in system performance; but the denominator would change from the performance characteristics to cost characteristics. Corresponding to a 10 percent increase in the investment in the subsystem, what will be the corresponding increase in the performance of system characteristics?

Whether considered in terms of performance or cost, the accent is on the rate of change. By how much will system performance change for either a given change in subsystem performance or subsystem cost? If for a 10 percent change in subsystem performance, system performance changes by 10 percent, the rate of change is $10\%/10\% = 1$, or 100%. If system performance changes by only 3% when subsystem performance changes by 10%, then the rate of change is $3\%/10\% = .3$, or 30%. If, on the other hand, system performance improves by 40% corresponding to a 10% change in subsystem performance, the rate of change is $40\%/10\% = 4$, or 400%. The reasoning remains the same whether the denominator is performance changes or cost changes.

The profile of an MIS (IIS) with respect to the *relative* effectiveness content of decision-making can now be identified in terms of the relative effectiveness in performance and cost. The relative effectiveness in fact measures the *sensitivity* of the system whether to the performance of the subsystem or the cost of the subsystem. We define sensitivity as

Proportionate change in system performance
Proportionate change in subsystem performance
or subsystem cost

Notice that the subsystem can be any one or more of the several subsystems

---

[1] Winston S. Churchill, *The Grand Alliance* (Boston: Houghton Mifflin, 1951), p. 45.

of the system. As a matter of fact, management would be interested in varying the inputs, i.e., the changes in the subsystem. It may want to know the rate of change in system performance when different subsystems are changed, either individually or collectively. Again, it may be interested in changing one or two subsystems, while holding the others constant, and investigating the sensitivity of the system to the single or multiple subsystems. The changes may of course be with respect to either the performance, or the cost, or both.

We can incorporate these three types of relative performance into the profile of MIS (IIS) matrix as in Table 6.5:

11 uncertain, unstable
    111111 uncertain, unstable, gestation, foregone, system, performance
    111112 uncertain, unstable, gestation, foregone, system, cost
    111113 uncertain, unstable, gestation, foregone, system, performance/cost
    111121 uncertain, unstable, gestation, acquired, subsystem, performance
    111122 uncertain, unstable, gestation, acquired, subsystem, cost
    111123 uncertain, unstable, gestation, acquired, subsystem, performance/cost
    111131 uncertain, unstable, gestation, foregone, sub-subsystem, performance
    111132 uncertain, unstable, gestation, foregone, sub-subsystem, cost
    111133 uncertain, unstable, gestation, foregone, sub-subsystem performance/cost
    . . . .
    117231 uncertain, unstable, death, acquired, sub-subsystem, performance
    117232 uncertain, unstable, death, acquired, sub-subsystem, cost
    117233 uncertain, unstable, death, acquired, sub-subsystem, performance/cost

The six variables can be subscripted, respectively, by i, j, k, m, n, and p: Context E becoming E_i, Context T becoming T_j, life cycle stage S becoming S_k, cost C becoming C_m, effectiveness—absolute, F, becoming F_n, and effectiveness—relative, G, becoming G_p.

MIS (IIS) Matrix

In the above sections we developed the four principal elements of MIS (IIS) which correspond to the four principal elements in OR/SA approach to

Table 6.5: Context E-T, Stage of Growth, Cost, Effectiveness—Absolute by Effectiveness—Relative

Context E-T, Stage of Growth, Cost, Effectiveness—absolute	Effectiveness—relative		
	Performance Change	Cost Change	Performance/ Cost Change
Uncertain, Unstable, Gestation, Foregone, System (11111)	(first) 111111	111112	111113
Uncertain, Unstable, Gestation, Foregone, Subsystem (11112)	111121	111122	111123
Uncertain, Unstable, Gestation, Foregone, Sub-subsystem (11113)	111131	111132	111133
Uncertain, Unstable, Gestation, Acquired, System (11121)	111211	111212	111213
Uncertain, Unstable, Gestation, Acquired, Subsystem (11122)	111221	111222	111223
Uncertain, Unstable, Gestation, Acquired, Sub-subsystem (11123)	111231	111232	111233
Uncertain, Unstable, Birth, Foregone, System (11211)	112111	112112	112113
Uncertain, Unstable, Birth, Foregone, Subsystem (11212)	112121	112122	112123
Uncertain, Unstable, Birth, Foregone, Sub-subsystem (11213)	112131	112132	112133
Uncertain, Unstable, Birth, Acquired, System (11221)	112211	112212	112213
Uncertain, Unstable, Birth, Acquired, Subsystem (11222)	112221	112222	112223
Uncertain, Unstable, Birth, Acquired, Sub-subsystem (11223)	112231	112232	112233
. . . .	. . . .	. . . .	. . . .
Reduced Risk, Stable, Death, Acquired, System (33721)	337211	337212	337213
Reduced Risk, Stable, Death, Acquired, Subsystem (33722)	337221	337222	337223
Reduced Risk, Stable, Death, Acquired, Sub-subsystem (33723)	337231	337232	337233 (last)

decision-making situations. As a safeguard against the tendency to equate information with data, and to identify rapidity of data processing with reliability of insight, 9 Context E-Context T combinations have been identified. These combinations are the proper context of decision-making because they combine the elements of external demands and internal capabilities, of customer preferences and technological performance.

By structuring the input of information to explicitly recognize the twin influences of environment and technology, the MIS (IIS) matrix emerges as a six-dimensional matrix. To make possible the representation in the form of a table, we split up the MIS (IIS) matrix by stage, with the first three variables, Context E_i, Context T_j, and Stage S_k as constants. Thus, uncertain environment, unstable technology, and the gestation stage together are represented as 111. The next stage of birth is represented by 112; and so on until the last stage, viz., that of death, is represented by 117.

We develop 7 figures, 1 for each stage, ranging from 111 through 117. The entity represented by 111, can be broken into two terms: cost as opportunity foregone (1111), and cost as opportunity acquired (1112). With each of the two types of costs can be associated three types of performance: system performance, subsystem performance, and sub-subsystem performance. Using the concept of cost as opportunity foregone, we have three types of effectiveness: system performance (11111), subsystem performance (11112), and sub-subsystem performance (11113). Similarly, using the concept of cost as opportunity acquired, we also have three types of effectiveness: system performance (11121), subsystem performance (11122), and sub-subsystem performance (11123).

Each of the *absolute* performance measures can be associated with three types of *relative* performances, or rate of change of effectiveness: system performance change (111111), system cost change (111112), and system per-formance/cost change (111113). Similarly, with 11112 can be associated 111121, 111122, 111123. Thus we have 18 elements of the MIS (IIS) matrix in stage 1, gestation, for the uncertain environment and the unstable tech-nology. These 18 elements are presented in Figure 6.1.

How important are the data on each of the 18 elements? The simplest assumption is that all the 18 elements are equal in importance. Similarly, which of the 7 stages is most important? We can assume that all the stages are equally important. Assigning equal weights to each of the 7 stages, we find that 111 (uncertain environment, unstable technology, and gestation stage of growth), has a weight of $(100\% \div 7 \simeq)$ 14.4%. In the gestation stage, if we assume that each of the 18 elements is of equal weight, we find that each element gets the weight of $(14.4\% \div 18 =)$ 0.8%. It should be noted that we have given a weight of 14.4% instead of 14.3% to each of the 7 stages to permit the obtaining of a round figure of 0.8% for each of the 18 elements.

In real life, every stage, and every element, does *not* have equal weight.

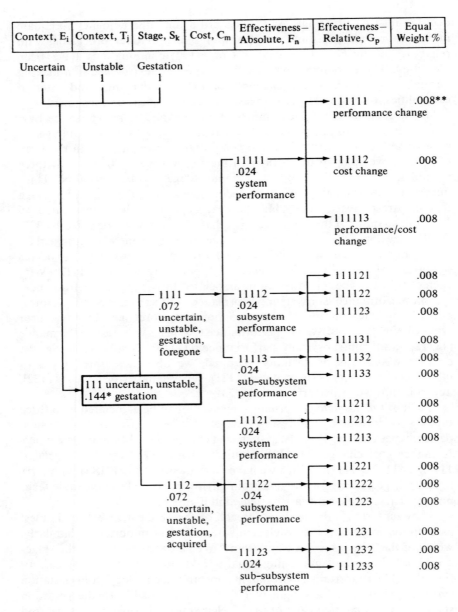

Context, E_i	Context, T_j	Stage, S_k	Cost, C_m	Effectiveness—Absolute, F_n	Effectiveness—Relative, G_p	Equal Weight %

Uncertain   Unstable   Gestation
1   1   1

111111 .008**
performance change

11111 .024 system performance

111112 .008
cost change

111113 .008
performance/cost change

111121 .008
111122 .008
111123 .008

11112 .024 subsystem performance

111131 .008
111132 .008
111133 .008

11113 .024 sub–subsystem performance

1111 .072 uncertain, unstable, gestation, foregone

111 uncertain, unstable, .144* gestation

111211 .008
111212 .008
111213 .008

11121 .024 system performance

111221 .008
111222 .008
111223 .008

11122 .024 subsystem performance

1112 .072 uncertain, unstable, gestation, acquired

111231 .008
111232 .008
111233 .008

11123 .024 sub–subsystem performance

*Assigning equal weight to each of the 7 stages ($100 \div 7 = 14.4\%$).

**Assigning equal weight to each of the 18 elements of each stage ($14.4\% \div 18 = 0.8\%$).

Figure 6.1: MIS (IIS) matrix by stage: I uncertain, unstable, (1) gestation

166

For the same product, different stages become important at different times. And, within the same stage, different elements become important at different times. By assuming equal importance for each of the stages and elements, we have a basis to compare the actual weights with the hypothetical situation of equal weights.

Figures 6.2 through 6.7 successively represent the other 6 stages of growth from birth to death.

So far, we have represented the MIS (IIS) matrix for only one combination of Context E_i, T_j, i.e., 11, uncertain environment, unstable technology. By similar reasoning, we shall have 7 figures for each of the 9 Context E_i-Context T_j combinations. With 18 elements per stage, each stage has (18 x 7 =) 126 elements. With 126 elements in each Context E_i-Context T_j combination, there is a total of (126 x 9 =) 1,134 elements in the MIS (IIS) matrix.

The 1,134 elements together cover all possible decision-making situations which can be specified in terms of the 6-dimensional MIS matrix. In Table 6.6, the distribution of the elements by stage of growth is shown, as well as the percentage of weight. The percentage of weight on the basis of the assumption of equality of weights provides a basis for comparison of the various information inputs developed from the organism's MIS (IIS). For instance, an organism which is heavily technology oriented would probably register a much heavier weight than the 1.296% for gestation registered in column 1. By the same token, an organism with a large number of products with a high degree of obsolescence will register a much larger quantity for rapid growth in column 4 than 1.296%, and so on.

Profile of MIS (IIS) Use

The proof of the MIS (IIS) is in its influence upon the control exercised by management. Control is exercised by the different elements of the decision-making hierarchy—organismic, strategic, and tactical. In chapter 3 we recognized the concurrent, conflicting context of decision-making which is imposed upon each decision-maker by the fact that he has to be *simultaneously* at the organismic level, strategic level, and tactical level. Recognizing the need for an MIS (IIS) at levels other than that of the absolute organismic level decision-maker, such as the president of a billion dollar corporation, we stated that an MIS (IIS) is required by a PDM at the strategic and even tactical level of the organism. A working definition would specify a PDM as one who has responsibility for 200 employees and/or $1,000,000.

Objectives and PDM roles by utilization

We can now combine the objectives hierarchy with the PDM roles. Since the objectives hierarchy of the organism is the controlling variable, we

167

Table 6.6: MIS (IIS) Matrix: 1,134 Elements—Stage by Context

	(1) Gestation	(2) Birth	(3) Infancy	(4) Rapid Growth	(5) Maturation	(6) Decline	(7) Death	(8) Total
1. Uncertain, unstable	18	18	18	18	18	18	18	126
	.144*	.144	.144	.144	.144	.144	.144	1.008**
2. Uncertain, quasistable	18	18	18	18	18	18	18	126
	.144	.144	.144	.144	.144	.144	.144	1.008
3. Uncertain, stable	18	18	18	18	18	18	18	126
	.144	.144	.144	.144	.144	.144	.144	1.008
4. Risk, unstable	18	18	18	18	18	18	18	126
	.144	.144	.144	.144	.144	.144	.144	1.008
5. Risk, quasistable	18	18	18	18	18	18	18	126
	.144	.144	.144	.144	.144	.144	.144	1.008
6. Risk, stable	18	18	18	18	18	18	18	126
	.144	.144	.144	.144	.144	.144	.144	1.008
7. Reduced risk, unstable	18	18	18	18	18	18	18	126
	.144	.144	.144	.144	.144	.144	.144	1.008
8. Reduced risk, quasistable	18	18	18	18	18	18	18	126
	.144	.144	.144	.144	.144	.144	.144	1.008
9. Reduced risk, stable	18	18	18	18	18	18	18	126
	.144	.144	.144	.144	.144	.144	.144	1.008
	162	162	162	162	162	162	162	1134
	1.296	1.296	1.296	1.296	1.296	1.296	1.296	9.072

*Assigning equal weight to each of the 7 stages ($100 \div 7 \simeq 14.4\%$).

**The extra eight-tenth of one percent makes it possible to assign a round figure to each of the 18 elements of each stage ($14.4\% \div 18 = 0.8\%$) in Figures 6.1 through 6.7.

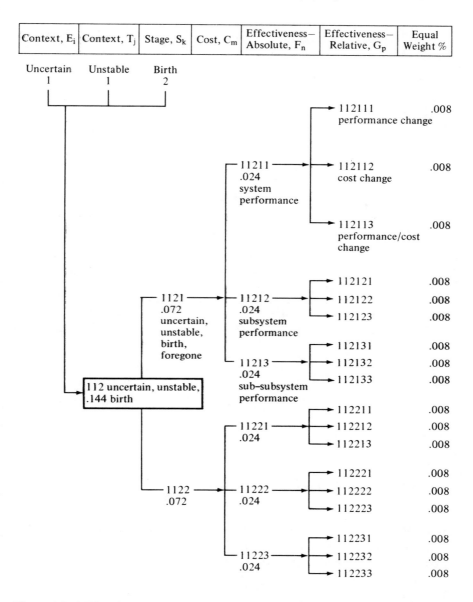

Figure 6.2: MIS (IIS) matrix by stage: I uncertain, unstable, (2) birth

hold that constant, and say that 11 represents the organismic level and the PDM role. With respect to the organismic level, a PDM can be at the

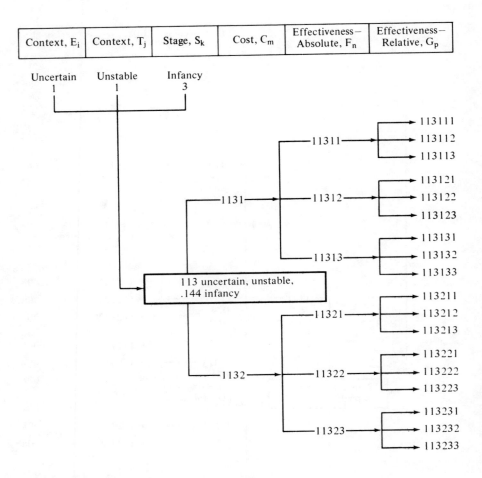

Context, E_i	Context, T_j	Stage, S_k	Cost, C_m	Effectiveness—Absolute, F_n	Effectiveness—Relative, G_p

Figure 6.3: MIS (IIS) matrix by stage: I uncertain, unstable, (3) infancy

sub-PDM level (e.g., a corporate vice-president). We represent this in Table 6.7 by 12: organismic sub-PDM. Similarly, 13 would represent organismic hierarchy, and sub-sub-PDM role.

Use of the MIS at each of these levels varies. We can designate the frequency of use as infrequent, intermittent, and frequent. We can associate with each combination of objectives hierarchy and PDM roles, one of the three levels of use as shown in Table 6.8. Incorporating the three characteristics simultaneously, we have:

    111 organismic, PDM, infrequent
    112 organismic, PDM, intermittent
    113 organismic, PDM, frequent

Context, E_i	Context, T_j	Stage S_k	Cost, C_m	Effectiveness— Absolute, F_n	Effectiveness— Relative, G_p

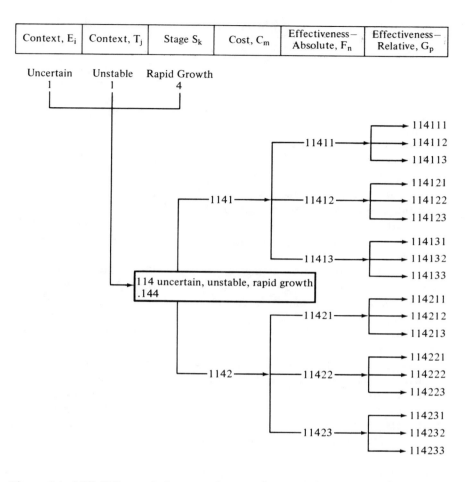

Figure 6.4: MIS (IIS) matrix by stage: I uncertain, unstable, (4) rapid growth

121 organismic, sub-PDM, infrequent
122 organismic, sub-PDM, intermittent
123 organismic, sub-PDM, frequent
131 organismic, sub-sub-PDM, infrequent
132 organismic, sub-sub-PDM, intermittent
133 organismic, sub-sub-PDM, frequent

Hierarchy by forecasting time period

In chapter 1 we established that the rationale for MIS (IIS) lies in the aid it provides the decision-maker to influence the behavior of the organism

Table 6.7: Objectives Hierarchy by PDM Roles

	PDM Roles		
Objectives Hierarchy	PDM	Sub-PDM	Sub-sub-PDM
Organismic	11 (first)	12	13
Strategic	21	22	23
Tactical	31	32	33 (last)

in a prespecified manner. Since the decisions are made at time t and it takes at least Δt to process the data, which itself is Δt behind, $t - \Delta t$, the earliest data that can be converted into information which influences the behavior of the organism is $t - 2\Delta t$ old, i.e., $3\Delta t$ beyond the latest data point. The earliest control that can be exercised will not be at time t, but at least Δt later, or at time $t + \Delta t$.

We can divide the forecasting as relating to the immediate $(2 - 3\Delta t)$, the intermediate $(3 - 4\Delta t$ to $6\Delta t)$, and the indefinite $(7\Delta t$ and beyond). To simplify notation, we may use $3\Delta t$ to represent the immediate, $6\Delta t$ to represent the intermediate, and $9\Delta t$ to represent the indefinite. The advantage of associating Δt with each time horizon is that for each organism and for each PDM role, Δt has to be explicitly defined. Once Δt is defined, it signals the pace of the data collection activity, as well as the pace of the conversion of the data into information. Further, it requires the PDM to think through the process of influencing the behavior of the organism via his decision-making. It separates the decision-making from the pressures of both data collection and data conversion. Data collection is usually done by the lower PDM roles; data conversion is usually done by staff services within the organism, or under contract with outside organisms—in either event, outside the direct control of the decision-maker. By making it necessary for the decision-maker to visualize the influence that his decision-making will have upon the behavior of the organism, he can make an intelligent demand upon the data collection activity as well as upon the data conversion activity.

We can now incorporate the forecasting time period into the utilization by hierarchy and decision-making roles as shown in Table 6.9:

  1111 organismic, PDM, infrequent, $3\Delta t$
  1112 organismic, PDM, infrequent, $6\Delta t$
  1113 organismic, PDM, infrequent, $9\Delta t$
  1121 organismic, PDM, intermittent, $3\Delta t$
  1122 organismic, PDM, intermittent, $6\Delta t$
  1123 organismic, PDM, intermittent, $9\Delta t$
  1131 organismic, PDM, frequent, $3\Delta t$

Table 6.8: Objectives Hierarchy, PDM Roles by Utilization

Objectives Hierarchy, PDM Roles	Frequency		
	Infrequent	Intermittent	Frequent
Organismic, PDM (11)	111 (first)	112	113
Organismic, Sub-PDM (12)	121	122	123
Organismic, Sub-sub-PDM (13)	131	132	133
Strategic, PDM (21)	211	212	213
Strategic, Sub-PDM (22)	221	222	223
Strategic, Sub-sub-PDM (23)	231	232	233
Tactical, PDM (31)	311	312	313
Tactical, Sub-PDM (32)	321	322	323
Tactical, Sub-sub-PDM (33)	331	332	333 (last)

1132 organismic, PDM, frequent, $6\Delta t$
1133 organismic, PDM, frequent, $9\Delta t$
1211 organismic, sub-PDM, infrequent, $3\Delta t$
1212 organismic, sub-PDM, infrequent, $6\Delta t$
1213 organismic, sub-PDM, infrequent, $9\Delta t$
1221 organismic, sub-PDM, intermittent, $3\Delta t$
1222 organismic, sub-PDM, intermittent, $6\Delta t$
1223 organismic, sub-PDM, intermittent, $9\Delta t$
1231 organismic, sub-PDM, frequent, $3\Delta t$
1232 organismic, sub-PDM, frequent, $6\Delta t$
1233 organismic, sub-PDM, frequent, $9\Delta t$
1311 organismic, sub-sub-PDM, infrequent, $3\Delta t$
1312 organismic, sub-sub-PDM, infrequent, $6\Delta t$
1313 organismic, sub-sub-PDM, infrequent, $9\Delta t$
1321 organismic, sub-sub-PDM, intermittent, $3\Delta t$
1322 organismic, sub-sub-PDM, intermittent, $6\Delta t$
1323 organismic, sub-sub-PDM, intermittent, $9\Delta t$
1331 organismic, sub-sub-PDM, frequent, $3\Delta t$
1332 organismic, sub-sub-PDM, frequent, $6\Delta t$
1333 organismic, sub-sub-PDM, frequent, $9\Delta t$

Hierarchy by data weighting

In chapter 5, both the form and content of raw data inputs were considered separately from the point of view of converting them into pre-information. Under form, we considered equal and unequal weighting

Context, E_i	Context, T_j	Stage, S_k	Cost, C_m	Effectiveness— Absolute, F_n	Effectiveness— Relative, G_p

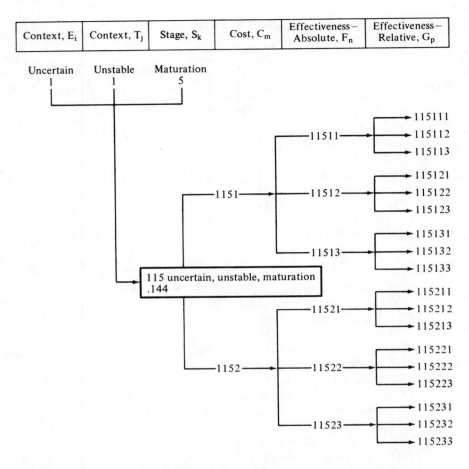

Figure 6.5: MIS (IIS) matrix by stage: I uncertain, unstable, (5) maturation

of the different data points. Under content, we considered three types of problems: solution oriented, structure oriented, and structural solution oriented.

With each of the forecasting time periods, we can associate the equal or unequal method of weighting the data. Under equal weighting, we have linear and nonlinear methods. Under the unequal weights method, we have discussed exponential smoothing in which the data are divided into "recent," and "remote." The size of the two periods changes; so does the weight expressed in the form of the smoothing constant, α. The data weighting methods for forecasting can be divided into (1) polynomial linear, (2) polynomial nonlinear, and (3) exponential smoothing.

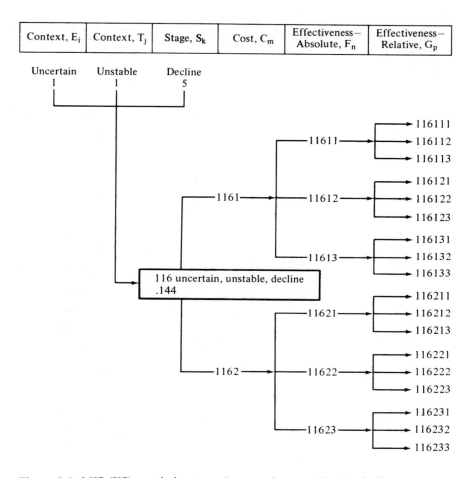

Figure 6.6: MIS (IIS) matrix by stage: I uncertain, unstable, (6) decline

We can now incorporate the data weighting methods into the MIS (IIS) utilization matrix as shown in Table 6.10:

11111 organismic, PDM, infrequent, $3\Delta t$, linear
11112 organismic, PDM, infrequent, $3\Delta t$, nonlinear
11113 organismic, PDM, infrequent, $3\Delta t$, exponential
11121 organismic, PDM, infrequent, $6\Delta t$, linear
11122 organismic, PDM, infrequent, $6\Delta t$, nonlinear
11123 organismic, PDM, infrequent, $6\Delta t$, exponential
11131 organismic, PDM, infrequent, $9\Delta t$, linear
11132 organismic, PDM, infrequent, $9\Delta t$, nonlinear

175

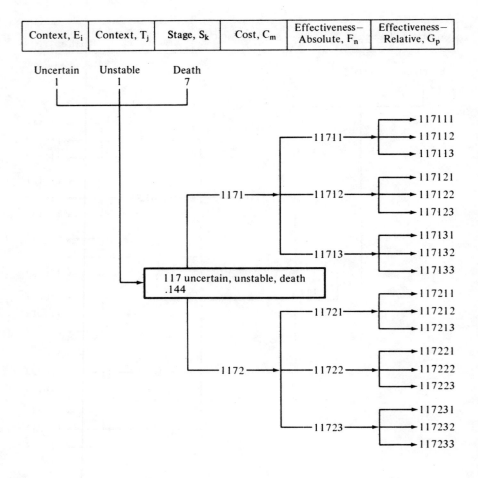

Context, E_i	Context, T_j	Stage, S_k	Cost, C_m	Effectiveness— Absolute, F_n	Effectiveness— Relative, G_p

Figure 6.7: MIS (IIS) matrix by stage: I uncertain, unstable, (7) death

11133 organismic, PDM, infrequent, $9\Delta t$, exponential

. . . .

33333 tactical, sub-sub-PDM, frequent, $9\Delta t$, exponential

Hierarchy by problem category

While the weighting of the data points can be done with little regard to the underlying phenomena, it is essential to appreciate the content of the problem and the predominant characteristics of the phenomenon in order to apply the appropriate analytical methodology which will permit an

Table 6.9: Objectives Hierarchy, PDM Roles, Utilization by Forecasting
Time Period

Objectives Hierarchy, PDM Roles, Frequency	Forecasting Time Period		
	$3\Delta t$	$6\Delta t$	$9\Delta t$
Organismic, PDM, Infrequent (111)	1111 (first)	1112	1113
Organismic, PDM, Intermittent (112)	1121	1122	1123
Organismic, PDM, Frequent (113)	1131	1132	1133
Organismic, Sub-PDM, Infrequent (121)	1211	1212	1213
Organismic, Sub-PDM, Intermittent (122)	1221	1222	1223
Organismic, Sub-PDM, Frequent (123)	1231	1232	1233
Organismic, Sub-sub-PDM Infrequent (131)	1311	1312	1313
Organismic, Sub-sub-PDM, Intermittent (132)	1321	1322	1323
Organismic, Sub-sub-PDM, Frequent (133)	1331	1332	1333
Strategic, PDM, Infrequent (211)	2111	2112	2113
Strategic, PDM, Intermittent (212)	2121	2122	2123
Strategic, PDM, Frequent (213)	2131	2132	2133
Strategic, Sub-PDM, Infrequent (221)	2211	2212	2213
Strategic, Sub-PDM, Intermittent (222)	2221	2222	2223
Strategic, Sub-PDM, Frequent (223)	2231	2232	2233
Tactical, Sub-PDM, Frequent (333)	3331	3332	3333 (last)

assessment of the particular features of the problem that may be relevant to decision-making. The alternative methods of weighting can be applied to each of the three problem categories as shown in Table 6.11:

Table 6.10: Objectives Hierarchy, PDM Roles, Utilization, Forecasting by Weighting

Objectives Hierarchy, PDM Roles, Frequency, Forecasting	Weighting		
	Linear	Non-Linear	Expo-nential
Organismic, **PDM**, Infrequent, $3\Delta t$ (1111)	11111 (first)	11112	11113
Organismic, **PDM**, Infrequent, $6\Delta t$ (1112)	11121	11122	11123
Organismic, **PDM**, Infrequent, $9\Delta t$ (1113)	11131	11132	11133
Organismic, **PDM**, Intermittent, $3\Delta t$ (1121)	11211	11212	11213
Organismic, **PDM**, Intermittent, $6\Delta t$ (1122)	11221	11222	11223
Organismic, **PDM**, Intermittent, $9\Delta t$ (1123)	11231	11232	11233
Organismic, **PDM**, Frequent, $3\Delta t$ (1131)	11311	11312	11313
Organismic, **PDM**, Frequent, $6\Delta t$ (1132)	11321	11322	11323
Organismic, **PDM**, Frequent, $9\Delta t$ (1133)	11331	11332	11333
Organismic, **Sub-PDM**, Infrequent, $3\Delta t$ (1211)	12111	12112	12113
Organismic, **Sub-PDM**, Infrequent, $6\Delta t$ (1212)	12121	12122	12123
Organismic, **Sub-PDM**, Infrequent, $9\Delta t$ (1213)	12131	12132	12133
Tactical, **Sub-sub-PDM**, Frequent, $3\Delta t$ (3331)	33311	33312	33313
Tactical, **Sub-sub-PDM**, Frequent, $6\Delta t$ (3332)	33321	33322	33323
Tactical, **Sub-sub-PDM**, Frequent, $9\Delta t$ (3333)	33331	33332	33333 (last)

111111 organismic, PDM, infrequent, $3\Delta t$, linear, solution
111112 organismic, PDM, infrequent, $3\Delta t$, linear, structure
111113 organismic, PDM, infrequent, $3\Delta t$, linear, structural solution
111121 organismic, PDM, infrequent, $3\Delta t$, nonlinear, solution
111122 organismic, PDM, infrequent, $3\Delta t$, nonlinear, structure
111123 organismic, PDM, infrequent, $3\Delta t$, nonlinear, structural solution
111131 organismic, PDM, infrequent, $3\Delta t$, exponential, solution
111132 organismic, PDM, infrequent, $3\Delta t$, exponential, structure
111133 organismic, PDM, infrequent, $3\Delta t$, exponential, structural solution
. . . .
333331 tactical, sub-sub-PDM, frequent, $9\Delta t$, exponential, solution
333332 tactical, sub-sub-PDM, frequent, $9\Delta t$, exponential, structure
333333 tactical, sub-sub-PDM, frequent, $9\Delta t$, exponential, structural solution

MIS (IIS) Utilization Matrix

After developing an MIS (IIS) matrix of 1,134 elements in which provides for decision-making situations the systematic use of raw data in the survival and growth of products and/or services, as well as that of organisms—both profit-making and nonprofit-making—we raise here the question of MIS (IIS) utilization.

It is one thing to convert raw data into pre-information; it is quite another to convert pre-information into information by utilizing the raw data. To aid management in exercising control, the latest time period of raw data is time $t - 2\Delta t$. The data on time $t - 2\Delta t$ must be converted into a forecast of what the data would be at time $t + \Delta t$. Knowing what the forecast is, management can take the necessary decisions to implement corrective actions at time t. In addition to the *what* (forecast provided by the MIS (IIS) matrix), it is necessary to raise the question of *who* (uses the forecast).

By structuring the objectives hierarchy of the organism to explicitly recognize the types of problems and the types of data conversion, the MIS (IIS) utilization matrix emerges as a 6-dimensional matrix. To make possible the representation in the form of a table, we split the MIS (IIS) utilization matrix by frequency of use. Thus, (1) the organismic level of the objectives hierarchy and (2) the PDM roles are held constant, and (3) the frequency of use is changed. We have organismic, PDM represented by (11) and the three frequencies of use—infrequent, intermittent, and frequent—combined to give 111 in Figure 6.8, 112 in Figure 6.9, and 113 in Figure 6.10.

179

Table 6.11: Objectives Hierarchy, PDM Roles, Utilization, Forecasting, Weighting, by Problem Category

Objectives Hierarchy, PDM Roles, Frequency, Forecasting, Weighting	Problem Category		
	Solution Oriented	Structure Oriented	Structural Solution Oriented
Organismic, PDM, Infrequent, 3△t, Linear (11111)	(first) 111111	111112	111113
Organismic, PDM, Infrequent, 3△t, Nonlinear (11112)	111121	111122	111123
Organismic, PDM, Infrequent, 3△t, Exponential (11113)	111131	111132	111133
Organismic, PDM, Infrequent, 6△t, Linear (11121)	111211	111212	111213
Organismic, PDM, Infrequent, 6△t, Nonlinear (11122)	111221	111222	111223
Organismic, PDM, Infrequent, 6△t, Exponential (11123)	111231	111232	111233
Organismic, PDM, Infrequent, 9△t, Linear (11131)	111311	111312	111313
Organismic, PDM, Infrequent, 9△t, Nonlinear (11132)	111321	111322	111323
Organismic, PDM, Infrequent, 9△t, Exponential (11133)	111331	111332	111333
Tactical, Sub-sub-PDM, Frequent, 9△t, Linear (33331)	333311	333312	333313
Tactical, Sub-sub-PDM, Frequent, 9△t, Nonlinear (33332)	333321	333322	333323
Tactical, Sub-sub-PDM, Frequent, 9△t, Exponential (33333)	333331	333332	333333 (last)

With each of the combinations of the three variables can be associated three forecasting periods—$3\Delta t$ (1111), $6\Delta t$ (1112), and $9\Delta t$ (1113). To each time period, three types of data weighting can be associated—linear (11111), nonlinear (11112), and exponential (11113). Each of the data weighting procedures refers to three types of problems—solution oriented

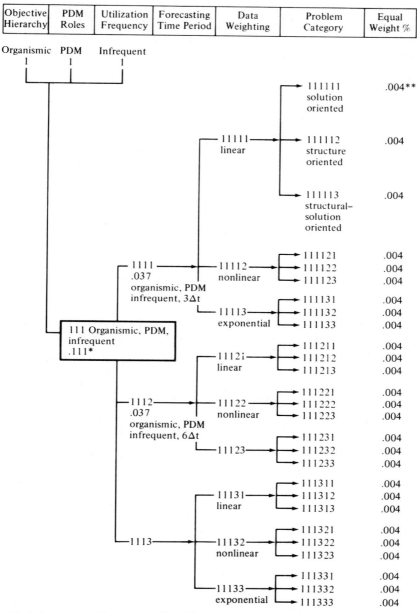

Objective Hierarchy	PDM Roles	Utilization Frequency	Forecasting Time Period	Data Weighting	Problem Category	Equal Weight %

Organismic   PDM   Infrequent

111111
solution
oriented   .004**

11111 ——→ 111112
linear   structure
              oriented   .004

              111113   .004
              structural–
              solution
              oriented

1111 ——→ 11112 ——→ 111121   .004
.037   nonlinear   111122   .004
organismic, PDM   111123   .004
infrequent, 3Δt

            11113 ——→ 111131   .004
            exponential   111132   .004
                          111133   .004

111 Organismic, PDM,   1112i ——→ 111211   .004
infrequent   linear   111212   .004
.111*   111213   .004

1112 ——→ 11122 ——→ 111221   .004
.037   nonlinear   111222   .004
organismic, PDM   111223   .004
infrequent, 6Δt

            11123 ——→ 111231   .004
                          111232   .004
                          111233   .004

            11131 ——→ 111311   .004
            linear   111312   .004
                          111313   .004

1113 ——→ 11132 ——→ 111321   .004
            nonlinear   111322   .004
                          111323   .004

            11133 ——→ 111331   .004
            exponential   111332   .004
                          111333   .004

*Assigning equal weight to each of the 9 frequencies (100 ÷ 9 = 11.1%).

**Assigning equal weight to each of the 27 elements of each frequency (11.1% ÷ 27 = 0.41%).

Figure 6.8: MIS (IIS) utilization matrix by frequency: I organismic, PDM (1) infrequent

Objectives Hierarchy	PDM Roles	Utilization Frequency	Forecasting Time Period	Data Weighting	Problem Category	Equal Weight %

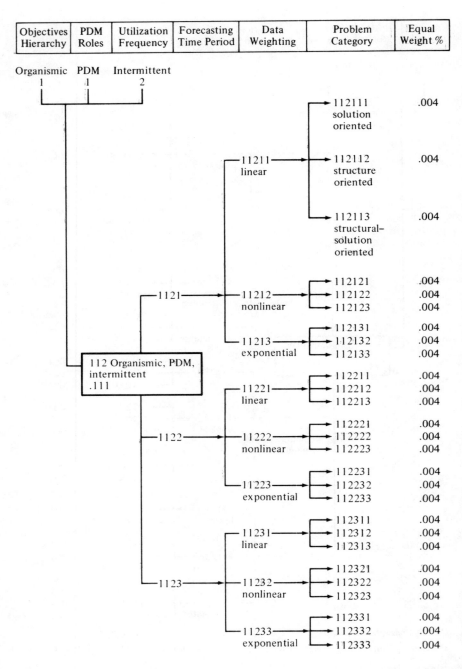

Figure 6.9: MIS (IIS) utilization matrix by frequency: II organismic, PDM (2) intermittent

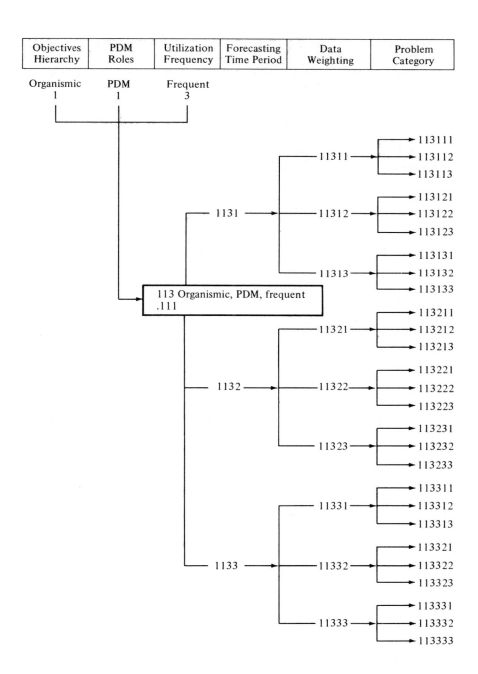

Objectives Hierarchy	PDM Roles	Utilization Frequency	Forecasting Time Period	Data Weighting	Problem Category
Organismic 1	PDM 1	Frequent 3			

113 Organismic, PDM, frequent
.111

Figure 6.10: MIS (IIS) utilization matrix by frequency: III organismic, PDM (3) frequent

(111111), structure oriented (111112), and structural solution oriented (111113).

Thus we have 27 elements of the MIS (IIS) utilization matrix for the organismic objective, PDM role, and infrequent use, which is designated 111. Similarly, we have 27 elements for organismic objective, PDM role, intermittent use, which is designated 112. And similarly, we have 27 elements for organismic hierarchy, PDM roles, and frequent use, which is designated 113. Or, a total of 81 elements for the three utilization frequencies of organismic, PDM combination. How many such combinations exist? We find in Table 6.12 that there are 9 such combinations, giving rise to (81 x 9 =) 729 elements for the MIS (IIS) utilization matrix.

How important is the utilization represented by each of the 27 elements? The simplest assumption is that all the 27 elements are equal in importance.

Table 6.12: MIS (IIS) Utilization Matrix: 729 Elements—Frequency by Hierarchy and Decision Roles

	Infrequent	Intermittent	Indefinite	Total
1. Organismic, PDM	27 elements .111*	27 .111	27 .111	81 .333
2. Organismic, Sub-PDM	27 .111	27 .111	27 .111	81 .333
3. Organismic, Sub-sub-PDM	27 .111	27 .111	27 .111	81 .333
4. Strategic, PDM	27 .111	27 .111	27 .111	81 .333
5. Strategic, Sub-PDM	27 .111	27 .111	27 .111	81 .333
6. Strategic, Sub-sub-PDM	27 .111	27 .111	27 .111	81 .333
7. Tactical, PDM	27 .111	27 .111	27 .111	81 .333
8. Tactical, Sub-PDM	27 .111	27 .111	27 .111	81 .333
9. Tactical, Sub-sub-PDM	27 .111	27 .111	27 .111	81 .333
	243 .999**	243 .999	243 .999	729 2.997

*Assigning equal weight to each of the 9 frequencies (100 ÷ 9 = 11.1%).

**The omission of one-tenth of one percent makes it possible to assign a round figure to each of the 27 elements of each frequency of utilization (11.1% ÷ 27 = 0.41%).

Similarly, which of the hierarchy, decision role combination is most important? We can assume that all the 9 are equally important which will give organismic, PDM, infrequent represented by 111 a weight of (100% ÷ 9 =) 11.1%. If all the 27 elements in 111 have equal weight, each element gets a weight of (11.1% ÷ 27 =) 0.41%. It should be noted that we round off to 0.4% the weight for each of the 27 elements, instead of carrying the 0.41%.

In real life, every utilization frequency and every element do *not* have equal weight. The weights obtained by assuming equal weight serve as a point of departure. Depending upon the external demands and internal capabilities of the organism, and depending upon the type of management, the percentage of use will vary by the hierarchy and decision role, and the frequency of utilization, which variation can be compared against the profile of equal weights for MIS (IIS) utilization.

Of the 729 elements, the organismic hierarchical level is assigned 243 elements; so also the strategic hierarchy, and the tactical hierarchy. If we give weights in the ratio $3:2:1$ to the organismic : strategic : tactical hierarchy, it could mean that instead of the equal weight figures of

organismic	strategic	tactical
.999	.999	.999

we would have

1.499	.99	.499

The 81 individual elements for each of the hierarchical levels can then be assigned appropriate weights.

No matter how the split is made between the hierarchical levels and their component elements, there is no doubt that if some use is not made by at least some of the hierarchy levels, there is no justification for the development of the MIS (IIS) matrix. *Use makes the MIS (IIS).*

Summary

In this chapter we developed the profile of an MIS matrix, and the profile of an MIS (IIS) utilization matrix. To construct a profile which is applicable to profit-making as well as nonprofit-making organisms in both the public and private sector, we developed the 4 principal elements of MIS (IIS) which correspond with the 4 principal elements of OR/SA approach to decision-making situations. The 4 elements are: (1) context, (2) cost, (3) effectiveness—absolute, and (4) effectiveness—relative.

The MIS (IIS) elements relate to the context of both the decision-making environment (E), and the technical capabilities of the organism (T). Combinations of Context E-T are associated with the 7 stages in the life cycle of a product, process, and/or organism: (1) gestation, (2) birth, (3) infancy, (4) rapid growth, (5) maturation, (6) decline, and (7) death.

Cost as opportunity foregone is generally recognized; but not cost as opportunity acquired, which nonmarginal consideration applies to every situation in which a different capability from the one which was existing theretofore emerges.

The absolute measures of how well the organism performs in relation to its desired level of performance can be measured in terms of the system as a whole, its main subsystems, and/or sub-subsystem performance.

Turning to the relative performance, we need to consider the rate of change of performance corresponding to a rate of change in cost, and vice versa. Further, to determine if the proposed changes are desirable, we need to determine the rate of change of performance by pointing to the rate of change of cost.

Associating each cost, absolute effectiveness, and relative effectiveness measures with the Context E-T combinations by each stage of the life cycle gives rise to an MIS (IIS) matrix of 1,134 elements. The MIS (IIS) matrix says *what* (information) is available. It is necessary to raise the question of *who* uses the MIS (IIS).

Use of MIS (IIS) in decision-making is to exercise control. The control is exercised at the organismic, strategic, and tactical levels. The decision-maker finds himself in a context of concurrent conflict insofar as he is obliged to assume the three simultaneous roles of organismic, strategic, and tactical hierarchies. His use of the MIS (IIS) must therefore be calibrated, not only by the hierarchy level, but also by the role of decision making (PDM—principal decision-maker).

An MIS (IIS) utilization matrix is constructed with the combination of objectives hierarchy and PDM role as the governing factor. The MIS (IIS) is utilized by each such combination in three ways: infrequent, intermittent, and frequent.

The frequency of utilization depends upon the conversion of the raw data into pre-information. From the point of view of the decision-maker, his decision horizon can be specified in terms of the period to which the forecast makes reference. Recognizing the inevitable time lag between the origin of raw data, its conversion into pre-information, and the earliest time period at which management can influence the behavior of the organism, we say that the immediate time period is $3\Delta t$, the intermediate $6\Delta t$, and the indefinite, $9\Delta t$.

The forecast that relates, respectively, to $3\Delta t$, $6\Delta t$, and $9\Delta t$, is arrived at by giving equal weights to all the instances of data, or unequal weights. Equal weights are given by linear, or nonlinear methods; unequal weights are represented by the method of exponential smoothing.

From the point of view of management, the type of forecast is governed by the type of problem. It may be one in which a constant is derived as the solution, suggesting that so many units of such and such product and/or service should be produced in order to maximize the profit and/or the service rendered by the organism. Or, it may be a problem in which the method of finding a solution is more important than the actual solution itself. In the case of the first lunar landing, the problem was to learn about the man-machine interaction in each stage: suborbit, earth orbit, lunar orbit, etc., to apply learning to the *next* stage. Or, the problem may be one in which features of both the structure and the solution are important.

Associating the combination of objectives hierarchy, and decision-making roles with the forecast period, the weighting methods, and the problem categories by each frequency of utilization, we derive an MIS (IIS) utilization matrix of 729 elements.

In the case of both the MIS (IIS) matrix and the MIS (IIS) utilization matrix, the percentage value of each element is shown on the basis of equal importance. In real life, every stage and element, every utilization frequency and element *do not* have equal importance, the value in the two matrices providing a useful point of departure for the individual profile of the elements of MIS (IIS) and the elements of MIS (IIS) use.

QUESTIONS

Chapters 4, 5, and 6 of Part II deal with the MIS sequence—from raw data to information. In chapter 6, the principal elements of the third part of the sequence, i.e., information, as well as the use of information, were discussed. The purpose of the following questions is to develop an appreciation for the MIS matrix of 1,134 elements, and the MIS utilization matrix of 729 elements.

A. CONTEXT E-T, STAGE OF GROWTH

1. Why is the stage of growth important to the information for management decision-making?
2. Interpret element 315 in the MIS (IIS) matrix.

B. COST

3. How is cost as opportunity acquired different from cost as opportunity foregone?
4. Interpret element 3152 in the MIS (IIS) matrix.

C. EFFECTIVENESS—ABSOLUTE

5. Define effectiveness.
6. How would you arrive at a composite measure of effectiveness?
7. Interpret element 11713 in the MIS (IIS) matrix.

D. EFFECTIVENESS—RELATIVE

8. Define sensitivity.

9. In what terms must system performance changes be measured?
10. How would you measure the impact of additional subsystem dollar expenditure?
11. Interpret element 117132 in the MIS (IIS) matrix.

E. MIS (IIS) MATRIX

12. How many elements are there in the MIS (IIS) matrix and why?
13. How would you index the MIS elements so that they could be used as a basis to compare the actual importance of the elements of your own MIS (IIS)?

F. MIS (IIS) UTILIZATION MATRIX

14. What are the principal elements of use of MIS (IIS)?
15. How many elements are there in the MIS (IIS) utilization matrix and why?
16. Interpret element 111123 in the MIS (IIS) utilization matrix.
17. How would an MIS (IIS) utilization matrix for a chemical industry firm differ from an MIS (IIS) utilization matrix assuming equal importance to every use?

Part III
MIS (IIS) Types

7
M-Zero MIS (IIS)

TECHNICAL OVERVIEW / When the technology is stable, the production is so well controlled that an inspection of 100 light bulbs out of 10,000, i.e., an inspection ratio of 1 percent, would give adequate guarantee of performance. The 1 percent ratio can be expressed as 10^{-2}, making the M in $10^M = -2$, or M-Negative. In the present instance, we allow for an inspection ratio of $10^0 = 1$ or 100 percent, making the $M = 0$, or M-Zero. We allow for every single product produced to be examined to guarantee satisfactory performance.

A public sector and a private sector real-life situation are discussed to illustrate M-Zero MIS (IIS). The public sector problem is that of producing Weapon System W. What are the MIS (IIS) requirements for the principal decision-maker (PDM)? The decision-making environment is *risky* because the applicable probability distributions can be specified as to *form*, but not as to the parameters themselves. The probability distributions specify how weapon systems similar to Weapon System W have fulfilled customers' demands in the past. The technology is *quasistable,* because enough is known about the performance characteristics of similar weapon systems so that the components of Weapon System W do not have to be inspected more than 100 percent, i.e., $M = 0$ in 10^M—yielding $10^0 = 1$.

In addition to Context E (for environment)—risky—and Context T (for technology)—quasistable—a third context, viz., Concurrent Conflicting Context of decision-making, emerges as an essential consideration. Context C identifies the PDM (principal decision-maker) as simultaneously being at the organismic level with respect to sub-subordinates such as personnel supervisor, at the strategic level with respect to the director of the missile or aircraft system, and at the tactical level with respect to the director of offensive weaponry. The fact that he is *simultaneously* at all three levels of decision-making imposes upon MIS (IIS) conflicting demands. Further, he finds himself in alternative Context C of concurrent conflict with respect to the Director of Defense Research and Engineering, the U.S. House Subcommittee on Appropriations, etc.

The identification of applicable probability distributions is pursued with respect to finance, manpower, schedule, and technology.

One of the primary requirements of the MIS (IIS) is to tell the program manager of Weapon System W the prospects of program completion. The manager exercises control through managing the prime contractor, who, in turn, exercises control through subcontractors. The positive leverage that the program manager can exercise emerges as the attractiveness of the incentive payments for improved schedule of production by the prime contractor. The negative leverage would be penalties attached to the delay in delivery beyond the schedule. In both cases, the program manager has to start from the forecasts of job completion.

The raw data on performance should reflect time, cost, and schedule, all of which should be specified in terms of the status of the product with respect to its completion. An index is constructed to incorporate all three elements on an integrated basis.

While the immediate responsibility of the PDM is the physical completion of Weapon System W, he has to bear in mind the peculiarity of the production for defense, i.e., the production is for *nonuse,* the success being determined not by how well the product performs, but how well its nonuse has been insured. Because of this unusual emphasis upon nonuse, the PDM should acquaint himself with potential changes in the requirements for justification by him of Weapon System W. Even on the performance of the Weapon System W, he should acquire performance data from outside to compare with his own.

Turning from the public sector to the private sector MIS (IIS), the change in orientation is immediately brought to the fore by the product being for *use,* and not nonuse. The product in question is the core of a new ten-ton jet engine, originally developed by General Electric (GE) for the B-1 bomber. It was to be used in the development of the new jet engine system in partnership with a government-owned French Company, SNECMA.

The $400 million to develop the technology for civilian market was to be shared by GE and SNECMA. The French share of the investment in the development was much less important than the new business that would be generated in France and Europe for the subsonic planes which use the new jet engine with the core of the engine element developed at GE.

Clearly, there are not only economic factors (in the form of sale of subsonic planes) but also political factors which have to be reckoned with. In particular, the development of the core element having been sponsored by U.S. military research and development, the approval of the United States Government to export the technology to France is indispensable. And, since the company is French Government-owned, the jet engine assembly cannot proceed without the blessings of the same.

The principal decision-maker, who is the manager of the GE Program in France, must identify his economic and political hierarchy. Since approval for the program has reportedly come from the White House, the PDM would be at the tactical level with respect to the White House, and strategic level with respect to GE group vice-president for international operations. Similarly, on the French side also, the PDM would be at the tactical level with respect to the counterpart of the White House in the French government. So also, the PDM would be at the tactical level with respect to the airline companies using the jet engine. The PDM will be at the strategic level with respect to the European or American airplane manufacturer.

The political and economic objectives are identified with respect to the *demand* for the core element of the jet engine. The other side of the coin, i.e., *supply*, refers to the manufacture of the core element itself. Here again, there are two distinct objectives of the hierarchy. With respect to the manufacture of the core element of the jet engine in the United States, the PDM is at the organismic level. When it comes to the assembly of the jet engine by SNECMA, the PDM is at the strategic level.

What is the rationale for describing the environment as one in which the fulfillment characteristics have applicable probability distribution(s)? The applicable distribution comes from the experience with the integration of a number of component parts of a large unit, such as spacecraft or aircraft. The integration of the core element into the jet engine requires well-coordinated effort; and experience with the integration of components produced by several different manufacturers does provide applicable probability distributions, the form of which is known, but not the exact parameters themselves which apply to the present instance of integrating the core element with the jet engine assembly. The parameters themselves will be different because of the language differences and the protection of proprietary interests in contributing to the larger unit.

In the M-Zero decision-making context, not only is the environment one of risk, but also the technology is quasistable. The quasistability comes from the different requirements of performance in the civilian market: it is known that the core element does work in the B-1 Bomber; what is not known is whether adaptation to the civilian market would work effectively. For instance, the consideration of pollution would have been far less significant a constraint in the military market than in the commercial.

What are the requirements of the forecasts for decision-making by the PDM? Political prospects—in the United States and in France—are the variables on which the PDM requires reliable forecast. From the point of view of the United States, the establishment of the credibility of U.S.-European technical cooperation is the most important variable; on the French side, the political capital that can be made in France on the basis of technical cooperation on the jet engine would probably be the chief consideration.

The substratum of the political measures is the technical performance of the jet engine assembly, which is largely dependent upon the technical performance of the core element. The PDM must therefore, of course, have available to him forecasts of both the technical performance of the core element and of the jet engine into which the core element is incorporated.

From the point of view of the private sector, profit is the prime motive; therefore, the success of the political prospects in the U.S. and in France as well as the technical performance capabilities of the core element in the United States and the jet engine in France should all be evaluated from the point of view of the difference it makes in the market for GE products. The forecast that the PDM needs with respect to the American and European market is: At this rate, what is the expected number of airplanes in which the GE core element is utilized?

The raw data requirement for the forecasts of political prospects, technical performance, and market prospects are generic: they are applicable, *mutatis mutandis* (with appropriate changes), to any organism which finds itself confronted with risky environment and quasistable technology. The specific raw data elements would, of course, vary with the organism and with time, for the same organism. What has been set out here is simply the basic *types* of raw data which are indispensable to an MIS (IIS) in light of the forecasts that it has to provide the decision-maker.

EXECUTIVE SUMMARY / On the basis of the capability of the products and/or services to satisfy the wants of the market, on the one hand, and of the technical performance characteristics of the products and/or services themselves on the other, we can classify the requirements for MIS (IIS). When there are applicable prior experiences with similar decision-making environments, we know how often customers have been satisfied with different products and/or services.

When the production technology is reasonably stable, it means that the technical performance characteristics can be assured with a relatively small number of inspections. If, however, the technology is not sufficiently stable, then the ratio of number of units inspected to the total number of units produced could be as high as 100 percent. If the ratio is 10^M, M will be 0 when the ratio is as high as 100 percent in the combination of risk, quasistable decision-making situations which we designate as M-Zero.

A public sector problem and a private sector problem illustrate M-Zero MIS (IIS) in real-life situations. The former pertains to the production of a billion dollar Weapon System W; the latter refers to the commercial development of the new ten-ton jet engine using the core element that was developed for the B-1 Bomber by General Electric (GE).

In addition to the Context E (for environment)—risky—and Context T (for technology)—quasistable—a third context, viz., Concurrent Conflicting Context of decision-making, emerges here as an essential consideration. Conflict comes from the fact that the principal decision-maker (PDM) has to be at top level, middle level, and lower level management—all at the same time. At the top level, he looks at the long term, at the middle level, at the intermediate term, and at the lower level, he looks at the short term. These points of view are in conflict with each other. The PDM finds himself in such a conflict because he is at the top level of management (organismic level) with respect to his sub-subordinate staff, like personnel supervisor; at the intermediate level (strategic level) with respect to the director of the missile or aircraft system; and at the lower level (tactical level) with respect to the Director of Offensive Weaponry.

In performing his function as PDM, he seeks to obtain applicable prior experiences on finance, manpower, schedule, and technology.

As PDM, he has to estimate the prospects of program completion. The PDM exercises control through the prime contractor who controls the performance of the subcontractors. How well each is performing should be stated in terms of time, schedule, and cost. Each has to measure the progress that has yet to be made toward the completion.

The immediate responsibility is to complete production. However, Weapon System W (as any other weapon system) is produced, *not* for use, but for *nonuse*. It means that the PDM requires the latest information on the demands for justification of his weapon system production, in conjunction with all other weapon systems: for, changes in the international political balance, as well as superpower negotiations, can indeed affect the continuation of the billion dollar weapon system production.

Turning from the public sector MIS (IIS) to the private sector, the difference is obvious in that the ten-ton jet engine is produced for *use*, unlike Weapon System W which is produced for *nonuse*.

The major payoff to the GE-French venture is the increase in the medium range, subsonic planes that use jet engines which use the GE core element. However, to reach that estimate of the *market* prospects, two other elements have to be continuously and carefully monitored: political prospects and technological prospects.

The political prospects are those which relate to the willingness of the United States to let General Electric export the technology that has been developed for the B-1 engine. The main impetus for the export comes from U.S.-European technical cooperation and the interest that the United States has in making U.S.-European cooperation credible. The French have a definite political interest in the joint GE-SNECMA (French Government-owned company) venture. It is in the political credibility that the joint venture will provide via French technological enhancement.

The basis upon which the political prospects depend is the technical performance, first of the core elements manufactured in the United States, and second of the jet engine assembly made in France.

The raw data requirement of the MIS (IIS) stems from the three major forecasts of (1) political prospects, (2) production prospects, and (3) market prospects, that the PDM requires for decision-making. In discussing the public sector and the private sector examples, the basic *types* of raw data which can be used by the PDM are identified as indispensable to an MIS (IIS) for the forecast it has to provide the PDM for decision-making.

An index of decision-making situations was constructed in chapter 3 as a combination of Context E (for environment) and Context T (for technology). Context E refers to the *demand* for the products and/or services of the organism, and how well the decision-maker estimates that the products and/or services are fulfilling the demand: environmental status of *fulfillment characteristics*. Context T refers to the *supply* of the products and/or services of the organism, and how well the decision-maker estimates that the organism is capable of technically producing the products and/or services: technological status of *performance characteristics*. An MIS (IIS) should reflect both.

We have seen in chapter 3 why the inspection ratio is M-Positive when Context E is uncertain and Context T is unstable. Why would the inspection ratio be M-Positive when Context E is reduced risk? Reduced risk means that there has been enough precedence for the decision-making situation, i.e., for estimating by the decision-maker of the *fulfillment characteristics*. However, so long as the technology (performance characteristics) continues to be unstable, the customer is likely to inspect more and accept less—because he has little assurance that even if the product and/or service passes inspection at time t, that it will perform in time $t + \Delta t$. The reduced risk characterization means that the producer has been dealing with the same product and/or service or same type of product and/or service for sufficient length of time to feel confident that his

Table 7.1: Inspection Ratios in Decision-Making Situations

	Context T		
Context E	Unstable	Quasistable	Stable
Uncertain	M-Positive (11)	M-Zero (12)	M-Negative (13)
Risk	M-Positive (21)	M-Zero (22)	M-Negative (23)
Reduced Risk	M-Positive (31)	M-Zero (32)	M-Negative (33)

commitments to perform are warranted. Nevertheless, to the customer, the product and/or service is too new to accept without question. Therefore, *he* would raise the inspection ratio, keeping the total inspection ratio M-Positive.

By similar reasoning, M-Negative inspection ratio will hold for three combinations: (1) uncertain, stable; (2) risk, stable; and (3) reduced risk, stable. The three M-Zero inspections ratios will hold for three combinations: (1) uncertain, quasistable; (2) risk, quasistable; and (3) reduced risk, quasistable. These are shown in Table 7.1.

We will consider in this and chapters 8 and 9, public and private sector decision-making situations characterized by each of the three inspection ratio indices: M-Zero, M-Negative, and M-Positive.

APPLICATION 4
PRODUCTION OF WEAPON SYSTEM W

We now turn to a *public sector* problem concerned with rendering a "service." The context is military. The objective is the building of a weapon system in the interests of national security. We will assume that $1 billion is the budget for the system. To determine the type of MIS (IIS) that would best serve its needs, we first develop the objectives hierarchy and then identify the Context C of decision-making before proceeding to identify the Context E-Context T combination.

Objectives Hierarchy

The $1 billion budget is approximately 0.8 percent of the Department of Defense Budget. As such, Weapon System W will be expected to contribute approximately 0.8 percent to the fulfillment of the objective of the Department of Defense.

What is the objective of the Department of Defense? It has been discussed operationally elsewhere.[1] Without repeating the arguments, it will

[1] George K. Chacko, *Systems Approach to Public and Private Sector Problems* (Amsterdam: North-Holland, 1976), chapter 5, section 5.1.

merely be stated that the three major objectives of deterrence, victory, and restoration depend upon the credibility of one's capability by the would-be adversary. In other words, the would-be adversary has to be convinced of the destructive capability of the weapon systems that have *never* been used in anger, without any direct knowledge of its capabilities.

The unknown capabilities have to be compared with the known capabilities of the would-be adversary's own weapon system. It is hard enough to make a judgment when the magnitude and accuracy of each weapon system is known. But, with only the knowledge of one's own weapon systems and guesses about the would-be adversary's weapon systems, the task becomes even more difficult. The difficulty is enormously increased when the knowledge of even one's own capabilities is nothing more than that of laboratory tests and not based on field experience. To make matters worse, it is *not* today's balance of terror that matters, but tomorrow's. The weapon systems of tomorrow have been predetermined by the choices that were made from the technical options which were available 3, 4, 5 years ago. What was the particular option that was chosen by the would-be adversary at that time? What are the chances of success in his development of those options? What are our own chances of development? The credibility is the firm conclusion that has to be based upon these and other considerations, which are far from firm.

Assume that Weapon System W is now authorized to be produced in quantity. It means that the technological promises seen in the system a few years ago have been so sufficiently borne out that its deployment as an operational weapon has now been established. However, it is one thing to be convinced that Weapon System W could work; it is quite another to manufacture it, translating laboratory findings into the assembly line of the manufacturing plant. The manufacture itself does not necessarily take place under the same roof. It is parcelled out to a number of manufacturers, each of whom has the responsibility for a small portion of Weapon System W. The responsibility of the program manager, who is the PDM, is to make sure that the $1 billion yields the planned number of operational units of W.

Even before the first complete unit of Weapon System W has been assembled, it is being held accountable to make its contribution to approximately 0.8 percent of the objective of the Department of Defense. That objective being the achievement of credibility through capability, Weapon System W will be expected to make its contribution—as will similar weapon systems. If Weapon System W is an aircraft, it is contributing to the credibility of our aircraft capabilities. If it is a missile system, it is contributing to the credibility as one of the missile systems. Being one among many, Weapon System W is both a *contributor* to and *competitor* with other weapon systems of the same kind. It is a contributor, because it performs certain fulfillment characteristics as no other aircraft system or missile system does; therefore, its contribution is significant to the total picture of credibility of the capability of the aircraft system or the missile system. At the same time, it is competitive with the other aircraft and missile systems because it is competing for funds.

Both missile systems and aircraft bomber systems are part of the offensive weaponry. Similarly, offensive weaponry is part of the national arsenal to accomplish the national defense objective. To achieve the objectives, not only offensive, but also defensive, weaponry is required.

The defense objective is an important, but not the only, objective of the nation. We could include under the heading "development" all the national objectives pertaining to human and natural resources. We can now set forth the hierarchy of objectives with the national objectives at the top, and the missile Weapon System W at the bottom of the hierarchy as shown in Figure 7.1.

Context C

The objectives hierarchy shows Weapon System W at the tactical level in Round 2. In Round 1, the tactical objective is offensive weaponry, which becomes the organismic objective in Round 2. With the offensive weaponry as the organismic objective in Round 2, Weapon System W becomes the tactical objective in Round 2, as shown in Figure 7.2.

The program manager in charge of Weapon System W is indeed at the organismic level with respect to the supervisors at the various functional levels. The managers for personnel, finance, production, etc., would be at the strategic level; the respective supervisors would be at the tactical level, as shown in Figure 7.3. Now we see that the PDM is at the organismic level with respect to the supervisors in the functional areas. He is at the strategic level with respect to the particular weapon systems group, i.e., missile system or aircraft system. He is at the tactical level with respect to offensive weaponry. In other words, the PDM is *simultaneously* at the organismic, strategic, and tactical level, as shown in Figure 7.3.

There are alternative ways of viewing this simultaneous conflict. As the program manager for Weapon System W, the PDM is subject to the supervision of his own service, such as the Army, Navy, Air Force. Insofar as research is involved in the production of the weapon system, it is of interest to the Director of Defense Research and Engineering (DDR&E). In other words, the PDM is at the strategic level with respect to the service, and at the tactical level with respect to DDR&E.

It is also possible that as a $1 billion item in the budget (or several items adding to $1 billion), Weapon System W is likely to attract congressional interest. The PDM may well have to justify the $1 billion budget for his

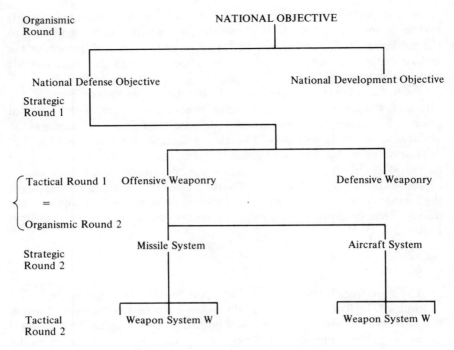

Figure 7.1: Objectives hierarchy—round 1 and round 2

particular weapon. His testimony will, of course, be asked for through the Secretary of Defense. In this context, the PDM is at the strategic level with respect to the Secretary of Defense, and at the tactical level with respect to the U.S. House Committee on Appropriations.

These various elements of Context C are shown in Figure 7.4. The elements have an important bearing on the MIS (IIS) data requirements because the forecasting by MIS (IIS) has to meet the needs of the PDM in the various roles. For instance, the PDM would need, at some time or other, forecasts on the performance characteristics of the Weapon System W Program for:

1. U.S. House Subcommittee on Appropriations
2. Director of Defense Research and Engineering
3. Offensive Weaponry Directorate
4. Secretary of Defense
5. Missile Systems or Aircraft Systems Directorate
6. Secretary of the Army, Navy, or Air Force, as applicable

These (and other similar requirements) are *external* to the PDM's control requirements which are *internal* to Weapon System W. To run the

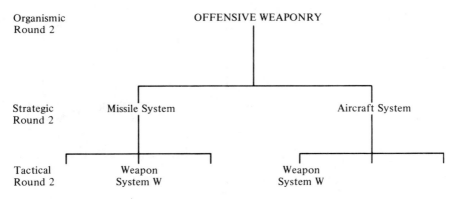

Figure 7.2: Objectives hierarchy—round 2

Weapon System W costing a billion dollar budget, the PDM would want to have forecasts of the different elements of finance, personnel, production, etc. In addition, different forecasts need to be made available to external sources as called for.

Risk of Environment, and Quasistability of Technology

Unlike in the case of unstable technology where every product has to be examined several times, in the case of quasistable technology, fewer inspections are needed. The ratio of inspected items to the total is closer to 1, making the M in 10^M to be 0. The designation of M-Zero for the MIS (IIS) suggests that the decision-maker situation is one of risk, and the technology is quasistable.

Risky environment

Risky environment is one in which the fulfillment characteristics do have applicable probability distribution(s). Its form is known but not its parameters. How is the probability distribution known?

Weapon systems have been manufactured in the past, and will continue to be manufactured in the future. Weapon System W has a budget of $1 billion. Many other weapon systems may not be equal in size. However, the fact that other weapon systems have been built does give rise to the possibility of identifying the fulfillment characteristics of one or more weapon systems as being close to the present one. True, each product is unique, in the sense that it has not been made before. However, something *similar* had in fact been constructed.

201

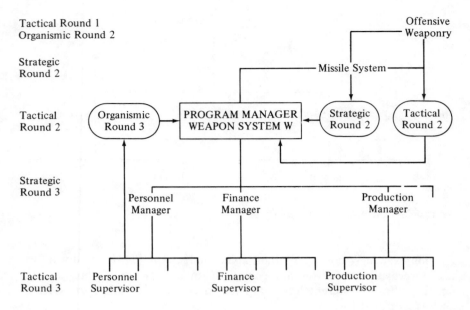

Figure 7.3: Context C of concurrent conflict

The first step is therefore to find an analogous production situation. It could be another billion dollar weapon system production; it could be another weapon system in the same category—missile or aircraft system category. The budgetary dimensions may be the same or similar.

The probability distribution requires the specification of the parameters. Mean and standard deviation are two parameters. However, to arrive at these two, one needs several observations. When we say that we do not know the parameters, what we are saying is that we do not have enough experience with a number of similar weapon systems to warrant saying: a billion dollar weapon system takes, on the average, so many months. However, we have some idea that there are enough similarities between another program(s) and the present Weapon System W program to suggest a similar curve for its fulfillment characteristics.

What are some of the fulfillment characteristics? To meet the needs of the environment, the organismic capabilities are converted into the production of a number of operational units of Weapon System W, the main factors which affect the fulfillment characteristics being finance, manpower, schedule, and technology. The last one, being related to technology, should properly be discussed in the next section.

What is the applicable experience of other weapon system productions which can be applied to Weapon System W? Such experience can be used to estimate the requirement for *funds* which have to come from external

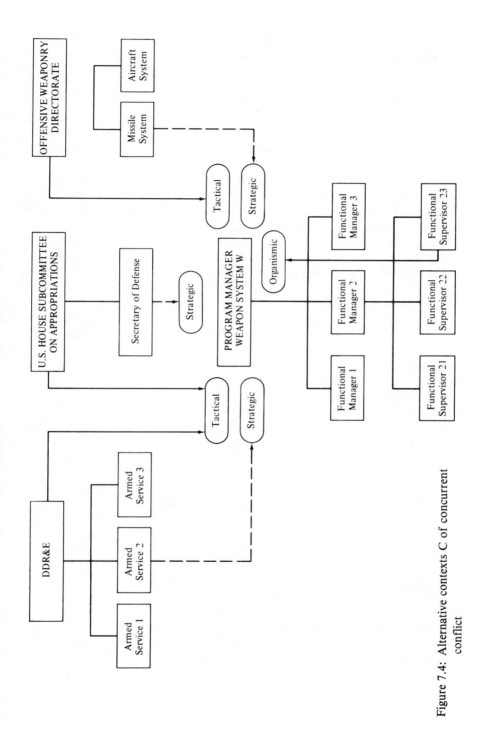

Figure 7.4: Alternative contexts C of concurrent conflict

sources, such as the U.S. Congress, which is external to the Weapon System W program management. If the demand for funds is uniform and if there are 10 time periods, the $1 billion budget will be split into $100 million in each of the time periods. If, on the other hand, more is required at the beginning, much more at the middle, and much less at the end, the probability distribution of the fund requirement again for 10 periods may suggest: $200 million for the first time period; $50 million for the second period; $50 million for the third period; $100 million for the fourth period; $350 million for the fifth period; $100 million for the sixth period; $75 million for the seventh period; $25 million for the eighth period; $25 million for the ninth period; and $25 million for the tenth period. Or, alternatively, the requirement for funds may be very small at the beginning and at the end, the concentration being in the middle time period. These three distributions are shown in Figure 7.5. The contribution of experience from previous programs is reflected in the change from the first curve, which simply assumes that each time period has an equal demand for funds.

The *manpower* group probability distribution should reflect the differences in the types of pools of experience that are required in each phase of the program. It is quite likely that grade A labor would be much more in demand at the beginning of Weapon System W production, and grade C would be much more in demand toward the end of the manufacture. The demand could be shown in terms of the distribution of the total grade A labor over the time periods, i.e., say, 30 percent of the total grade A labor in the first time period, 10 percent over the next time period, 15 percent in time period three, 15 percent in time period four, and 5 percent each in time periods 5, 6, 7, 8, 9, and 10. A different breakdown for grade B, grade C, and grade D labor could also be outlined. In all instances, the basic point of departure is that of equal weights in all the time periods for all types of labor, i.e., 10 percent of each grade labor for each time period.

Of course, both the distribution of funds and of manpower by grade will be custom-tailored to the Weapon System W program. The advantage that can be gained from similar experiences is that the hypothesis of ignorance, i.e., equal share of funds and manpower in each of the time periods, can be modified from the outset. If, for instance, $200 million is really required for the first time period, as shown in Figure 7.5b, and only $100 million had been requested, as in Figure 7.5a, that would create a considerable problem in getting the program off on the right foot. As soon as actual data are acquired, they can be utilized to modify the hypothesis of ignorance, and provide applicable prior experience in the form of probability distributions.

The probability distribution of the *schedule* can also start from the hypothesis of ignorance, i.e., assigning 10 percent of the total production to be completed in each of the time periods. The percentage of schedule completion would be particularly important to the control of Weapon System W. The concept is not unlike that of arranging the schedule of

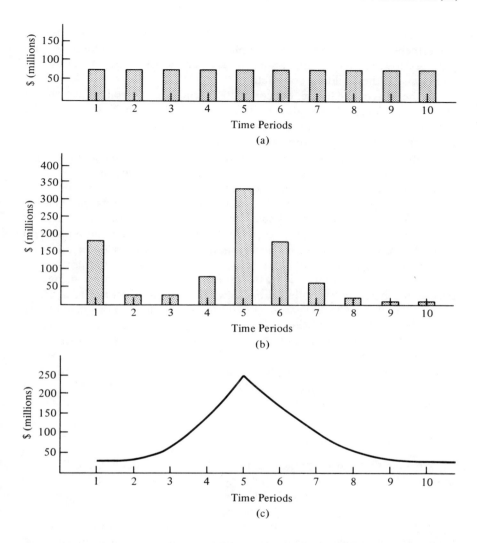

Figure 7.5: (a) Equal demand for funds: hypothesis of ignorance; (b) Unequal demand for funds distribution; (c) near-normal distribution of demand for funds

progress payments on a construction loan. In building a house, foundation completion counts as, say, 7 percent, roof installation as 19 percent, etc. These are abstract figures, because the house is not usable until all the work is completed. To say that the foundation represents 7 percent of the house is not to suggest that the house is 7 percent *usable*. Similarly, when the roof is

205

on, it does not mean that the house is (7% + 19% =) 26% usable. Nevertheless, such concepts of completion have to be developed, so that progress toward completion of the house can be calibrated to authorize payments to the building contractor.

In the case of the house, the completion schedule is specified in terms of the major elements. So also in the case of Weapon System W; the completion can be stated in terms of the major components such as propulsion, guidance, command and control, payload, etc. Unlike the house, though, work is progressing on probably all the elements at the same time, making it necessary to break down the components of Weapon System W in such a way that, at each state, the progress in the many different components can be represented as the progress toward Weapon System W itself. To construct such an index, it is necessary to order the major components in terms of their contribution to what Weapon System W is designed for. The mission accomplishment depends upon the joint activity of all of the elements. However, a relative ordering of importance is necessary, so that remedial measures may be undertaken to bring the production back on schedule. Setbacks will occur, and the priority of effort to remedy the setbacks has to be in terms of the importance of the particular element to mission fulfillment. If every component is judged to be equally important (and therefore equally unimportant), then every setback will command equal attention. On the other hand, the assignment of unequal weights would enable the differential allocation of resources to remedy schedule setbacks, as well as to assess progress toward the end objective of Weapon System W itself.

Quasistable technology

We said that the discussion of the technology element in the Weapon System W program properly belongs to this section. What does the technology group do for the PDM of Weapon System W, and what is the quasistability of the technology that they deal with?

A billion dollar missile system would normally have two components: (1) research and development (R&D), and (2) procurement or production. The reason for the R&D element is the belief that the performance characteristics of the major components of the missile system can be improved. The improvement would come in the form of better performance characteristics of the components themselves, or in the form of improved methods of fabricating them.

In the production process, it may be found that certain elements are not performing as well as they should. There may be a problem with the propulsion system, the guidance unit, the payload, etc. The technology group is charged with the responsibility to not only record the technical difficulties as they occur, but also to anticipate them. The technology itself

206

is by no means uncertain. The general principles and practices of fabricating the weapon system are known. However, some changes may be required in the application of that technology to the particular weapon system production. It is these particular problems which make the technology more stable than the uncertain technology, but less stable than a mass production technology.

The technological problems, when anticipated, will be an important input to the management of manpower problems because the technical difficulties may well indicate the demand for higher grade labor over and above that which was originally planned. That requirement, in turn, would translate itself into the need for additional funds. Therefore, the finance group should be promptly appraised of the increased demand. There will also be an impact upon the schedule group, because the technical problems mean that the schedule of completion will have to be slipped. If slippage is not permissible, it would mean that additional resources will have to be employed to rectify the technical problem situation.

Requirements of Forecasts for Decision-Making

Given that the environment is risky and that the technology is quasistable, what types of forecasts are needed from the MIS (IIS) in support of the program manager of Weapon System W?

Program completion prospects

The 0.8 percent share of the Department of Defense budget requires that Weapon System W pull its weight by contributing to the expected credibility of our position to the would-be adversary. The capability is operational capability. It means that the weapon system is ready for immediate operational employment. The success of the operational employment depends upon the success of each of the major components of the system. Therefore, the question from the organismic viewpoint of program management is: At this rate, what is the expected success of Weapon System W performance?

The emphasis upon *performance* is different from the emphasis upon *production*. Notice that the required forecast is not simply on the size and time of the production unit, but instead on the performance. The performance is a *potential* measure: potential because it is only the projected performance under conditions of hostile encounter which, by definition, are not obtained. Therefore, the PDM has not only to project the production completion of Weapon System W, but also its hypothetical performance under hypothetical conditions.

To make the performance measure a reasonably accurate portrayal of the projected performance, it would be advisable to establish a direct relationship between the percent of the weapon system completed and its performance. In other words, what the schedule management group should do is not only to specify an index of completion of the physical product, but also its capability to perform under hostile encounter conditions.

Index of physical completion

What the PDM is held primarily accountable for is the physical delivery of the operational Weapon System W on time and at the scheduled cost. While he does not have to answer questions about its projected performance capabilities, he does have an obligation to deliver the physical system. Therefore, what he needs is a forecast of the *physical completion* of the required number and type of Weapon System W production, apart from whatever projection may be made of the performance of the system.

To use an analogy from home construction, the quality of living in a house is separate from the physical completion of the structure itself. The building contractor is responsible for the physical completion of the house; the quality of living is a matter of use by the owner. If, however, there are physical defects in the structure which would interfere with the quality of living within the house, that responsibility is of course that of the contractor. If the program manager of Weapon System W ensures that it conforms to the physical specifications, but if the performance does not match the specifications, that would indeed affect the estimate of performance under hostile conditions. Unlike in the case of the owner of the house, the weapon system is not likely to be put to immediate use or even remote use. Therefore, unlike the owner who would directly discover physical defects in the construction of the house that impair the quality of living, the program manager of Weapon System W has little recourse to firsthand experience in the conceivable future. His judgment must therefore be confined to *experimental* observations performed on a *sample* of units. He can have greater confidence in the physical delivery of the actual units than in their projected performance.

INDEX OF COMPLETION—CONTRACTOR

Program management of a large weapon system effectively comes down to managing the prime contractor. The measures that the program manager uses to exercise control over the prime contractor must include program accomplishment and program cost. Instead of looking at the past by questioning how much has been accomplished and at what cost, the program manager could look into the *future:* How much remains of the work and the money? The work itself has two characteristics, that of product and of time. If 50 percent of the time is available for 50 percent of the job, and 50 percent of the money remains, we could say that project completion is on schedule. If, however, 50 percent of the job remains to be done and only 25 percent of the money remains, we can arrive at an index of money-time or *cost-schedule* of (25% ÷ 50% =) 50. If 50 percent of the job remains to be done and 75 percent of the money remains, we will have an index of (75% ÷ 50% =) 125 on a scale of 0–100.

Now we can relate the time remaining with the job remaining. If 50 percent of the job remains to be done and there is only 25 percent of the time left, then we have a time-job or *time-schedule* index of (25% ÷ 50% =) 50 on a scale of 0–100. Combining the previous index, a job 50 percent of which remains to be done with only 25 percent of the money (25/50) and 25 percent of the time (25/50) will have a *time-schedule-cost* (TSC) index of (50/100 x 50/100 =) 25/100.

INDEX OF COMPLETION—SUBCONTRACTORS

The prime contractor himself has to exercise control through forecasts that he can make of the program completion prospects of his subcontractors. Sometimes the program manager asks for and obtains access to the records of the subcontractor(s). Generally, however, the prime contractor would be reluctant to allow the program manager such direct access. If there are problems with the program, the prime contractor may want to bring in the program manager, both to acquaint him with the problem and to have him use his extra leverage.

Whether or not the program manager has direct access to the raw data on the subcontractors' program completion, he should insist on the *forecast* of such completion. Unless such forecasts are made available, the program manager can do little more than ask the prime contractor to perform his duty. With forecasts on the subcontractors' performance, the program manager can look into the *specific* problem areas and make contributions to their solution.

Program control mechanism—incentive contract

How can the program manager stimulate better compliance on the part of the prime contractor and the subcontractors to keep the program on schedule?

As the person who has to approve progress payments to the prime contractor, the program manager can and will insist upon satisfactory performance. In negotiating the contract, the program manager may want to have written into the contract incentive payment provisions. The incentive payments are for more efficient performance, above and beyond the normal compliance with the program. This incentive can be tied to the schedule, the cost, and/or the performance. When it is tied to the schedule, the prime contractor derives the benefit of the incentive when he finishes ahead of time. If it is tied to the cost, the contractor is given a share of the savings on the cost of the program as originally envisaged. If it is tied to performance, the contractor is rewarded when the actual performance of the product is superior to that of the required performance characteristics.

Of the three, the last would be the most difficult to achieve because that would require R&D efforts beyond those devoted simply to fabrication. With respect to the second, as long as the savings are not turned back to the contractor in full, he may not be inclined to perform beyond the specifications of the contract. The incentive applied to the schedule would appear to be more reasonable because it would mean that the contractor had achieved savings in the time schedule by diligent utilization of his resources.

The positive leverage that the program manager can exercise thus depends upon the attractiveness of the incentive payments for improved schedule of production to the prime contractor. The negative leverage would be penalties attached to the delay in delivery beyond the schedule period. In both cases, the program manager has to start from the forecasts of job completion.

Raw Data Requirements of Production MIS (IIS)

The types of raw data depend upon the type of forecasts that are to be made.

Raw data on performance

The particular performance characteristics that make up the weapon system performance would vary with the system. From the point of view of the organismic decision-maker who is most concerned with the contribution of the particular weapon system to overall defense capability, what matters most is the specific role that Weapon System W can fulfill. In other words, the program manager should find the types of mission assigned to his weapon system, and put W in the context of contributions by similar weapon systems. It means that the program manager should acquire performance data from outside to compare with his own.

Raw data on program completion

The program manager needs raw data to construct the time-cost-schedule (TCS) index. All three are specified in terms of the status of the project with respect to its completion.

On a large program with many interacting components, the delay in one can affect several others. Therefore, it is customary to start with a Program Evaluation and Review Technique (PERT) chart. In fact, there may be several PERT charts which specify a number of connected activities to complete each task, and the associated time for the performance of each task. Of the three time estimates—optimistic, pessimistic, and most likely—associated with each PERT activity, the particular estimate which emerges as most accurate most of the time would suggest improvements in the PERT calculations in the future, in addition to guiding the present estimates themselves. If, for instance, it is found that the pessimistic time estimate is what turns out to be the appropriate one for a number of major activities, then in constructing PERT networks for the next time period, the pessimistic estimate may be given more weight than the optimistic. (This would be different from the customary weights of 1 each for optimistic and pessimistic and 4 for most likely estimate.)

The raw data for the calculation of the time-cost-schedule index would include the particular choice of the PERT forecasting mechanism. The index itself will be based upon the time estimate which is most appropriate: in this instance, the pessimistic estimate.

Raw data on technological problems

In the context of quasistable technology, any problem that requires extensive attention on the part of the program manager would necessarily indicate the existence of technical problems, either of manufacture or of a more fundamental nature. The basic input comes in the form of technical observations by the technical personnel. These should be translated into the nature and magnitude of corrective measures that have to be taken in order to get the program back on course. Thus, if the contractor, or one of his subcontractors, reports technical difficulties with the propulsion system, then it will be necessary to localize the problem as soon as possible. The raw data should reflect the particular importance of the individual items, not only as a small component of a large subunit, but also in terms of its own contribution to Weapon System W as a whole.

Raw data on applicable probability distributions

The very characterization of the problem as one of risk environment and quasistable technology suggests that there is applicable experience. It should be established that such experience is indeed applicable. Therefore, the raw data on the basis of which the applicability has been initially hypothesized must be explicated and updated to indicate whether the parallel continues to apply.

Raw data on external demands upon MIS (IIS)

One of the unique features of the military system is that the production emphasis is on *nonuse* as opposed to *use*. It is hoped that the capability of the weapon system would provide enough credibility that it would not be necessary in fact to exercise the capability. This emphasis on nonuse makes special demands on the PDM.

Since an important element of the continuing support for the Weapon System W program depends upon the goodwill that others have for the program, it is necessary that the program manager acquaint himself with the potential changes in the requirements for justification by him of the program. This will include the comments and views of congressional decision-makers on the defense posture in general, and the role of the particular type of weapon system, e.g., missile systems, aircraft systems, in particular. He should also be aware of the emphasis upon new insights that are obtained from the weapon system programs of which Weapon System W is a part. Further, major developments, such as the progress of the SALT negotiations, should be calibrated to provide the newer context for the performance characteristics that Weapon System W is called upon to provide.

These are some of the types of raw data that can facilitate the creation of forecasts for the PDM to assist him, not only to physically complete the Weapon System W production on schedule and within budget, but also to enable him to effectively present the contribution that Weapon System W is able to make to credibility through capability.

APPLICATION 5
DEVELOPMENT OF NEW JET ENGINE

Weapon System W just discussed is clearly a military application with the unique feature that the production is for *nonuse*. In the private sector, a product or service is produced with the expressed intent of its *use* as well as that of making a profit.

Military R&D and Commercial Development

Military R&D has been a major source of new ideas. The research has been primarily mission oriented, and has been carried out both in government laboratories and in private industry research facilities. When done under contract with the private sector, military R&D offers the possibility of converting into commercial development what was originally a military discovery. Such adaptation is subject to the requirement that the primary mission of national security would not be in any way compromised by the commercial development.

In August 1972, General Electric (GE) applied for an export license to collaborate on the production of a new jet engine system in partnership with a government-owned French company. The application was denied on the following grounds:

The engine's core element is a strategic system necessary for national defense. It was developed with Pentagon funds for the B-1 bomber.

The engine was constructed by GE with Defense Department money, or in other words, the money of the American taxpayers.

Constructing the engine with a French company instead of building it completely in the United States and exporting it reduces the number of workers who could be employed by the project.[2]

Ten months later, the White House reversed its earlier ban. The reversal was based on locating in the United States the manufacture of the core of the engine, and exporting the system to France where the French Government-owned Societe Nationale d'Etude et Deu Construction de Moteurs d'Aviation (SNECMA) would complete the engines. It was reasoned that by manufacturing the technologically most advanced part in the United States, it would not only protect American technology, but also provide employment to Americans.

International and intersectoral cooperation

According to press reports, President Nixon told French President George Pompidou of the reversal of the decision in their meeting in Iceland in June 1973. It indicates the high level of importance attached to the joint venture between the American private sector and the French public sector. It would not at all be surprising if this particular effort is held forth as an instance of the third dimension of U.S.-European cooperation. In his speech to NATO in 1969, President Nixon referred to the need for cooperation between the U.S. and Europe, which had already worked together on the military and the political dimensions, to work jointly in a third dimension, viz., social. It is also probably not accidental that France, which hosted the Vietnam peace talks and was the site of the Paris Agreement, would be chosen as the site for a demonstration of technical cooperation between the U.S. and Europe. The signing of the Vietnam Peace Agreement in January 1973 could have provided added reasoning to the reversal of the rejection before the peace agreement of the application for export license.

[2] Clyde H. Farnsworth, "White House Backs GE-French Jet Engine Plan," *The Courier-Journal and Times,* Louisville, Ky. (June 24, 1973), p. B8.

The Context of Development Decision-Making

To determine the type of MIS (IIS) that would serve the needs of decision-making in intersectoral and international technical cooperation, we need to identify the objectives hierarchy and the Context C of decision-making before discussing the nature of Context E-Context T combinations.

Considered in terms of financial investment, the $400 million shared by GE and SNECMA to develop the technology for the civilian market, the joint venture is by no means a large undertaking. Therefore, political factors in addition to economic factors have to be reflected in the choice of the objectives for the project.

Economic considerations

The technology represented in the core element for a jet engine is novel, but its potential market is reasonably well established. The core is part of the 10-ton engine. It would be only 40 percent of the weight of a DC 10. The lower engine weight with higher engine thrust provides an attractive option to medium-size subsonic planes of the Boeing 727 type:

> The engine would be used to power airliners that have not yet been built, but which aircraft companies in Europe and the United States think will be dominating the market from the end of the 1970's to the end of the 1980's.

> These would be medium-sized subsonic planes needing shorter runway space, to fly medium-range routes—planes that in effect would replace present DC 9's, Caravelles and Boeing 727's.

> Aircraft industry sources see a market for between 4,000 and 6,000 of the 10-ton engines, which would be worth upward of $4 billion.[3]

Political factors

The first major political cooperation on a technology problem in Europe was represented in the Concorde Supersonic Transport (SST) that France and Britain agreed to build together. With the cancellation of the Supersonic Transport program in the United States in 1971, and the subsequent cancellation of the options held by several American airlines to purchase the Concorde Supersonic Transport from Europe, a severe blow was dealt the prospects of a viable European SST.

In the discussions on the GE-SNECMA technical cooperation, the

[3] Ibid.

French made it clear that they attached great importance to the joint venture of the two countries. One could look upon this importance as political importance, against a background of economic necessity. It is possible to recognize the political importance of technological cooperation, the objective of which is the political credibility through enhanced economic capability.

Jet engine development: objectives hierarchy

Both the economic and the political motivations must be reflected in the organismic objectives of the U.S.-French venture. On the economic side, it is the establishment of General Electric in the international market for medium-size subsonic planes for medium-range routes. Such planes are expected to be in use both in the United States and in Europe; and the economic objectives should reflect both the domestic and international markets for the plane. Since there can be no guarantee that a given market will in fact materialize, the best that the organismic objective can stipulate is the expected share of the market. In other words, the MIS (IIS) should answer the PDM's question: At this rate, what is the expected share of the market of medium-size subsonic planes in the next decade?

Whatever share of the $400 million needed for commercial development that GE can obtain from SNECMA is of much less importance than what the investment will generate in the form of new business from France for GE. Obviously, the new business will be in areas where the U.S.-French cooperation shall have proven it most worthwhile for the French. Therefore, the MIS (IIS) should indicate to the PDM the *French* estimate of what the cooperation represents in enhancing France's own technological capability. It should be recalled that France did not sign the partial nuclear test ban treaty, which suggests the French desire to keep her options open in nuclear development for military purposes. Somewhat coincidently, just at the time of the reversal of the White House ruling on GE's application for the export license, the state-owned French electric monopoly announced contracts to GE for two nuclear power stations. What is most important here is the political credibility that France sees in the technical capability of the nuclear power stations. The MIS (IIS) for the PDM should reflect the political factors: At this rate, what is the expected enhancement of the political credibility through technical capability of France?

The objectives hierarchy has thus two clearly defined elements: political and economic. Of the two, the political is more important, because without political approval, the technological and economic capabilities would simply not have a base to operate from. Therefore, we should recognize the objectives hierarchy of the political dimension as being more important than that of the economic dimension.

Political objectives hierarchy

The political objectives are not only those of France, but also those of the United States. However much the French may desire the technical capabilities of GE, without an export license GE would not be able to honor the requests from the French. In other words, the PDM should recognize the political objectives of the United States which are furthered by the joint venture agreement. That objective can also be stated in terms of the credibility generated by capability. Europe has heard promises of the willingness of the United States to share American technology, but the call for cooperation in space, for instance, has not materialized so far. Neither has the call for cooperation in the third dimension. From the point of view of the political objectives of the United States, establishment of the credibility of U.S.-European technical cooperation is perhaps the most important objective. The MIS (IIS) should answer the question of the PDM: At this rate, what is the expected increase in the credibility of U.S.-European technical cooperation?

The PDM is at the tactical level with respect to the White House decision-maker who is concerned with U.S. credibility on U.S.-European technical cooperation. The press reports indicated that Henry Kissinger —then President's Assistant for National Security—was the decision-maker who reversed the earlier rejection of GE's application for export license. The program manager for the venture would report to GE's group Vice-President for International Operations, who, in turn would have to persuade Kissinger that the U.S. political objectives are in fact fulfilled through the joint venture. Similarly, on the French side, also, the PDM would be at the tactical level with respect to the counterpart of Kissinger in the French Government.

Economic objectives hierarchy

Turning to the economic objectives, the customers for the medium-size subsonic planes would be U.S. and European airlines. As customers, they will be at the organismic level. GE is manufacturing only the core element of the jet engine, the engine itself being assembled in France. The engine would be a major component of the jet airplane, which could be manufactured in the U.S. or in Europe. Bearing in mind both the U.S. and the European market, the PDM can be at the tactical level with respect to the European airline company, on the one hand, and at the tactical level with respect to the U.S. airline company, on the other. In both cases, the strategic level will be occupied by the airplane manufacturer—European or American.

The political and the economic objectives have been identified with respect to the *demand* for the core element. The other side of the coin, i.e., supply, refers to the manufacture of the core element itself. Here again, there are two distinct objectives hierarchy. With respect to the manufacture of the element in the United States, the PDM is at the organismic level. When it comes to the assembly of the jet engine by SNECMA, the PDM is at the strategic level because of the importance of the core element to the assembly of the jet engine itself. In the manufacture of the core element in the U.S. also, the PDM can be viewed as being at the strategic level with respect to the manufacture of jet engine parts.

Risk of Environment, and Quasistability of Technology

We have classified the MIS (IIS) as belonging to the M-Zero category in which the decision-making situation is one of risk and the technology is quasistable.

Risky environment

Risky environment is one in which the fulfillment characteristics do have applicable probability distribution(s). This applicability is indicated by the fact that the *form* of the probability distribution is known, but not its parameters. How is the form known?

While the technological cooperation between U.S. private sector and French public sector to undertake the commercial development of a technology which grew from military R&D is new, technical cooperation between companies is nothing new. As a matter of fact, as was pointed out earlier, the program management of a large weapon comes down to the management of a number of subcontractors by the prime contractor, of many companies by one company with respect to the large system, which happened to be a military weapon system. Compared to the complexity of elements that go into the making of large weapon systems, integrating the core of the engine manufactured by GE with the rest of the jet engine is a small matter. However, language enters as an element of complexity here: in the fabrication of large systems where different companies have cooperated in the past, the physical integration has always taken place within the United States.

Unlike in the case of a spacecraft subunit assembly, which can be performed on the basis of engineering concepts which are communicated in the *same* language, it may be necessary to make allowances for the extra time required in making a translation of concepts from one technology to another. It may require an awareness on the part of the French on how the core element fits into the jet engine itself. Since there is definite intent on

217

the part of the United States to protect the technology represented in the core element, the necessity for an understanding of how the element fits into the engine has to be tempered by the need for protecting the U.S. technological novelty.

Again, in integrating the component parts of a spacecraft, there has had to be provision to protect proprietary interests on the part of the many subcontractors, while fulfilling the requirement that all the subunits function together as a unit. The requirements that the prime contractors have imposed upon the subcontractors are in terms of the performance characteristics which the various components have to fulfill. What is proprietary is the particular manner in which the subcontractor fabricates the component or element that he has contracted to provide. The same principle can be applied to international technological collaboration also. The *production* of the core element is what is proprietary; the *performance* of the core element is mandatorily required by the contractual obligations. To ensure the fulfillment characteristics, the core element has to be united with the jet engine assembly; and the details of that union have to be laid out in great detail long before the actual assembly itself.

Quasistable technology

The core element was developed for use in the B-1 bomber. Subsequent work has resulted in getting higher engine thrust with lower engine weight. Operational experience with the engine to date makes the technology reasonably stable as far as its performance is concerned. We consider the technology stable when its performance characteristics can be specified within small limits.

Why is it then that we consider the technology of the jet engine core to be *quasistable*? The principal reason is that the technology has to be developed for the civilian market. This development is estimated to cost $400 million, which will be shared by GE and SNECMA. What the results of this conversion will be is not known. However, it has been established that a 10-ton engine can fly. The quasinature comes from not the performance characteristics of the engines themselves, but from the fulfillment characteristics of the environment. In other words, what has been quite successful in the military context may well be partially or barely successful as a commercial venture. Comfort, which is an essential element of air travel and the minimization of pollution now injected into the use of any technology are *not* primary considerations in the military success of the 10-ton engine technology. It is hoped that the engine will succeed as a commercial venture, but how it will perform can be stated only within broad limits on the basis of projected experience from similar events in the past. Hence, we characterize the technology as quasistable.

Requirements of Forecasts for Decision-Making

Given that the environment is risky and the technology is quasistable, what type of forecasts are needed from the MIS (IIS) in support of the program manager of GE-SNECMA?

U.S. credibility prospects: U.S.-European technical cooperation

The very existence of the GE-SNECMA joint venture depends upon its political viability. This viability has two different elements: domestic and foreign. Of the two, the domestic outweighs the foreign because without the sanction and support from domestic political sources (meaning thereby the decision-makers in authority), the export license could be revoked, and there will be no further basis upon which to build the political objectives hierarchies of the foreign sources. Therefore, the first and primary forecast that the PDM should be able to obtain from his MIS (IIS) is: At this rate, what is the increase in the credibility of U.S.-European technical cooperation? It should be recognized that the GE-SNECMA venture is only *one* of a number of possible international technical cooperation efforts. As such, the whole weight of continuing international cooperation should, of course, not be put upon the first such venture. Nor should the PDM be obliged to bear the brunt of the entire U.S. foreign policy in the technical sphere. Therefore, the PDM should have an appreciation of the *specific* area of potential success in technical cooperation that the GE-SNECMA is designed to contribute. If it is one of, say, five such ventures and if all are equally important, then the apportioned share of the national technical foreign policy of the GE-SNECMA will be 20 percent. Therefore, the PDM's concern is with the increase in the 20 percent share of the credibility of U.S.-European technical cooperation. The credibility prospects could therefore address that particular share, and not the entire U.S.-European technical cooperation.

French credibility prospects: political credibility through technical capability

The second most important element that the PDM should be apprised of is the prospects for enhancement of credibility for the French of *their own* technological capabilities. After all, insofar as the French have to pay for the technical cooperation (and not receive it as technical aid), they have an interest in it of not only meeting the immediate technical needs, but also reducing future dependence upon the aid that they are receiving at the moment. In other words, the very success of technical cooperation means an early termination of the same. It is conceivable however, that the technical dependence could be transferred to other allied areas which GE can then proceed to fulfill.

It is really not the technology that is transferred that matters, but what the host country *perceives* as having been transferred. The degree of transfer depends upon the capability of the host technology to absorb the new knowledge. As far as the country itself is concerned, their eyes are upon the *political* capital that can be made out of the technical transfer. Even if the technical transfer were successful, but the political pickings were slim, that could spell trouble for GE. In other words, what the PDM needs to know is: At this rate, what is the *French* estimate of the increase in their political credibility on the basis of technological capability?

GE performance prospects: U.S. production

As program manager, the PDM has to deliver the core element of the jet engine. Its performance in accordance with the specified characteristics is crucial. He will be subject both to time and money constraints upon the delivery of the finished product. Just like the program manager of Weapon System W, his concern is with the index of completion. A time-schedule-cost index, which measures the actual completion of the job and the budget in terms of preestablished standards, would be essential for the PDM.

GE performance prospects: engine assembly in France

Even while production of the core element progresses at home, preparation for the jet engine assembly abroad must be well laid. If there are changes in the performance characteristics of the core element, as may well be the case in the context of commercial development of military technology, the PDM would want to make sure that the preparations for engine assembly do take these into account. A parallel division between performance and production as discussed with respect to Weapon System W is also applicable in this instance. In the former case, the performance characteristics were of interest to the higher levels of command. In the present case, the performance characteristics are what is of interest to the customer. One distinction between the two is the fact of production for *nonuse* in the case of the weapon system, and production for *use* in the case of the jet engine. Therefore, instead of the emphasis upon the *potential* performance of the weapon system for *credibility* by high levels of command, the *present* performance of the core element is what has to be used in future *production* of the jet engine. Therefore, the PDM must have the answer to the question: At this rate, what is the impact of the projected performance characteristics of the core element upon the assembly of the jet engine?

GE market prospects: U.S. airlines

The medium-size subsonic airplanes that are projected for the U.S. market are the prime customers for the GE core element which goes into the jet engines. Development of the technology for the civilian market is undertaken in the hope of realizing gains from the future market. Therefore, the PDM must inform himself about the development of market prospects, even as commercial development is progressing. This means convincing airplane manufacturers, as well as airline companies, that the GE product delivers more power and less pollution for the same money. Since options are taken by the airline companies well ahead of the actual production, a tangible measure of the success of the PDM's function would be the size of the orders (options) placed by the airline companies for the medium-size subsonic aircraft utilizing the GE core element: At this rate, what is the expected number of airplanes in the U.S. in which the GE core element is embodied in the engine?

GE market prospects: European airlines

Similar considerations apply to the European market also. The fact that the core element is embodied in a jet engine which is produced jointly with France may add to the appeal to European customers. The forecast that the PDM needs with respect to his European market is: At this rate, what is the expected number of airplanes in Europe in which the GE core element is utilized?

Raw Data Requirements of Development MIS (IIS)

The types of raw data depend upon the types of forecasts that are to be made.

Raw data on political prospects: United States

The primary forecast that the PDM requires is perhaps the hardest one to develop. The forecast itself is an American estimate of how well Europe believes U.S.-European cooperation is progressing. It will be necessary to identify the sources upon which the White House decision-maker depends to give him an assessment of the European attitude. The sources are as varied as their stature. For instance, the public utterances at a technical meeting by a European scientist of U.S.-European technical cooperation may be given far *less* weight than the private comments of an influential political personage. The White House decision-maker himself is quite *unlikely* to be knowledgeable in the technical details, and, therefore, likely to be less sympathetic to the myriad problems of working across languages and oceans, with the pressure of preserving the proprietary interests, on the one hand, and the pressure to open up the floodgates of technology to the public sector in another country, on the other. The raw data elements themselves will have to be calibrated for their relevance, reliability, and repeatability.

Raw data on political prospects: France

Even more difficult will be the identification and pursuit of raw data elements on the political disposition of a foreign country. It should be remembered that their interest is probably much less with the technical capability than with the *fact* of the existence of the machinery for cooperation. A prime raw data source would, of course, be the counterpart of the White House decision-maker who has a vested interest in preserving the technology transfer or technological cooperation between the two countries. To whom is he most sensitive? It could be another official, a legislator, a party functionary. The PDM will do well to identify these raw data sources, because if they are not identified by design, they may well reduce by default the effectiveness of the technological cooperation in part or altogether.

Raw data on GE performance prospects

Perhaps the most tractable of all the raw data elements are those relating to the physical production of the core element in the United States, and the jet engine assembly in France. For, in spite of linguistic and cultural differences, the communication has to be precise and carried out in the common language of technical specifications and drawings.

Raw data on market prospects

The markets for the jet engines to be utilized in medium-size subsonic transport are well specified: they are the airplanes in which the jet engines can be used. What is not known is *which* airlines would be the early customers for the particular type of jet engines. Given the airline customers, the next question, of course, is: Which airplane manufacturers would be most likely to respond to the commercial demand? To assess the prospects, whether at home or abroad, the demand for the medium-size subsonic jet planes themselves must be assessed. Who are the travelers, what are their requirements today and tomorrow? In other words, the demand for jet planes is a *derived demand*. In the case of any derived demand, the principal influences upon the derivation of the demand is most important. We will discuss further the situation of derived demand in chapter 9, using a numerical illustration.

The raw data requirements to enable the forecasts of political prospects in the United States and in France, as well as the technological performance and market prospects are generic: they are applicable *mutatis mutandis* (with appropriate changes) to any organism which finds itself confronted with risky environment and quasistable technology. The specific raw data elements would, of course, vary with the organism and with time for the same organism. What has been set out here is simply the basic *types* of raw data which are indispensable to an MIS (IIS) in light of the forecasts that it has to provide the decision-maker.

QUESTIONS

Chapters 7, 8, and 9 deal with MIS (IIS) types: M-Zero, M-Negative, and M-Positive. In chapter 7 the first of the three types was discussed, as well as its application to real-life problems in the public and the private sectors. The purpose of the following questions is to develop an appreciation for the raw data requirements of MIS to provide forecasts for the principal decision-maker (PDM).

A. M-ZERO MIS (IIS)

1. Distinguish between M-Positive and M-Zero contexts of MIS (IIS).
2. How would you establish applicability of prior experience in M-Zero situations?

B. APPLICATION 4

3. Who is the PDM in the production of Weapon System W?
4. Identify the Context of Concurrent Conflict of the PDM of Weapon System W.
5. Indicate the interaction between technological quasistability and the fulfillment characteristics of manpower.
6. What are the requirements of forecasts for the PDM in Weapon System W production?
7. What types of raw data are required to provide the forecasts for the PDM?

C. APPLICATION 5

8. What is the principal difference between military and nonmilitary systems?
9. Discuss the two different objectives hierarchies in the GE-SNECMA Project.
10. Why is the MIS (IIS) for GE-SNECMA termed M-Zero?
11. What are the requirements of forecasts for the PDM in the GE-SNECMA Project?
12. What types of raw data are required to provide forecasts for the PDM?

8
M-Negative MIS (IIS)

TECHNICAL OVERVIEW / From the combination of risky and quasistable decision-making situations designated as M-Zero, we turn to M-Negative situations. When the technology is stable, the production is so well controlled that inspection of 100 electric bulbs, out of 10,000, i.e., an inspection ratio of 1%, would give adequate guarantee of performance. The 1% ratio can be expressed as 10^{-2}, making the M in $10^M = -2$, or M-Negative.

As in chapter 7, real-life situations, one in the public sector and one in the private sector, are discussed here to illustrate M-Negative MIS (IIS). The public sector problem is that of delivery of hospital care, and the private sector problem is the sale of durable products.

It is necessary to define what constitutes hospital care. To be considered meaningfully, health must take into account physical, mental, and environmental elements. Health would have to be recognized as the rule, with ill health as the exception. For the present, only ill health as pertaining to treatment in hospitals is considered.

The index of service rendered by the hospital should be considered in terms of the relative improvement in the physical capability to follow one's pursuits. It would mean that the accent is not on any absolute physical capability, but, instead, upon a relative measure which is *individual oriented*.

The reason why it should be an individual-oriented index is that health is personal. And, unless measured in individual terms, health of a community or of a nation has little basis in reality.

An index which takes into account individual evaluation is developed: (1) patient evaluation of his well-being; (2) hospital evaluation of individual physical well-being, and (3) hospital days of stay. These three elements can be given numerical values. The third item is readily available because the hospital keeps records of the number of hospital-days. On the second item, the hospital has qualitative statements about the condition of the patient as he (she) is admitted; all that is needed is to translate those qualitative statements onto a numerical scale, say, from 0 to 100. Similarly, on the first item, the patient expresses *qualitatively* his estimate of physical well-being at the time of admission; he should be asked to express a similar evaluation at the time of his exit or soon thereafter—making the evaluations at the time of entry and exit on a scale of 0 to 100.

We have classified the fulfillment characteristics of the object of the hospital as being reduced risk. It means that not only are the probability distributions of the fulfillment characteristics known, but also their parameters are specified. For instance, patient arrivals, assignments, and operations are reasonably well documented from other experiences with service facilities similar to the particular hospital. Observation on the pattern of arrivals, waiting, and operations can be made on as short a time period as a day, and estimates can be made of the parameters of the service facility operations. Close correspondence can in fact be obtained with the real-life experience on the basis of a relatively *small* amount of real-life data through the use of simulation, making it possible to arrive at reasonably reliable estimates of the parameters of the probability distributions applicable to the given situation, which we call reduced-risk situations.

The performance characteristics of the various diagnostic facilities and prescriptive facilities of the hospital operate under stable technology, i. e., the inspection ratio is less than 100%, making the M in the 10^M negative. The inspection ratio encompasses the performance of the *diagnostic* facilities, such as radiology facilities, and the technical performance of medication; and the performance of the *prescriptive* facilities, such as quality of nursing care, wholesomeness of hospital diet, and correctness of the diagnosis by the physician. The inspection ratio applied to all the diagnostic and prescriptive facilities can be specified as M-Negative.

What type of forecasts does the hospital administrator, as the principal decision-maker (PDM), require? First, the PDM requires the health improvement index expectation: At this rate, what is the expected value of the health improvement index? What he is interested in is the *rate of change* of the index, the administrator not having to be concerned as long as the index is maintained at a specific level or within a specific range.

The health improvement index indicates the acceptability of the "product" that the hospital produces or the "service" that the hospital renders. Supporting the flow of services are the twin facilities of diagnosis and prescription. The administrator can exercise control over the outputs through the two main inputs of diagnostic facilities and prescriptive facilities. The MIS (IIS) should answer the question of the PDM: At this rate, what is the utilization index of the diagnostic and the prescriptive facilities?

The raw data inputs are governed by the requirements of the forecast. The data on the first encounter with the patient become an important element in this context. Massachusetts General Hospital and Harvard Medical School have a joint research unit, Laboratory of Computer Science, which carries out a continuing program of hospital research utilizing a specially developed, interactive, interpretive programming language. The integrated record of a single patient is used by the health care professional in the daily patient care activity. The data are also used to produce statistical reports for accounting and long-range planning purposes.

Turning from the public sector MIS (IIS) to the private sector, we consider a product, instead of a service. The product is not a single one, but rather a *generic product* which shares the features of reduced risk and stable technology.

We make a distinction between "need-values" and "want-values." We will consider only the want-values in the present instance, and only those which can be considered to be stable. The want-value(s) satisfied by a product(s) of the organism is considered to be well established. The performance characteristics of the product(s) are also considered to be well established.

From the point of view of the PDM, he needs to know how the want-values of the market are being satisfied by the particular product(s). These vary with the life cycle stage of the product. The distinct stages of the life cycle—(1) gestation, (2) birth, (3) infancy, (4) rapid growth, (5) maturation, (6) decline, and (7) death—are applicable to any phenomenon, whether it be product, service, or relationship.

The PDM is particularly interested in the specific stage of life cycle that the given product is heading toward in the next decision period. If the product is in the stage of rapid growth at this time, it will soon be entering the stage of maturation, requiring reduction in the resources devoted to its production. If, however, the product is entering the stage of decline in the near future, the PDM should have already introduced, or be able to do so in the immediate future, the new product which will be a substitute for the product in the phase of decline. To be effective, the product P_2, which is replacing product P_1, must be able to compete with not only P_1, but also with all the products of other organisms which are all competing with P_1, i.e., $P_{11}, P_{12}, \ldots$.

The PDM will generally be concerned with not only a single product, but also a number of products at the same time. He has to be especially careful if the majority of his products are entering the maturation stage shortly, for he should have long since brought out replacement products for them.

The PDM should have the capability to group several products by the want that is being satisfied by the particular product group. Each product group satisfies different market segments. Owing to no fault of the given product, the demand for the product may decline, simply because the nature of the particular market segment has undergone change. Therefore, the forecast would indicate the significance of the want satisfied by the particular product in the particular market segment, as well as the significance of the product to the organism itself.

The types of raw data required to yield the forecasts for the PDM relate to the expectation of the fulfillment characteristics of the product. The question of the expected index of fulfillment of the want values by the products can be answered (1) in the aggregate (relating to all the products), (2) or on an individual product-by-product basis, with respect to (3) the market segment of major products, and (4) the market segments of a single product.

The raw data requirements of the MIS (IIS) to indicate how the products are fulfilling the wants of the market, by themselves and in comparison with the performance of competing organisms, are based upon the requirements of the PDM for decision-making. In discussing the public sector and private sector examples, the basic *types* of raw data are identified as indispensable to an MIS (IIS) for the forecasts it has to provide the PDM for decision-making.

EXECUTIVE SUMMARY / When the production technology is stable, fewer units of the product need to be inspected to assure quality performance than when the production technology is unstable or quasistable. To use the example of the light bulb production, by inspecting only 100 out of 10,000 light bulbs, or 1%, the production performance of the bulbs can be well assured. The inspection ratio of 1% can be represented as 10^{-2}, making the M in 10^M equal to -2, giving an MIS (IIS) which is M-Negative.

A public sector problem and a private sector problem are used to illustrate M-Negative real-life situations. The former relates to the delivery of hospital care, and the latter to the sale of durable products.

It is necessary to define what constitutes hospital care. Health must be recognized as the rule, and ill health the exception. Not all of the ill health, but only that which is treated in hospitals is considered here.

Health is personal; therefore, measurement of hospital care must be in terms of the individual. At present, the individual patient's evaluation is not recorded quantitatively. The hospital's evaluation of the patient is available from the qualitative diagnosis at the time of entry, as well as subsequently. The number of hospital-days, is, of course, quantitatively recorded.

A Health Improvement Index which combines the evaluation of his (her) health status by the patient, the evaluation of the hospital, both at the time of entry and exit from the hospital, as well as the number of hospital-days, is developed. It can be instituted with little additional effort.

The Health Improvement Index indicates the acceptability of the "product" that the hospital produces, or of the "service" that the hospital renders. The flow of service in the hospital can be identified with reference to diagnostic facilities and prescriptive facilities. The arrival of patients, their waiting, and operations performed on them can be stated in terms of well-defined curves which relate the frequency of occurrence of each hospital phenomenon by type of hours and/or number of patients. The advantage of such a specification is that the raw data obtained from very small periods can be used to give a close enough description of the phenomenon if observations were to be made over a long period of time. Therefore, decisions made with reference to the use of the facilities can be treated as though they belong to the well-defined curves. Similarly, the performance characteristics of the various diagnostic and prescriptive facilities of the hospital can also be specified rather precisely, making it necessary to inspect just less than 100% of the diagnostic and prescriptive facilities.

The question that the administrator wants answered is: At this rate, what is the utilization index of the diagnostic and the prescriptive facilities? The utilization index itself should help answer the question: At this rate, what is the expected value of the Health Improvement Index? The raw data inputs are governed by the requirements of these forecasts.

Turning from the public sector to the private sector MIS (IIS), we consider a *product* which exhibits the features of reduced risk in decision-making and stable technology in performance characteristics.

The particular product fulfills certain want-values which may or may not have a basis in need-values of the customers. The PDM will recognize that the want-values served by his particular product are also served by other products. Further, he himself will have a line of products which serve a group of related want-values.

The PDM is especially interested in the particular stage of life cycle that the given product is heading toward in the *next* decision period. If the product will enter the maturation stage, then the PDM has to prepare now to reduce the resources devoted to its production. If the product is entering the stage of decline, then the PDM has to identify a new product which should be ready to be introduced on short notice to replace the particular product in the stage of decline. The particular product serves a market which has several segments. The capability to satisfy the different segments varies; therefore, the PDM should know how the particular product is faring in the different market segments so that corrective actions may be taken in the market segments where demand is declining. The PDM needs forecasts which relate not only to the individual market and its segments, but also the different products and their segments, so that he may have a composite index of performance of all his products in fulfilling the want-values of the customers.

The question of the PDM is: At this rate, what is the expected index of fulfillment of the want-values by the product(s)? It can be answered with respect to all the products, an individual product, market segments of major products, and market segments of a single product. The raw data requirements of the MIS (IIS) are based upon the requirement of the PDM for decision-making. In the present discussions of public sector and private sector problems, we have identified not the individual elements of raw data, but the basic *types* of raw data which are most germane to the forecasts required for decision-making by the PDM.

From the risk environment and quasistable technology combination of decision-making situations discussed in chapter 7, we now turn to reduced-risk environment and stable technology combinations. The first is a public-sector problem dealing with the delivery of hospital care; the second is a private-sector problem concerning the sale of durable products. We will discuss decision situations in which not only the form of the applicable probability distributions of the fulfillment characteristics is known, but also the parameters are known, or can be assumed to be known, making the decision-making environment one of reduced risk.

APPLICATION 6
DELIVERY OF HOSPITAL CARE

The relative increase in the size of the budget for health, education, and welfare reflects the importance attached to the issue of health by the federal government, as mirrored in the mood of the times. There were some 47 bills in Congress in 1971, all seeking to legislate for one aspect or other of production and/or delivery of national health care. There seems to be little question that everyone is entitled to good health however it may be defined; the question is, How can it be brought about?

Hospital Care as a Subsystem of Health Delivery

To be considered meaningfully, health must take into account physical, mental, and environmental elements. Health would have to be recognized as the rule, with ill health as the exception. This focus on the positive characteristics of health would enable the proper incorporation of the environmental elements which are so influential in maintaining good health. Further, the use of medical facilities, whether in or out of a hospital, would then be properly considered as an interim measure, designed to prevent and to cure when prevention is not possible, rather than as an end in itself. For the maintenance of good health, health care has to be *produced*, and *delivered*.

Individual-oriented health index of hospital service

A hospital is a service facility. The units arrive, wait for operations (in the generic sense of service activities, and not in the restrictive sense of surgical services), and leave (AWOL). The arrival is in an impaired condition; the leaving is in improved condition, in most instances. The departure from one hospital service facility could be back to home, to another hospital, to a nursing home, back to work, or by death. Each of the exits can be characterized in terms of the primary objective of improved health at the time of exit compared with the impaired health at the time of entry. By improved health, we could designate the capability to follow one's pursuits at least as well as before the impairment which brought the person to the hospital. The impairment may be physical, psychological, or both (ignoring the environmental process of, or contribution to, the impairment). It is quite likely that only the more pronounced impairment would be recognized; therefore, we will confine discussion to the *physical* impairment to the following of one's pursuits (ignoring the equally, if not more, important impairment to psychological well-being).

The index of the service rendered by the hospital is thus the *relative* improvement in the physical capability to follow one's pursuits. It would mean that the accent is not on any absolute physical capabilities, but, instead, upon a relative measure which is individual oriented. If someone entered the hospital with only 40 percent capability to follow his pursuits and exited the hospital with the capability increased to 50 percent, the relative improvement would be (50 percent − 40 percent/40 percent =) 25 percent. By the same token, if someone entered the hospital with 80 percent capability and exited with 100 percent capability, the relative improvement will also be (100 percent − 80 percent/80 percent =) 25 percent.

The *relative* improvement in the capability to follow pursuits of one's choice can thus have two principal components: hospital evaluation and patient evaluation. If we give equal weights to both evaluations, then the index can be obtained by adding one to the other. Thus, if the patient's evaluation put his capability to follow his pursuits at the time of entry at 80 percent (reflecting both the quantity and quality), and if the hospital evaluation put it at 70 percent, the index at entry would be (80 percent

+ 70 percent =) 150. Similarly, at the exit, if the patient places his capability at 100 percent and the hospital also places its evaluation at 100 percent, the combined index, giving equal weights to both, would be (100 percent + 100 percent =) 200. The relative improvement then will be (200 percent − 150 percent/150 percent =) 33 1/3 percent.

We have thus a narrow objective for the hospital segment of the human flow from the pre-hospital environment to the post-hospital environment. It is measurable, and is now qualitatively expressed. The additional effort is minimum, i.e., providing two numbers between 0 and 100 by the patient and the physician at the time of entry (or shortly before or after) and the time of exit (or shortly thereafter). Many more than the single number are now provided by the hospital in its evaluation charts. All that is required is to simply provide one composite number between 0 and 100 to reflect what is now qualitatively expressed about the physical capabilities of the patient at the time of entry into the hospital and exit from it.

Reduced Risk of Environment, and Stability of Technology

We have classified the fulfillment of the organismic objective of the hospital as being one in reduced-risk environment and stable technology. What is the reduced risk, and what is the stability?

Reduced-risk environment

In a reduced-risk environment, the fulfillment characteristics should be not only known, but also specified in terms of form and parameters of the applicable probability distributions. What are the main elements of the external demands upon the hospital which are fulfilled by the services, and how can they be specified?

PATIENT ARRIVALS

The arrivals of patients at a hospital facility, i.e., the demands for fulfillment, are easily identifiable. The experience of any one hospital in any one time period would be different from the experience of another hospital, and from its own experience at another time. However, taken over a reasonably long period, the arrival of patients can be specified reasonably closely. The frequency of arrivals by type can be constructed from past records of the same hospital, or projected on the basis of limited experience of its own, or of other hospitals of similar profile. Within the same hospital itself, the demand for services in the different departments can also be ascertained with a good deal of precision on the basis of one's own or similar institution(s)' experience.

PATIENT ASSIGNMENTS

As a service facility, the orientation must always be to the units that arrive for service, i.e., the patients. It is traumatic when patients have to wait for what appears to be an eternity in the emergency room. The very reason why an emergency ward has been chosen by the patient (at the direction of a doctor) would indicate the gravity of the ill health; anything but instantaneous attention given to the incoming patient would strain the endurance of the patient and of the immediate family. Therefore, delays in the emergency ward in the assignment of the patient to a diagnostic or treatment facility would perhaps reflect most adversely upon the service rating of the hospital.

PATIENT OPERATIONS

The results of the diagnostic tests and analysis of the specimens constitute raw data for use by the physicians. The separation between raw data production and raw data utilization is institutionalized clearly in the hospital environment, the former being the responsibility of the diagnostic facilities, and the latter the responsibility of the prescriptive facilities.

Clearly, the prescriptive facilities are dependent upon the diagnostic facilities for the appropriate raw data input. Both facilities depend upon trained manpower, and the problem of health manpower was the subject of the Presidential Commission on Health Manpower which published its report in 1968.[1] In it, the increase in the demand for manpower resources is seen to outstrip the supply, requiring the use of paramedical personnel to supplement the growing disparity between supply of and demand for health manpower, particularly in the prescriptive facilities. There is also identified an increasing deficiency in the diagnostic facilities as pointed out by the Presidential Commission on Health Facilities, which published its report in 1969.[2]

The shortage of manpower in diagnostic facilities is illustrated by the demand on the radiologist's time:

The annual increase in the demand on the radiologist's time has been estimated by Morgan[3] at 6.7 percent and by the National Advisory Committee on Radiation[4] at 7.2 percent. The amount of hospital patient cost incurred in the radiology department has increased in a similar

[1] President's Commission on Health Manpower, *Report* (Government Printing Office, Washington, D.C., 1968).

[2] President's Commission on Health Facilities, *Report* (Government Printing Office, Washington, D.C., 1969).

[3] R. H. Morgan, "The Emergence of Radiology as a Major Influence in American Medicine," *American Journal of Roentgen* 111 (March 1971): 449–462.

[4] National Advisory Committee on Radiation, *Protecting and Improving Health Through Radiological Sciences* (U.S. Government Printing Office, Washington, D.C., 1966), p. 9.

manner; at the Massachusetts General Hospital, the increase was from $1.2 million in 1961 to $2.9 million in 1967[5], representing an average compounded annual increase of 15.8 percent. . . .

Professional manpower in radiology has been estimated by Knowles[6] to be increasing at the rate of only 5.7 percent per year.

To compensate for this trend, every radiology department in the country is striving continuously to improve the efficiency of its operations.[7]

With the pressure upon increased efficiency, the hospitals find that the behavior of the diagnostic facilities, such as the radiology department, can, in fact, be described in terms of probability distributions whose parameters are known.

Stable technology

We have characterized the performance characteristics of the hospital system as being in the stable technology category. When the technology is stable, as in the case of the production of light bulbs, the method of making bulbs is so well established that the technical performance characteristics can be specified quite precisely, i.e., with small variation. This fact is reflected in the small fraction of the total production that needs to be inspected to ensure that the variations are minimum.

Our classification of the hospital system in the stable technology group merely suggests that the inspection ratio is less than 100 percent. If it were 100 percent, the M in 10^M will be zero, giving us M-Zero MIS (IIS). It can be maintained that the majority of facilities in use in a hospital do in fact fulfill this requirement. Where new inventions are used, a higher inspection ratio, i.e., 50 percent or even 99 percent, may be indicated. Even if the technical performance results of the new inventions among the diagnostic facilities were to be examined 200 percent, i.e., the test results are inspected by at least two technicians (not for diagnostic purposes, but for testing that the equipment does in fact function dependably), when we take into account the inspection of all the hospital facilities (diagnostic and prescriptive), the inspection ratio will be well below 100 percent.

It should be recognized that this statement about the inspection ratio covers the consistency of performance of not only the equipment, but also that of medication, surgical procedures, etc. Further, the statement includes

---

[5] J. H. Knowles, "Radiology—A Case Study in Technology and Manpower," Part II, *New England Journal of Medicine* 280 (12 June 1969): 1323–1329.

[6] J. H. Knowles, *Ibid*, Part I, *New England Journal of Medicine* 280 (5 June 1969): 1273–1278.

[7] George Revesz, Francis J. Shea, and Marvin C. Ziskin, "Patient Flow and Utilization of Resources in a Diagnostic Radiology Department," *Radiology* 104 (July 1972): 21.

the continuing quality performance of the technical characteristics of the human resources: correctness of the diagnosis by the physicians, effectiveness of the regimen, quality of nursing care, wholesomeness of hospital diet, and so on. Taken as a whole, we can state that the technology performance characteristics of the hospital operations are in fact in a stable technology.

Requirements of Forecasts for Decision-Making

Given that the environment is one of reduced risk and that the technology is stable, what types of forecasts are needed from the MIS (IIS) in support of the hospital administrator?

Health improvement index expectation

No matter what particular type of hospital is considered, the prime criterion of any service facility is the effectiveness of its service. Health being personal, the index of performance of the hospital must take into account the individual evaluation of each instance of service. The improvement in health also is personal, depending upon the individual, his prior condition, and the circumstances which are unique to each incidence of hospital stay. What should the hospital administrator require from the MIS (IIS) which is designed to support him in the control of the activities of the hospital?

Earlier we indicated the three elements of the index of relative improvement in the health of the patient: (1) patient evaluation, (2) hospital evaluation, and (3) hospital-days. What the administrator requires is the *rate of change* in the index of health improvement. So long as the index is maintained at a specific level, it would mean that the administrator does not need to intervene. On the other hand, if the rate of change reflects more than minor variation, then the administrator should be alerted to the possibility that significant changes may be occurring in one or more of the principal elements comprising the Health Improvement Index. He would want to set up his own guidelines for action; he requires not only the recording of past values of the Health Improvement Index, but also the *forecast* of where, at this rate, the index is headed. The MIS (IIS) therefore should answer the hospital administrator's question: At this rate, what is the expected value of the Health Improvement Index?

Diagnostic facilities expectation

The Health Improvement Index indicates the acceptability of the "product" that the hospital produces, or the "service" that the hospital

235

renders. Supporting the flow of service are the twin facilities of diagnosis and prescription. In order to control the quality of output, the administrator should be able to exercise control through the two main inputs of diagnostic facilities and prescriptive facilities. We have referred to the increasing demand for one of the diagnostic facilities, i.e., the radiology department, which is rising at a faster rate than the supply of qualified technical manpower. Nor is the situation peculiar to radiology. Other departments are also in similar situations. Therefore, the pressure is upon the administrator to make sure that the diagnostic facilities (and prescriptive facilities) are utilized as efficiently as possible. Based on simulation studies of radiology departments, it would be apparent that if the utilization of the radiology department is increased, then it would serve to reduce patient waiting time, which is a continuing source of dissatisfaction. More importantly, improved utilization of diagnostic facilities would suggest that the diagnostic process is carried out on a timely basis, enabling early diagnosis, which, even if it were to be only one day earlier than at present, that itself can mean a possible decrease in the number of hospital days of the patient, for whom every day counts.

The MIS (IIS) should therefore answer the question of the hospital administrator: At this rate, what is the utilization index of the diagnostic facilities?

Prescriptive facilities expectation

The output of the diagnostic facilities serves as input to the prescriptive facilities. It is one thing to have the radiologist take the X-rays; it has to get to the attending physician on time before the X-ray can be interpreted. Even if the X-ray were made today, if it does not reach the attending physician before his rounds of the wards tomorrow evening, then the utilization of the diagnostic facilities will have not borne fruit in possibly reducing the number of hospital days for the patient through early diagnosis and prescription. Therefore, the utilization ratio of facilities should be considered not only separately, as diagnostic and prescriptive facilities, but also *jointly* as a diagnostic-prescriptive facilities system.

The utilization of prescriptive facilities refers not only to the number of hours of work performed by the prescriptive staff, but also to the quality of the prescription that they make. As diagnostics becomes highly specialized, and the literature on the specialized knowledge is far-flung, the efficient utilization of prescriptive facilities must reckon with the access that the prescriptive facilities have to the latest diagnostic research.

The path from research abstract to diagnostic aids is by no means direct or easy. Even when such diagnostic aids are available, they would probably be out of the reach of the physician in remote parts of the country. It is clear that the idea of a computer utility, similar to the notion of public utilities like telephone, telegraph, electricity, gas, etc., is particularly appropriate. If the diagnostic aids are available on a fee-for-use basis whenever and wherever needed, it would mean that the physician in the remotest parts of the country would be able to gain access to the diagnostic devices. All that he needs would be a computer terminal which he can use as he would a typewriter. Such access is parallel to the use of a switch to turn on electric current which is maintained at the appropriate pressure at any time of day or night, so that a single flick of the switch puts the world of electricity at one's command.

The MIS (IIS) should answer the question of the hospital administrator: At this rate, what is the utilization index of the diagnostic and prescriptive facilities? The answer should incorporate not only the utilization of the working hours of the prescriptive resources (physicians) but also their access to diagnostic devices and the use of the medicine-dispensing activities of the hospital.

Raw Data Requirements of Hospital Care Delivery MIS (IIS)

The types of raw data required depend upon the forecasts that are to be made.

Raw data on health improvement index

The use of the data created at the first demand made upon the hospital by the patient is subject to continuing research to identify better methods of utilization. The tendency is toward automation, to make it possible to minimize errors and maximize diagnostic and prescriptive activities. Ideally, the notes made by the physician must be preclassified in terms of diagnosis and prescription. They should provide for alterations in the diagnosis and prescription, and should specify the particular diagnostic tests that need to be performed upon the patient.

Invariably, the patient record is limited to the *hospital* evaluation of the patient at the time of entry. It is not customary for it to show the *patient* evaluation of his own status. However, we saw earlier that provision must be made for the patient evaluation at the time of entry and exit, so that the hospital evaluation of the patient at these same times can be used as an "objective basis" for the evaluation of the "subjective" basis of the patient evaluation. Incorporation of this particular piece of raw data is not at all difficult, because one of the first questions asked by the physician is: How do you feel today? For our purposes, what we need is the question: How well are you able to perform your normal activities?

Since 1967, the Department of Medicine at Massachusetts General Hospital and Harvard Medical School have used a near-English, user-oriented interpretive programming language, which has reportedly excellent capabilities for data base management in a remote-access, multi-user, time-sharing environment, called Massachusetts General Hospital Utility Multi-Programming System (MUMPS).[8,9] MUMPS is patterned after JOSS, a high level interpretive language developed at the Rand Corporation in 1964 by J. C. Shaw.[10] According to the director of the Laboratory of Computer Science, which is the joint research and development unit of the hospital and Harvard:

Since 1967, MUMPS has been used exclusively for all computer activity of the MGH (Massachusetts General Hospital) Laboratory of Computer Science in both research and development and in operational patient care systems. All application programs are written in this language and run in the MUMPS time-sharing environment. The commitment of the Laboratory is the development of a medical information system that is incorporated in the ongoing daily functioning of the hospital through the creation of a series of modules that are linked together to form an expanding data base of patient medical records. The specific areas of application were selected on the basis of:

A. Presumptive impact on improving patient care, by facilitating information processing activities considered to be important (and often onerous) by the professional staff;
B. Feasibility for rapid development of a workable and reliable computer-based system; and
C. Potential for transferability of the completed program or technique to other medical facilities and to private industry.

The modules which are operational involve information processing activities concerned with:

A. Clinical laboratory data processing (chemistry and bacteriology);
B. Ordering and preparation of intravenous medication mixes;
C. Ambulatory care medical records;
D. Management and interpretation of data on patients in acute respiratory failure;
E. Automated medical history acquisition;

---

[8] G. Octo Barnett and Robert A. Greenes, "High-Level Programming Languages," *Computers and Biomedical Research* 3 (1970): 488–494.

[9] Morton Ruderman and A. Neil Pappalardo, "The Hospital Computer Comes of Age," *Computers and Automation* 19 (June 1970): 2–6.

[10] J. C. Shaw, "JOSS: A Designer's View of an Experimental On-Line Computing System," 1964 Fall Joint Computer Conference, AFIPS (Rochelle Park, N.J.: Hayden Publishing Company, 1964).

F. Management of clinical data in the Intensive Care Unit.

Modules still in the development stage include:

A. Data management involved in ordering, administering, and charting all medications;

B. Radiology scheduling, x-ray folder inventory, and radiology reporting;

C. Problem-oriented medical records in a Nurse Practitioner Clinic.[11]

Module C is "Ambulatory Care Medical Records." It is a universal data requirement. The Laboratory of Computer Science and the Harvard Community Health Plan (HCHP), which is a prepaid group plan, have worked together on the medical records system which has been in operation since November 1969. At present, data on 22,000 patients are kept by the system.

According to the Laboratory:

Thus two types of data are available within the system. The integrated record of a single patient is used by the health care professional in the daily patient care activity. The aggregate data are used to produce statistical reports for the administrators for accounting and long range planning. Both types of information are available to the health care researcher for medical audit and epidemiological studies.[12]

If the final status report of the patient shows that the patient is discharged, then we need an additional index of how the hospital evaluates the status of the patient, i.e., the estimate by the hospital of the ability of the patient to resume pre-admission activities. We also need the patient evaluation of how much activity he has been able to resume after a week or two, so that the two evaluations may be compared. Incorporating the hospital's evaluation of the patient's capability to resume normal activities should be relatively simple. The patient should report on his post-discharge status by mail or phone if a personal visit is difficult or judged to be unnecessary.

Raw data on facility utilization

Barnett indicates radiology scheduling as one of the modules still in the development stage as of 1973. Of course, the scheduling of X-ray facilities is only a part of the problem of diagnostic facilities utilization. Other

---

[11] G. Octo Barnett, "The Modular Hospital Information System," in Bruce Waxman, and Ralph W. Stacy (eds), *Computers and Biomedical Research* 4 (1973), pp. 13–14.

[12] Massachusetts General Hospital, and Harvard Medical School, "Laboratory of Computer Science" (Boston, Massachusetts, 1972), p. 6.

equipment in radiology and other laboratories must be scheduled; not only must the physical resources be scheduled for optimum utilization, but also the manpower resources.

Similar comments apply to the utilization of scarce facilities, including physician time. A number of studies have been made on the problem, and these studies continue. The devising of an appropriate raw data form for the utilization of diagnostic and prescriptive facilities must be responsive to the needs of forecast of the rate of utilization for decision-making by the administrator.

APPLICATION 7
SALE OF PRODUCTS

The delivery of hospital care is part of the larger question of the delivery of health care. Delivery presupposes production. Discussion so far has, however, been confined simply to the delivery process, and that too limited to the hospital. A number of agencies, both public and private, are engaged in the delivery of hospital care but, by and large, they are all not-for-profit operations.

We now move to a private sector profit-making operation characterized by a reduced risk and stable situation. The reduced risk, stable environment, it will be recalled, is a decision-making situation in which the fulfillment characteristics can be specified by parameters whose form and content are known; similarly, the performance characteristics of the products and/or services are specifiable within narrow limits.

To make the problem manageable, we will confine our attention to product, i.e., to the exclusion of service. Among products themselves, there are consumer goods and durable goods. An example of the former is hamburgers; an example of the latter is furnitures and fixtures. Our intent is to discuss not a particular product, but a generic product, so that the features of reduced risk and stable technology applicable to a large number of products can be discussed.

In chapter 4, three principal elements of internal data were identified as applicable to an activity generating a product and/or service. These elements were demand factors, supply factors, and profit factors. The demand factors identify the "humanly determined values." We made a distinction between the two types of such values: need-value and want-value. The "humanly determined values" apply to both need-values and want-values. Our present concern is, however, only with *want-values*.

What does the PDM require from the MIS (IIS) on demand factors? He wants to be assured that present customers are satisfied, and that he is taking advantage of the changes in the demand factors to prepare ahead to meet them. It will be recalled that Alfred Sloan, Chairman of General

Motors, introduced the annual automobile model to the American customer, thereby not only anticipating what the customer would want in the next year, but also influencing the customer in his expectation of the "novelties-always-to-come."

The requirement of the forecast is not as wide-ranging in the case of reduced-risk environment. Our reference is to a well-established want-value(s) that is satisfied by a product(s) of the organism. Therefore, the accent is on the preservation of the market by continuing to sell essentially the same product(s) with a minimum of modification.

Turning from the demand factors to the supply factors, the stability in the performance characteristics of the product(s) would require that the first unit of the year be identical in all essential respects of performance with the last unit on the last day of the year. We have often used the example of light bulb manufacturing. The first bulb as well as the millionth bulb will have the same capabilities of performance. If anything, as time goes on, better performance characteristics are achieved by the bulbs. In terms of the mechanism of production, stable technology is one in which the variations between products are so insignificant that they may be considered to be the same for all practical purposes. In other words, the production process is so well established that what comes out of the pipeline can be specified with great precision. When the performance characteristics of a product can be so specified, it stands to reason that advantage be taken of the assembly line method of production. The assembly line concept requires the breaking up of all jobs into small components, and the dovetailing of the components of one segment of the process into the other. Such a process is an excellent candidate for automation, i.e., a continuous stream from raw materials to finished product which runs with such precision that the minor variations can be detected and corrected by machines themselves.

Henry Ford, the originator of assembly lines, recognized the interrelationship between mass production and mass consumption: "The necessary, precedent condition of mass production is a capacity, latent or developed, of *mass consumption*, the ability to absorb large production. The two go together, and in the latter may be traced the reasons for the former." The MIS (IIS) should therefore be one which reflects the forces of both mass production and mass consumption. To consider the problem comprehensively, a number of elements should be incorporated, such as advertising of the wares, both to create want-values and to induce the customer to try the products of the organism; scheduling of the production facilities, both human and mechanical; management of inventory of products to meet the demand of customers expeditiously, and to reduce the finished goods waiting in warehouses for customer orders to materialize; scheduling of distribution facilities to move goods from production locations to locations of consumer demands, etc. For the present, we shall concentrate on an aspect of demand factors, viz., the elements of MIS (IIS) which assist the PDM in assessing the market for the products in the immediate future.

Reduced Risk of Environment, and Stability of Technology

We have classified the fulfillment characteristics of the sale of durable products as being in the reduced-risk environment and stable technology. What is the reduced risk, and what is the stable technology?

Reduced-risk environment

The fulfillment characteristics, i.e., the capability of the products to satisfy the demand for them, are not only known, but they can also be specified in terms of probability distributions whose form and parameters are known. What are the underlying factors of the phenomenon which make possible the specification of the fulfillment characteristics?

The stages of growth vary from product to product, and from industry to industry. Anything which is born, dies. Before it dies, it declines; and before it declines, it matures. Before maturation, it is likely to experience a stage of rapid growth, which follows the period of infancy. The seven distinct stages of life are applicable to any phenomenon, whether it be product, service, or relationship, so long as it gets born. Before birth comes the gestation period which, in the case of products like color television, is the research and development (R&D) stage. In chapter 5 the life cycle stages of growth were identified as a means of weighting the available data on any phenomenon. We will discuss here the general method of exponential smoothing applied to the life cycle stages of growth of the fulfillment characteristics of the products on sale.

FORECASTING IMPLICATIONS

What are the implications for product sale of the life cycle stage-of-growth point of view? For one thing, it forces the organism to *anticipate* the next stage in the product's life cycle on the basis of present knowledge. For another, given such knowledge of the coming stage of growth, there are actions that ought to be taken by the organism.

The fulfillment characteristics which the decision-maker is interested in pertain not just to product P_1, or its substitute replacement, product P_2. He will have a line of products, say 5 or 10, or 100 or 1,000. In the choice of the products, the principal guiding criterion is that there be some complementarity of demand: that Product 1 *and* Product 2 may share the same or similar fulfillment characteristics. In fact, the products could even be competing with each other. The risk is the investment that he has to make in the increased production of the products on the assumption that either the present product will have experiences similar to the one which he knows, or experiences different from the one which he knows.

The rapid growth stage is not the only stage that the decision-maker is interested in. He also wants to know ahead of time when the change from rapid growth to maturation will take place, lest he overproduce and consequently build up a sizeable inventory which would remain unused for a long time to come.

A new implication arises with respect to the *product portfolio* of the organism. It is no longer the single product, but a *group of products* moving from one stage to the other, responding to which requires the inventiveness of the decision-maker. He requires not only the knowledge of the individual life cycle stage of each product, but also the group life cycle stage. Further, he needs to know how the present product portfolio fares with respect to the fulfillment characteristics. Is his product line as a whole in the rapid growth stage? In that case, if he looks simply at the total number of units sold or the total dollar volume of sales, he will be in for a rude awakening; buoyed by the rapid growth stage, the *present* volume of sales would be high, leading him to hope that it will continue. However, the logic of the life cycle demands that whatever is in one stage passes on to the next stage sooner or later. If the products are in the rapid growth stage, the next stage happens to be that of maturation followed by decline. His sales will decline in the declining stage, but by then it will be too late to find replacements for the products that are now declining in their ability to fulfill the want-values of the market. He should have started long ago to bring in new products to take the place of those which are phasing out.

MEASUREMENT OF FULFILLMENT CHARACTERISTICS
AGGREGATE SALES OF PRODUCT I. How well are the products satisfying the want-values of the market? The satisfaction is *at a price*; the demand for the product is not an absolute demand, but a relative one—relative to the price per unit. Therefore, a direct measure of how well a product satisfies the demands of the market is an index of quantity and price.

One could consider the number of units of the product sold, because the number of units have been sold at the given price. Thus, if 100,000 units of a product, P_2, are sold at a given price, compared with 50,000 units of a competing product, P_1, then P_2 may be said to be twice as effective as P_1 in its fulfillment characteristics, provided the prices are nearly the same and the market profile is also sufficiently similar.

There is one danger in the inspection merely of the *total* quantity sold. That danger comes from the fact that it does *not* differentiate between the different want-values of the market itself. Different people buy the same product for different reasons, i.e., there are different want-values which are satisfied by the same product in different market segments. The function of advertising is to convince the different market segments that the given product will satisfy its particular want-value. The want-values themselves are subject to the logic of the life cycle, i.e., they too grow, mature, and decline. Therefore, it behooves the decision-maker to know how the fulfillment characteristics perform in the different segments of the market, with respect to the different want-values which are sometimes created through advertising, but always sought to be sustained by advertising.

The decision-maker must therefore *weigh* the contribution that the particular market segment makes to the total demand for his product by the stage of life cycle of the particular market segment. Consider the case of Product Group I, the total sales of which in the year Y_1 are about 24 million units. Data for years Y_1–Y_7 are available. A five-year plan comprising years Y_8–Y_{12} has to be developed for submittal to the executive vice-president for approval.

A major component of Product Group I is Product I which alone accounted for 17 million units out of the 24 million in year Y_1. In order to chart a course for Product Group I, the performance of *Product I*, i.e., the segment of Product Group I represented by the market for Product I, would be of great value. As it turns out, the market for Product I is not homogeneous, but heterogeneous. Therefore, we repeat the process and identify the particular major market segment of Product I, just as we went ahead establishing the market segment for Product Group I. Customer Industry I has been purchasing between two and three million units of Product I during the years Y_1–Y_7. During the same period, Customer Industry II demand demonstrated a phenomenal rise from 40,000 units to about 1.5 million units. These are shown in Figure 8.1.

The sale of Product I to any segment of the United States economy can be identified using the SIC code. Division A comprises agriculture, forestry, and fisheries; Division B, mining; Division C, contract construction; Division D, manufacturing. Since we are confining our attention to a product instead of a service, the product in this case is being sold to components of Division D. Major groups 19–39 are components of Division D. Major Group 19 consists of Ordnance and Accessories establishments; Major Group 20, Food and Kindred Products; and so on until Major Group 39, Miscellaneous Manufacturing Industries which are not classifiable under any of the preceding establishments.

The extent of satisfaction derived by the respective customers from the purchase of Product I can be measured by the fraction that the total purchase value of Product I represents in the total purchase of similar items by the customer industry. Thus, if Product I is purchased as an input to manufacture some other products, the denominator would be the total expenditure on similar inputs. Measuring the vital nature of the want satisfied by Product I, it is important to notice how the significance of the product in the total purchases of the industry itself changes over successive time periods. It is important also to know the contribution of Product I to

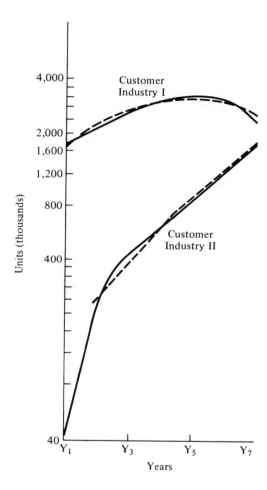

Figure 8.1

Industry Group V_1, of which the Customer Industries V_{11}, V_{12}, V_{13}, V_{14} are components.

We note in Table 8.1 that in the Year Y_1, 22.8 percent of the total sales of product I was made to Industry Group V_1. The corresponding fraction in the year Y_2 was 26.2 percent, and in Y_3, 26.9 percent. How were these sales distributed among the components of the major industry group?

Customer Industry I was sold 14.3 percent of the total Product I sales in the Year Y_1, and in the next two years, 15.5 and 16.0 percent, respectively. Customer Industry IV purchased 5.7, 5.6, and 5.5 percent of the total sales of Product I in the three years; Customer Industry II—1.7, 3.3, and 4.0 percent; and Customer Industry III—1.1, 1.8, and 1.4 percent. It is these percentages that determine the V-Index for the four Customer Industries,

245

since they are all components of the industry group satisfying the most vital need V_1.

Turning to the importance attached to the purchase of product I by the industries it serves, we find that more than a fifth of the total sales of the product to Industry Group V_1—food and kindred products—represented only 0.009 percent of the total purchase of products similar to Product I by Major Group 20. The next year, Y_2, 26.2 percent of the total sales of Product I was made to Major Group 20, but this represented only 0.011 percent of the total purchase of kindred products by the industry. Similarly, in the third year, 26.9 percent of the total sales of product I represented only 0.013 percent of the total purchases of kindred products by Major Group 20.

What is the story that emerges out of these different measurements? (1) The sales of Product I to Major Group 20 are an important constituent of the sales of Product I. (2) While the absolute magnitudes of the purchase of Product I by the Major Group 20 are nominal, the relative direction is consistently upward. (3) Customer Industry I is the most important constituent of Major Group 20 as far as sales of Product I by the organism are concerned. Since the sales of Product I to Customer Industry I represent two-thirds of the sales to Major Group 20, the possible course of future sales of Product I to Major Group 20 can be gauged from the trend of sales to Customer Industry I. (4) The downward trend of sales of Product I to Customer Industry IV, as well as the vacillation in the sales to Customer Industry III, are more than offset by the upward trend in Customer Industry I and II purchases of Product I. (5) Significance of sales to other industry groups, similar to Major Group 20, has to be determined in order to chart the probable course of Product I sales—particularly because only a little over a fifth of sales is accounted for by the sales of Product I to Major Group 20.

What has been the significance to the organism of the total product sales? We find from Table 8.2 that the dollar value of the sales of Product P represented about 13 percent of the total sales revenue of the organism. It probably means that the product is one of the seven or eight major contributors to the total revenue of the organism; it definitely means that the contribution of Product P to the organism is approximately one-eighth to one-seventh of the total sales. In order to make the percentages of contribution to organismic sales by different products comparable, we may want to weight the percentage of the product sales in the total by its rate of growth.

Thus, in the year Y_1, Product P sales were 91.7 percent of the sales in the year Y_0. Multiplying the 13.5 percent that Product P sales contributed to the total sales of the organism in year Y_1 by the rate of growth between the periods Y_0 and Y_1, 13.5×91.7 percent, we obtain the weighted percentage of growth as 12.4 percent. Similarly, weighting the 13.5 percent fraction for the year Y_2 by the growth between years Y_1 and Y_2, 143.7 percent, we obtain a weighted percentage of sales of 19.4 percent. Similarly, for the

Table 8.1: Illustrative empirical elements of V-Index of Product I presumably sold to four customer industries in Major Group 20

V-Index Measures	Time (Year)			Direction
	Percent, Y_1	Percent, Y_2	Percent, Y_3	
V_1 — FOOD AND KINDRED PRODUCTS				
Product I Sales to Major Group 20				
Major Group 20 *total* purchases of kindred products	0.009	0.011	0.013	↑
Product I Sales to Major Group 20				
Total Product I sales	22.8	26.2	26.9	
V_{11} — CUSTOMER INDUSTRY I				
Product I Sales to Component I of Major Group 20				
Major Group 20 Component I's *Total* Purchase of kindred products	0.049	0.064	0.078	↑
Product I Sales to Component I of Major Group 20				
Total Product I sales	14.3	15.5	16.0	
V_{12} — CUSTOMER INDUSTRY IV				
Product I Sales to Component IV of Major Group 20				
Major Group 20 Component IV's *Total* purchase of kindred products	0.009	0.003	0.004	
Product I Sales to Component IV of Major Group 20				
Total Product I sales	5.7	5.6	5.5	

Table 8.1 (continued)

	Time (Year)			
V-Index Measures	Percent, Y_1	Percent, Y_2	Percent, Y_3	Direction
V_{13} – CUSTOMER INDUSTRY II				
Product I Sales to Component II of Major Group 20				
Major Group 20 Component II's *Total* purchase of kindred products	0.001	0.003	0.004	↑
Product I Sales to Component II of Major Group 20				
Total Product I sales	1.7	3.3	4.0	
V_{14} – CUSTOMER INDUSTRY III				
Product I Sales to Component III of Major Group 20				
Major Group 20 Component III's *Total* purchase of kindred products	0.001	0.003	0.002	
Product I Sales to Component III of Major Group 20				
Total Product I sales	1.1	1.8	1.4	

years Y_3 and Y_4 we have the weighted percentage of growth, respectively, of 11.7 and 12.3 percent. The "raw" percentage of Product P sales for Y_3 and Y_4 are quite close: 12.80 and 12.67 percent. However, since 12.80 percent was the fraction of the total organismic sales in a year when the growth was 91.2 percent, and since 12.67 percent was the fraction of the total organismic sales in a year which had a growth of 102.8 percent, the lower figure represents a higher weighted percentage of sales in the total picture. The purpose of the weighting is to incorporate into the absolute sales figures an appropriate growth factor, so that the contribution of the particular product(s) may be given recognition with respect to not only its absolute sales, but also its stage of growth.

Table 8.2: Fulfillment Characteristics of Product I Sales

Satiability Measure and Significance	*Time (Year)*					
	Y_0	Y_1	Y_2	Y_3	Y_4	Y_4/Y_0
A. Satiability of total *Product P* sales to all customers						
Quantity (Units)	60,684	55,296	79,509	72,570	74,691	
Dollars (1000)	15,323	16,980	22,640	18,350	18,870	
Price elasticity	+1.39		+10.35	+0.56	−0.57	
Percent of growth, quantity	91.7		143.7	91.2	102.8	123.5
Stage of growth						G_2
C. Significance to organism of total product sales						
Percent of organismic sales		13.5	13.5	12.80	12.67	
Weighted percent of sales		12.4	19.4	11.7	12.3	

We see in Table 8.3 that Product I sales to Customer Industry II grew 141.0 percent between years Y_1 and Y_2. The sales in year Y_2 represented 3.0 percent of the total organism's sales. Product I sales to Customer Industry III grew 125.0 percent between years Y_1 and Y_2. Product I sales to Customer Industry III represented 1 percent of the total organismic sales in Y_2. The growth of Product I sales to Customer Industry IV was 142.5

Table 8.2 (continued)

Satiability Measure and Significance	Time (Year)					
	Y_0	Y_1	Y_2	Y_3	Y_4	Y_4/Y_0
B. Satiability of total *substitute* Product SP sales to all customers						
Quantity (units)	32,554	30,046	39,826	26,857	30,809	
Cross-elasticity		+1.20	−7.70	+2.08	+2.86	
Percent of growth, maturity		90.0	132.7	67.3	114.5	94.8
Stage of growth						G_3
D. 1. Satiability of partial product sales to major customer I						
Percent of total product sales		37.4	26.7	26.4		
Percent of total customer purchase						
Percent of product growth				92.1	92.3	
Stage of growth						G_3
D. 2. Satiability of partial product sales to major customer II						
Percent of total product sales		14.5	11.0	8.3		
Percent of total customer purchase						
Percent of product growth				100.7	92.2	
Stage of growth						G_3

percent and its share of organismic sales 0.2 percent. The weighted growth of three segments of Product I are, respectively, 4.2, 1.3, and 0.3 percent. The weighted sales of the three segments of Product I sales by stage G_2 is the sum of these weighted percentages of growth of the Product I sales to Customer Industries II, III, and IV, the sales to which of Product I are in the rapid growth stage, G_2.

Table 8.3: Products Satiability Illustrative Empirical Situation: Product I Sales to Customer Industries

Growth Stage	Sales Segment	Growth Rate, Percent	Percent Share of Organismic Sales	Weighted Sales Percent of Segments by Growth
	Product I sales to:			
	Customer Industry II	141.0	3.0	4.2
	Customer Industry III	125.0	1.0	1.3
	Customer Industry IV	142.5	0.2	0.3
Stage G_2	Weighted growth rate by stage G_2			5.8
	Product I sales to:			
Stage G_3	Customer Industry I	93.0	5.4	5.0
	Weighted growth rate by stage G_3			5.0

We also find that Product I sales to Customer I declined between years Y_1 and Y_2, the rate of growth being 93.0 percent. In the year Y_2, Product I sales to Customer Industry I represented 5.4 percent of the total sales of the organism, which, when weighted by the growth rate of Product I sales to Customer Industry I, becomes 5.0 percent.

In this illustrative empirical situation, we find that Product I sales to Customer Industries II, III, and IV are in the stage of rapid growth, and Product I sales to Customer Industry I are in the maturation stage. If these were the only customers for Product I sales, we find that the weighted growth rate in the rapid growth stage is almost nearly equaled by that in maturation.

AGGREGATE SALES OF PRODUCTS I, II, III, IV, V, AND VI. We pointed out earlier that the implications of the life cycle point of view to the decision-maker require the assessment of the stage of growth of his product line *as a whole*. It is not one product, or two products, or the important market segments of one product or two products that the decision-maker is concerned with; instead, it is the product line as a whole, and the important market segments of the product line as a whole.

We now turn from the consideration of a single product, Product I, and look at the fulfillment characteristics of six products of the organism. We find in Table 8.4 that Product I is in stage G_2; there are other customers, outside of Customer Industries I, II, III, and IV, the sales to which are a standoff in growth. The total sales of Product I represent 19.0 percent of the total sales of the organism. Product II sales amount to 0.2 percent of the organism's sales; Product III, 3.6 percent; Product IV, 4.3 percent; Product V, 0.8 percent; and Product VI, 26.1 percent. It should be noted that the total fraction of the organismic sales represented by the sales of these six products is not 100 percent, but only 54 percent. In fact, these six products constitute a Product Group of the organism. When the respective contributions of the products to the total organismic sales are weighted by the respective growth percentages, we find that the products representing 54 percent of the total sales are equivalent to 66.0 percent of weighted sales.

In Figure 8.2 the weighted growth rate percentages by stage are shown in diagrammatic form. In the empirical situation, G_2 and G_3 predominate. When a product enters G_3, it should have its replacement from research and development ready, while a product entering G_4 should have immediate replacement from research and development. Since the research and development process takes time, the replacement for the products entering stages G_3 and G_4 should be initiated sufficiently early, allowing for the time lag.

PERIODIC TABLE OF PRODUCT DIVERSIFICATION. How can the decision-maker visualize the performance of the product line *as a whole*? He needs to know how each product is performing in terms of its fulfillment characteristics. He needs to know how each major segment of the market for each

Table 8.4: Products I, II, III, IV, V, VI Sales

Growth Stage	Products	Growth Rate, Percent	Percent Share of Organismic Sales	Weighted Growth by Product
Stage G_1	Product II	67.6	0.2	0.1
	Weighted growth rate by stage G_1			0.4
Stage G_2	Product I	113.5	19.0	21.6
	Product III	137.6	3.6	4.9
	Product IV	200.8	4.3	8.6
	Weighted growth rate by stage G_2			35.1
Stage G_3	Product VI	115.3	26.1	30.1
	Weighted growth rate by stage G_3			30.1
Stage G_4	Product V	91.1	0.8	0.7
	Weighted growth rate by stage G_4			0.7
	Total		54.0	66.0

product is performing. He needs to know how the group of products which satisfies essentially the same fulfillment characteristic is performing. He needs to know how his product portfolio as a whole is performing with respect to the life cycle stage, so that he may bring reinforcements from research and development to replace products which are phasing out and to step up production of products entering the rapid growth stage.

The question that the decision-maker asks is: What products are feasible from the marketing point of view?

A similar question was posed in the 1870s: What "elements" are structurally feasible? Dimitri I. Mendeleyev formulated the Periodic Law of chemical elements, the ingenuity and skill in formulating which depended upon the discovery of a particular *structural arrangement*. The structure runs in terms of the properties that the chemical elements should satisfy. On the basis of his insight into the particular properties which are of the essence in distinguishing one element from the other, he was able to develop a table, the Periodic Table, whose contribution was in identifying

Figure 8.2

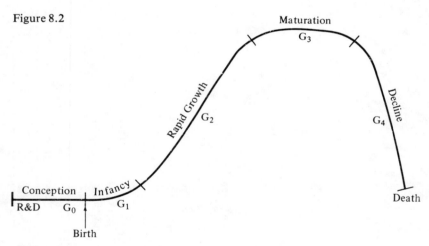

Share of Sales:

Stage G_1 0.1%
Stage G_2 35.1%
Stage G_3 30.1%
Stage G_4 0.7%

In the Empirical Situation:

1. G_2 and G_3 predominate.
2. Product entering G_3 should have *ready* replacement from R&D
3. Product entering G_4 should have *immediate* replacement from R&D.
4. Allowing for time lag, R&D replacement program should have started X years ago.

elements which "ought to be" in the missing cells: Mendeleyev found that by changing 17 elements from the positions indicated by their atomic weights which had been accepted for them into new positions, their properties could be correlated with those of other elements. Mendeleyev was also able to predict the existence of many of the properties of undiscovered elements.

We can apply the logic of the Periodic Table to answer the question: What products "ought to be" offered by the organism? We attempt an answer through the arrangement of the cells of a table which reflects the profile of the fulfillment characteristics of the entire portfolio of products of the organism at a given time. Table 8.5 presents the Periodic Table of Product Diversification. The great usefulness of the periodic table is that it provides for *preventive investment* in R&D ahead of time in such a way that the "death" of the organism, or its components, is possibly prevented. Its strength is derived from the fact that all the component elements are empirical and relate to both sides of the coin, the fulfillment characteristics of the products on the one hand, and the want-value of the customer as reflected in the purchases of the product on the other. The periodic table seeks to emphasize that it is the successful satisfaction of want-values that will ensure the successful operation of the organism. The table underscores an often neglected fact of alternative sources of want-value satisfaction, sometimes provided by the same organism in competition with some other outputs of its own. Should there be a perceptible movement toward the substitute products (either its own or that of other products), the organism can be protected early through the periodic table and manage to foster such shifts in demand to its own advantage.

Stable technology

We can characterize the production of durable products considered in this section as being in the stable technology category.

It is clear that stable technology is obtained in products which have been made and sold for several years. The inspection ratio becomes smaller and smaller with the increase in production experience.

Not all the products of the organism are necessarily products of stable technology. For instance, new products and novel products must be experimented with in order to develop replacements for products which mature and decline. The experimental products will require inspection ratios to be greater than zero.

However, the experimental products are but a very small percentage of the total production of the durable goods manufactured. Taken as a whole, we can say that the performance characteristics of the durable goods production are in fact in a stable technology.

Requirements of Forecasts for Decision-Making

Given that the environment is one of reduced-risk and that the technology is stable, what types of forecasts are needed from the MIS (IIS) in support of the sales PDM?

Index of fulfillment characteristics expectation

No matter what particular type of product is considered, the prime criterion of any product sales organization is the continuance of the expectation on the part of the customers that the products will in fact fulfill the want-values of the customer. The continuance of customer demand depends upon the satisfaction that the customers have derived from present and past performances of the product(s) to fulfill want-values. Of course, the want-values themselves are subject to change, with no reference to the performance characteristics of the products themselves. The composite of all the various pressures upon the demand for the product to satisfy the want-values is reflected in the sales figure. What is of interest to the decision-maker is *not* what the past sales have been (although that is of interest to him), but what the *future* sales will be of the particular product. The question that the MIS (IIS) should answer is: At this rate, what is the expected index of fulfillment of the want-values by the product(s)? The same question can be answered (1) in the aggregate (relating to *all* the products), (2) or on an individual product-by-product basis with regard to (3) the market segments of the major products and (4) the market segments of a single product.

Index of future life cycle stage

The expected value of the fulfillment characteristics would indicate how well the product line is serving to meet the want-values of the customer. The measurement could be in terms of the expected share of the market and the actual share of the market; or it could be in terms of the actual return on investment of the particular organism versus the rate of return for the industry of which the particular organism is a part. In any event, the measurement is an evaluation from the *outside* of what the product is doing with respect to the want-values which seek satisfaction from the product.

Now we turn to the evaluation from *inside* to satisfy the want-values. To meet the demand from outside, production by the organism has to be stepped up. That depends upon the particular stage of growth of the product, and its present relative size in terms of the quantity of units produced. The question that the MIS (IIS) should answer is: At this rate,

Table 8.5: Periodic Table of Product Diversification

Product Satiability

(1) Stage	(2) Product Name	(3) P_{jk} Product Number	(4) P_{jk} Total Product Sales	(5) P_{jk} Percent of Growth	(6) P_{jk} As % of Total Organismic Sales	(7) P_{jk} Weighted Growth by Product
	P_{01}	P_{01} : Satiability				
		: Significance				
	P_{02}	P_{02} : Satiability				
G_0 : Conception		: Significance				
	P_{03} * * *					
Weighted Growth by Stage G_0						
	P_{11} P_{12}					
	P_{13}	P_{13} : Satiability				
G_1 : Infancy		: Significance				
	P_{14} * * *					
Weighted Growth by Stage G_1						
	P_{21}	P_{21} : Satiability				
		: Significance				
G_2 : Rapid Growth	P_{22} * * *					
Weighted Growth by Stage G_2						
	P_{31} P_{32} P_{33} P_{34}	P_{34} : Satiability				
G_3 : Maturation		: Significance				
	* *					
Weighted Growth by Stage G_3						
	P_{41} P_{42} P_{43} P_{44} P_{45}	P_{45} : Satiability				
G_4 : Decline		: Significance				
Weighted Growth by Stage G_4						

Table 8.5 (continued)

					V_1					
					Y_0 Y_1 Y_2 Y_3 ***					
					V_{11} Customer Industry			V_{12} Customer Industry		
			Want Intensity		Y_0	Y_1	Y_2	Y_0	Y_1	Y_2
(8) SP_{jk} Substitute Product Total Sales	(9) P_{jk} Price Elasticity of Demand	(10) SP_{jk} Cross Elasticity of Demand	(11) SP_{jk} Percent of Growth	(12)	(13)	(14)	(15)	(16)	(17)	(18)
				$\dfrac{P_{01}\text{ sales to }V_{11}}{V_{11}\text{ purchase total}}$	*	*	*			
				$\dfrac{P_{01}\text{ sales to }V_{11}}{P_{01}\text{ sales total}}$	*	*	*			
				$\dfrac{P_{02}\text{ sales to }V_{31}}{V_{31}\text{ purchase total}}$						
				$\dfrac{P_{02}\text{ sales to }V_{31}}{P_{02}\text{ sales total}}$						
				$\dfrac{P_{13}\text{ sales to }V_{22}}{V_{22}\text{ purchase total}}$						
				$\dfrac{P_{13}\text{ sales to }V_{22}}{P_{13}\text{ sales total}}$						
				$\dfrac{P_{21}\text{ sales to }V_{32}}{V_{32}\text{ purchase total}}$						
				$\dfrac{P_{21}\text{ sales to }V_{32}}{P_{21}\text{ sales total}}$						
				$\dfrac{P_{34}\text{ sales to }V_{12}}{V_{12}\text{ purchase total}}$				*	*	*
				$\dfrac{P_{34}\text{ sales to }V_{12}}{P_{34}\text{ sales total}}$				*	*	*
				$\dfrac{P_{45}\text{ sales to }V_{21}}{V_{21}\text{ purchase total}}$						
				$\dfrac{P_{45}\text{ sales to }V_{21}}{P_{45}\text{ sales total}}$						

Table 8.5 (continued)

	V_2							V_3												
	Y_0 Y_1 Y_2 Y_3 ***							Y_0 Y_1 Y_2 Y_3 ***												
V_{13}	V_{21} Customer Industry			V_{22} Customer Industry			V_{23}	V_{31} Customer Industry					V_{32} Customer Industry					V_{33}		V_{39}
	Y_0	Y_1	Y_2	Y_0	Y_1	Y_2		Y_0	Y_1	Y_2	Y_3	Y_4	Y_0	Y_1	Y_2	Y_3	Y_4			
(19)	(20)	(21)	(22)	(23)	(24)	(25)	(26)	(27)	(28)	(29)	(30)	(31)	(32)	(33)	(34)	(35)	(36)	(37)	(38)	(39)
								*	*	*	*	*								
								*	*	*	*	*								
				*	*	*														
				*	*	*														
													*	*	*	*	*			
													*	*	*	*	*			
	*	*	*																	
	*	*	*																	

what is the expected number of units of the particular product(s) which have to be produced in order to meet the demand for the products?

Raw Data Requirements of Product Sales MIS (IIS)

The types of raw data required depend upon the forecasts that are to be made.

Raw data on fulfillment characteristics

The sales record is a basic raw data input upon which all the forecasts depend. To meet the immediate demand, data on the number and quantity of the type of products have to be collected. However, much more than the mere sales record is required for the MIS (IIS) to be of value to the sales PDM. For instance, he needs to know: (1) the type of customer by SIC classification; (2) the importance of the product-sale to the particular customer industry; (3) the importance of the sale of the product to the organism; (4) the capability of substitute products (whether of the same organism or competing organism) to satisfy the fulfillment characteristics; (5) the life cycle stage of the sales demand of the product as a whole, and (6) with respect to the major customers; and (7) the weighted growth rate of the product portfolio by stages of growth.

In other words, the sales order is only a part of the number of elements required by the PDM. The MIS (IIS) needs raw data on the many different aspects of the sales of the particular product. The particular elements of raw data will vary with the product and time. However, to fulfill forecast requirements, raw data in answer to each of the above mentioned categories and other similar categories must be obtained.

Raw data on comparative organismic performance

In the previous section, emphasis was exclusively upon the experience of a single organism. No organism exists in isolation; in fact, each competes with other organisms in fulfilling identical, or closely similar, want-values. Therefore, if the PDM concentrates only upon the internal forecasts of production and the external indicators of fulfillment characteristics, he would be cutting himself off from a valuable external measure, i.e., the experience of other organisms. As mentioned in chapter 4, several federal publications based on SIC coding do provide comparative measures of performance which the organism can use in the context of other organisms which are part of the same industry. The raw data input to the product sales MIS (IIS) should necessarily include applicable external experiences of comparative organismic performance.

The raw data requirements to enable the forecast on fulfillment characteristics and comparative organismic performance are generic: They are applicable, *mutatis mutandis* (with appropriate changes), to any organism which finds itself confronted with reduced-risk environment and stable technology. The specific new data elements would, of course, vary with the organism and, with time, for the same organism. What has been set out here is simply the basic *types* of raw data which are indispensable to an MIS (IIS) in light of the forecasts that it has to provide the decision-maker.

QUESTIONS

Chapters 7, 8, and 9 deal with MIS (IIS) types: M-Zero, M-Negative, and M-Positive. In chapter 8, the second of the three types was discussed, as well as its application to real-life problems in the public and private sector. The purpose of the following questions is to develop an appreciation for the raw data requirements of MIS (IIS) to provide forecasts for the principal decision-maker (PDM).

A. M-NEGATIVE MIS (IIS)
1. Distinguish between M-Zero and M-Negative contexts of MIS (IIS).
2. What additional data on performance are needed to convert M-Zero into M-Negative?

B. APPLICATION 6
3. Why is an individual-oriented health index necessary?
4. Develop the elements of a numerical index of individual health (in the context of health care production and delivery in the hospital).
5. Why is the health care delivery an M-Negative context?
6. What are the requirements for forecasts for the PDM in the hospital?
7. What types of raw data are available within the Ambulatory Care Medical Records of MUMPS? What additional elements are necessary to develop a medical information system?

C. APPLICATION 7
8. What is the reduced risk and stable technology of durable products sale?
9. What are the requirements of forecasts for the PDM in durable goods production and sale?
10. What types of raw data are required to provide forecasts for the PDM?

9
M-Positive MIS (IIS)

TECHNICAL OVERVIEW / An index of decision-making situations was constructed in chapter 3 as a combination of Context E (for Environment) and Context T (for Technology). When the technology is stable, as in the manufacture of light bulbs, lots of 10,000 can be accepted by inspecting only a small fraction, say, 100 bulbs. If the technology is unstable, the number of units inspected would be far more, every unit being likely to be inspected over and over again. Designating the ratio of total number of units inspected to the total number produced by 10^M, when M is a positive quantity greater than 0, the ratio is greater than 1; for instance, when $M = 2$, $10^M = 10^2$ which is equal to 100, giving an inspection ratio of 100 indicating the repeated inspection of the same production unit(s) as many as 100 times. We characterize this inspection ratio in terms of M—as M-Positive.

When the technology is so uncertain, the decision-maker has no prior applicable probability distribution which he can apply to the *fulfillment characteristics* of his product(s) and/or service(s), i.e., the capability of his product(s) and/or service(s) to satisfy external demands. We combine the uncertainty in Context E and the unstable technology in Context T to designate M-Positive MIS (IIS) situations.

A public sector and a private sector real-life situation are discussed in this chapter to illustrate M-Positive MIS (IIS).

The Employment Act of 1946 assigned to the public sector the responsibility to make up the deficiency in demand for goods and services by the private sector. A quarter century later, the abrupt slowdown in the increased public sector demand for aerospace employment, in a sense, reversed the roles, the public sector becoming the one causing deficiency in demand. Public Law 91-373 reflects the importance of unemployment, in part aggravated by the deficiency in public demand. The law looks at the problem from the point of view of *un*employment in requiring the Secretary of Labor to carry out "a continued and comprehensive program of research to evaluate the unemployment compensation system."

This research into unemployment is put in the perspective of the Department of Labor, whose organismic objective is *employment*. A working definition of the organismic objective is developed. The MIS (IIS) should provide the answer to the question of the Secretary of the Department of Labor: At this rate, what is the expected probability of 96% *employment*; and to the extent that the expected value falls short of the 96%, what is the expected probability of success of corrective measures?

The uncertainty stems from the major change in the character of unemployment. It is no longer the unskilled who becomes unemployed, but the highly skilled as well. The extent of unemployment compensation will depend upon the rapidity with which those with developed skills (as well as unskilled skills) can be reemployed. And the reemployment itself depends upon the private sector. As to the Department of Labor itself, they can only react to the end result in the form of employment, unemployment, or reemployment. The uncertainty comes from the fact that there is no experience applicable to the major changes in the profile of employment, in particular, skilled employment.

A reemployment matrix is constructed which indicates the relationship between reemployment skills and periods: The most highly skilled are reemployed in the area of primary training/experience in the short run; the least skilled being reemployed in the area of tertiary training in the long run; and so on.

What are the requirements of forecasts for decision-making by the principal decision-maker (PDM) who is the Secretary of Labor in this instance?

Since only the employed can become unemployed, the maximum number of man-weeks of unemployment insurance available in the 50 states can be directly related to the changing number of employed in the different states: the ratio of the total number of man-weeks of unemployment insurance to the total man-weeks of unemployment insurance available, i.e., the actual/available ratio. To estimate the expected ratio of actual/available ratio, it is necessary to obtain the transition probabilities from worker (W) to claimant of unemployment insurance, (C), or W-C, as well as C-C, C-W, and W-W.

To construct the appropriate probabilities of transition, reliance has to be placed upon the state records on Continuous Wage Benefits History (CWBH). The Department of Labor issued a guide for the CWBH Program in 1966 for use by the states. There are three basic raw data elements: (1) the Wage Record/Annual Summary Card, (2) Claimant Annual Summary Card, and (3) Master Control Card. Six years later, following the passage of the Public Law 91-373, the Department of Labor sent out a Field Memorandum on October 24, 1972 to determine the current status of the CWBH Data Bank system in each state. The returns indicated that only 6 states record all 14 items of data recommended on the Wage Record Annual Summary Card. With respect to the data on the unemployed worker, only three states collect the data on the 21 items recommended by the Department of Labor, and the 14 items of the Master Control Card are collected by only three states. A detailed breakdown on the status of the CWBH collection by the states is provided. Further, it is found that the number of man-years utilized for the CWBH Program is extremely small, 38 states report utilizing one man-year or less for the CWBH Program.

Even if the minimum of 40 items of data suggested in the Department of Labor Guide for CWBH Bank were collected, that would be inadequate to generate the type of forecast that the PDM would require on the status of unemployment research. The direct basis for the study of the substance of unemployment insurance compensation payments is worker data across a number of years; however, the chances of conducting such longitudinal studies are quite slim on the basis of current CWBH data. In addition to the longitudinal history of *worker* experience, it is necessary to develop the longitudinal history of employment by the different *firms*, so that the possibilities of reemployment in the different firms may be ascertained. Both longitudinal histories can only refer to the visible *results* of underlying technological changes. To anticipate future technological changes, it is necessary to understand the interindustry relationships. These relationships can suggest *changes* over the years in the demand group of industries; these changes can then be translated into potential employment figures. In short, the raw data requirements of the unemployment compensation MIS (IIS) are derived from the impact of future technological changes upon the present profile of employment.

Turning from the public sector MIS (IIS) to the private sector, there is a major difference in orientation. In the public sector, the orientation is the "service"; in the private sector it is the "profit." We make a distinction between a *need*, a basic necessity, and a *want*, not a basic necessity. The service that the public sector renders is fulfilling a *need-value*, which can be distinguished from what the private sector offers to fulfill in the form of *want-values*.

In discussing the role of the *private sector* in maintaining effective employment, i.e., utilizing the skills and capabilities of its own resources most effectively, it should be remembered that without the possibility of profits, the need-values would not be translated into want-values. Thus, the need-value of employment security would do little to induce the private sector to create employment or to maintain it unless such activity can become profitable, in the sense of fulfilling a want-value.

One of the elements of want-values is the number of different ways in which they can be satisfied: which, therefore, give rise to the basis for product differentiation. The differentiation can be real or imaginary because the customer is committing resources for *potential satisfaction* of the perceived want. The basic need for transportation can, for instance, be met by public or private means. However, even in private transportation, several features are offered by competing manufacturers which have very little to do with the basic need for transportation, but has mostly to do with style, prestige, and other factors. The basis for the fulfillment by different manufacturers of the want-values is precisely in the area of nonessential elements in the fulfillment of the need.

The instability in the fulfillment characteristics stems from the private sector process of creating want-values on the basis of need-values. The record of congressional legislation in recognizing need-values has by no means been clear-cut or uniform. Therefore, to the extent that they depend on the need-values, they are governed by the uncertainties of the need-values themselves. Does the passage of the Environmental Act of 1970 mean that electric cars will be made mandatory by early 1980s? Or, should the industry concentrate upon making anti-pollution devices to be installed in present-day automobiles?

Even if antipollution devices were judged to fulfill want-values stemming from the need-values, there are no applicable probability distributions to suggest how the worker who is used to an *assembly-line* production job will perform on a custom-job production of single items. When the manufacturer finds that the number of units of output is comparably less than his production on the assembly line, is the production due to deficiencies in human skills, or instability in the technology itself?

In the context of unstable technology, what types of want-values are most profitable to pursue? With no prior applicable experience the choices become critical: the choices as to what constitutes acceptable need-values and what constitutes possible want-values. From the point of view of effective employment, the most important assets become that of being able to create viable want-values. The prize goes not to the one who creates the want-values, but to the one who is able to satisfy them, and possibly at comparatively lower cost. The more efficient the production, the less will be the unit cost; and the edge in competitive efficiency comes from the human skills which can be put to different uses, rather than from the machines which can produce only the same type of products and/or services.

Combining the major elements, we can say that the forecast that the MIS (IIS) should provide to the PDM must be a combination of three ratios: At this rate, what is the expected value of availability × novelty × adaptability, signifying the capture of the fraction of total available want values, the degree of novelty in the products and/or services, and the capability of the human skills of the organism to adapt to the new demands.

The raw data requirements to enable the forecast of availability, novelty, and adaptability are generic: they are applicable, *mutatis mutandis* (with appropriate changes), to any organism which finds itself confronted with uncertain environment and unstable technology. The specific raw data elements would, of course, vary with the organism and, with time, for the same organism. What has been set out here is simply the basic *types* of raw data which are indispensable to an MIS (IIS) in light of the forecasts that it has to provide the decision-maker.

EXECUTIVE SUMMARY / To determine the information needs of management for decision-making, it is necessary to identify the two major elements that are germane to decision-making. The organism produces a product(s) and/or service(s) to fulfill a demand, which *fulfillment characteristics* will depend in part upon the *technical performance characteristics* of the products and/or services. Effective decision-making should take into account both the characteristics.

All decision-making situations can be divided into three aspects on the basis of the two characteristics. When the technology is stable, as in the case of light bulb manufacture, the number of units inspected to the total number produced would be a small ratio: 100 bulbs/10,000 bulbs. However, in the manufacture of a spacecraft for the first time, not only the whole unit, but also every major component has to be examined several times over, raising the inspection ratio well beyond 1, to 3, or 30, or 40 or more.

When the technology is unstable, as in the case of spacecraft manufacture, the decision-maker has little applicable prior experience on how well the customer wants will be fulfilled by the technical performance of the products and/or services. He does not have a record of how often customers have been satisfied or dissatisfied with the characteristics of the products and/or services or similar products and/or services. He is uncertain.

The combination of *uncertain* environment and *unstable* technology of performance characteristics requires the inspection ratio to be high. If the ratio is expressed as 10^M, M will be greater than 0 in the combination of uncertain, unstable decision-making situations, which we designate as M-Positive.

A public sector problem and a private sector problem are used to illustrate M-Positive MIS (IIS) real-life situations. Both of them pertain to employment.

Public Law 91-373 requires that the Secretary of Labor carry out a "continued and comprehensive program of research to evaluate the unemployment compensation system." The objective of the Department of Labor is employment, not *un*employment. Therefore, to determine the requirements of MIS (IIS), unemployment is put in the context of the objective of the Department of Labor as a whole. The uncertainty in the environment stems from the fact that the unemployed today are not merely the unskilled, but also the highly skilled. Their reemployment depends upon what the private sector will do in order to employ highly skilled resources. The increased demand in the public sector for highly skilled labor for accelerated space effort in the 1960s was abruptly withdrawn in the 1970s. Reemployment of the highly skilled would depend upon the demand for products and/or services which require space-related technology. The private sector works for a profit, therefore, it has to be able to find products and/or services which can use the space technology and which have a market.

Private sector reaction is by no means certain, because there is no parallel to the sudden unemployment of a sizeable segment of scientists and engineers. Of interest to the public sector concerned with unemployment is the capability of the private sector to reemploy the highly skilled unemployed.

Reemployment should take into account the time it takes for the unemployed to find employment. Further, it should take into account the relationships between the pre-unemployment skills and the post-unemployment skills. If a highly skilled person finds reemployment in a highly skilled profession, and both are in the area of his primary training, then it is most acceptable from the point of view of reemployment. If such reemployment occurs in the short term, that would be doubly welcome. A reemployment matrix which incorporates the skill levels in the pre- and the post-unemployment period and the length of time between unemployment and reemployment is constructed.

The basic data available to the Department of Labor come from the records that they keep on employment and on unemployment compensation. The state records on Continuous Wage Benefits History (CWBH) are far from complete. The results of a Department of Labor Survey on CWBH data status are given. Even if the minimum of 40 items of data suggested by the department were available, the labor force experience of a number of individuals in different employment categories of primary-skills training needs to be studied: the chances of conducting such studies with the spotty data are slim indeed.

To answer the question of the principal decision-maker (PDM), who in this instance is the Secretary of Labor, not only must the labor force experience of individuals over a period of time be studied, but also the employment experience of different types of manufacturing and nonmanufacturing companies. Further, the changes in employment come from basic changes in the structure of demand for the products and/or services of a particular industry by all the others. In addition to the experience over time of employment of the individual and of the different employers, we should also study the long-term changes in the structure of the American economy as a whole as reflected in the technological composition of interindustry relationships.

Turning from the public sector MIS (IIS) to the private sector, the question is still one of employment: effective employment of resources by the individual company in the face of major technological changes. The motivation is different: rendering a "service," i.e., meeting basic necessities is the concern of the public sector, while the meeting of a *want* is the concern of the private sector. The difference between a need and a want is the incorporation of factors other than that of the fundamental requirements in meeting a basic need. The need for transportation can be fulfilled either by public or private means. However, the *wants* for prestige, for color, for chromium, etc., are not indispensable to the meeting of the *needs* for transportation itself.

Alfred Sloan, Jr., Chairman of General Motors, introduced the American consumer to the want of an annual automobile model, which differs little from the previous years' model in its capabilities to fulfill the primary need for transportation. Production of obsolescence is by design and the question is: What particular want-values will the customer pay for?

There is a relationship between the need-values and the want-values; to some extent, the embodiment of need-values in congressional legislation can give direction to want-values. The declaration that we need a cleaner environment, does not, however, give rise directly to want-values; they have to be created. Further, the want-values have to be satisfied, and satisfied possibly at a lower cost.

What information does the PDM require to employ his resources effectively? He needs the identification of the majority of viable want-values; he needs to know the necessary minimum element of novelty which will make the want-values operational; and he needs to know the capabilities of the human skills to adapt to the new want values. These three major elements are combined into an index of availability $\times$ novelty $\times$ adaptability.

The raw data requirements are governed by the forecast requirements of

MIS (IIS). In discussing the public sector and the private sector examples, the basic *types* of raw data which can be used by the PDM are identified as indispensable to an MIS (IIS) for the forecasts it has to provide the PDM for decision-making.

From the decision-making situation of reduced-risk environment and stable technology, we now turn to an uncertain environment and unstable technology.

APPLICATION 8
EMPLOYMENT SECURITY

The reversal of the role of the public sector from *curing* demand deficiency in employment to *causing* it has been reflected in recent legislations.

Public Law 91–373

The Employment Act of 1946 stated it to be the policy of the government to secure "maximum" employment; however, the Environmental Act of 1970 put a constraint upon "maximum" employment of resources in the immediate in favor of the long term. Three years later, two opposing forces gave rise to yet another law. On the one hand, the unemployment of human resources due to the discontinuance of the space-generated increase in demand, and on the other, the pressures against increase in industrial employment due to environmental awareness, joined forces to generate Public Law 91–373. The act required the Secretary of Labor to establish a "continuing and comprehensive program of research to evaluate the unemployment compensation system." Unemployment compensation, of course, is an interim relief to a longer-term problem. The real interest is of course, not in unemployment, but in the *employment* of human resources which would make unemployment compensation unnecessary.

What are the requirements of an MIS (IIS) for the Department of Labor services to the unemployed? The problem is broader than that of merely administering unemployment insurance; a "continued and comprehensive program of research" is required by law not merely into unemployment, but, more importantly, into employment itself. If we can state the objective of the Department of Labor, we can then so guide the collection of raw data and the development of forecasts based upon them that they would further, if not fulfill, the objectives of the department.

Transitional probability of employment

"The continuing and comprehensive research" required under PL 91–373 is addressed to the unemployment compensation program. However, in light of the objective of the department to maintain *employment*, the particular aspects of interest will be the *transition* from employment to unemployment, and from unemployment to employment. Department interests in the maintenance of employment will include the impact of technology upon the requirements for skills and for *changes* in skills. If changes in skills requirements can be anticipated, it could help initiate retraining programs to augment current levels of skills in preparation for new skills. Similarly, the forecast of new skills required for the maintenance of employment could assist in the planning for and execution of retraining programs to assist the unemployed at time t to reenter the work force at time $t + \Delta t$, or more generally, $t + k\Delta t$, where $k = 0,1,2, \ldots, n$.

The continuing study of the unemployment compensation program is therefore to actively assist in the reentry of the unemployed into the work force. We may define the organismic objective of the Department of Labor as:

The maintenance of employment of approximately 96% of U.S. citizens able and willing to work by facilitating to update the human capabilities to achieve self-fulfillment through systematic application of the capabilities to produce goods and/or services.

The exercise of human capabilities requires that there be a demand for the resources at a given price for the supply of the resources. The demand is specified, and tends to be increasingly technical with the intensification of technological innovations. Therefore, the objective of updating human capabilities takes *explicit* account of technological changes which requires changes in technical skills. Unemployment, then, becomes the result of imbalance between technological requirements and human capabilities. The MIS (IIS) should provide the answer to the question of the Secretary of Department of Labor: At this rate, what is the expected probability of 96% employment, and to the extent that the expected value falls short of the 96%, what is the expected probability of success of corrective measures?

Uncertainty of Environment, and Instability of Technology

We have classified the fulfillment of the organismic objective of the Department of Labor as being one in uncertain environment and unstable technology. What are the uncertainties and instabilities?

Uncertain environment

The uncertain environment is one in which the fulfillment characteristics do not have an applicable probability distribution. Surely, people have been employed and unemployed for many years and decades, and unemployment insurance has been in force only since the 1930s. Therefore, what is uncertain about the decision-making regarding the unemployment compensation?

The uncertainty stems from the major change in the character of unemployment. It is no longer the unskilled who becomes unemployed. If it were so, public works programs can be considered a means of solving the problem. However, the unemployment resulting from the decision to deemphasize space has been not that of the unskilled but that of the highly skilled. The unknown factor is precisely the nature and magnitude of the developed skills involved in the unemployment picture.

There are several components essential to the determination of the probability of reemployment: (1) the probability of public sector initiation of programs to absorb the supply of developed skills; (2) the probability of private sector initiation of programs in which developed skills can be absorbed, (3) the probability of private sector demand for increased public sector demand for advanced technology (e.g., space technology); (4) the probability of converting public sector technology into private sector products and/or services; (5) the probability of demand for private sector products and/or services utilizing developed skills; (6) the probability of adaptation of developed skills to the changes in private sector demand from those of the public sector; (7) the probability of physical mobility of the highly skilled from public sector facility locations to private facility locations; (8) the probability of timely transition from the public to the private sector, etc.

The uncertainty of decision-making with respect to the unemployment compensation system stems from the lack of applicable experience in some or all of the foregoing probabilities.

Unstable technology

We have characterized M-Positive situations as those in which the environment is uncertain and the technology is unstable. The instability of the technology is with reference to the particular performance characteristics of the products and/or services offered by the organism. What is the instability of the technology with respect to the service offered by the Department of Labor—in particular, with respect to the unemployment compensation system?

The service that the unemployment compensation provides is temporary relief to the unemployed. The object of the relief is to support the unemployed while he relocates himself. This service must, therefore, be considered in terms of *not* the number of people who are paid the unemployment insurance, but rather by the number of people who *outgrow* the need for unemployment compensation.

A physical example of the unstable technology has been the manufacture of semiconductors in the 1960s; the instability was the fact that the manufacturer could not guarantee that the product would fulfill the performance characteristics expected of it. In the present instance, to avoid instability the performance characteristics of the unemployment compensation system need to be specified in terms of the frequency of reemployment of its recipients. Reemployment itself could be characterized with respect to their skills. It does make a big difference whether an unemployed scientist or engineer can get back to the field of his primary training and experience, or if he reenters the labor market, say, as a taxi driver.

SKILLS FACTOR

To pinpoint the performance characteristics of the service rendered by the unemployment compensation system, we may refer to three types of reentry: (1) reentry into the profession of primary skills, (2) reentry into the profession of secondary skills, and (3) reentry into the profession of tertiary skills. This classification takes into account the technological displacement brought about by the discontinuance of the increased demand in the public sector, and takes into account the national reservoir of skills represented in the highly skilled unemployed.

TIME FACTOR

In addition to the type of skills, we should also recognize the timing of the reentry. This is particularly important from the point of view of the unemployment compensation system. The period during which unemployment compensation is paid is fixed by law; and one of the important questions of legislative interest is what changes should be made in the length of the period of compensation.

We can associate the skills factor with the time factor. Since the unemployment compensation system looks at the time factor as the primary category, we can develop a matrix of unemployment compensation periods by level of reentry skills of the unemployed. The short-term primary skills would be the most desirable event, because it means that the highly skilled unemployed worker has been able to relocate himself in the profession which demands his primary skills within a short period. We can make the length of the time segments coincide with the different periods of unemployment compensations, beginning with the thirteen-week period as the short term. The least desirable alternative would be the long-term tertiary skills designating the prolonged period of unemployment compensation payments, at the end or near the end of which the unemployed has to find a make-do job, almost totally unrelated to anything that he has had been trained for or has acquired experience in.

The depiction of the performance characteristics of the service performed by the unemployment compensation system helps to give precision to the notion of unstable technology. Instability stems from the fact that the relationship between the insurance period and the reentry skill levels can by no means be guaranteed.

REEMPLOYMENT MATRIX

The service offered by the Department of Labor is not only for the unemployed with advanced skills, but includes the unemployed with all kinds of skills. Since the classification of reentry levels makes reference only to pre- and post-unemployment, it is a consistent classification which can be applied to any kind of unemployed person. As it stands now, reentry into a profession or job requiring similar skills by a nuclear physicist and by a ditch digger would both be represented by an entry in the cell (short-term, primary skills). We need to differentiate between the levels of training and experience embodied in the practice of ditch digging and of nuclear physics. The technical content of training and experience would be the principal criterion by which ditch digging and nuclear physics would be clearly separated. It would be impractical to incorporate all the different disciplines recognized in the National Roster of Scientific and Technical Manpower, which the National Science Foundation maintained for more than a quarter of a century, for in the National Roster, mathematics has 125 subdivisions and psychology some 50 subdivisions.

The technical content of one's training can be (poorly) approximated by the number of years of post-high school level training. If we consider one year of advanced training to be equal to one year of applicable experience, we shall have an initial indexing of the technological content of the skills. High school level training offers little technical content of comparable degree to that of post-high school training. Therefore, it would be hard to incorporate the high school level training into the technical content of the skills inventory. On the scale that counts as 1 unit a year of *post*-high school training, high school training for a year would count as, say, 0.3; and pre-high school training as, say, 0.1. The numbers are illustrative; they can be changed without prejudice to the principle of *technical content* represented in the skills of the unemployed. The advantage of a numerical scheme is that it permits the comparability of diverse backgrounds and training in a large number of unrelated fields. On the basis of the total number of years of technical content, four classifications appear to be in order: very high, high, medium, and low.

Now, each of the primary skills can be classified into one of the four technical content categories. With three types of skills—primary, secondary, and tertiary—there are (3 × 4 =) 12 skills classifications. Each of the

12 classifications may find reemployment within one of the 12 classifications (12 × 12 =) 144 possibilities, each of which can occur in one of three ways: (1) short term, (2) intermediate term, and (3) long term, making (144 × 3 =) 432 possibilities for the matrix to depict the major categories of reemployment in terms of the length of unemployment insurance payments.

Requirements of Forecasts for Decision-Making

Given that the environment is uncertain and the technology is unstable, what type of forecasts are needed from the MIS (IIS) in support of the unemployment compensation program? We said earlier that the MIS (IIS) should provide the answer to the question of the Secretary: At this rate, what is the expected probability of 96% employment, and to the extent that the expected value falls short of the 96%, what is the expected probability of success of corrective measures? The unemployment compensation system is a small part of the larger question of the 96% employment. It focusses attention upon the 4% or more unemployed.

Expected value of actual/available

Dealing only with the unemployment compensation system, we need to rephrase the organismic objective of the Department of Labor in terms of the strategic objective of the Manpower Administration of the department. Unemployment compensation is by definition an interim measure. Its scope is to cushion transitions. Therefore, a proper objective of the system is in providing the cushion in such a way that the unemployed can make their transition into the ranks of the employed. In other words, the object of unemployment compensation is to make it as short as possible and as small as possible because the recipients have rapidly outlived or overcome their need for unemployment insurance. The maximum period of unemployment compensation payment is fixed by law. Therefore, the shorter the number of weeks that a person receives unemployment insurance, the better will be the achievement of the objective of the system. Treating all unemployeds on the same footing, the number of man-weeks of unemployment insurance payments can be expressed as a fraction of the maximum number of weeks of unemployment insurance available in a year in a given state. Since only the employed can become unemployed, the maximum number of man-weeks of unemployment insurance available in the state can be directly related to the changing number of employed in the state. Modification can be made on a yearly, quarterly, monthly, or weekly basis. No matter how often the data are updated, the ratio of the total number of man-weeks of unemployment insurance to the total man-weeks of unemployment insurance available, i.e., the actual/available ratio, becomes a good measure of the achievement of the strategic objective.

Given the strategic objective of minimizing the actual/available ratio of unemployment insurance, the MIS (IIS) should help answer the question: At this rate, what is the expected ratio of actual to available unemployment insurance?

Expected probability of transition

To answer the question of expected probability of transition, it is necessary to ascertain the probability of someone who is a worker (W) becoming a claimant of unemployment insurance (C). So also, having become a claimant, what is the probability of remaining a claimant (C-C)? Further, it is necessary to determine the probability of a claimant (C) becoming a worker (W), or C-W. Similarly, what is the probability of a worker remaining as a worker (W-W)?

What the raw data should provide is the basis to estimate each of the probabilities. The workers can be grouped into categories of work, levels of skills, length of employment, and so on. By following the history of each worker for a sufficient length of time and for a sufficient number of workers, the percentage of the time that the worker maintained his status as a worker (W-W) or *changed his status* (W-C) can be ascertained on a weekly, monthly, quarterly, yearly, or other time-period basis. If we ignore the entry into the work force of new workers, and the exit from the work force through retirement, permanent disability, permanent change of residence abroad, or death, we can characterize the critical events of interest to the unemployment compensation program as those of *maintaining or changing* one's state of employment, or unemployment, as shown in Table 9.1. The object of the raw data inputs into the unemployed compensation MIS (IIS) is to associate a probability value with each of the four changes of state: (1) worker to worker state (W-W), (2) worker to claimant state (W-C), (3) claimant to claimant state (C-C), and (4) claimant to worker state (C-W).

Raw Data Deficiencies of Unemployment Compensation MIS (IIS)

Currently, even the minimum of 40 items of data suggested in the Department of Labor Guide for Continuous Wage Benefits History (CWBH) data bank is far from uniformly available in the 50 states, District of Columbia, and Puerto Rico. Yet, the CWBH data bank system is considered the basic source to conduct a "continuing and comprehensive program of research to evaluate the unemployment compensation system,"

Table 9.1: Reemployment Matrix

	Primary Training				Secondary Training				Tertiary Training			
	Very High	High	Medium	Low	Very High	High	Medium	Low	Very High	High	Medium	Low
Primary Training												
Very high	S,I,L	S,I,L	S,I,L	S,I,L	S,I,L	S,I,L	S,I,L	S,I,L	S,I,L	S,I,L	S,I,L	S,I,L
High	S,I,L	S,I,L	S,I,L	S,I,L	S,I,L	S,I,L	S,I,L	S,I,L	S,I,L	S,I,L	S,I,L	S,I,L
Medium	S,I,L	S,I,L	S,I,L	S,I,L	S,I,L	S,I,L	S,I,L	S,I,L	S,I,L	S,I,L	S,I,L	S,I,L
Low	S,I,L	S,I,L	S,I,L	S,I,L	S,I,L	S,I,L	S,I,L	S,I,L	S,I,L	S,I,L	S,I,L	S,I,L
Secondary Training												
Very high	S,I,L	S,I,L	S,I,L	S,I,L	S,I,L	S,I,L	S,I,L	S,I,L	S,I,L	S,I,L	S,I,L	S,I,L
High	S,I,L	S,I,L	S,I,L	S,I,L	S,I,L	S,I,L	S,I,L	S,I,L	S,I,L	S,I,L	S,I,L	S,I,L
Medium	S,I,L	S,I,L	S,I,L	S,I,L	S,I,L	S,I,L	S,I,L	S,I,L	S,I,L	S,I,L	S,I,L	S,I,L
Low	S,I,L	S,I,L	S,I,L	S,I,L	S,I,L	S,I,L	S,I,L	S,I,L	S,I,L	S,I,L	S,I,L	S,I,L
Tertiary Training												
Very high	S,I,L	S,I,L	S,I,L	S,I,L	S,I,L	S,I,L	S,I,L	S,I,L	S,I,L	S,I,L	S,I,L	S,I,L
High	S,I,L	S,I,L	S,I,L	S,I,L	S,I,L	S,I,L	S,I,L	S,I,L	S,I,L	S,I,L	S,I,L	S,I,L
Medium	S,I,L	S,I,L	S,I,L	S,I,L	S,I,L	S,I,L	S,I,L	S,I,L	S,I,L	S,I,L	S,I,L	S,I,L
Low	S,I,L	S,I,L	S,I,L	S,I,L	S,I,L	S,I,L	S,I,L	S,I,L	S,I,L	S,I,L	S,I,L	S,I,L

S – Short term
I – Intermediate
L – Long term

required by PL 91–373. Therefore, it is necessary to improve the CWBH data banks in all the states in preparation for building a viable MIS (IIS) for the administration of the unemployment insurance program.

Longitudinal analysis of worker status

The direct basis for the study of the substance is worker data across a number of years. Workers could be classified by skills level as reflected in Table 9.1, or on the basis of more inclusive and exhaustive characteristics. In any event, the labor force experience of very high skilled, high skilled, medium skilled, and low skilled workers needs to be constructed. How long does the worker in each category maintain his status in the profession or job of primary skill? Does he move from the primary skill to secondary or tertiary skill in making a transition in employment? What are the time delays associated with each type of transition? These and other questions reflect the substantive data required to make meaningful decisions on the administration of unemployment compensation.

Raw data requirements for the unemployment compensation MIS (IIS) must specify these decision-making requirements. Judging from the current state of the CWBH data bank, it is clear that the chances of conducting longitudinal studies are quite slim. It may be necessary to develop a composite picture of the employment profile, based upon comparable data by skills categories in the different states.

Longitudinal study of employment by firms

The persistence in the state of being employed or the transition from the state of being a claimant to that of a worker are both contingent upon the existence of employment opportunities. The data on employment by groups of firms, all of which belong to the same category, i.e., 4-digit SIC Code, are available from the Census of Manufactures conducted every five years, and supplemented by the Annual Census of Manufactures. The breakdown into categories may not be suitable for analysis by technical level of content: very high, high, medium, and low. Of course, finer breakdowns under each technical content level of skills will be more than welcome. If statements can be made about types of job categories, it, of course, will be a decided advantage.

Until such data are available, however, the medium of the Annual Census of Manufactures may be employed to determine the *change* in the complexion of the labor force in successive years. This would require data on individual firms, instead of industry aggregates. Change in the fraction of the total employees in very high, high, medium, and low levels of skills from year to year provides a basis against which to compare the labor force experience of the workers in four (or more) categories of skills.

The Department of Labor currently seeks projections of the number of employees in different categories of selected firms. The intent is to identify shifting patterns of employment. It is understandable that the forecast will tend to be conservative, the safest assumption being that things will continue unchanged. Wherever possible, these forecasts should be related to the *actual* changes in the profile of the firms.

The raw data requirement for an unemployment compensation MIS (IIS) must thus include longitudinal history of *worker experience* and longitudinal history of *employment history* of firms.

Input-output analysis

Both longitudinal histories can only refer to the visible results of underlying technological changes. To anticipate future technological changes, it is necessary to understand the interindustry relationships. In 1936, Leontief developed the first interindustry table for the United States, representing the transactions among industrial sectors in 1919. The reason for the input-output table structure was the explicit recognition of the interdependence among industries: e.g., steel being an input to automobiles, iron being an input to steel, pig iron an input for iron, and so on. In subsequent analyses based on the input-output model, the method of "triangulation" has been suggested to identify the groups of industries which generate demand for a given industry. If the industries which generate a demand can be identified, the *changes* over the years in this group would presage technological changes. Such technological changes can be translated into potential employment figures.

In short, the raw data requirements for the unemployment compensation MIS (IIS) are derived from the necessity to incorporate the impact of future technological changes upon the present profile of employment.

APPLICATION 9
EFFECTIVE EMPLOYMENT

Maintenance of the level of employment, it was found in the 1930s, could not be left to the private demand; it had to be supplemented by public demand. Since labor is perishable, in the sense that if not utilized at a given time it is lost forever, Keynes theorized that ways should be found to maintain employment, even if it meant spending more than what is obtained from taxes by the government.

In the 1970s, it is the demand by the public sector which seems to be in need of supplementing by the private sector. The increased demand for employment in the aerospace industry was suddenly brought down significantly. Labor still remains a perishable commodity, therefore the deficiency in the demand—whether it be of the public or the private sector—needs to be made up lest labor go to waste.

Profit Motivation

In the previous section, Public Law 91-373 was referred to as a result of awareness of legislators of the unemployment problem, partly due to the slowdown in the aerospace industry. The motivation is that of rendering a "service" to the public. However, to the private sector, the motivation is not service, but profit. Profit requires customers for the products and/or services that the private sector can offer. Labor is only one component in creating such products and/or services. Peter Drucker points out that the products and/or services are really abstract values:

> The business enterprise produces neither things or ideas but humanly determined values. The most beautifully designed machine is still only so much scrap metal until it has utility for a customer. ...

> Inside and outside the business enterprise there is constant irreversible change; indeed, the business enterprise exists as the agent of change in an industrial society, and it must be capable of both purposeful evolution to adapt to new conditions and of purposeful innovation to change the conditions.[1]

The profit motive of the private sector should therefore be translated into its capability to satisfy "humanly determined values." Such values would be both responsive and adaptive: responsive to the new demand, and adaptive in taking advantage of the willingness to change in the environment.

Production of obsolescence

In one sense, both the public and the private sector are stimulated by values. In the case of the public sector, the values stem from an interpretation of the role of the government in providing the needs of the population. For instance, health has come to be regarded as a *right*, much as the constitutional guarantees of life, liberty, and the pursuit of happiness. In other words, to be healthy has become a *need*: a basic necessity. The Employment Act of 1946 accented the *need-value* of employment security to be guaranteed by the instrumentality of the federal government. Again, the Environmental Act of 1970 reflects another need-value—environmental health, or livable environment—to be guaranteed by the instrumentality of the federal government. In a sense, the incompatibility between the two need-values represented in the acts of 1946 and 1970 is what gave rise to the

---

[1] Peter F. Drucker, *Technology, Management & Society* (New York: Harper and Row, 1970), p. 197.

Employment Security Amendments of 1970: the need-value of employment security, which is a reaffirmation of the need-value in the 1946 act, made necessary by the slowdown in aerospace which, in a sense, can be interpreted as the consequence of another need-value, i.e., clean environment, to work toward which funds have to be diverted from outer space to inner cities.

While the public sector is guided by *need-values*, the private sector is guided by *want-values*. It is guided only to the extent that the private sector is able to create a want-value that it can fulfill, or help fulfill directly or indirectly, the need-values recognized in the public sector. Thus, the need-value of employment security would do little to induce the private sector to create employment or to maintain it unless such an activity can become profitable, in the sense of fulfilling a want-value. The need for a clean environment by no means translates itself into devices to cut down on automobile pollution unless it affects directly the stimulation of and the service to a want-value. If only electric cars can be sold, say, by 1990, then the private sector has to create want-values for different types of electric cars, each of which will fulfill the need-value criteria of clean environment, but *in addition* will serve to meet some *want-values*. If want-values cannot be created, it will be difficult to maintain product and/or service *differentiation*. Without differentiation, there is little possibility of rewards for meeting want-values.

Unlike need-values, want-values are far more variable. In a sense, the difference between them represents a measure of affluence. Since want-values begin where need-values leave off, the success of want-values is highest when they are identified with need-values. Two-car garages become standard equipment when not one, but two, cars are found to be the basic minimum that a family comes to expect as essential for its very existence. More than the *quantity*, want-values trade on the *quality* of differentiation. Both quantity and quality fulfill utility, which is *potential satisfaction*. The potential nature of the satisfaction underscores the fact that satisfaction is not of the essence, but the potential for satisfaction is what is of the essence. In other words, what the private sector should succeed in doing is the creation of the belief in the customer's mind that the product and/or service has the most potential to offer for its satisfaction. The satisfaction is with respect to the customer's perceived want; that want, if created by the manufacturer, can be designed to find fulfillment best in the products that the manufacturer himself offers.

The qualitative nature of the potential satisfaction is the basis for the production of obsolescence. If the same products and/or service can continue to fulfill the want-values of the customer, then the manufacturer has not induced any changes in the want-values so that the customer requires different products and/or services to meet real or imaginary differences in want-values. Change must become desirable *for its own sake*.

The change itself does not have to be real; it can be imaginary. In other words, it is not change that the customer should ask for or be taught to ask for, but the *idea of change*.

Uncertainty of Environment, and Instability of Technology

The first problem examined the uncertainty of environment and instability of technology associated with the need-value of employment security. Can we identify uncertainties and instabilities with respect to the effective employment of human resources in the private sector?

Uncertain environment

As we have observed, the fact of employment itself is well established. Therefore, what is uncertain about the decision-making regarding employment in the private sector? The uncertainty stems from the major change in the character of need-values which form the substratum upon which want-values are constructed.

Need-values have not followed a steady or predictable course. The Environmental Act of 1970 by no means represented public willingness to cut down on the consumption of energy, the unconsumed part of which becomes pollution. On the contrary, the demand for energy has been increasing at a rapid rate. Thus, the need-value, as embodied in the Environmental Act of 1970, proclaims anti-pollution. At the same time, the demand for energy consumption, by its rapid and sustained increase, proclaims pollution. The two are incompatible; the private sector which seeks to create want-values within the framework of need-values will be found in the position of simultaneously running with the rabbits (away from pollution) and hunting with the hounds (contributing to pollution).

To manage its human resources skillfully, the private sector must have means of effectively utilizing its pool of skills in one, or both, of these opposing value-needs, as reflected in the public pronouncement on the one hand, and the public action on the other. Should the private enterprise abandon the manufacture of automobiles, and go into the production of pollution-combatants; or should the private enterprise engage in developing both automobiles *and* pollution-combatant devices for them at the same time? The *specificity* of the skills required in the production of both products and/or services contributes greatly to the uncertainty of the decision-making environment. There is no applicable experience of decision-making *for* and *against* pollution.

Unstable technology

PRODUCTION PROCESS

Effective employment is an instance in which not only is the environment uncertain, but also the technology unstable. The instability of the technology is, of course, with reference to the particular performance characteristics of the products and/or services offered by the organism. What is the instability of technology with respect to profitability in the form of want-values, which are to be created by the organism?

The instability stems from the fact that the "effectiveness" of employment is hard to define, and harder to measure. If an employee who has been producing automobiles were to be switched to producing antipollution devices for smoke stacks, there are two types of instabilities: instability of the state of the art, and instability in the adaptability of the worker. Of the two, the former is more serious. An understanding of the nature of pollution in stationary smoke stacks is essential before appropriate devices to combat the pollution can be fabricated. The difficulty in the definition process is shown by the long delay experienced in even the *initial* specification of the pollution dimensions of just one pollutant—sulphur dioxide. It took more than $3\frac{1}{2}$ years for the government to come up with initial levels of sulphur dioxide pollution that would be the basis for legislation regarding the level that can be generated in industrial processes, such as coal production. The standards were immediately challenged by the coal industry and other manufacturers. If even a single pollutant required prolonged periods for the devising of initial standards, how firmly can the industry develop anti-pollution devices?

MANAGEMENT PROCESS

The emphasis upon the creation of new want-values places the onus more upon the management process than upon the production process. The production process is primarily responding to the promises of potential satisfaction that the management process has created in the minds of the customers.

In the context of unstable technology, what type of want-values are most profitable to pursue? With no prior applicable experience, the choice becomes critical: the choices as to what constitutes acceptable user needs and what constitutes possible want-values. The need to differentiate between need-values and want-values is well illustrated in the experience of Edison who got his first patent for a telegraphic vote-recording machine:

> He had developed this machine while he was reporting the votes of Congress over the press wires, and he noticed the time lost in polling the members for their voice votes. With his invention, at every roll call each

congressman would simply press a button at his seat, immediately registering his vote at the Speaker's desk, where the votes were counted automatically. But Edison's instant vote recorder would have abolished one of the traditionally cherished opportunities to filibuster. "Young man," declared the chairman of the congressional committee to whom Edison had just given a demonstration, "that is just what we do *not* want. Your invention would destroy the only hope that the minority would have of influencing legislation ... and as the ruling majority knows that some day they may become a minority, they will be as much averse to change as their opponents." This taught Edison a lesson that he never forgot; thereafter, as Edison himself noted, he would aim at a "commercial demand."[2]

Boorstin characterizes Edison as a *social* inventor, who would aim at "commercial demand." In dealing with unstable technology, the management process has to be judged in terms of its social inventiveness. The same consideration applies whether it is lunar landing or pollution fighting that is the need-value of the moment. Employment efficiency in the 1960s meant that human resources whose primary training had been electrical engineering, mechanical engineering, economics, psychology, etc., had to be fashioned into an "aerospace team." A mere rechristening would not do the trick; there had to be a reorientation in the collective thinking of the team.

Requirements of Forecasts for Decision-Making

Given that the environment is uncertain and the technology is unstable, what type of forecasts are needed from the MIS (IIS) in support of effective employment of human resources by the organism?

Social inventiveness

As Edison learned from experience, "commercial demand" is the basis of the success of the organism. In our terms, it is the capability to identify present and/or potential want-values. In the context of effective employment, this means matching internal capabilities with external employments, which is the essence of our definition of forecasting in chapter 1.

From the point of view of effective employment, the most important asset becomes not that of meeting a want-value, as much as being able to create such a want-value. This creation cannot be accomplished by mere advertisement. Before advertising can be effectively launched, it is neces-

---

[2] Daniel J. Boorstin, *The Americans: The Democratic Experience* (New York: Random House, 1972), p. 528.

sary to identify the particular want-value which is most likely to succeed. The most important forecast, therefore, that an MIS (IIS) in support of employment effectiveness should provide is: At this rate, what is the expected ratio of success of the actual/available want-values? The presumption is that there are several want-values which may well be identified: one or several of which would lead to the effective utilization of the assets in the form of human skills that are at the disposal of the organism. The ratio of actual/available opportunities for want-values indicates the measure of success in the forecasts that management exercises.

Meeting of "commercial demands"

It is one thing to create want-values; it is quite another to satisfy them. Both the identification of want-values and their satisfaction are competitive efforts. The competitiveness is with other sources which can also satisfy the want-values in a comparable manner. The prize goes not to the one who creates the want-values, but to the one who is able to satisfy them, and possibly satisfy them at comparatively lower costs. The more efficient the production of the products and/or services, the less the unit cost. Efficiency in production requires the assets of human skills to be convertible into the new products and/or services with minimum delay. The delay is a function of the employment heretofore of the particular group of human resources. Taking together the social inventiveness and the capability to meet the demands for new or novel products and/or services, the most advantageous combination is want-values which are most different from current ones, but least different in their production processes from the current set of products and/or services.

Functional adaptability of human skills

The edge in competitiveness comes from the human skills which can be put to different uses, rather than from the machines which can produce only the same type of products and/or services. Therefore, given the need for a change, the degree of success depends upon the rapidity with which current assets can be converted into newer skills. To express this measure, we need to represent the new skill requirement in terms of the old. The degree of overlap in the skills requirements between the old and the new production processes can be used as a direct measure. If the overlap is complete, i.e., 100%, then there is no difference between the production requirements. However, since the idea of novelty is at the heart of the unstable technology, the ratio has to be less than 1, or less than 100%. The adaptability of the human assets skills is expressible in terms of the timeliness of the adaptability. Thus, if the new product and/or service were required in, say, three months and was delivered within three months, then the adaptability can be given an index of 100. However, if the requirement was for delivery within a three-month period but took place within six months, the index of adaptability would be $(3/6 \times 100 =)$ 50. If delivery takes place within twelve months, compared with the three-month requirement, then the index of adaptability is reduced to $(3/12 \times 100 =)$ 25. If, on the other hand, delivery occurs in two months, instead of the requirement for three months, then the index rises to $(3/2 \times 100 =)$ 150.

The more novel the product and/or service, the less will be the degree of overlap, and possibly greater will be the time lag between actual delivery and ideal delivery. If the overlap is 50% and if the delivery is on time, the combined index would be $(.50 \times 1.0 =)$ 0.50. If, however, the overlap is 50%, but completion is ahead of schedule, then the combined index would be $(.50 \times 1.5 =)$ 0.75.

We can use a combined index of novelty-adaptability (NA). The organism's survival depends upon the social inventiveness of the management, which can be applied to as many segments of the human resource assets as possible. It requires a knowledge of both internal capabilities and external requirements. The "available" want-values refer to the maximum number of ways in which the human assets of the organism could be employed with a reasonable degree of retraining. The ratio of actual/available can reflect management's perception of the number of alternatives open to them.

The forecast that the MIS (IIS) should provide to the organism in uncertain environment with unstable technology can be expressed as a combination of all three ratios: At this rate, what is the expressed value of availability × novelty × adaptability?

Raw Data Requirements of Effective Employment MIS (IIS)

The type of raw data should depend upon the type of forecasts that are to be made.

Raw data on availability

Our discussion of want-values has been almost exclusively in terms of need-values formally embodied in acts of Congress. While they do not signify immediate or even remote want-values, they can be useful bellwethers of coming changes in public attitudes on what constitutes minimum levels of public service to which it is entitled and for which it will pay.

From the point of view of the organism, the provisions of congressional legislation do *not* become raw data until they are translated into present and/or potential want-values. From the larger group of want-values, those which are of particular relevance to the organism itself must be isolated.

Raw data on novelty

The basic question underlying novelty is: What *is* novel? As Boorstin puts it:

Ironically, Henry Ford's faith in the Model T was an Old World Faith: a belief in the perfectible product rather than the novel product. And it was his old-fashioned insistence on craftsmanship and function rather than on consumer appeal that eventually left him behind. . . .

"The great problem of the future" Sloan [Alfred P. Sloan, Jr., General Motors] wrote to Lawrence B. Fisher, Maker of the Fisher Bodies, on September 9, 1927, "is to have our cars different from each other, and different from year to year." The annual model, then, was part of a purposeful, planned program. And it was based on creating expectations of marvelous, if usually vague, novelties-always-to-come. . . . The American economy, then, would have to grow by *displacing objects that were still usable.*[3]

The novelty has to be defined quite precisely in terms of the successive generations of products and/or services. It should be expressed to permit the determination of the ratio of overlap between the old and the new product and/or service represented in their respective technology.

Raw data on adaptability

The instability of the technology makes the determination of the adaptability hard. It is hard because today's product would be *un*like yesterday's; and tomorrow's product will be more unlike today's product than today's was with respect to yesterday's. The raw data used to estimate the extent of adaptability of the present human assets to the potential needs of tomorrow have to include the record of past adaptabilities, but must resist the temptation to say that tomorrow will be like yesterday.

The raw data requirements to enable the forecast of availability, novelty, and adaptability are generic: they are applicable, *mutatis mutandis* (with appropriate changes), to any organism which finds itself confronted with uncertain environment and unstable technology. The specific raw data elements would, of course, vary with the organism and, with time, for the same organism. What has been set out here is simply the basic *types* of raw data which are indispensable to an MIS (IIS) in light of the forecasts that it has to provide the decision-maker.

[3] Ibid., pp. 551, 552, 554.

QUESTIONS

Chapters 7, 8, and 9 deal with MIS (IIS) types: M-Zero, M-Negative, and M-Positive. In chapter 9, the third of the three types was discussed, as well as the application to real-life problems in the public and the private sector. The purpose of the following questions is to develop an appreciation for the raw data requirements of MIS (IIS) to provide forecasts for the principal decision-maker (PDM).

A. TYPES OF MIS (IIS)

    1. How can inspection ratio be used to calibrate MIS (IIS)?
    2. Show how both the demand and supply factors are incorporated in the MIS (IIS) categories.

B. EMPLOYMENT QUESTION

    3. What is the implication of large, public sector-sponsored, technological spectaculars?
    4. In the context of unstable technology, how does the motive of profit compensate for the deficiency in public sector demand?

C. APPLICATION 8

    5. What is the real focus of the research on unemployment compensation?
    6. What are the uncertainties and instabilities in the employment question?
    7. What are the requirements of forecasts for the PDM in the Department of Labor?
    8. Identify the limitations of unemployment compensation data.
    9. Discuss the focal point of the MIS (IIS) from the point of view of the PDM.

D. APPLICATION 9

    10. Distinguish between need-values and want-values.
    11. What are the uncertainties and instabilities in the employment question from the point of view of the private sector?
    12. What are the requirements of forecasts for the PDM of the organism?
    13. Compare the raw data requirements of the private sector with those of the public sector.

Part IV
MIS (IIS) Development

10
MIS (IIS) Sequence 1:
From Staff Position to
Dry Run

TECHNICAL OVERVIEW / From the discussion of the types of MIS (IIS) which respond to the combination of different fulfillment characteristics of the environment, and different performance characteristics of the technology—M-Zero, M-Negative, and M-Positive—we turn to the sequence in setting up an MIS (IIS).

Seven steps are identified as comprising the sequence. The MIS (IIS) manager must report to the PDM because it is the PDM who has to use the MIS (IIS) forecasts in his decision-making. Since the forecasts apply to the organism as a whole, and not to an individual department or activity, it is quite likely that the MIS (IIS) recommendations would cut across and override individual departmental considerations. If the MIS (IIS) manager were in a line position, he would be competing for resources with other line managers, each of whose activities he has to assess from the point of view of the PDM. Therefore, the MIS (IIS) manager should be a staff position reporting to the PDM.

The MIS (IIS) manager should identify two or three key areas of performance changes anticipated as a result of the MIS (IIS). These areas should be identified *ahead* of time before the institution of the MIS (IIS) so that the PDM can know well in advance what he is buying in the MIS (IIS).

MIS (IIS) is an agent of change, and change is not usually welcomed. As soon as these areas are identified, the MIS (IIS) manager should work with the appropriate line managers who would be most affected by the changes. Line managers are the ones who could carry out the new ways of doing business, and they are also the source of valuable raw data for the MIS (IIS).

The raw data provided by the line managers must be based on an equivalent return. The MIS (IIS) manager and the line managers should agree clearly ahead of time as to what each is providing the other and receiving in return.

While the input of raw data comes from individual departments, the output, i.e., pre-information as well as information for the PDM, must take into account *all* the departments of the organism. It is not the multitude of printouts that makes the difference, but the few items that the PDM *uses*. Therefore, the MIS (IIS) manager should establish the particular format in which the MIS (IIS) forecast will be furnished to the PDM. Every MIS (IIS) activity should be keyed to what the PDM is able to use.

The usefulness of the MIS (IIS) inputs to decision-making would depend largely on how well the raw data have been decoded by the MIS (IIS) activity. Patterns have to be established from among the raw data entries with reference both to the *form* and/or *content*. How well insights are derived from the raw data depend upon the ingenuity and skill of decoding procedures and their selection—an activity in which the MIS (IIS) personnel would find themselves pretty much alone.

Only the wearer of the shoe knows where it pinches. Therefore, it is essential that the MIS (IIS) Manager undertake a dry run of his system to know where it gives rise to problems which were not anticipated and could not be anticipated without actual experience. In particular, the dry run should determine if all the raw data inputs that have been promised by the line management are in fact available, how well the conversion of the raw data into pre-information and of pre-information into information forecasts in the specified format are used by the PDM.

It will be noticed that in the seven steps for setting up an MIS (IIS), automation has been carefully excluded because it is not indispensable to MIS (IIS), but forecasting for control is.

EXECUTIVE SUMMARY / Having identified the three major types of MIS—M-Zero, M-Negative, and M-Positive—we now turn to the sequence in setting up an MIS (IIS).

Seven steps are identified as comprising the sequence. The MIS (IIS) Manager should report to the PDM in a staff position. The staff position is required because otherwise he would be competing for resources with the same line managers, forecasts of whose activities he has to make as part of the projected performance of the organism. The MIS (IIS) manager should report to the PDM, because the PDM is the only one who can make decisions affecting the organism as a whole, as recommended by the MIS (IIS) manager.

The MIS (IIS) manager should specify two or three key areas of change which can be anticipated as a result of the institution of MIS (IIS). The concurrence of the PDM in key areas would enable the MIS (IIS) manager to select those matters which are of the utmost concern to the PDM. They would further tell the PDM what he could expect from the new activity called MIS (IIS).

The areas of change in the performance of the organism necessarily implies line activity. The MIS (IIS) manager should establish working relations with the line manager whose activity would be affected by the MIS (IIS) forecasts. As a visible token of cooperation, the line manager should be promised something in return for the raw data that the line manager would provide the MIS (IIS).

The MIS (IIS) manager should establish the particular form in which he would furnish forecasts and recommendations to the PDM for his decision-making. It should preferably specify a regular time set apart for discussion between the PDM and the MIS (IIS) manager of the forecasts and recommendations for decision-making.

To make such forecasts and recommendations most useful, the form as well as the content of the raw data should be analyzed by the MIS (IIS) activity using appropriate analytical methods. These have to be chosen and applied by the MIS (IIS) activity itself, with almost no help from line management or the PDM except in assessing the applicability of the analytical characterization.

The MIS (IIS) manager should make a dry run to determine, among other things, how well the raw data inputs are made available by line management; how well patterns are discovered from the raw data; and how well the PDM is able to use the forecasts and recommendations made by the MIS (IIS) manager.

Notice that nothing has been said of the automation aspects of the MIS (IIS). Automation is not indispensable to MIS (IIS), but forecasting for control is.

Throughout this volume, we have emphasized that the primary rationale for any MIS (IIS) is its *utilization*. Therefore, the first consideration of an MIS (IIS) is *not* how fast the computer can store or retrieve data, but how well the decision-maker can *use* the data. The decision-maker does not really use raw data, the latest data at best relating to the time period $t - 2\Delta t$, while the decision he has to make pertains to the earliest period at which a change can be effective, i.e., $t + t\Delta t$. Therefore, the PDM uses for his decision-making the forecast of the past into the future. What he wants to accomplish is to *change* the future as forecast by means of his decisions at time *t*.

Establish a Staff Reporting Position to PDM

The only decision-maker who would have real use for the forecasts provided by the MIS (IIS) is the one who can exercise control, i.e., bring about *changes* in the manner and method of operation of the organism. Such a person is the principal decision-maker (PDM): the decision-maker who commands a unit of significant resources and authority which is charged with an identifiable objective. Notice that the PDM must have adequate authority, responsibility, and resources.

What should be the relationship of the MIS (IIS) manager to the PDM? If the MIS (IIS) manager were a line manager, reporting to the PDM, then, by definition, the MIS (IIS) manager must have line responsibilities to produce a product or provide a service as part of the products and/or services that the organism is providing. If he has these responsibilities, he must compete for the resources of the organism with all others who are in the similar position of providing products and/or services.

However, the primary function of the MIS (IIS) is to provide forecasting which will enable the PDM to exercise control. The control is exercised from the point of view, not of an individual department, division, or group of divisions, but from the view of the organism *as a whole*. To determine what is good for the organism as a whole, the MIS (IIS) must present the forecasts for every segment of the activity of the organism, as part of the whole. In other words, the MIS (IIS) must have a point of view which transcends that of any department or division or other units within the organism. Therefore, the MIS (IIS) manager *cannot* be a line manager who, by virtue of his line responsibility, will necessarily have to take a parochial point of view as opposed to an organismic one. It is necessary, therefore, that the MIS manager be a *staff* manager.

What should be the reporting level of the MIS (IIS) manager? He should report to the PDM for whom he is producing the forecast. The MIS (IIS) manager has to do more than merely pile up computer printouts on the desk of the PDM. If he were only doing that, the computer programmers whose activity gives rise to the printouts could each send their output directly to the PDM, and eliminate the MIS (IIS) manager altogether. The manager's primary responsibility is to provide forecasts which induce management action. It is not the numbers themselves which will induce management action, but the selection, presentation, and *interpretation* of the forecasts as they affect the survival and growth of the organism, which are the two principal concerns of the PDM. In order to perform the interpretation, the MIS (IIS) manager must necessarily know the intent of the PDM, and interpret the intent with respect to the changing circumstances. He may find it necessary to ask for more detailed forecasts of certain elements, to discontinue some other forecasts, and to initiate new forecasts. Additional data may have to be acquired, depending upon the changing needs of the forecasts which impact upon organismic policy. All of this requires that the MIS (IIS) manager be attuned to the PDM: which can be best done, if the MIS (IIS) manager is reporting directly to the PDM in a staff capacity.

Identify Key Performance Changes

Why should the PDM establish a staff position of MIS (IIS) manager? An inappropriate criterion is the savings that the MIS (IIS) would bring about. Such arguments have been the bane of existence of a number of MIS (IIS) activities. Automation is not indispensable to establish MIS (IIS), but with any decent size organism, the use of a computer (directly on the premises, or indirectly through time-sharing) would sooner or later become necessary. It is here that the ill-advised promise of savings to be effected through the displacement of manual chores by mechanical means entraps the advocate of MIS (IIS). The emphasis is clearly short-sighted, because it has not taken the point of view of the PDM and his decision-making, but of the computer and its data processing. As a rule, cost will increase, not decrease, in the initial stages of the installation and operation of a computer facility. It may well be two or three years before the increase in the cost stabilizes.

If, on the other hand, the emphasis is placed upon the *change* in the decision-making by the PDM, then the PDM must necessarily give his consent to, or at least consider seriously, what the *future* contribution of the new MIS (IIS) facility should be. It is quite likely that the changes that the PDM would like to see brought about may not be the changes that the MIS (IIS) manager would have foreseen. What is important is that one or two significant changes in the decision-making by the PDM should be identified *ahead* of time, before an MIS (IIS) is instituted.

Such a selection of key areas of change in the behavior of the organism does presuppose a grasp of the functioning of the organism itself. Clearly, such a grasp is not easy to come by, and it is unlikely that it will have been formally expressed in any company document. Even where such an objective is stated explicitly, it is rare that such statements will have been given an operational content. For instance, the statement, increase the net return on investment, while a laudable goal from the point of view of company reports to the share-holders, does not suggest the elements that could enter into the MIS (IIS). The reason is that the net return on investment is a result, which has to be influenced by other factors. The MIS (IIS) should focus its attention upon those elements which can be influenced by the action of the management, such as the production and distribution of products and/or services, and, to a lesser extent, the demand for the products and/or services. Again, the injunction to sell more does not provide operational directives to the MIS (IIS). The reason is that the customer is not asking for the products and/or services for their own sake, but, instead, is asking for them in order to serve a need-value or want-value. Therefore, the MIS (IIS) should reflect the particular need-value and/or the want-value that the customer is seeking to satisfy through the products and/or services of the organism. It is this identification which will be hardest to achieve; it is quite likely that even the principal decision-maker may not have devoted enough attention to articulating the particular need-values and/or want-value of the customer that should be satisfied.

It is precisely because the need-values and/or want-values are the ones which determine the maintenance and/or increase of customer demand for the products and/or services of the organism that their profile should be identified, and two or more specific areas where *operational* changes can be brought about be identified by the MIS (IIS) manager. In making management accept the version of need-values and/or want-values that the particular products and/or services are fulfilling, the MIS (IIS) manager involves management in the need for and the design of the MIS (IIS) at the very outset. By mutually agreeing to concentrate upon two or three major areas where the MIS (IIS) results in improved decision-making, and therefore of improved performance in the production and/or delivery of products and/or services as well as in maintenance, improvement, and/or creation of demand for products and/or services, the MIS (IIS) manager states unequivocally how his professional performance can be judged. Such a commitment *ahead of time* protects both the PDM and the MIS (IIS) manager. It protects the PDM because he is not led to undue expectation of miracles simply because he has invested in an MIS (IIS); it protects the MIS (IIS) Manager because the obligation to be specific requires him to think in concrete terms of the particular organism, and to select conservatively achievable goals, rather than engage in arm-waving.

Establish Working Relations with Line Managers

The MIS (IIS) is a staff activity. It brings about changes by design through changes in management decision-making. The changes that management plans to bring about are in the line activities of the organism, and are with respect to what the course of events would have been if there were no management decisions. In other words, what would have been the sales of a particular product(s) and/or service(s), which is what the MIS (IIS) would provide as an input to management decision-making. However, to provide the input, MIS (IIS) requires raw data, and these raw data come from the line management itself. Therefore, it is mandatory that working relations be established with the key line activities which are significant sources of raw data.

The raw data that line management should provide include not only the elements that are produced in the course of ordinary operations, such as the sales order, the production schedule, etc., but also the whole series of "soft" data, such as market intelligence, trade rumors, and so on. Line sales management is directly in touch with the customers and are therefore in a position to acquire such data which are essential to the interpretation of the sales orders—why they behave the way they do. Further, operational insights from line management are most valuable to the MIS (IIS) in determining the appropriateness of the various forecasting methods to the particular situations. Their insights are especially valuable to the MIS (IIS) in choosing forecasting methods pertaining to the content of the raw data on sales, production, etc., because there are underlying forces in the market which the sales management have a far better "feel" for than others.

There is another important reason why working relations should be established at the outset. Notice that the MIS (IIS) is committing itself to change, and the change means that the line management will be affected. If there are no changes, then status quo prevails, and there is no necessity for an MIS (IIS) dedicated to bringing about change. If the MIS (IIS) is doing its job, it is inevitable that change is to be brought about; and since these changes are to be brought about in the particular line management activities, they should be the ones who are aware of the coming changes. It will be surprising if line management welcomes changes in their operations with open arms, for, change really means that there are better ways of doing things than theirs. No manager who, by definition, is paid to perform to the best of his ability will want to directly acknowledge that he is not so doing. However, if the MIS (IIS) persuades the line manager that the MIS (IIS) will *help* him do his job better, rather than show him up, then he will be willing to cooperate. In fact, he will probably be willing to make additional raw data available, knowing that he is going to receive in return something greater in value than the value of his investment in the form of resources devoted to raw data input.

Identify Quid Pro Quo Basis

Cooperation is easier promised than obtained. After all, the MIS (IIS) manager, as staff to the PDM, has the ear of the PDM which he, the line manager, does require from time to time. Therefore, the line manager would agree to cooperate *in principle*. However, to convert the agreement *in principle* to reality *in practice* is another matter altogether. The basis for such conversion would be the establishment of a quid pro quo. What is the line manager going to receive in return for the raw data he provides the MIS (IIS) manager?

This question was discussed in chapter 4, where it was pointed out that the basis for the quid pro quo is the intelligence output for raw data input, i.e., the line manager will get *information* in return for the raw data. Since information is data when they affect behavior, the line manager should get something which will affect his behavior. However, the primary obligation of the MIS (IIS) is to affect the behavior, not of the particular line activity, but that of the organism *as a whole*. It is quite likely that in discharging the primary obligation, the MIS (IIS) manager would, in fact, have to override the sectional interests of different line managers.

Nevertheless, the MIS (IIS) manager receives inputs from several line managements, and is therefore in a position to offer something in return to each of them which is more than what they put in. While the recommendation that the MIS (IIS) manager makes to the PDM will probably be different from what the individual line manager would like to see from his own point of view, projection of the individual raw data itself would, in fact, be something more than what line management contributes to the MIS (IIS). In other words, the MIS (IIS) manager could provide line management with the forecasts of the form: At this rate, the performance characteristics of the products and/or services for which you are responsible will be such and such; or, at this rate, the fulfillment characteristics of your products and/or services will be such and such.

In chapter 4 the quid pro quo was developed with respect to 12 different managerial activities of a large corporation. In each case line management specified the particular contribution in the form of raw data input that they would make, and stated specifically the outputs they would receive from the MIS (IIS). Notice also that the quid pro quo was agreed to by the appropriate authority within line management who can commit the resources for the raw data input, and he affixed his signature to the agreement. The one-page statement becomes a written contract which stipulates the particular elements of understanding between line management and MIS (IIS) manager.

Establish Information Input and Decision Output

The primary obligation of the MIS (IIS) manager is, of course, to the PDM. We discussed earlier the elements of the "contract" between the PDM and the MIS (IIS) manager, viz., the two or three key areas of organismic activity where changes of a specified nature within a specified time are promised. How can they be carried out?

Clearly, the MIS (IIS) manager is only making recommendations to bring about change; at this rate, say, a car will run over the cliff. Any change in the direction, and in the eventual outcome, must be made by the decision-maker, the driver. However, in order for the driver to take action, he needs to be told that he would soon be driving over the cliff in sufficient time to take remedial action: either to put the brakes on and change direction, or to eject himself out of the car which cannot be prevented from going over. The decision-maker must have *effective time for action*, which the MIS (IIS) manager should specify in his forecast.

The decisions that the PDM have to make are probably not as catastrophic as the one in the above illustration. However, the principle holds, i.e., that there must be time for effective action. In the course of day-to-day decision-making by the PDM, a pattern should be established for the briefing by the MIS (IIS) manager of the forecasts applied to the various segments of the organismic activities, so that the PDM will *habitually* look for the forecasts and recommendations by the MIS (IIS) manager. The briefing does not have to be on a daily basis, but it should be on a *regular* basis. The advantage of the regular briefing is that a conversational mode is established; as time goes on, there is no need for repeated explication of the assumptions and the implications, but instead, ideas can be communicated effectively and easily.

To facilitate the communication of the forecasts and their implications, and to minimize the need to reiterate the basic premises, it is preferable to establish an input-output structure. From the point of view of the PDM, the output is the decision-making, and the input is the MIS (IIS) forecast. The decisions are of three kinds: (1) continue unchanged, (2) change in a negative direction, (e.g., reduce the cost of production), and (3) change in a positive direction, (e.g., increase the sales). In all three types of decisions, there has to be an "ideal" value with which the "actual value" is compared to arrive at the alternative decisions. The "actual" from the point of view of the MIS (IIS) is, in fact, the forecast of the fulfillment characteristics or the performance characteristics of the products and/or services. The "ideal" values are derived from the organismic objective established ahead of time. In order to fulfill the organismic objectives, certain "ideal" values have to be accomplished. Will they be accomplished? The forecast answers: At this rate the "actual" values will be such and such. The input from MIS (IIS) should not merely compare the actual and the ideal, but also suggest the nature and magnitude of the action that will be required on the basis of the comparison between the ideal and the actual (as represented in the forecast).

Consider, for instance, a sales organization. The line activity is sales of, say, durable products. Let us say that the entire sales are accomplished through one, and only one, medium, the company salesmen. In this instance, the organismic objective of increasing the net return on investment can be translated into increasing the particular types of sales of products which, in turn, most fulfills the want-values of the customers. Not only must the profile of demand by the customers be identified, but also must it be translated into particular products, and particular products handled by particular salesmen who are located in particular territories. The need for the cooperation of line management in identifying the peculiarities of the customers' want-values is quite apparent. It is also apparent that the mere record of sales orders will do little to arrive at the future want-values of the customers, and how they can be translated into the particular products sold by the particular salesmen in the particular territories. The "ideal" values would include what the individual salesmen "ought to" sell of each product in each territory in a given period, say, next year.

The input-output format for the PDM should include: (1) the forecast of the projected sales of the individual salesman in the individual territory for the next time period; (2) the "ideal" sales by the particular salesman in the particular territory in the next month, on the basis of the organismic objective for the *whole year*; and (3) the index of the comparison between the "actual" (the forecast) and the "ideal," indicating whether the difference between the two is zero, negative, or positive.

The output is the decision-making by the PDM. He has to decide on the basis of his experience whether the "ideal" is too high to be realized, or too low, depending upon which the (actual/ideal) ratio for PDM action would vary. If the "ideal" were pegged too high, the PDM may decide that the ratio of 80% would be considered acceptable performance in fulfilling the "ideal." Depending upon the value of the ratio chosen, the corrective action for the different performance values would vary. If 100% were the "ideal," a salesman with a 70% ratio might be considered in need of remedial action, while if the 80% ratio were the "ideal," then the salesman accomplishing 70% might be considered acceptable, and the level of remedial action may be pegged to the salesman achieving 50%. The particular percentage of acceptable performance could be varied, thereby altering the corresponding decision on remedial action with respect to the salesman.

The input-output format in this instance is relatively straightforward. The PDM should see the actual dollar sales by the salesman, this month, and year to date; the comparison with the corresponding figures for similar salesmen serving similar territories and selling similar products; the "ideal" figures for the individual salesman and the group of salesmen for the month, and year to date; the actual/ideal percentage. The PDM can set up his own percentage for acceptable performance; the MIS (IIS) manager can indicate the particular salesmen and the particular corrective measures required corresponding to different levels of achievement that the PDM selects as acceptable.

If the PDM is used to seeing the MIS (IIS) input in such a specified, simple, and direct format, he can ask for alternative inputs and additional inputs on the basis of what he habitually receives. His involvement becomes direct and continuing, and he asks for more information on the basis of proven results of past forecasts supplied by MIS (IIS).

Identify Applicable Modeling Approaches

In chapter 6 we identified the problem category as an important element in the preparation and use of MIS (IIS). The role of the problem category is in identifying the particular features of the given problem, so that the raw data *content* may be judiciously used for forecasting with particular reference to the peculiar features of the given problem. The problem category is not a necessary consideration for the forecasts of raw data simply on the basis of *form*: the requirement is simply to identify a repeating pattern of numbers. Such form forecasts must be compared with *content* forecasts which take into account the particular features of the problem category. In chapter 5 raw data content was used to identify three problem categories: solution-oriented, structure-oriented, and structural solution-oriented problems. The MIS (IIS) manager must classify the major aspects of the decision-making situation facing the PDM into one or more of the three categories. With such an identification, the MIS (IIS) manager can choose the appropriate methods of forecasts of the raw data.

Further, identification of the problem categories is important from the point of view of hypothesizing alternative outcomes which may result from specified action. If, for instance, the problem suggests that sales are likely to be responsive to an increase in the commissions paid to the salesmen, then, it would have a major impact upon the organism's pursuit of increased sales. Of course, it is only a hypothesis that an increase in sales commissions would result in a corresponding increase in total sales. Before the policy change can be instituted, the PDM would want reasonable logical evidence that in fact an increase in the sales could be construed to be dependent upon, or directly related to, an increase in the sales commission. Even if it is granted that the two increases go hand in hand, the PDM would want to know how much the increase in the sales commissions should be before sales increases can be anticipated; what the time lag is between the introduction of an increase in commissions and the realization of increased sales, etc. If there are no past data on a change in the sales commission and the corresponding changes (increase or decrease) in total sales, then the representation of the relationship between sales commissions and total sales becomes an activity of critical importance.

The general activity of representing a physical phenomenon by means of abstract relationships in such a way that the representation is adequate for the purposes on hand (including decision-making) may be called modeling. Admittedly, modeling is an abstraction, and the value of the results of the modeling depends upon the appropriateness of the representation of the physical phenomenon by the model. A direct relationship between a desired outcome from the point of view of the PDM, and the changes in a single element as suggested by the increase in the sales commissions leading to an increase in the total sales, may *not* be the rule; it would probably be the exception. Whether the model is simple or complex, for MIS (IIS) purposes the mandatory requirement is that the modeling must be designed to represent the interrelationships among the elements of the physical phenomenon in such a way that insights can be gained to better achieve the PDM objective. In other words, the modeling must be decision oriented.

Neither the PDM nor the line management is likely to be of any significant assistance to the MIS (IIS) manager in his modeling efforts, except as sources of knowledge about the physical functioning of the phenomenon, i.e., production, distribution, sales, etc., of the organism. It will be the MIS (IIS) manager's professional responsibility to identify the modeling approaches that are most adequate and appropriate: adequate for the decision-making purposes on hand, and appropriate to the phenomenon. He has to insure that the various modeling approaches are sound and applicable, the choice of the models being governed by relevance to the decision-making, rather than by the elegance of the mathematical formulation. His modeling could result in unorthodox or unexpected results. He should stick by them in spite of skepticism on the part of line management and/or the PDM, and force a discussion of the characteristics of the phenomenon that have been incorporated into the model, as well as features that were not incorporated into the model. If competently conceived and carried out, the modeling should be presented as evidence which has to be reckoned with, rather than as an edict or exercise for its own sake. The PDM may well decide to override the results of the modeling—not because they contradict his intuition, nor because he does not understand the mathematical properties of the variables which represent the phenomenon of the organismic activity, but because he, as PDM, has reason to believe that corrective forces are at work, which will avert the findings of the model or that the organism is at a stage of development where the courting of the results of the model is a calculated risk. It should be noted that whether or not the modeling results are accepted as presented, and whether or not the action taken is in line with, or opposed to, the findings of the model, the value of the modeling itself is recognized in the decision-making process.

Establish an Initial Operational Mode

The dictum "don't undertake vast programs with half-vast ideas" is quite appropriate to the installation and operation of an MIS (IIS). As a safeguard against half-vast ideas precipitating an avalanche of MIS (IIS), we have stipulated that two or three significant changes have to be agreed upon to be brought about through the medium of MIS (IIS) *ahead of time*.

The particular areas marked for bringing about changes by design will be the logical candidates for a dry run of the MIS (IIS). Can the raw data inputs be obtained in adequate form and quantity, and will the appropriate persons with the right knowledge and talent be designated by the line management to carry out the function of raw data input? If the system is exercised on a dry run basis for, say, a week or a month, on a *manual* basis, the problems of operation which can only be identified from actual experience will surface. Such problems can exist not only in the raw data input, but also in the transformation of raw data into pre-information, and in the use of information by the PDM (and other decision-makers). With respect to the transformation of raw data into information, the weighting of raw data, using only the *form* of the data, as well as the weighting of the raw data on the basis of content of the data need to be demonstrated as workable. Also, are the lines of communication between the MIS (IIS) manager and PDM clear and regular? Is there a particular time every week on the PDM's calendar set apart for the discussion of the inputs to decision-making furnished by the MIS (IIS) manager?

Notice that the entire spectrum of activities is *manual*. Even if some of the data inputs are currently automated, it is advisable to transcribe them onto manual forms for the trial period. The forecasts that are based on the data should also be derived manually, just to insure that such transformation of raw data into information is physically feasible within the MIS (IIS) structure. It should be recognized that no matter how fast computers run, and no matter how fast they produce reams of output, it is not the weight of the computer printout that will improve the decision-making, but the use made by the PDM of perhaps a very small part which details the present and future performances of the various segments of the activities of the organism. The PDM's decision-making could, of course, set in motion the need for more and more detailed forecasts of activities of segments of the organism where control is to be exercised.

All That Is Automated Is Not MIS (IIS)

In chapter 2 we used the same title for a section as the one above. The reference there was to eight ADP systems in products, service, and research which apply to a wide range of activities from American Airlines' reservation system to IBM's products schedule. Every one of the ADP systems uses a significant amount of computer time and activity. However, *none* of them qualifies as an MIS, because none of them is designed to forecast the organismic performance in order to enable the PDM to exercise control. In spite of their elaborate and extensive data files, and even updating of raw data, all of them remain at best as data update systems, whether of products, service, or research.

Notice that in the seven steps for setting up an MIS (IIS) automation has been carefully excluded. Automation is not indispensable to MIS (IIS), but forecasting for control is. Having identified the seven steps that are indispensable to the development of an MIS (IIS), we shall now turn to the computer considerations of the question.

QUESTIONS

Chapters 10 and 11 deal with the development of MIS (IIS). In chapter 10, 7 essential steps in setting up an IIS were discussed. The purpose of the following questions is to develop an appreciation for the organizational and operational relationships of the MIS (IIS) activity with the rest of the organism.

A. MIS (IIS) UTILIZATION
1. Why should MIS (IIS) activity be under a staff manager, and not a line manager?
2. How can the MIS (IIS) be set up to ensure its use by the PDM?

B. MIS (IIS) INPUTS
3. What is the basic antagonism between the line departments and MIS (IIS)?
4. What is the advantage of a quid pro quo basis of exchange between line managers and MIS (IIS)? Develop quid pro quo contracts for your own organism using chapter 4 as a point of departure.

C. MIS (IIS) PROCESSING
5. What aspect of MIS (IIS) activity would be the exclusive responsibility of MIS (IIS) personnel?
6. Why is a dry run important to the MIS (IIS) program?

11
MIS (IIS) Sequence 2: Computer Considerations

TECHNICAL OVERVIEW / The computer considerations in this chapter are twofold: (1) four functional criteria in selecting a computer, and (2) seven customizing criteria in tailoring computer capabilities to the special needs of the organism.

The 729 categories of utilization of MIS (IIS) by PDM developed in chapter 6 should be used to construct a profile of potential utilization for the particular organism. Given that the MIS utilization matrix indicates a *prima facie* justification for considering automating the MIS (IIS), how should the different alternative computer configurations be evaluated?

Four functional criteria are developed to select a computer system. They are:

1. Efficiency as a matter of hardware-software combination
2. Ease of writing vs. cost of overhead
3. Access time vs. processing time
4. Control over computer operations

Given two manufacturers, both of whom are developing new computer hardware, preference must be given to the one who is also simultaneously expending significant efforts for developing appropriate software.

The closer the programming language is to English (or mathematics) the greater the need for a more complex translation mechanism, which usually means higher cost. Translation is not the only item of cost. In the computers of tomorrow, the capability to find a pattern on the basis of limited problem-solving experience may well be incorporated, which would be a part of the computer overhead. In making selections—whether of language, instructions, storage, or operations—it should be borne in mind that you get what you pay for, and you pay for what you get.

Computer operations are *location* oriented: the computer does something to something located at some place. Before something can be done to the entity at a given location, the computer has to get to it. How soon the computer can get to the desired location depends upon where that location is.

Computer overhead reduces significantly the available locations in the central processing unit. Therefore, fixed allocations of space mean that they are not available for operations until the specified operations are completed. On the other hand, if the limited space is allocated on a need-basis as in *dynamic storage* allocation, it would facilitate better utilization of the computer facilities.

It is one thing to allocate the limited space that is available in the computer to perform operations; it is quite another to physically carry out operations in the assigned locations. Core cycle specifies the time taken to *read*, i.e., clear a word from magnetic core storage, and *write*, i.e., insert or reinsert the word in the same storage.

Once having reached the desired location in the computer, how long does it take to perform the operations? Because the computer takes no more time to do the most elaborate addition than the simplest addition, combining of data into batches on the basis of the processing to be performed on them, *batch processing*, is an important consideration in reducing the time for operations. Another is the capability of the computer to create, update, and transfer data.

Among other considerations pertaining to computer operations are the capability to extend instructions, as in the use of macro instructions which permit the programmer to explicitly specify groups of operations by a single name(s); the implicit extension of instructions by letting the computer discover patterns and apply them, as in heuristics; the capability to interrupt repetitive processes, as in flexible iterative operations; and the process of transferring control over the variables as in releasing data.

One of the important features of modern computers is the control programs which can be looked upon as the mechanical managers. In more recent vintage computers, there are *processing programs* which operate under the control of the control programs to perform translations and other chores.

The four functional criteria are ordered *illustratively*. Software is given a maximum score of 60 and hardware a score of 40. Some functions, e.g., access time vs. processing time, are a combination of hardware and software, therefore their scores are a combination of the two:

Hardware		*Software*	
		Improvement of communication with the computer via program-ming language	25
		Ease of writing vs. cost of over-head	15
Access time vs. processing time	15	Access time vs. processing time	5
Control over computer operations	25	Control over computer operations	15
	40		60

Turning from the selection of a computer to custom-tailoring the computer capabilities to the special needs of the organism, 7 criteria are discussed:

1. Alternative access
2. Communication capabilities
3. Staff support
4. Internal education
5. Concrete contract
6. Data input–decision output
7. Automating order

The significant increase in the speed of computer operations from the 1946 ENIAC's 1/5000 of a second to perform an addition to the 1970 CDC 7600's 1/10,000,000 of a second—and the projected billionth of a second and even less—puts great pressure on utilizing the computer as fully as possible. When computer operations increase 1,000-fold in speed, if the demand for the operations does not increase correspondingly, the computer will be idle, costing money. One way of reducing the idle time is by increasing the demand for operations and sharing time on the same computer.

The viability of *time-sharing* depends not only upon the availability of computer hardware, but also upon the variety of computer programs needed for the prosecution of the different activities that a particular MIS (IIS) will require. The greatest common factor would govern the availability of software in a time-sharing system to serve as many users as possible. However, the existence of significant groups, such as hospitals, insurance companies, has underscored the group-specific demand for computer programs and set the stage for the evolution of *computer (public) utility*.

The use of time-sharing and computer utility and other alternate accesses to computer capabilities is limited by the *user* capabilities to communicate with the computer. A simple questionnaire is developed to ascertain these capabilities.

Where the computer systems services (CSS) should be located organizationally is a crucial question. In chapter 10, the MIS (IIS) manager was proposed as a staff position reporting to the PDM. Where should the CSS be located? The organizational location should be one which facilitates the functioning of CSS in a supporting staff capacity. The supportive role is in relation to demand factors, supply factors, and profit factors. CSS activities should be oriented to these three major factors. They can be well served if the CSS is a supportive staff function reporting to a vice-president for staff services who will be in charge of service functions related to the maintenance, operation, and development of human skills and mechanical capabilities, as well as the acquisition of new facilities, mergers, etc.

The best computer systems can be total failures if they are not accepted by the organism. Therefore, a continuing program of in-house education is essential—education covering the higher levels of users as well as the lower levels of direct liaison with the CSS. The CSS functions have to be presented as not only service functions, but also as technical and professional functions, the justification for which may not be apparent to those not initiated.

The CSS is a significant investment—$1,000,000 per year and more. As in every major *financial* investment, a clear-cut statement of what is being bought should be spelled out in a contract. The contract can only specify what the CSS can do; it is up to the users to decide how to exploit the opportunities so offered. How will the PDM use the outputs of the CSS as presented by the MIS (IIS) manager? How will other decision-makers utilize forecasts made by the CSS? The drawing up of input (data) and output (decision) forms is one way of specifying how the organism is gearing up to utilizing the CSS.

Utilization will vary from department to department. Demand, supply, and profit are a reasonable set of factors to determine the level of inputs to be made by each department to CSS and the level of outputs to be derived, and the degree of automation in each area.

Whether manual or mechanical, the MIS (IIS) is an aid to decision-making designed to exercise control. Automation should be subordinate to the overriding consideration of better decision-making today through the use of yesterday's data as reflected in tomorrow's outcome.

EXECUTIVE SUMMARY / The computer considerations of MIS (IIS) are divided into (1) four functional criteria in selecting a computer, and (2) seven customizing criteria in tailoring computer capabilities to the special needs of the organism.

Is this computer really necessary? To answer the question, an individual profile of the particular organism should be drawn up in terms of the applicable categories from among the 729 categories of MIS (IIS) utilization by the PDM developed in chapter 6. If the profile indicates that automation is likely to be worthwhile, there are four technical considerations in selecting a particular computer capability.

The first criterion is the combination of hardware (the machine itself) and software (the programs that run the machine), not one or the other by itself. Such a combined consideration will permit the recognition of the computer manufacturer who makes the investment in designing more suitable languages for *human* communication with the computer.

The second criterion is the question: Is this computer overhead necessary? It is somewhat similar to selecting an automobile, which can be equipped with a large number of extras. In a pickup truck, white-wall tires will be out of place, and the car telephone would certainly require demonstrable need for instant communication. Similarly, in the case of the computer it should be borne in mind that you get what you pay for; and you pay for what you get.

The third criterion is the question: What is the turnaround time? It depends upon where the data are; how they are transmitted to the central processing unit where operations are performed; how long it takes to perform the specified operations and to print out the results.

The fourth criterion is the question: How does the computer manage its own operations? Management by the computer refers to both the data and the computations. The reference in the second criterion to the overhead is primarily addressed to the translation of the human programming language into computer language. There are processing programs which perform this chore (and others). Processing programs are under the command of the control programs, which are really the mechanical managers in the computer. Much depends upon the efficiency of the mechanical manager both in utilizing space in the computers and in performing the operations.

How much weight should each of the four criteria be given in selecting the computer capability for the organism? In our illustrative weighting, software is given a maximum of 60, and hardware a score of 40. Some of the functions combine both hardware and software, therefore, their scores are a combination of the two:

Hardware		Software	
		Criterion 1	25
		Criterion 2	15
Criterion 3	15	Criterion 3	5
Criterion 4	25	Criterion 4	15
	40		60

Turning from the selection of the computer to custom-tailoring computer capabilities to the special needs of the organism, there are seven criteria:

1. Alternative access
2. Communication capabilities
3. Staff support
4. Internal education
5. Concrete contract
6. Data input–decision output
7. Automating order

To use a computer, it is not necessary to physically locate it on-site. Time on the computer can be rendered by the hour or the minute, as needed. *Time-sharing* is a possibility; so also is *computer (public) utility*. The advantage of the utility is that it is more specifically oriented to a smaller group of specialized users than time-sharing which has a larger clientele, not unlike a car pool compared with public transportation.

Whether the computer is located on-site or is accessed through time-sharing or computer utility, its utilization is limited by the capability to communicate with it. How well can the line and staff people dealing with demand factors, supply factors, and profit factors communicate with the computer?

One of the functions of the computer systems services (CSS) is to provide education to the user. Such education would be twofold: an appreciation course for the high levels of management, and a hands-on training for the lower levels of management. The CSS should serve all the factors—demand, supply and profit—i.e., be a supportive staff function. Therefore, the manager of CSS should report to the vice-president for staff services.

The CSS is a significant investment—$1,000,000 per year and more. Therefore, what the organism is getting for its money should be spelled out in a contract.

Utilization of computer capabilities will vary from department to department; so will the need for automation. Both can be specified by identifying the major input (data)–output (decision) forms for demand factors, supply factors, and profit factors.

Whether manual or mechanical, the MIS (IIS) is an aid to decision-making designed to exercise control. Automation should be subordinate to the overriding consideration of better decision-making today through the use of yesterday's data as reflected in tomorrow's outcome.

Automation is not indispensable to MIS (IIS); forecasting for control purposes is. Forecasting can be manual, mechanical, or both. No matter what the means of obtaining the forecast, they are of no value unless used.

Therefore, the starting point in the discussion of computer considerations of MIS (IIS) is the utilization matrix developed in chapter 6.

MIS (IIS) Matrix and Utilization

There are 1,134 types of forecasts that the PDM can receive from the MIS (IIS) and 729 categories of utilization of the MIS (IIS) by the PDM. The first step is to identify the profile of MIS utilization by the PDM.

Potential utilization

Recalling the suggestion in chapter 10 that a manual mode of operation be established to ensure that the system is in fact workable, it may be added here that the *potential utilization* profile is critical. After all, the MIS (IIS) utilization matrix *cannot* be filled in until the MIS (IIS) is installed and operated. However, the *potential utilization* has to be carefully constructed: What type of forecast would the PDM need for the type of decisions that he makes? This potential profile of MIS (IIS) utilization would serve to identify a number of candidates for structure-oriented, solution-oriented, and structural solution-oriented types of problems of the organism, for the solution of which the medium of computers would be most helpful, if not indispensable.

Analytical aspects

This profile of potential utilization will indicate, in general terms, the degree of sophistication that may be required of computer operations. If, for instance, statistical computations of a theoretical nature are expected to occur with reasonable frequency, then it is clear that the computer facility, whether owned by the organism, leased, or time-shared, or computer utility-shared, must have the ready capability to serve the theoretical statistical calculations. Similarly, if a number of simulations are to be performed on a regular basis, the capability of the computer system to operate simulation languages becomes an important consideration.

Empirical aspects

Again, turning from the analytical aspects to the empirical aspects of the use of the computer, the data handling capability of the computer is of particular importance for any organism. In chapter 5 we discussed the concept of data management as an element of operating systems. The analytical edifice is built upon the foundation with the building materials provided (preferably) by empirical data.

It is the empirical data which invest the organisms with proprietary rights, whether the empirical data relate to the environmental status of fulfillment characteristics, or the technological status of performance characteristics. For instance, if the organism wants to claim new capabilities for a particular product, that must be based upon the carefully collected and evaluated data on performance characteristics obtained from laboratories of field tests. These data are acquired at significant cost and, therefore, are treated with the care and concern that is due any valuable property. Similarly, data on the market of the product are acquired through careful cultivation of present and past customers, and are supplemented by investigative data developed by company personnel for use by the company. These environmental data—data on the environment of the company—are not only valuable, but also sensitive data, which are accorded the treatment due any valuable property.

The best analytical method can only be as good as the raw data, in this instance empirical data. In fact, the sanctity of the empirical data sometimes leads the organisms to opt for a more expensive on-site computer installation in preference over an off-site facility shared with others. Even when the analytical capabilities are adequate under a time-sharing system, fear of unauthorized access to one's empirical data on the environmental status of fulfillment characteristics and technological status of performance characteristics—their secure storage, rapid retrieval, accurate processing, ready results, and secure return to storage—may lead the organism to incur extra expenditures in their computer operations.

Forecast period

The analytical and the empirical aspects of computer operations of the MIS (IIS) must be of sufficient magnitude to warrant the use of automated data processing and computing facilities. Once the profile of potential MIS (IIS) utilization is identified, the question must be raised: Will the decisions made *with* the MIS (IIS) be significantly different from the decisions made *without* the automated MIS (IIS)? In other words, the nature and frequency of use of the forecasting time period becomes quite important. As discussed in chapter 6, the Δt can be an effective index of the significance of MIS (IIS) to the decision-making process. If the majority of decisions have to be made in very short time, making Δt very small, then speed is of the essence, thereby indicating the necessity for automated transformation of raw data into information. If, on the other hand, most of the decisions relate to the long term, there will be less pressure on the turnaround time between raw data and information for decision-making purposes. The question is *not* how fast the data can be transformed into information, but how fast can the PDM *use* it?

Functional Approach to Computer Performance

Given that the MIS (IIS) utilization matrix indicates a *prima facie* justification for considering automating the MIS (IIS), how should the different alternative computer configurations be evaluated?

We have indicated that the facility to perform analytical operations, as well as the facility to handle empirical data, must be considered at some length, because the forecasts that the MIS (IIS) provides for purposes of management control depend exclusively upon the particular empirical data and the analysis performed upon them. There are four functional criteria for the selection of a computer system for MIS (IIS). These draw upon the functional approach to programming languages criteria developed elsewhere.[1] The four criteria are:

1. Efficiency as a matter of hardware-software combination
2. Ease of writing vs. cost of overhead
3. Access time vs. processing time
4. Control over computer operations

1. Efficiency as a matter of hardware-software combination

Developments in both hardware and software do reflect the importance attached to the type of operations in demand at different periods of time.

HISTORICAL DEVELOPMENT

Business computations generated the first development. For instance, in the 1950s the emphasis was upon data processing, which grew out of the accounting applications of automation. Files of data had to be accessed for updating purposes and for performing simple operations. The software of the times was Symbolic Optimum Assembly Program (SOAP) for use with IBM 650, a business-oriented computer which was introduced in 1956.

Next, development of scientific computation led to the first professional presentation on FORmula TRANslating System (FORTRAN) in 1957. To meet the needs for accuracy in scientific computations, the new IBM 704 was developed for use with which FORTRAN II was released in 1958.

Emphasis upon accurate mathematical computations led to the parallel development overseas of IAL (International Algebraic Language) which subsequently became known as ALGOL (ALGOrithmic Language), whose purpose was to provide a computer language which was as close to standard mathematical notation as possible. The first version of ALGOL appeared in 1958 as indicated by the term ALGOL 58.

---

[1] George K. Chacko, *Computer-Aided Decision-Making* (New York: American Elsevier, 1972), chapters 7, 8.

In 1960 data-handling problems were given recognition in the development of the Common Business-Oriented Language (COBOL). The federal government stipulation that all computers purchased by the government should accept COBOL stimulated the use of the language.

With FORTRAN dedicated to scientific computations and COBOL dedicated to data-handling in business (and other) problems, it was only natural that the features of both would be attempted to be incorporated into a new language, which IBM announced after three years of effort in 1966: Programming Language (PL/I), the I indicating the first version.

Hardware developments

One of the implications of considering a hardware-software combination, instead of one or the other by itself, is the explicit emphasis upon the developmental efforts of the different computer manufacturers on behalf of programming languages and other elements of software. Promises of fourth generation computers as being imminent in the late 1960s were soft-pedalled by the early 1970s. However, current selection of a computer system must take into account potential developments which are in the offing as represented by fourth generation computers. Nor must the considerations be confined to the hardware. What is the nature of the programming language that will accompany the new computer hardware? Given two manufacturers, both of whom are developing new computer hardware, preference must be given to the one who is also simultaneously expending significant efforts to develop appropriate software.

Not to be overlooked are the potentials of the minicomputers. While they may not represent any new capabilities, the fact that they are able to accomplish equivalent operations with less investment of resources would make their candidacy attractive. Further, the development of computers devised for experimental purposes should be considered, even if it be only to appreciate the possibility of custom-tailoring computers to the organism's special needs.

Augmentation of human reasoning

Before the selection of a computer is made, it would be worth while for the organism to conduct a state-of-the-art survey, particularly with reference to computer architecture, and the efforts to augment human reasoning through a variant of the learning process imbedded in the computer. Artificial intelligence may not become available tomorrow, but developments in the process of identification of *problem-solving* have much to offer to the planning of the utilization of MIS (IIS) for decision-making purposes.

2. Ease of writing vs. cost of overhead

The programs which drive the computer are written in programming languages. The function of any language is communication. For communication to take place, the originator and the receiver of symbols should transmit identical meaning. This requirement can be expressed in the essential element of a legal contract: the minds must be *ad idem* (at one).

The medium of communication between man and computer is *not* the same set of symbols. The computer requires machine language for communication, while man requires something other than machine language. The computer needs to understand in every instance whether or not an electric impulse must be present or not (on or off). Depending upon where the impulse is (location), the computer performs a number of alternative activities (operations). In other words, the essentials of the language that the computer understands are signals for off, or on, of electric impulses in specific locations. The beeps and blips which are meaningful to the computer are alien to the human language.

When two parties want to communicate with each other but they speak different languages, a translator is required. A vivid illustration of the translation process in the computer is available with IBM 650, wherein the program written in SOAP I will be physically returned by the computer in another language, SOAP II, the number of cards being 25 to 30 percent more than the program written in SOAP I. After the programmer checks the computer translation into SOAP II, he resubmits the program, and the computer again performs another translation.

The number of program cards has now nearly doubled. Further, as space is allocated for computer operations on each of the variables through the successive translations, it would not be unusual for the programmer to find that some of the variables no longer had adequate space for the operations; he would have to go back to the drawing board for a rewrite of the program in SOAP I.

Modern computers do not give the successive translations back to the programmer for checking. Instead, whether a single translator or several are required, they are performed within the computer itself, until the programmer instructions are translated into beeps and blips for the computer. If there are any inconsistencies—in the programming and/or in the translating—the computer will submit a "diagnostics."

One of the disadvantages of not receiving successive translations of programs is that the sizable space taken up in the computer for the translation process is no longer visible. It is like the driver not recognizing the automatic shifting of gears by the modern automobile which he would have more readily recognized had he to shift the gears himself. With automatic driving, all he has to do is put the gear in D for drive. Of course, the cost of the automatic shift is greater than that of manual shift. Consider that now, in addition to the automatic shifting of gears, the automobile also selects a route as soon as the driver punches the desired destination. In automated highways of the future, the automobile is visualized as having the facilities to receive commands from a central computer, which will guide it at a steady speed through the highway portion, shift to the appropriate off ramp, change the speed, and steer to the exit at the appropriate place. When these operations thus become automated, the manual functions of the driver will have been reduced, but it is also likely that with every added feature, there is added cost.

The cost of automated operations in the computer are not confined to the translation of human language instructions into machine language instructions alone. To use the automobile analogy, if the automobile were to run its course on the highway on the basis of inquiries that it makes en route and on the basis of the experience that it gains, that would take over some of the problem-solving approaches of the driver. In the computers of tomorrow, the capability to find a pattern on the basis of limited problem-solving experience may well be incorporated, which would be a part of the computer overhead. In making selections—whether of language, operations, instructions, or storage—it should be borne in mind that you get what you pay for, and you pay for what you get.

3. Access time vs. processing time

Computer operations are location oriented: the computer does something to something located at some place. Before something can be done to the entity at a given location, the computer has to get to it. How soon the computer can get to the desired location depends upon where that location is. To use the library analogy, the ease of reaching a desired book in the library depends upon how the books are arranged. The location of any book can be specified in terms of the particular shelf, row, and number; however, the reader must first locate the book in the library catalog, which is done by means of author and subject card catalogs. He has to get a "key" from the author and subject file, usually in the form of Dewey Decimal System identification. The reader then has to match the specific identification with the location, first of the shelf, then of the row in the shelf. On the particular row, he moves in a given order, probably from left to right, to get the book.

ACCESS TIME: A MATTER OF LOCATION

Of the two elements of computer operations, i.e., location and operation, access time pertains to the location.

STORAGE ALLOCATION. The data in the computer can be stored on-line or off-line. If it is off-line, the data will have to be brought back to where it needs to be processed. The space in a computer is at a premium, especially, in the central processing unit (CPU) where the calculations have to be performed. Approximately half the spaces in the CPU are taken up by computer overhead—which comprises everything required to carry out the instructions except data—leaving only half the space available for the operations. With the progressive reduction in the time required for the operations as the number of operations per minute increase to the order of billions, there is increasing pressure to keep the computer in operation for as much time as possible—which means using as much storage space as possible in the central processing unit. If several cells are reserved for successive values of different variables, it may result in "dead" storage, meaning thereby their unavailability for performing operations until the particular problem or processing is completed.

From the point of view of computer utilization, storage allocation, i.e., allocation of computer locations to hold data or perform operations, is of critical importance. FORTRAN allocates storage locations prior to the commencement of program execution. Every location is preassigned and is dedicated to a particular operation or data.

However, in ALGOL and PL/I storage allocation is dynamic, meaning that the information structures are created at the beginning segment of the program and deleted at the end. Of course, this does not include creating permanent locations of storage, which can be made by a simple command. PL/I has dynamic storage allocation, with wider types of dynamic options. It should be remembered that in dynamic storage allocation, the data and/or instruction are moved around in the course of performance of the operations, so that special accounting has to be maintained of what is in the location at any given time; therefore, if the data or operation locations are moved around, the computer better keep track of the changing occupants of the locations, lest the wrong things be done to the wrong data at any given location. Such bookkeeping chores go with the advantages of dynamic storage allocation. In addition, the computer has to have an idea of the nature and magnitude of upcoming operations for which appropriate space has to be reserved. It means that some scheduling operations have also to be performed. Again, additional increases in the overhead.

CORE CYCLE. It is one thing to allocate the limited space that is available in the computer to perform operations; it is another to physically carry out operations in the assigned locations. How soon can the data be stored in a given location? How soon can the data be taken from storage and brought up for processing? Access time in terms of hardware capabilities must include both operations, which is designated by the term, *core cycle*. It consists of the *read* operation of clearing a word from magnetic core storage and the *write* operation of inserting or reinserting the word in the same storage. Of course, if the data are stored away from the main storage, say on discs, access time would include the disc access time, over and above that of the core cycle.

PROCESSING TIME: A MATTER OF OPERATION

Once having reached the desired location in the computer, how long does it take to perform the operations?

BATCH PROCESSING. The operations are performed in accordance with a preestablished hierarchy of operations. For instance, multiplication and division must be performed before addition and subtraction. Since multiplication is successive addition, and division is successive subtraction, what the computer does is to add and subtract. Integration and differentiation can also be expressed as additions and subtractions of very, very small quantities over very, very small intervals. The computer takes no more time to do the most complex addition than the simplest. It takes as long to add 1 and 1, as to add two 10-digit numbers. In fact, subtracting 1 from 1 is a very elaborate process. Since it works in one direction only, it cannot simply go back one step from 1 to zero. Instead, the minus 1 is set in as 9,999,999,999, i.e., 10 billion minus 1. It then adds 1 to 9,999,999,999. The advantage therefore is to combine a number of similar operations in a *batch*. Of course, the sequence of the operations to be performed on each set of variables has to be observed carefully, and the progression of a particular piece of data from one location to another should be meticulously kept track of through a number of successive operations.

DATA HANDLING. The capability to create files of data, maintain them, and move them back and forth is an important criterion in selecting a computer. It will be recalled that the importance of data handling was behind the development of COBOL in 1960 and the federal government's decision to require the capability to accept COBOL as a prerequisite to federal purchase (lease) of computers.

The basic raw data files mostly remain the same for the entire organism. What changes is the way that each user uses the data. In the simplest instance, the number of units of a particular product (service) purchased by a customer is a piece of data which is of interest to the sales department (sales revenue), the shipping department (requirement for shipping facilities), production department (quality control), purchasing department (raw material requirements), finance department (billing and collection), and so on.

In other words, each activity of the organism requires the rearrangement of the identical piece of data to suit its own individual needs. If the computer has the facility to create a file, change it, and re-create with a minimum of direct instruction, this would facilitate more frequent and widespread use for the same data file. PL/I uses the word GET to obtain data and the word PUT to report data, provided the data are in the form of a continuous stream of data items associated with a particular set of variables. The user can determine the particular list(s) of data items that he is going to handle by means of a *pointer*.

COMPUTER COMMANDS. The computer is used to augment human reasoning. Therefore, if human reasoning in the form of computer instructions in a program can be extended by the computer, to that extent the need for human programming will be decreased. One of the ways of extending instructions is to use *macro* instructions. Using macros, by means of a single command, called SUM, the operation of finding two or more entities and storing the SUM of the entities in a specifiable location can be repeated as often as needed, thus avoiding the necessity for the repetition of the same instruction. As more is understood about the repeating patterns which represent any phenomenon, macro facilities can be employed to shorten the programming effort by extending the logic of discovered patterns.

HEURISTICS. In the use of heuristics, the operation has to be identified and explicitly specified, so that the computer can repeat it. Instead of the *explicit* extension of instructions in using the macro facility, implicit extension of instructions can be achieved with programs in which the computer is instructed to discover patterns and to repeat them. Much remains to be learned about how humans solve problems before their discovery pattern can be translated into computer capability to discover and apply patterns in one phase of the problem to another. In the selection of a computer, such capability to extend implicitly the human instructions would be a useful asset.

COMPUTER COMMANDS FOR ITERATIVE OPERATIONS. Taking advantage of the reliability in the repetition of operations of any computer, the instruction can be given: Repeat such and such operation beginning with one value and increasing by a specified increment, until a terminal value is reached. Greater flexibility of computer instruction is obtained if such a repetitive process can be *interrupted*, i.e., perform the operation for successive values until a given value is reached; then proceed in one direction or the other depending upon the outcome until a terminal value is reached. PL/I offers the flexibility of iterative operations which not only repeat the same operations, but also repeat the operations subject to the given condition. The capability to let the computer monitor its own processes in accordance with the prespecified logic, permits much greater flexibility than having to carry out an entire sequence of operations, then compare the values, and then issue instructions for a different set of repeated operations.

CONTROL TRANSFERS. In discussing access time, mention was made of the time required to move the data from wherever it is located to wherever it is needed to perform the operations upon them. It is equally important to release the data after given operations so that other operations may be performed upon them. The computer does this by transferring control over the variables in accordance with the given conditions. The flexibility of changing the control mechanism, i.e., letting different operations be performed upon a given set of data as certain conditions are fulfilled (or not fulfilled), is an important consideration in effectively utilizing computer capabilities so that processing time may be kept to a minimum.

4. Control over computer operations

In chapter 5 attention was given to operating systems. An *operating system* has been defined as "an organized collection of programs and data that is specifically designed to facilitate the creation of computer programs and control their execution on a computer system."[2] The operating system comprises control programs and processing programs, the latter operating under the control of the programs and existing as a unit of work of the system.

Control programs can best be looked upon as the mechanical managers of computer systems. These programs are resident within the computer, and manage the utilization of computer resources (locations and operations) to achieve the objective of the system, i.e., to maximize computer utilization. The role of the mechanical managers is increasingly important when one considers modern computers, whether purchased, rented, or leased, and further, if the use of a time-sharing facility or a computer utility network is contemplated. The reason is that in all instances, to make the computer operations viable, the data have to be created, maintained, and accessed, and the operations should be grouped together wherever possible, consistent with the accurate and speedy performance of the operations. This function is increasingly vested in the mechanical managers. For this reason, operating systems in general, and control programs in particular, occupy a very important place in the functional approach to computer selection.

An Ordering of the Functional Criteria

How can the various criteria be ordered to apply them to computer system selection?

In the first criterion, efficiency as a matter of hardware-software combination, software considerations should be weighted more than hardware. Computer languages, the medium of communication with the computer, must be selected with care to provide not only capability today, but also flexibility tomorrow. Therefore, the past record and the present

---

[2] Harry Katzan, Jr., *Operations Systems: A Pragmatic Approach* (New York: Van Nostrand, 1973), p. 3.

performance of the computer manufacturer with respect to the development and maintenance of computer languages would be a prime consideration.

If hardware and software were equal, they would share a total score of 100 in 50:50 ratio. To give primacy for software, let us associate an index of 60 with software. Out of 60, the continuing improvement of communication with the computer via programming languages would get a weight of, say, 25.

The second criterion, ease of writing versus cost of overhead, can be given a score of 15 out of 60.

Access time versus processing time, the third criterion, is a combination of hardware and software—more hardware than software. Therefore, we assign a score of 5 out of 60 on the software side; and a score of 15 out of 40 on the hardware side, making a total maximum score of $(5 + 15 =)$ 20 for access time versus processing time.

In the last criterion, control over computer operations, a mixture of hardware and software features should be considered. The operating system is part of software; but, being resident in the computer and essentially not subject to major changes by human intervention from the outside, it should be considered more hardware than software. We assign 15 out of 60 from the software side; and 25 out of 40 from the hardware side, making a total maximum score of $(15 + 25 =)$ 40 for the operating systems.

These weightings are, of course, illustrative. However, they give an initial ordering which can be used as a point of departure in the functional approach to the evaluation computer selection.

Customizing Computer Capabilities

From the technical and general considerations of computer selection developed so far, we now turn to organismic and particular considerations in tailoring the computer capabilities to the special needs of the organism. We shall discuss customizing criteria in selecting a particular computer capability in support of MIS (IIS). The seven criteria are:

1. Alternative accesses
2. Communication capabilities
3. Staff support
4. Internal education
5. Concrete contract
6. Data Input–Decision Output
7. Automating order

Alternative accesses

Even as management becomes increasingly complex, the technology of computer operations makes it possible to handle more and more operations with modern equipment. The rapid rise in the speed of computer operations, say, from 1,000,000 to 1,000,000,000 operations per minute, would, other things being equal, *reduce* the unit cost of operations unless the increase in computer cost is 1,000-fold and/or computer utilization has decreased substantially.

There is a certain amount of interdependence between the complexity of MIS (IIS) operations and the capability of computer operations. A solution-oriented problem such as linear programming with 77 variables and nine constraints took 120 man-days of calculations to arrive at *a* solution. The same problem took twelve minutes on one of the very early computers; and the computer could evaluate not just a few selected combinations, but the whole set of possible calculations, so that the answer could be determined to be *the* solution. Before the computer, such a reduction from 120 man-days to twelve minutes, i.e., 1/14400 or roughly a reduction to one fourteen-thousandth of the time, would have been unimaginable.

INCREASE IN COMPUTER SPEED

In the 1950s, the first mathematical computer, Electronic Numerical Integrator and Computer (ENIAC), performed an addition in 1/5000 of a second. The largest computer in the United States in the 1960s was the Weather Bureau's STRETCH (so named because it was hoped that it would stretch man's knowledge) which was able to do the same addition in 1.5 millionths of a second, or 300 times as fast. In the 1970s Control Data Corporation's CDC 7600 can do 10 million calculations per second, or 2,000 times as fast as ENIAC. The CDC 7600 is performing between 10^7–10^8 operations per minute. The foreseeable future speeds are in the range of 10^{11}–10^{12} operations per minute. When the upper range on future speeds is attained, *1,000 billion* operations will be performed in a minute. When one billion operations are performed in a second, the speed of an operation is *one nanosecond*. When the upper range of the projected future speed is attained, a single computer operation would take approximately 1/16th of a *nanosecond*.

KEEP THE COMPUTER BUSY

Decrease in the unit cost can be realized only if the computer is kept fully occupied. If, for instance, the computer can be given only one million operations to do, while it can perform one billion units operations, then the 999/1000 minute is available for use.

COMPUTER COSTS AND TIME-SHARING

According to George S. Walker, business manager of Yale University's Computer Center, a second-generation machine costs $2 million to buy, while a third-generation machine might cost another $6 million.[3] The high cost of purchasing computers led to the growth of the computer-leasing industry. The principle of leasing is the differential depreciation between the manufacturer and the lessor. The manufacturers depreciate computing equipment over 50 months; leasing companies depreciate over 10 years. This means that on a million-dollar computer, a manufacturer charges off $20,000 per month, while a lessor writes off $8,000.[4]

The total cost of computer operations, of course, is not limited to the cost of the equipment itself. Other expenses are personnel, site preparation, supplies, contracts, etc. Of these, personnel is expected to rise significantly, if not steadily, having risen from 5 percent in the early 1950s, to 50 percent in 1965, and over 70 percent in the 1970s—i.e., programming cost as percent of total data processing cost, including hardware, programming, and maintenance.[5]

The significant costs, both initially for hardware and subsequently for maintenance, have made the possibilities of time-sharing quite attractive. The advantages of time-sharing include the fact that it pays for what you use instead of what you own. The disadvantage is that when you need it, the computer (time) may not be available. One way of circumventing such a predicament is to use time-sharing facilities of more than one manufacturer, so that if one fails the other can be used as a backup. The experience of the Simulation and Computers (SIMCOM) Directorate of the Industrial College of the Armed Forces (ICAF) which is organized under the auspices of the Joint Chiefs of Staff clearly endorses time-sharing:

> Prior to the establishment of SIMCOM, the accepted idea at ICAF was to install a computer. Fortuitously, in early 1967, the long-awaited time-shared systems were becoming reality. . . . Original estimates for a computer were $2.5 million. Estimates for software, environmental modifications, and personnel were an additional $3 million. SIMCOM leases time from several different time-shared systems for less than $0.1 million per year.[6]

---

[3]"Campus Computers: Federal Budget Cuts Hit University Centers," *Science* 192 (22 Sept. 1969): 1337.

[4] "Computer Leasing Is Here to Stay," *Computopics* (Dec. 1968): 8.

[5] Earl C. Joseph, "Computers: Trends Toward the Future," Paper presented to International Federation of Information Processing Societies (Edinburgh, Scotland, Aug. 1968), p. 28.

[6] William Thane Minor, "Current and Future Uses of Time-Sharing in Education Simulation," in *Time Sharing Innovation for Operations Research and Decision-Making*, eds. Hugh V. O'Neill and Donald W. King (Washington, D.C.: Washington Operations Research Council, 1969), p. 99.

COMPUTER NEEDS AND UTILITY

The viability of the time-sharing depends not only upon the availability of computer hardware, but also upon the variety of computer programs needed for the prosecution of the different activities that a particular MIS (IIS) will require. As far as the manufacturer who is renting time on the computer is concerned, he would want to carry the software which serves the largest number of users. In other words, the *greatest common factor* would determine the availability of software in a time-sharing system.

Suppose there is a group of users who have common programming needs which are not satisfied by the lowest common factor. Among themselves they would have need for computer uses of a specialized kind. For instance, a group of hospitals have several special needs which will not be shared by the many other computer users; for example, the facility to diagnose diseases on the basis of symptoms; the requirement to provide medication, to compare the subsequent behavior of the patient, and to change the medication if necessary; the scheduling of patients in diagnostic facilities, such as radiology, laboratory, etc. Similarly, a group of insurance companies would also have group-specific MIS (IIS) needs. For instance, they would need the updating of experience of life insurance policies; changes in the classification of property from the point of view of insurance premiums on the basis of acquired experience, and so on.

The existence of such significant groups whose MIS (IIS) requirements of computer usage are group-specific set the stage for the evolution of *computer public utility*. Parkhill says:

> . . . historically, many of our present public utilities began as limited subscribers of private ventures. Even today, despite the fantastic growth of the public systems, many organizations continue to operate their own private power plants or internal communication systems.

> In this same pattern the first rudimentary examples of computer utilities were of private type, regardless of whether they were general-purpose or special-purpose in function. . . .

> . . . the computer utility is a general-purpose public system that includes features such as:

> (1) Essentially simultaneous use of the system by many remotely located users.

> (2) Concurrent running of different multiple programs. . . .

> (5) A capacity for indefinite growth, so that as the customer load increases, the system can be expanded without limit by various means including:

>   (a) the addition of extra computers within the utility service area,

>   (b) the addition of special modules such as extra random-access storage, extra arithmetic units, etc.,

(c) connecting with other information utilities to draw on their unused capacity. . . .

In fact, as such a utility grew it might eventually embrace the entire nation and service not only industrial, government, and the business customers, but also private homes, until the personal computer console became as commonplace as the telephone.[7]

Within the context of the computer public utility in general, the role of computer utility networks in health care MIS (IIS) may be mentioned. In chapter 2 reference was made to the work of the University Computing Company (UCC) in Dallas, Texas. Hospital data management needs provide the basis for the computer concept of the University Computing Company:

The cornerstone of the UCC utility concept is regional marketing service through a national network of users providing economies of scale. . . . Hospitals and other health care organizations utilizing the services of Health Data Net become members of user group organizations. These user groups play a key role in defining critical areas of need which can benefit from the application of automation techniques.[8]

In this connection, another utility may be mentioned. In chapter 8 the use of an interactive language, MUMPS, was discussed with reference to diagnosis, medication, and other similar functions, as distinguished from the initial primary concentration upon the financial areas in the UCC network. MUMPS is also developing a utility concept. It has in fact acquired a number of users, and they are in the process of forming a group of users who can share the MUMPS system:

There are now a number of different institutions which have implemented MUMPS systems, and several commercial vendors market MUMPS Systems and MUMPS application programs on a utility basis. A MUMPS user's group is being formed to enhance communication between various MUMPS users, to facilitate sharing of programs, and to promote standards in regard to language definition and documentation.[9]

---

[7] D. F. Parkhill, *Challenge of the Computer Utility* (Reading, Mass.: Addison-Wesley, 1966), p. 5.

[8] Douglass M. Parnell, Jr., Julius Aronofsky, and Thomas G. Paterson, "Role of Computer Utility Networks in Health Care," Paper presented to AAAS National Meeting, Washington, D.C., December 29, 1972, pp. 8, 12.

[9] Massachusetts General Hospital and Harvard University, "Laboratory of Computer Science," Boston, Mass., 1972, p. 1.

Communication capabilities

The alternative accesses provided by the different ways of utilizing computer capabilities raise the important question of *user* capabilities to communicate with the computer. A brief questionnaire is offered to elucidate the organism's own capability in the matter:

1. How would you characterize the users of your computer system —present or potential—in terms of their capability to communicate with the computer?
   a. Can they write programs in one or more languages, or can they learn to do so within, say, two to three months?
   b. Can they formulate their questions in the required sequence of steps, or would they expect it to be done for them?
   c. Will they interpret the computer outputs themselves by poring over them, or will they expect it to be done for them?
2. In the light of the answers to question 1, how would you characterize the relative preference for the ease of writing versus the cost of overhead?
   a. How rapidly would you expect the computer installation to be producing outputs which would be relevant to decision-making?
   b. How frequently would the computer outputs have to be re-formatted before use by decision-makers?
   c. What is the fraction of the processing by the computer in which extensive calculations predominate, as distinguished from handling of large-scale data?
3. In the light of the answer to question 2(c), how would you characterize the importance of the functional criteria of computer commands?
   a. Computer commands to handle data more important than computer commands to extend instructions (data processing more important).
   b. Computer commands to extend instructions more important than computer commands to handle data (mathematical calculations more important).
   c. Computer commands for control transfers more important than computer commands for iteration (flexible computations more important).

Staff support

In chapter 10 the first step in the development of an MIS (IIS) was identified as that of establishing a staff position reporting to the PDM. Equal care must be exercised in the establishment and operation of the computer facility within the organism.

"No place for ADP in our organization structures"

John Diebold, writing in 1964, discussed the problem of ADP—The Still Sleeping Giant:

We still have no place for ADP *in our organization structures.* . . .

Finally, and of paramount importance, will be the *creation of a place in the organization structure* for ADP. This is no simple task. Today's business organization structure is a legacy of the first industrial revolution; specialization of labor has been followed by organization around specialties. However, the new technology makes it imperative that we build information systems which break through the compartmentalized structure of traditional business organization.[10]

Where should the computer systems services be located? The MIS (IIS) manager is at a staff position, reporting to the PDM, deriving the justification for his existence from the contribution he is able to make to the decision process of the PDM himself. The MIS (IIS) manager is supporting the PDM by providing forecasts and insights into forecasts, as well as recommendations for alternative decision courses.

The computer systems services (CSS) should serve the organism as a whole. The MIS (IIS) manager would be one of the principal *users* of CSS in the organism, but not necessarily the only one. It would be unwise to make the MIS (IIS) manager also the CSS manager, because the computers themselves are items of major investment; managing those resources, which runs into a million dollars or more a year, does require a manager apart from the MIS (IIS) manager.

Comptroller control of computers

Where should the computer systems services be located organizationally?

The earliest use of data processing facilities to run the company payroll on data processing equipment led to the control of CSS being invested in the comptroller's office. However, this is not necessarily a logical location, for the comptroller is dealing with the third major type of raw data input, profit factors. Profit factors are a derived set of figures, *derived* from the first two set of factors, demand and supply factors.

The comptroller is a very important user of the computer system, because accounting data, payroll, and associated elements of representations of the operations of the organism are usually the first operations to be put on the computer. However, these are *not* directly related to the production, the demand for, or the supply of, products and/or services by the organism. After all, it is the demand for the products from the outside that justifies the very existence of the organism. Therefore, the most

[10] John Diebold, "ADP—The Still Sleeping Giant," *Harvard Business Review*, 1964.

important use of CSS should be by those who are dealing directly with these external *demand* factors. Next in importance are those who deal with the *supply* of products and/or services, i.e., the utilization of the production capabilities of the organism: manual, mechanical and/or both. A third group of users is the *distribution* facilities which deliver the products and/or services to the different demand points.

User orientation of computer system services (CSS)

Thus we have a logical view of the different types of users who would be customers for CSS. They can be ranked in decreasing order of importance as those relating to demand factors, supply factors, and profit factors. If the use of the computer facility is oriented toward these three major factors, then there would be a rational apportionment of the time and resources available to these functions. Of course, if they are equally weighted, the share of each would be 33-1/3%, which means that each of the operations in the three categories will share the budget of the computer systems according to their share. The CSS costs would be an overhead item; therefore, the sharing of the budget by each facility devoted to one of the three factors would be a *pro forma* entry rather than an actual one.

But the total cost of operations are a real entity, and it has to be assigned to those who use the facility. If the share of the CSS costs borne by each major activity were visible and used in the planning and operations, then the user would be encouraged to think in terms of the concrete results that would be yielded by CSS and not the mere glamour of the hardware itself. In other words, the obligation is upon the user to insure that the decision-making is in fact responsive to the changes that the computer system operations will have yielded. If such results cannot be established, then the value of the use of the computer facility will be questioned, and an alternative user will have to be found.

In seeking alternative users, it becomes apparent that the *change in decision-making* holds the key. If present computer system operations results do not have any perceivable effect upon the decision-making by the different users, then either the computer system users should be changed, or new decision-making activities will have to be discovered. If the outputs are not used in decision-making over a significant period of time, then the particular user should really raise questions about the value of the computer system operations for him. It is precisely this situation that has been anticipated in chapter 10. It will be recalled that each user was asked to provide raw data input, in return for which he was promised certain outputs. Further, there was an indication of frequency of use report. What the continued nonuse of the system would indicate is that the initial estimates of inputs and outputs are not applicable and that they need to be revised. The total lack of use would suggest that the initial estimate was wide off the mark altogether.

COMPUTER SYSTEMS SERVICES AS PART OF MANAGEMENT SERVICES

The user levels must be identified with respect to the levels in the organizational hierarchy—organismic, strategic, and tactical—over and above that of merely the three factors of demand, supply, and profit. In order to make the outputs user-oriented at the organismic level, it is advisable to raise the level of reporting to the organismic level. Chapter 10 identified the MIS (IIS) manager in the staff reporting functions as reporting to the PDM. The CSS manager could also be reporting at the organismic level, but not to the PDM—the absolute PDM. The reason is that the MIS (IIS) manager deals with ideas and recommendations, while the manager of the computer systems operations has to deal with a million dollar operation, the returns on which have to be identified as worthwhile.

If the organism is sufficiently large, it could have an activity in support of management functions, *management services*. The CSS could logically come under this activity; so also could other supporting activity pertaining to demand, supply, and profit factors. The director of management services would himself report to the PDM or the vice-president for staff services. The latter will be in charge of not only computer systems-related operations, but also other service functions related to the maintenance, operation, and development of human skills and mechanical capabilities, as well as the acquisition of new facilities, mergers, etc.

Internal education

The best computer systems can be total failures if they are not accepted by the organism. Often the CSS speaks a different language all its own. And understandably so. However, if the entire communication with CSS is predicated upon everyone else learning the computer lingo, that is bound to reduce to a minimum the acceptance, and therefore use, of CSS.

TRAINING THE USERS BY CSS

The CSS manager must be oriented toward the *use* by the various elements of the organism of the computing operations. To facilitate corporate-wide use of CSS, an *initial training* of the major users of the computer system will be necessary. The initial training would be at least of two types: (1) an appreciation of the computing systems by the top- and middle-level management; and (2) a hands-on training for the lower levels of management. The former is intended to win the approval of the decision-makers for the facility itself, while the latter is to insure that the people who would most directly be involved in the use of CSS would know how to prepare the data and to present it for processing by the computer as well as to interpret the results.

FACILITATING THE FLOW OF INPUTS

In view of the unprecedented capability of the computer to handle data and of the vesting of corporate proprietary interests in the raw data peculiar to each entity, it is imperative that the CSS manager have an acute awareness of his customers, i.e., the particular needs of those within the organism who will now or in the future *use* the computer facility. CSS must make it possible and convenient for present and potential users of the system to input data, and to receive outputs, which often convey more insight than what they put in. Awareness on the part of the CSS manager of the capabilities necessary to meet the raw data input demands and the pre-information output demands require (1) knowledge of the data, i.e., the peculiar characteristics of the particular organism in terms of its fulfillment characteristics and performance characteristics; and (2) a knowledge of computers, i.e., the capabilities and limitations of the present computer system, in light of potential alternatives.

RECOGNIZING SUPPORTIVE STAFF FUNCTIONS

Unlike other supportive staff functions of the organism, CSS represents a significant investment of resources and requires considerable activity shrouded in technical jargon. The line manager may wonder what debugging is all about, and why it takes forever. Why should a program, which is after all written in near-English, take so much effort? It would be helpful to recognize the major types of functions that CSS has to perform.

Included in the staff functions served by the computer system operations are (1) initial training of the users, including the decision-makers and their line support; (2) interpretation of the problem requirements of the users into computer processing instructions; (3) development of equitable procedures to share the computer system facilities by all the users; (4) upkeep of the hardware; (5) upkeep of the software; (6) development of new applications of the computer software capability; (7) periodic training of the users in the computer capabilities that are of particular application to them; (8) maintenance of liaison with the technical computing professional community on the developments particularly in software; and (9) professional participation, both in the user groups and in the software groups.

These 9 functions can be grouped into three: technical functions, service functions, and professional functions. Considerable amount of misunderstanding has arisen in the past because of lack of understanding of the technical functions, and, to a lesser degree, the professional functions. The language used by the computer system personnel in discharging their technical functions would necessarily remain a closed book to all but those who are initiated. Therefore, the time that they have to spend in technical functions would be considered probably a waste of time by those who do not understand. The time spent in professional activities would not appear to generate immediate results, their contribution being the enrichment of the professional participants to enable more effective utilization of CSS capabilities at a later time. If these two types of activities account for, say, 20 to 25% of the time, and if they are not understood, it is quite likely that the expenditure of some $250,000 a year would be considered wasteful. This is a sizable figure, and it will attract considerable attention. Since defense of the technical and professional functions will use necessarily technical terms, it is likely that at times the explanation would also be less than satisfactory.

Since it is so easy to reject the entire computer system operations on the basis of lack of understanding of a portion of it, it is essential that long before the computer selection is made, the supporting levels develop an appreciation for this peculiarity of the operations. Great care must be exercised in *not* overselling the computer; and the significant expenditure in the care and feeding of CSS must be laid out well in advance to the vice-president for staff services, and through him, to the potential users of CSS.

Concrete contract

In chapter 6 an MIS (IIS) utilization matrix was developed with 729 categories. They include most of the *types of uses* that can be made of CSS.

CUSTOM-TAILORED MIS (IIS) UTILIZATION MATRIX

To ensure the user-orientation of CSS, a profile should be drawn up of the particular MIS (IIS) utilization matrix envisaged for the particular organism. If such a profile is not drawn up, it is quite likely that the decision to institute a computer facility would be left to the technicians. If technicians devise the operations, there is a distinct possibility that the system would succeed, but fail from a user point of view.

USER-INVOLVEMENT IN CSS DESIGN

In the survey of more than 2,500 executives undertaken on behalf of the 140 U.S. and overseas companies sponsoring the Diebold Research Program, it was found that technicians have been setting the goals for computer systems:

> The survey indicates that *technicians*, not management, are setting goals for computers. This is one of the prime reasons why companies often fail to realize the true potential from their data processing investment. . . .

> Most technicians cannot be expected to understand the needs or the opportunities of the corporation well enough to establish goals for

331

computer systems. Management itself must take the trouble to understand what new technologies make possible and what is necessary in
order to apply them effectively and imaginatively.[11]

The development of a user profile can help avoid the pitfalls of
overspecialization in the equipment at the expense of potential utilization.
The development of the profile is only a starting point in that it identifies
what the computer system should be able to do as perceived *before* it is
installed. Given the basis of its initial usage, the specialists in computer
programming should in fact plan for the particular profile of use in that
organism, and in addition allow for expansion. The user profile has two
advantages: (1) it brings the user into the loop; and (2) it specifies the
"before" computer installation status, so that an "after" comparison can be
made with the subsequent developments.

COMPUTER FACILITY SUITS BY USERS

Neither the user nor the technical personnel is likely to be a specialist in
the management of sizable financial investments. It should be remembered
that the computer system is in fact a significant investment, as Diebold
points out:

> The average company which responded reports spending just under
> $1,000,000 per year on ADP activities; 4.3% spend over $5,000,000 and
> 17% under $100,000 per year.[12]

Recognizing the investment in computers as a *financial* one, it is
important that the computer acquisition be treated as any other significant
investment of money would be treated, such as buying a house, an
automobile, etc. In these large purchases—large to the individual who buys
the house, the automobile—*written* representation of the product is
customary. The law requires that the automobile parts and accessories be
itemized and priced on a sticker that is displayed prominently in the new
automobile. The performances rendered by these parts and accessories are
well understood with respect to an automobile, but they are not quite well
understood with respect to the computer. Even if the hardware were to be
identified, that would be far from adequate because the applications are
what make the difference. Roy Freed, an attorney who has devoted a large
part of his practice to legal matters involving computers, reports:

> In April 1969, a data-processing service company was ordered to pay
> three automotive and electrical parts-distributing customers $480,811 in
> damages for losses suffered from misrepresentations concerning the
> capabilities of an inventory system which had been used to serve the

[11] John Diebold, "Bad Decisions on Computer Use," *Harvard Business Review* (January-
February 1969): 31–33.
[12] Ibid., p. 32.

company's customers; the misrepresentations were considered tantamount to fraud.[13] That incident is fast becoming merely another example of the large law suits brought by unhappy customers against suppliers of computers and computer service. . . .

In 1967, a computer manufacturer was sued by a textile manufacturer for $4 million in damages for breach of contract and fraudulent representations in connection with the lease of a large computer system in 1964. An injunction was granted against the removal of the equipment until alternative arrangements could be made by the lessee.[14]

Freed points out that such problems can be avoided by following sound procurement practices. He suggests a list of key points that should be covered in the negotiations:

> Descriptions of *all* goods and services to be furnished
> Specifications of those goods and services
> Acceptance tests
> Time of delivery
> Penalties for unexcused delays and other defaults
> Place of delivery
> Price, including discounts
> Terms of payment
> Warranties
> Protection against patent and copyright infringement
> Indication of the supplier's liability
> Action to be performed by the customer
> Options
> Duration of agreement[15]

It should be pointed out that the description of "services to be furnished" is more easily said than done. In particular, the capabilities of programming would make the difference between utilizing and not utilizing the hardware effectively. Therefore, it would be much harder to specify the "services" to be rendered, not only now, but also in the future. However, at least *minimum* standards should be specified as well as how these performances would be evaluated, i.e., the performance criteria. If the results of programming do not meet with the expected savings in the company operations such as inventory, transportation, etc., then it should not be immediately blamed on the computer programming; the problem

---

[13] Clements Auto Co. et al. vs. Service Bureau Corp., 298F. Supp. 115 (D. Minn. 1969). Decision reported in *The Wall Street Journal*, April 19, 1969.

[14] Spring Mills, Inc. vs. General Electric Co., U.S. District Court for District of South Carolina (Docket No. C.A. 67-544). Suit reported in *Electronic News*, September 11 and 25, 1967, and October 3, 1967.

[15] Roy N. Freed, "Get the Computer System You Want," *Harvard Business Review* (November-December 1969): 162.

could well be one of understanding the particular situation. If, however, the programs which deal with allocation of resources in inventory or transportation did not function technically satisfactorily, then that would be an area clearly attributable to computer programming. The important point is that both the limitations and possibilities of computer programming should be specified in writing at the time of the acquisition of the computer system services, whether through outright purchase or through leasing arrangements of one kind or another.

Data input–decision output

The profile of utilization only identifies the estimate of the potential utilization of different types of information for use by different decision-makers. It does not specify the particular format in which each user would receive forecasts.

It is important to identify the end product, i.e., the decision-making by the PDM. What is the information that the decision-maker will use? And, what difference will the information make to his decision-making? In chapter 10 it was suggested that an information input-output decision system profile be constructed at the outset, which would indicate the type of decisions for which the decision-maker would use the particular information input. This focus upon the *use* by the decision-maker—PDM as well as other echelons of decision-makers—will make it necessary to raise the question: Is this computer output really necessary? If it does not contribute to the information that the PDM, sub-PDM, or sub-sub-PDM would use, then there must be explicit justification for the computer printout itself and the processing which precedes the printout. A simulation would yield results which may not be immediately an input to the decision-maker. However, the results will yield *indirect* inputs in the form of new variables or relationships that the decision-maker ought to be aware of, over and above those currently considered. That would be a legitimate contribution to the quality of the decision-making.

Once the major *outputs* in the form of forecasts are identified, this can guide the designing of the corresponding raw data *inputs*. Each user should have a well-specified raw data input form, which identifies the precise inputs he would make, the precise outputs he will receive, and how often. In chapter 4 one-page statements of the inputs and the outputs from each of the major users of the computer system were illustratively identified.

In addition to the raw data input forms and the outputs expected in return, there must also be additional specification of applicable *modeling* concepts which will process the data. The processing would be open-ended, because the exact nature of the potential applications would not be known until the system is in operation. Nevertheless, it is important to identify in as specific terms as possible, the different uses to which the computer installation will be put, so that a minimum level of activity can be outlined at the outset.

Automating order

The computer systems does *not* generate information; it only converts raw data into *pre*-information.

It would be futile to consider the computer system to be one large furnace which melts widely different raw materials into a single major product. Even as the input of raw materials is individual oriented, so also will be the requirements of output. Therefore, it would be realistic to consider CSS as supporting the three major types of factors: demand, supply, and profit.

The individual needs of each of the supporting activities is different. Therefore, the degree to which each can utilize the facilities of CSS would also be different. For instance, payroll is certainly important, but work on them is fairly elementary from the point of view of the technical capabilities of the computer. On the other hand, the demands for a large-scale simulation of the operations of the company would require more sophisticated facilities. Solutions to the systems of equations representing the production processes would probably require even more sophisticated facilities.

The important thing is not to be carried away by the sophistication of the data processing or computing, but instead, to focus attention upon the level of complexity appropriate to the needs of the particular user. The requirements for automation, even as sophistication, would vary with the user and with the level of utilization. It should be custom-tailored to meet the particular problems and needs of each type of user. However, it is necessary to schedule the time required by each user to convert from a manual to a machine mode of operations. For instance, some preparation time would be needed to design the payroll forms which are most appropriate to the activity of a given organism. Similarly, the raw data inputs from the marketing group about incoming orders would also require the devising of appropriate computer forms. The distinction between data input–decision output forms and the present ones is that the forms discussed here are computer-oriented, while the previous ones were decision-oriented.

The automation sequence involves the totality of steps which transform a manual mode into a mechanical mode. It includes (1) design of input forms, (2) coding of the input forms, (3) verification of the coding, (4) recording of the forms in the computer storage, and (5) transfer to and from off-line storage. The number of steps in the sequence would vary, but, they have to reckon with the processes outlined in these steps. Clearly, the question of storage of data—whether it should be on-line or off-line—has to

335

be settled with respect to each of the three sets of data. In the three sets of data, there will be segments which can be accessed less frequently than others, and there will be those which need to be accessed more frequently. Therefore, some of the data can be stored on-line, and some others off-line with respect to the *demand* factors, the *supply* factors, and the *profit* factors. There would be changes in the status of the different data themselves, according to the nature of use made of the raw data.

If time-sharing is utilized, there is an added consideration of security. The principle of time-sharing is that the computer could be shared by a large number of users, each of whom could get to his particular set of data as needed. What guarantee is there that the raw data of one user will *not* be accessed by another? In a library, the books are stored according to the Dewey Decimal System and are accessed by the particular location in the library by the shelf; and there are really no barriers for a user to pick up one book instead of another in the same category, or in a different category. However, one organism's raw data should not be accessible by other organisms; and organisms which value their proprietary data may well choose the additional cost of an on-site CSS over the savings of a time-sharing system.

Yesterday's Data for Today's Decision

Whether manual or mechanical, the MIS (IIS) is an aid to decision-making designed to exercise control, i.e., bring about changes in tomorrow's outcome. MIS (IIS) provides forecasts, arrived at on the basis of decoding yesterday's data, of the shape of things to come tomorrow; these forecasts become information when the PDM uses them. The information will forever be incomplete because even in making instantaneous decisions, the latest data are at least an instant behind; and the content of the data is dictated by the PDM *not* asking for every bit of data on everything but in fact selectively ignoring considerable portions on any phenomenon. *Incomplete* information systems contribute to effective management by decoding yesterday's data into tomorrow's forecasts which the PDM seeks to affect by design by his decision-making.

QUESTIONS

Chapters 10 and 11 deal with the development of MIS (IIS). In chapter 11 computer considerations pertaining to setting up an MIS (IIS) were discussed. The purpose of the following questions is to develop an appreciation for the 4 functional criteria in selecting a computer, and the 7 customizing criteria in custom-tailoring the computer capabilities to the special needs of the organism.

A. FUNCTIONAL CRITERIA

1. Outline the role of analytical, empirical, and forecast period aspects in the potential utilization of computerized MIS (IIS).
2. Discuss briefly the functional criteria in selecting a computer system for MIS (IIS).

B. CUSTOMIZING CRITERIA

3. Answer the questionnaire on page 326 on behalf of your particular organism.
4. Why should computer systems services be a part of Management Services?
5. Identify the more important staff functions served by the computer systems services.
6. What are the major points to be covered in a contract for a computer system?

Answers to Questions

The intent of this section is merely to indicate what appears to be the most important elements of the answers to the problems. Therefore, the Answers are not exhaustive. It is hoped that the reader will use them as points of departure.

CHAPTER 1

A. DATA AND INFORMATION

1. Datum is *what is*. Data become information only when they affect behavior.
2. Forecasting and control.

B. INFORMATION SYSTEM

3. A manager is not saved by the multitude of data in which he immerses himself. The data cannot tell him where he should be with respect to the accomplishment of the objectives of the organism. It is he who has to interpret how well he is doing, which requires a perspective which goes beyond the past and the present, in which context he will find segments of the data to be irrelevant.
4. See Definition of Management.
5. See Definition of System.
6. The information system requires the conversion of data into information. The earliest data are yesterday's; the earliest projection of the data applies to today; and the earliest time at which any change can take place as a result of the decision made

today is tomorrow. There is an irreducible lapse of time between data and information; information and decision; and decision and consequence. The time elapsed may be made extremely small—on the order of microseconds—but it cannot be reduced to zero. Therefore, the information system will forever remain incomplete with respect to time.

It will also remain incomplete with respect to the characteristics in terms of which the information is presented. There are no "absolute" set of characteristics in terms of which information can be "complete" for any situation. The characteristics differ with the situation on hand; therefore, any information system will remain incomplete with respect to at least some of the uses to which it can be put.

7. See Definition of Forecasting.

CHAPTER 2

A. DATA UPDATE SYSTEMS

1. As each seat on each flight is booked, at any one of the 1,008 reservations and sales desks handling American Airlines passenger reservations, it is recorded in the master file of seats by flights.

2. The major difference will be with respect to the handling of *potential* demand for passenger seats. Instead of passively responding to the *present* demand for passenger seats, the incomplete information system will, for instance, alert management to the need for filling a particular flight with standby passengers including special-rate passengers, such as youth and military fares. Only if the probability of *not* filling the particular flight is known ahead of time can management institute a program to stimulate *potential* demands for passenger seats.

3. One modification is the estimate of the time at which the stock of a particular item will run out, so that substitute products may be promoted by the sales organization.

Another modification would be the incorporation of the unit profit of each item, so that the selection of substitute products, and the inducement to the customer to accept another similar product, may be planned from the point of view of the total profit, rather than from the total number of units of sale.

B. SERVICE STATUS REPORTS

4. Approximately 25%.

5. The purpose of a computer utility is to offer to a number of subscribers, each using a small portion, the capability of the services offered by the large computer utility. The reason it is advantageous to the large group of customers to utilize a specialized service offered by a utility, instead of a general services computer, is that the utility is *custom-tailored* to the special needs of the customers, such as those in insurance, those in hospital services, etc. The major element of cost is the writing of the programs to serve the special needs of the customers; therefore, if there is a large enough group who needs specialized handling of processes and products which are common to them, but quite different from those outside the group, it would pay to develop custom-tailored programs for their exclusive use because the economies of scale would reduce the individual cost.

C. PRODUCT STATUS REPORTS

6. AAS is the *accounting* system which handles the System 360 orders, while the CMIS handles the *manufacturing* side. Between the entry of an order and the installation of a computer, it is necessary to monitor the progress of the production of all components—involving some 20 million records and 27 million index records. Production takes place in 13 plants. Prior to the introduction of CMIS in 1968, each plant kept track of its production in its own way, making the process of reflecting even a moderate change in customer specifications an involved process. Therefore, a "common" manufacturing data system was developed, the word "common" emphasizing the uniform record-keeping system.

7. Forecasting is a "given" of CMIS, given by the "headquarters."

D. RESEARCH STATUS REPORTS

8. TRAIS is billed as being capable of providing the data to plan, control, and assess Department of Transportation Research and Development Programs. However, budget data appear to be the only data provided in addition to work in progress.

MARES does refer to "projected capabilities" of the Fleet Marine Forces to execute contingency and other plans. If capabilities are in fact projected, to that extent MARES incorporates forecasting, it thereby moves closer to information systems.

9. See ADP system (8): NTIS.

E. COMPUTER USAGE SURVEYS

10. Dollars and cents earned from the computer system investment are the prime *measurable* criterion used in the McKinsey Survey.

11. The value of the new information obtainable from computer-aided information systems is not taken into account by management which thinks in terms of "return on investment," such as reduction in labor due to computer calculations.

CHAPTER 3

A. OBJECTIVES AND ADMINISTRATIVE HIERARCHIES

1. The triad of objectives of an organism is a flexible concept which identifies three successive levels of decision-making related to each other in a logical fashion. Thus, the *organismic* level can be associated with top management, the *strategic* level with middle management, and the *tactical* level with lower management. The requirement is that the component elements of the triad be an integral part of the immediately higher levels: the tactical level must be a logical component of the strategic level, and the strategic level must be a logical component of the organismic level.

2. In the answer to question 1, the objectives hierarchy of organismic, strategic, and tactical levels has corresponded to the administrative hierarchy of top management, middle management, and lower-level management. However, the two need not correspond to each other. The objectives hierarchy is based on the *content* of decision-making, while the administrative hierarchy is based on the *form* of

organizational relationships. To the extent that perspective is not determined exclusively by one's organizational position, someone in lower management could well be at a strategic level with respect to a group of products, while the middle management to which he reports may be at the organismic level.

3. The formal levels of organization specify the formal lines of communication in the administrative hierarchy. However, in performing *managerial* functions the supervisor may well find that he has to think about what is good for the *organism*, and not merely for his section. If the supervisor is in the production department, he may find it necessary in performing his function of warehouse maintenance to find out from the marketing department the demand for the products in the warehouse. Further, there may be a need to touch base with the personnel department which has requirements of stability in production employment which may conflict with both the marketing department and the production department.

The administrative hierarchy requires that communication from the production supervisor go through the production manager and the production vice-president. Therefore, the supervisor will have to go through the chain of command in his department, which, at the vice-presidential level, will initiate contacts with counterpart(s) in the marketing and personnel departments. However, the operational data directly applicable to the warehouse supervisor is at least two levels below the vice-president. Therefore, the vice-president of marketing will have to search for the data at least two levels below him, and have the data transmitted back two levels up and across to the vice-president of production, who, in turn, will have to transmit two levels down to the warehouse supervisor. If the supervisor were to do any forecasting and control, he would need the inputs from his counterparts in marketing and personnel. Time could be of the essence. Therefore, the chain of communication laid down by the administrative hierarchy would impose considerable delay, which could be detrimental to the interests of the organism as reflected in the organismic hierarchy.

B. CONTEXT C

4. Any decision-making role in an organism would have another role immediately above and another role immediately below with respect to its relationships to the organismic objectives. With regard to the level directly below, the decision-maker is at the strategic level; with respect to two levels below, the decision-maker is at the organismic level. At the same time, with regard to the level immediately above, the decision-maker is at the strategic level, and with respect to the two levels immediately above, he is at the tactical level. The requirement that the same decision-maker be simultaneously at the organismic, strategic, and tactical levels produces the inherent conflict.

5. No single MIS (IIS) can be equally effective for decision-making at the organismic, strategic, and tactical levels of decision-making because the same set of data cannot produce equally effective inputs to long term, intermediate-term, and short-term policy questions. Different MIS (IIS) will have to be developed to meet the different hierarchical decision-making requirements; since decision-making roles do vary, it is necessary to build enough flexibility in the MIS to respond to the varying demands placed on it.

C. CONTEXT E

6. The raison d'être of the organism is to meet the external demands placed upon it; the extent to which these demands are met by the organism determines its survival and growth. Therefore, it behooves the organism to know what its customers expect of it.

7. The characteristics which the external environment expect to be fulfilled may have no known precedence (hence no probability distributions), as in the case of the customer trying to state in the 1940s what he would expect from the jet propulsion technology of the 1950s. At the other extreme are the well-known characteristics, as in the case of specifying the duration of light bulbs. In between the former (uncertain) and the latter (reduced risk) context is the intermediate situation of risky context, in which the customer has some knowledge of the expected performance, i.e., he knows the *form* of the probability distribution, but not the specific performance of the immediate product on hand, i.e., not the parameters of the distribution.

D. CONTEXT T

8. Context E is the characterization of the fulfillment characteristics (what needs the customer expects the products and/or services of the organism to fulfill), while Context T is the characterization of the characteristics of technology (what the state of the art is with respect to achieving desired performance characteristics). The customer may wish to travel at supersonic speeds; however, the technology of air travel may still be in the subsonic speed range. When the customer of the *future* product and/or service specifies what he wants the product and/or service to do to fulfill his needs or wants, it may well leapfrog what the technology might conceivably accomplish in the foreseeable period. Context E could be considered a shopping list by the customer, while Context T is the market basket. The former can be fanciful, but the latter has to be specific.

9. Consider in the early 1960s when the fabrication of semiconductors was by no means well known. The customers of the then futuristic semiconductors were computer and spacecraft manufacturers. When the customers asked for semiconductors, they probably specified wild specifications for the yet-to-be-made product.

At the same time, the technology being unstable, the performance characteristics would be far from established. Therefore, the technologists in the semiconductor industry could do little guaranteeing of performance to the manufacturers of computers and spacecrafts. The uncertainty of Context E interacts with the instability of the state of the art to make the situation one of not just double ignorance, but triple or quadruple ignorance.

E. THREE TYPES OF MIS (IIS)

10. The producer and the consumer inspect part of the total units to ensure acceptable characteristics. When the technology is stable, as in the case of light bulb manufacturing, only a small portion of the total number of units needs to be examined, while in the case of spacecraft manufactures, every element may well be examined several times, raising the total number of inspections quite high.

11. See sections on M-Negative, M-Zero and M-Positive.

F. DECISION CONTEXT

12. Data systems were passed off as management information systems. Since the data were not converted into information, management found them to be virtually useless.

No distinction was made between the data systems in terms of their technological performance characteristics or environment fulfillment characteristics. Therefore, management was offered data on well-established performance and environment (market) characteristics, such as light bulbs, to handle situations with little established performance characteristics and little established market, such as lunar landing.

13. By using the inspection ratio.

14. See Context C—Concurrent Conflicting Context.

G. MIS SEQUENCE

15. See MIS Sequence (1): Raw Data.

16. See Raw Data Processing.

17. See Four Elements of Decision-Making.

18. See Classification of Decision-Making Situations.

CHAPTER 4

A. RAW DATA INPUT

1. (1) *Who*—customers, (2) *what*—product and/or service, (3) *how much*—price, (4) *how many*—quantity, (5) *where*—delivery location, and (6) *when*—delivery time.

2. (1) men, (2) machinery, (3) materials, and (4) money.

3. Profit is the measure of a profit-making organism's performance evaluation, while service is the measure of a nonprofit-making organism's performance evaluation. A number of industry measures of profit are available for comparison of a given profit making organism.

B. APPLICATION 1

4. (1) Immediate use by the organism, (2) future use by the organism, (3) immediate or eventual sale of the patent rights to some other organism, and (4) immediate or eventual licensing of the patent by some other organism.

5. Potential outputs and present outputs are the concern of the entire organism, each part of which specializes in one or more aspects of the activity. In Figure 4.1 the different departments and their primary concentration—present or potential output—are shown; the *illustrative* raw data inputs from the different departments —patents and licenses, sales analysis, product management, marketing and new enterprises—indicate the area of their contribution. Tables 4.5 and 4.6 specify the particular inputs, each of which is important to arrive at the right decision on the disposition of the patents—to be used now or later by the organism itself or by other organisms. Only by knowing how the various departments plan their present and future activity can the value of the patents be assessed properly.

C. APPLICATION 2

6. National data on manufacturing establishments by:
   1. Size of establishments
   2. Type of organization
   3. Manufacturers' inventories
   4. Expenditures for new plant and new equipment
   5. Materials consumed
   6. Water used in manufacturing
   7. Concentration ratios in manufacturing
   8. Rates of change in sales and profits by industry
   9. Profits per dollar by sales by industry
   10. Annual rates of profit on stockholders' equity by industry
   11. Annual rates of profit on stockholders' equity by industry asset size and industry group
   12. Financial statements in ratio form by industry
   13. Financial statements in ratio form by asset size and industry group
   14. Financial statements in dollar amounts by industry
   15. Financial statements in dollar amounts by asset size and industry group
   16. Composition of the sample by total sample by total assets
   17. Shipment data
   18. Production workers, wages
   19. Capital expenditures
   20. Value added by manufacture

7. *Key Plants* provides the address, plant name, and number of employees in each plant to the nearest hundred. I would purchase the deck of cards on the 41,000 plants if the cost of purchase and processing would be significantly less than the sales revenue generated by their use. Unless I find that there are a large number of potential customers for what I have to offer among the 41,000 plants, the data would not be particularly valuable. The price to be paid for either the book or the deck of cards depends upon what the expected returns are.

8. The available national data give the sales data (shipment data) for the industry as a whole which may include 939 companies as in the case of Industry 2515: Mattresses and Bedsprings. To use the average figure for nearly 1,000 units to judge the performance of 1 out of 1,000, the composition of the industry, and the position of the particular firm within the industry have to be examined: Is the firm "above" average or "below"—in terms of sales, is the position tenable?

Again, with reference to the profits data, the overall profitability figures for the industry as a whole have to be tempered with the knowledge of the structure of the industry. The concentration ratios which provide information on the fraction accounted for by the 4, 8, 20, and 50 largest companies manufacturing each of the 1,200 classes of products are helpful in placing the individual firm in the context of the entire industry: Does it belong to the top groups or bottom groups, and where among the top or the bottom groups? The financial data do not disclose such a concentration; therefore, it is much harder to give meaning to the "average" profit figures for the industry as a whole as applied to the particular firm.

D. CIRS

9. The different pieces of data can be used to identify the present and/or potential capabilities of my company with respect to future products or improvement of present products that may be generated by the patent(s). Given the product(s) that will be generated, the tabulation of company strengths in the area of the product can be classified into:

1. Manufacturing capability
2. Sales capability
3. End-user interests (the company itself being a direct consumer)
4. Raw material capability
5. Near-unique facility availability
6. Activity plans into the area of the product(s)

10. Intelligence is insight derived from multidepartmental information which none of the individual pieces of information (data projected in time and/or space) could yield by itself.

11. In general, potential products relate to outputs which are sometimes a mere gleam in someone's eye, while present products are current realities. Therefore, the principal data implication of potential products is the *credibility* of the data.

The credibility is both personal and professional. The personal element of credibility examines the question: Who says so? If the person making the statement has a good track record, of having made ahead statements which were borne out by subsequent events, then he would command more attention than someone who has a poor track record.

The professional aspect of credibility is an index of the professional judgment of the person providing the data on the potential products. Track records may be hard to come by if the potential products are so novel that there are no similar products to compare. The credibility then becomes a matter of logical probabilites: degree of belief in propositions. How well the propositions are chosen, and how the potential products are fitted into the chosen propositions would determine the professional credibility. For instance, if the potential product is a "Cancer Cure," and if the professional estimate of the potential of the product is tied to the similarity of cancer to polio, the logical probability would say something like the following:

The Polio problem was primarily the identification of the virus. The virus inducing polio in the animal was the turning point. From the animal virus to the human vaccine was a direct step.

If the foregoing "logic" of propositions were to be applied to "Cancer Cure,"

The Cancer Problem is sufficiently similar to the Polio Problem. The virus inducing cancer in the animal has just been identified. Therefore, the step to "Cancer Cure" is a direct step.

See Figure 4.1 for the data sources for Present Products and Potential Products. For specific data input characteristics, see Figure 4.2, items 13, and 21 thru 23; Figure 4.3, items 7 and 8.

12. Without quid pro quo, the motivation of the data provider to collect, codify, and communicate data is absent; therefore, if he is forced to comply, probably the barest minimum of data would be provided, the quality of the data being quite suspect.

13. Answer varies.
14. Answer varies.

CHAPTER 5

A. COMPUTER OPERATIONS

1. See Library Analogy to Data Management.
2. Data become *input* when codified data are located in the storage (memory).
3. (1) Input, (2) storage, (3) processing, and (4) output.

B. OPERATING SYSTEM

4. Control programs and processing programs together comprise an operating system.
5. Data management functions:
   1. Assign space on direct access volumes
   2. Maintain a catalogue of data sets
   3. Perform support processing for input-output (I-O) operations, e.g., open, close
   4. Process I-O operations, e.g., I-O supervision, access routines, data set sharing

6. Virtual memory is a combination of hardware and software facilities that gives the user the operational advantage of having a large address space.

C. APPLICATION 3

7. What used to require special programming requires only simple instructions in ADMINS.
8. 1. Categories of information embodied as named lists of codes
   2. Relation norms
   3. Relation norms applied to cases
9. See Use of ADMIN System in Israeli Logistics

D. DATA ANALYSIS

10. The proportionate change in the efficiency and effectiveness of the resulting behavior of the organism indicates the desirable frequency of decisions. Data collection should be governed by the use that can be made of the data in decision-making.
11. Equal weights for all instances of data simplify computations; however, it also means that the GNP for 1874 is given just as much weight as the GNP for 1974 in arriving at the projection for 1975.

Unequal weights for different instances of data require the weighting of the data unequally, i.e., applying differential weights to different parts of the data, which is more difficult than according the same weight to every piece of data.

The choice between the two types of weighting must be based primarily upon the underlying forces that generate the data: if they have changed significantly over the period under study, *unequal* weights are indicated. However, if the underlying forces have remained essentially constant, equal weights can be given to all instances of data under study.

347

12. See page 138 for the three principal classes of filters: (1) fixed-memory, (2) expanding-memory, (3) fading-memory.

13. See χ^2 Criterion for Selection of α

14. Stages of growth are important to data analysis because the same set of figures for sales, for instance, could mean entirely different things to the organism. If the sales of the product refer to the maturation stage, the organism should anticipate an imminent decline in sales in the near future; however, if the sales of the product refer to the rapid growth stage, the organism could well anticipate an increase—and possibly substantial increase in the near future.

15. See Life Cycle Stages of Growth Based on α-Values

16. See Raw Data: Content—Problem Category for three types of problems by content: (1) Solution oriented, (2) Structure oriented, and (3) Structural-solution oriented.

CHAPTER 6

A. CONTEXT E-T, STAGES OF GROWTH

1. Information being projected as data is most sensitive to the identification of the particular stage of growth. For instance, if the product is in fact in the stage of maturation, and the projection is made on the assumption that it is in the rapid growth stage, management would expect a substantial growth and be shocked to find a tapering off of growth. Gearing up production to meet the rapid growth would lead to waste of productive capacity and the buildup of inventory.

Similarly, when maturation is assumed, contrary to the true state of rapid growth, the organism would have geared down to reduce production, when in fact increasing demand would require higher production, leading to loss of sales.

2. Element 315 of the MIS matrix designates a decision-making situation which is one of reduced risk, unstable technology, and maturation stage of growth.

B. COST

3. See Cost as Opportunity Acquired for a discussion of new capability acquired which has no parallel in the past, e.g., missile production being an opportunity acquired compared with airplane production. As the technological uncertainty increases, so does the *dissimilarity* of the new product to the old product, representing new capability *not* of the same kind.

4. Element 3152: reduced risk, unstable technology, maturation stage of growth, and cost of opportunity acquired.

C. EFFECTIVENESS—ABSOLUTE

5. Effectiveness is the ratio of observed performance over desired performance.

6. To arrive at a composite measure of effectiveness, it is necessary to project the *joint* effectiveness of two or more component parts, whose *individual* performances are known as probability distributions. Since the probabilities only refer to *group* behavior in the long run, the actual experience of a single component operating with another or others needs to be observed or established on the basis of simulated experience.

7. Element 11713: uncertain, unstable technology, death stage of growth, cost of opportunity foregone, subsystem performance.

D. EFFECTIVENESS—RELATIVE

8. Sensitivity is:

$$\frac{\text{Proportionate change in system performance}}{\text{Proportionate change in subsystem performance}}$$
or subsystem cost

9. Changes must be measured in terms of system performance characteristics. By how much do the system performance characteristics improve when the *subsystem* performance or subsystem cost is changed?

10. Again, according to system performance characteristics.

11. Element 117132: uncertain, unstable technology, death stage of growth, cost of opportunity foregone, subsystem performance.

E. MIS (IIS) MATRIX

12. There are 1,134 elements in the MIS matrix. As a safeguard against the tendency to equate information with data, 9 Context E-Context T combinations are identified. Each combination can refer to one of the 7 stages of growth of the product (service) in question. The entity in each stage of growth can be broken down into two types of costs as opportunity foregone and as opportunity acquired. To each of the two types of costs can be associated three types of performance. With 18 elements per stage, each stage of growth has (18 × 7 =) 126 elements. With 126 elements in each Context E-Context T combination, there is a total of (126 × 9 =) 1,134 elements in the matrix.

13. Every element in each stage can be assumed to be as important as any other. If each stage is equally important, the 7 stages have each a weight of (100% ÷ 7 =) 14.4%. Similarly, if each element is equally important, the 14.4% is divided into 18 to give 0.8% importance to each element.

In real life, each stage and each element are *different* in importance. Figures 6.1 through 6.6 present the importance of the elements and their combinations, which can be used to compare a particular MIS.

F. MIS UTILIZATION MATRIX

14. Objectives hierarchy, PDM roles, utilization, forecasting, weighting, problem category.

15. There are 81 elements for the three utilization frequencies of organismic and PDM combinations, and 9 such combinations give rise to (81 × 9 =) 729 elements of the MIS utilization matrix.

16. Element 111123 of the MIS (IIS) Utilization Matrix: organismic hierarchy, PDM, infrequent, $3\Delta t$, nonlinear, structural solution-oriented.

17. The MIS utilization matrix for a chemical industry firm would indicate considerably more emphasis upon the rapid growth stage for a number of its products, making the weight of that stage to be much higher than what it is in equally weighted stages. Therefore, the nonlinear projections in the $3\Delta t$ and $6\Delta t$ periods would be more important than the linear projections in the $9\Delta t$ time period.

CHAPTER 7

A. M-ZERO MIS

1. In M-Positive contexts the environment of fulfillment characteristics is uncertain, while in M-Zero contexts it is one of risk. The technological characteristics of performance are unstable in the M-Positive contexts while they are quasistable in M-Zero contexts.

2. Only the form of the probability distribution of performance characteristics is known in M-Zero situations, but not the parameters. Either logic or experience has to be employed to establish similarity of form of performance. It could be pointed out that the system under consideration is a new model of a system already in existence. Or, it could be pointed out that the performance of certain important constituents of the new system is similar to some known constituents of other systems. If the parallel is established by logic, it is important that it be verified by observation.

B. APPLICATION 4

3. The program manager of Weapon System W.

4. The PDM is simultaneously at:

Organismic level with respect to functional supervisors
Strategic level with respect to armed service 1, 2, or 3
Strategic level with respect to specific weapon system group
Tactical level with respect to offensive weapon group
Tactical level with respect to DDR&E
Tactical level with respect to U.S. House Subcommittee on Appropriations

5. In the production of Weapon System W, certain elements may be found to be performing at levels below what they should be: propulsion, guidance, payload, etc. The difficulties would probably be in the application of the principles to the particular system. When such difficulties arise or are anticipated, they have a direct bearing on the manpower requirements, e.g., higher-grade manpower. The uncertainty of the technology thus impinges upon the demand for manpower via the ability of manpower to fulfill the performance characteristics.

6. The PDM needs forecasts of program completion prospects—both the physical completion and projected performance of the weapon system under production. What he is held accountable for is more the *physical* completion of Weapon System W than the potential performance, and therefore, needs an index of physical completion. Insofar as the production is generally done by contractors, the PDM exercises control through his management of the prime contractor. How much of the work remains to be done, and how much of the money remains to be used? An index of time-schedule-cost (TSC) needs to be forecast. Since the prime contractor himself depends on the subcontractors to produce the System W, the PDM would need qualified access to the forecasts of subcontractor index of physical completion; qualified access, because the prime contractor is the one who is to exercise control over the subcontractor.

7. See Raw Data Requirements of Production

C. APPLICATION 5

8. Military production is for nonuse, while nonmilitary production is for use.

9. The two different objectives hierarchies are the political and economic. A market estimated at above $4 billion for the medium-size subsonic plane of the Boeing 727 type in which the General Electric engine could be installed after adaptation underscores the economic importance of the GE-SNECMA Project. Even more important is the political consideration, or the capability of the French to enhance their technological capabilities.

10. For M-Zero situations, the environment has to be one of risk, and the technology has to be quasistable. While technological cooperation between the U.S. and France to undertake the commercial development of a technology which grew from military R&D is new, the cooperation between a number of subcontractor companies in the production of a large system is by no means new; to the extent that prior applicable experience is available, the context is one of risk. The technology of the core element is also known insofar as it was developed for the B-1 Bomber and proved operational. It has to be applied to civilian needs, and that is not yet established, making the technology quasistable.

11. See Requirements of Forecasts for Decision-Making

12. See Raw Data Requirements of Development

CHAPTER 8

A. M-NEGATIVE MIS

1. In M-Zero contexts the environment of fulfillment characteristics is one of risk, while in M-Negative contexts it is one of reduced risk. The technological characteristics of performance are quasistable in M-Zero contexts, while they are stable in M-Negative contexts.

2. The parameters of the probability distribution of performance characteristics.

B. APPLICATION 6

3. Health is individual, therefore, an individual-oriented health index is necessary.

4. Hospital confinement indicates impairment of physical health, therefore, the individual health index should indicate the status of impairment of health on entry into the hospital, the status of improvement of health on leaving the hospital, and how long it took to improve.

5. Delivery of health care falls under the category of queuing situations in which units arrive for service, wait, are served, and discharged. To the extent that the fulfillment characteristics of queues are known, to that extent, the form and the parameters of the probability distributions describing the queues are known from similar situations. In fact, hospital queues themselves are known to some extent, so that for a given hospital operation, applicable form and parameters of probability distribution are available.

Not only is the environment one of reduced risk, but also the technology is stable. The number of inspections required is much less than 100% in the case of diagnostic equipment, such as radiology facilities. However, in some other areas, the inspection may have to be greater, e.g., the diagnosis by an intern may sometimes have to be checked by a more experienced diagnostician. However, when we take into account the inspection of all facilities, i.e., diagnostic and prescriptive facilities, the inspection ratio will be well below 100%.

6. See Requirements of Forecasts for Decision Making

7. See Raw Data Requirements (of Hospital Care Delivery MIS [IIS])

C. APPLICATION 7

8. The capability of the durable products to satisfy the demand for them are not only known, but they can also be specified in terms of probability distributions whose form and parameters are known. The context is one of reduced risk. As seen from chapter 6, the demand for products goes through different stages of life cycle. While the stage indicates what happens to the total number of units of product demanded, each product fulfills the demand in one or more specific segments of market demand, which can be studied to anticipate customer demand in different market segments.

The durable products themselves have been manufactured for sufficient length of time to specify the performance characteristics of the products within a very small range: the technology is stable.

9. At this rate, what is the expected index of fulfillment of the want-values by the product(s)? The question needs to be answered: (1) in the aggregate (relating to *all* the products) or (2) on an individual product-by-product basis; (3) the market segments of the major products; and (4) the market segments of a single product.

10. See Raw Data Requirements (of Product Sales MIS [IIS])

CHAPTER 9

A. TYPES OF MIS (IIS)

1. MIS should reflect both the context of *demand* for the products and services of an organism, and the context of *supply* of resources to meet the demand. The former is the Context E (environmental status of fulfillment characteristics), and the latter is the Context T (technical performance characteristics of products and/or services).

All decision-making situations can be divided into three types on the basis of these two characteristics. When the technology is stable, as in the case of light bulb manufacture, the number of units inspected to the total number produced would be a small ratio: 100 in 10,000 bulbs. However, in the manufacture of a spacecraft for the first time, not only the whole unit, but also every major component has to be examined several times over, raising the inspection well beyond 1 in 100, beyond 1 in 1, or 1 or 100%, to quite possibly 3, 30, or 40 (= 4,000%).

Turning to the performance characteristics that a customer would specify that the product and/or service should fulfill, in the case of the spacecraft manufactured for the first time, the customer has no prior experience to go by and is therefore uncertain. Not quite knowing what he is looking for, the customer is likely to perform inspections of his own of the new product. The combination of *uncertain* environment of decision-making and *unstable* technology of performance characteristics requires the ratio of total number of inspections to the total number of units produced, i.e., inspection ratio, to be high. If the ratio is expressed as 10^M, M will be greater than 0, say, 1 or 2 or more, in the combination of uncertain and unstable decision-making situations, which we designate as *M-Positive.*

When the technology is stable, it is likely that the customer knows what to expect, as in the case of light bulbs. He can specify the fulfillment characteristics of the light bulbs better than he can those of the very first spacecraft. The total number of inspections by the producer and the customer together will be a fraction less than 1: making the M in 10^M negative—*M-Negative.* In between is *M-Zero.*

2. The demand factors are embodied in the fulfillment characteristics of the environment: uncertain, risk, and reduced risk. The supply factors are embodied in the performance characteristics of the technology: unstable, quasistable, stable. The M-Positive category applies clearly to an uncertain and unstable combination; the M-Zero category applies to a risk and quasistable combination; and the M-Negative category applies to a reduced risk and stable combination, as developed in answer to (1). By extending the reasoning, M-Positive applies to all situations in which the technology is unstable, i.e., uncertain and unstable, risk and unstable, and reduced risk and unstable. M-Zero applies to all situations in which the technology is quasistable, and M-Negative applies to all situations in which the technology is stable.

B. EMPLOYMENT QUESTION

3. The two technological spectaculars of recent times are Manhattan Project and Project Apollo. Time was of the essence in both. Survival—physical in the first instance, and technological (competitive contest) in the second instance—was at stake. With survival at stake, the public sector can be persuaded to provide resources. However, once the survival issue itself is met, the impetus to carry on the technological spectacular disappears—having succeeded with the atomic bomb, there was little impetus to proceed at the same speed with the next bomb; having succeeded with the lunar landing, there was little impetus to proceed at the same speed with the next space spectacular. The implication for employment of highly skilled and trained personnel is that demand deficiency will follow in the public sector for their services just as soon as the survival issue has been settled: what goes up, comes down.

4. The survival imperative of the assault on the atom and on space made the *joint effort* on the part of the public and private sectors the most natural development. The research that the private sector undertook at the behest of the public sector, under contract, would offer the private sector the advantages of early application and early modification of the results of research sponsored by the public sector.

In both instances of the assault on the atom and on space, the public sector demand was strictly for *service*—the product whether it be the atomic bomb, or the spacecraft being *not* for direct consumption but instead for *indirect* performance of a valuable service, i.e., that of survival. The research, spawned by the technological spectaculars, has to be maintained by the private sector if it wants to reap the dual benefits of early application and early modification. If it does not keep up the momentum, the initial effort will have been wasted.

In the context of unstable technology, as in the case of the two technological spectaculars, the profit motive has to satisfy itself that the *indirect* performance of a valuable service can in fact be turned into an advantage in generating a product and/or service for *direct* consumption.

C. APPLICATION 8

5. Unemployment compensation is an interim relief to a long-term problem. The real focus of the research on unemployment compensation is, therefore, not really underployment, but employment.

6. Uncertainty of the decision-making with respect to the unemployment compensation system stems from the lack of applicable experience in some or all of the probabilities of reemployment, such as (1) probability of public sector initiation of programs that can absorb the supply of developed skills, (2) probability of private sector initiation of programs in which the developed skills can be absorbed, (3) probability of the timely transition from the public to the private sector, etc.

Instability of technology with respect to the unemployment compensation system stems from the lack of applicable experience in performance characteristics: (1) skills factor, (2) time factor, and (3) reemployment.

7. The forecasts for the PDM in the Department of Labor should provide the answer to the question: At this rate, what is the expected probability of 96% employment, and to the extent that the expected value falls short of 96%, what is the expected probability of success of corrective measures?

Unemployment compensation is a small part of the large question of 96% employment; it focuses attention upon the 4% or more *unemployed*. The MIS (IIS) should forecast: At this rate, what is the expected ratio of actual to available unemployment insurance, i.e., the ratio of the actual number of man-weeks of unemployment insurance to the total man-weeks of unemployment insurance available?

8. See Raw Data Deficiencies of Unemployment Compensation MIS (IIS)

9. Employment, not unemployment, is the focus of attention of the PDM. In particular, the MIS should facilitate the determination and the forecast of the impact of future technological changes upon the present profile of employment.

D. APPLICATION 9

10. A need is an imperative requirement which, if not met, will significantly impair the functioning of the organism; a want is a requirement which is *not* imperative. Peter Drucker has said that the most beautifully designed machine is still only so much scrap metal until it has utility for a customer. Utility is potential satisfaction; and the potentiality of satisfaction is an assessment made by the customer *before* he irrevocably commits resources, such as putting 15¢ in a coffee machine. Whether or not that cup of coffee is imperative for the functioning of the organism raises the question of "necessary" and "unnecessary", which, in turn, clearly implies a value system.

Applying the notion to transportation, if both public and private transportation are available, and if the private means is preferred over the public, it would be for reasons beyond those of the basic necessity of getting from one place to another. The private sector does have to depend on the creation of a *want-value*, i.e., more than the basic minimum need for transportation, in the form of the newness of the car, the noise it makes on acceleration, the weight of chromium on the bumpers, etc., to earn its dollar.

11. See Uncertainty of Environment, and Instability of Technology

12. The forecast that the MIS should provide to the organism in uncertain context with unstable technology can be expressed as a combination of all the three ratios: At this rate, what is the expressed value of: availability × novelty × adaptability?

13.   *Private Sector*   *Public Sector*

1. Raw data on availability   1. Expected value of actual unemployment compensation

2. Raw data on novelty   2. Available unemployment compensation

3. Raw data on adaptability   3. Transition probability of employment

CHAPTER 10

A. MIS (IIS) UTILIZATION

1. As a line manager, the MIS manager would be competing for resources of the organism with other line managers. However, MIS is supposed to provide the PDM with forecasts from the point of view of not an individual department, division, or group of divisions, but from the point of view of the organism *as a whole*. To do so, the MIS manager must be free of competition for the resources of the organism with the line manager.

2. By involving the PDM in the setting up of MIS, what are the questions for which the PDM needs answers? Identify two or three "before" and "after" key performance situations which specify changes in decision-making that will be brought about as a result of the MIS. Further, establish the IIS activity as a staff activity, which the PDM himself is instrumental in creating. The PDM should set apart a specific minimum period for receipt and review of MIS contributions to the PDM decision-making process.

B. MIS (IIS) INPUTS

3. The basic antagonism stems from the fact that MIS will bring about *changes*. If the MIS is worth its salt, it will show changes that would be advantageous to the organism as a whole, changes which were not apparent before instituting the MIS. Further, the changes would be not from the point of view of a particular activity, but from the point of view of the organism as a whole. The holistic viewpoint and the changes in the life-style of the line departments brought about by the MIS set it on a collision course with the line departments.

4. With a quid pro quo, the line managers are assured that they are getting something in return for what they contribute in the form of data. Further, the line managers would appreciate the necessity to feed the MIS the right inputs, because poor inputs would mean poor outputs for the line managers. In specifying the quid pro quo, the line manager becomes a user of MIS, and that provides for good working relationships between the recommender of changes (MIS) and the implementor of changes (the line departments).

C. MIS (IIS) PROCESSING

5. Input formatting and modeling.
6. See Establish an Initial Operational Code

CHAPTER 11

A. FUNCTIONAL CRITERIA

1. The 729 categories of utilization of MIS by the PDM were developed in chapter 6; 81 elements are identified for the three utilization frequencies of organismic and PDM combination, and 9 such combinations give rise to $(81 \times 9 =)$ 729 elements of MIS utilization matrix. The potential profile of MIS utilization would serve to identify a number of candidates for structure-oriented, solution-oriented, and structural solution-oriented types of problems for the organism, depending upon which the degree of sophistication that may be required of the computer operations varies. The sophistication of the analytical efforts depends upon the validity of the data for the analysis to be useful; where proprietary data are concerned, the empirical aspects of MIS should include considerations of secure storage, rapid retrieval, accurate processing, ready results, and secure return to storage. How the computer operations should be performed would be governed by the forecasting time period to which the forecasts apply: the short term, the intermediate term, and the long term.

2. See pages 000 through 000.

B. CUSTOMIZING CRITERIA

3. Answer varies.
4. The MIS Manager, as pointed out in chapter 10, should be a staff manager. The computer system should serve the organism as a whole, including MIS. Therefore, it would be unwise to make the MIS manager, who is himself a user of computer services, also the computer services manager. Instead, computer systems services should be a staff support function, a part of management services to support management and managers.
5. Three types of functions: (1) technical, (2) services, and (3) professional. See Internal Education.
6. See Concrete Contract.

Further Reading

MANAGEMENT CONCEPTS

Anthony, Robert N. *Management Control in Nonprofit Organizations.* Homewood, Ill.: Irwin, 1975.

Box, George E. P., and Jenkins, Gwilym M. *Time-Series Analysis: Forecasting and Control.* San Francisco: Holden-Day, 1976.

Campbell, Bonika J. *Understanding Information Systems: Foundations for Control.* Englewood Cliffs, N.J.: Winthrop, 1977.

Coleman, Raymond J., and Riley, M. J., eds. *MIS: Management Dimensions.* San Francisco: Holden-Day, 1973.

Davis, Gordon B. *Management Information Systems: Conceptual Foundations, Structure, and Development.* New York: McGraw-Hill, 1974.

Dermer, Jerry. *Management Planning and Control Systems: Advanced Concepts and Cases.* Homewood, Ill.: Irwin, 1977.

Greenberger, Fred. *Information Systems for Management.* Englewood Cliffs, N.J.: Prentice-Hall, 1972.

Harris, Roy D.; Maggard, Michael J.; and Lasso, William G. *Computer Models in Operations Research.* New York: Harper & Row, 1974.

Kanter, Jerome. *Management-Oriented Information Systems.* Englewood Cliffs, N.J.: Prentice-Hall, 1977.

Kirk, Frank G. *Total System Development for Information Systems.* New York: John Wiley, 1973.

Maciariello, Joseph A. *Program Management Control Methods.* New York: John Wiley, 1978.

Morton, Michael S. *Management Decision Systems: Computer-Based Support for Decision-Making.* Cambridge: Harvard University Press, 1971.

Murdick, Robert G. *Information Systems for Modern Management.* Englewood Cliffs, N.J.: Prentice-Hall, 1975.

Prince, Thomas R. *Information Systems for Management Planning and Control.* Homewood, Ill.: Irwin, 1975.

Radford, K. J. *Information Systems for Strategic Decisions.* Reston, Va.: Reston Publishing Co., 1978.

Roberts, Edward B., ed. *Managerial Application of System Dynamics.* Cambridge, Mass.: MIT Press, 1978.

DESIGN AND IMPLEMENTATION

Amey, G. K. et al. *Information Systems and Networks: Design and Planning Guidelines of Informatics for Managers, Decision-Makers and Systems Analysts.* New York: Elsevier, 1977.

Boulder, James P. *Computer Assisted Planning Systems: Management, Concept, Application and Implementation.* New York: McGraw-Hill, 1975.

Gildersleeve, Thomas R. *Data Processing Project Management.* New York: VanNostrand, 1974.

———. *Organizing and Documenting Data Processing Information.* Rochelle Park, N.J.: Hayden, 1977.

Herner, Saul, and Vellucci, Matthew J., eds. *Selected Federal Computer-Based Information Systems.* Washington, D.C.: Information Resources, 1972.

Lucas, Henry G., Jr. *The Analysis Design and Implementation of Information Systems.* New York: McGraw-Hill, 1976.

———. *Management of Information Systems.* New York: McGraw-Hill, 1978.

McLean, Ephraim R., and Soden, John V. *Strategic Planning for MIS.* New York: John Wiley, 1977.

Matthews, Don Q. *Design of Management Information Systems.* New York: Petrocelli, 1976.

Murdick, Robert G., and Ross, Joel E. *Information Systems for Modern Management.* Englewood Cliffs, N.J.: Prentice-Hall, 1976.

Putnam, Arnold O., and Barlow, Robert E. *Unified Operations Management: A Practical Approach to Management Information Systems.* Boston: Herman Publishing, 1977.

Sollenberger, Harold M. *Major Changes Caused by the Implementation of a Management Information System.* New York: National Association of Accountants.

Thierauf, Robert J. *Systems Analysis and Design of Real-Time Management Information Systems.* Englewood Cliffs, N.J.: Prentice-Hall, 1975.

DATA BASE MANAGEMENT

Date, C. J. *An Introduction to Database Systems.* Reading, Mass: Addison-Wesley, 1977.

Dolotta, T. A. et al. *Data Processing in 1980-85: A Study of Potential Limitations to Progress.* New York: John Wiley, 1976.

Katzan, Harry. *Computer Data Management and Data Base Technology.* New York: VanNostrand, 1975.

Lyon, John K. *The Database Administrator*. New York: John Wiley, 1976.

Martin, James. *Computer Data Base Organization*. Englewood Cliffs, N.J.: Prentice-Hall, 1975.

―――. *Principles of Data Base Management*. Englewood Cliffs, N.J.: Prentice-Hall, 1976.

Meadow, Charles T. *Applied Data Management*. New York: John Wiley, 1976.

SHARE 2nd Working Conference on Data Base Management Systems. Montreal, Quebec, *Proceedings*. Amsterdam, 1977.

Sundgren, Bo. *An Informal Approach to Data Bases*. Stockholm, 1973.

Tsichritzis, Dionysios C. *Data Base Management Systems*. New York: Academic Press, 1977.

Walton, Thomas F. *Communications and Data Management*. New York: John Wiley, 1976.

Wiederhold, Gio. *Data Base Design*. New York: McGraw-Hill, 1977.

COMPUTER NETWORKS

Blanc, Robert P., and Cotton, Ira W., eds. *Computer Networking*. New York: IEEE Press, 1976.

Chu, Wesley W. *Advances in Computer Communications*. Delham, Mass: Artech House, 1976.

European *Computing Conference on Communications Networks*. London, 1975.

Katzan, Harry. *Computer Organization and the System/370*. New York: VanNostrand, 1971.

NATO Advanced Study Institute on *Computer Communication Networks*. Sussex, England, 1973.

U.S. GOVERNMENT REFERENCES

OMB Circular A–71, *Computer Resource Management*.

DODD 4100.39 (31 March 72), *Selection and Acquisition of ADP Resources*.

DODI 4105.65 (29 June 70), *Acquisition of ADP Computer Program and Related Resources*.

DODI 4120.17 (29 Dec 72), *DOD Automated Data System Documentation Standards*.

DODI 4140.20 (18 Jun 73), *ADP Management Information System*.

DODD 5000.19 (12 Mar 76), *Policies for the Management and Control of Information Requirements*.

DODI 5000.19L (30 June 75), *OSD Listing of Recurring Information Requirements*.

DODI 5000.20 (7 Sept 73), *Management and Dissemination of Statistical Information*.

DODD 5000.29 (26 Apr 76), *Management of Computer Resources in Major Defense Systems*.

DODD 5100.40 (19 Aug 75), *Administration of DOD ADP Program*.

DODI 5100.45 (28 July 64), *Centers for Analysis of Scientific and Technical Information*.

DODD 5200.28 (18 Dec 72), *Security Requirements for ADP Systems*.

Army Regulation 18–3 (10 Nov 71), *ADP Management Information System*.

Marine Corps Pamphlet 4000.21A (12 Dec 74), *Data Acquisition Program Manual*.

Air Force Regulation 178–7 (29 Nov 76), *Management and Control Information Systems*.

Air Force Regulation 300–1 (15 Nov 74), *ADP Program Management*.

Air Force Regulation 800–14–1 (12 Sept 75), *Management of Computer Resources in Systems*.

Air Force Regulation 800–14–2 (26 Sept 75), *Acquisition and Support Procedures for Computer Resources in Systems*.

Military Standard S–52779, *Software QA Program Requirements*.

ENCYCLOPEDIAS

Computer User's Yearbook 1976. New York: International Publications Service, 1976.

Heyl, Carl, ed. *Automatic Data Processing Handbook*. New York: The Diebold Group, 1977.

Hoyt, Douglas B., ed. *Computer Handbook for Senior Management*. New York: Macmillan, 1977.

Ralston, Anthony, and Meek, Chester L., eds. *Encyclopedia of Computer Science*. New York: VanNostrand, 1976.

Sippl, Charles J. *Microcomputer Dictionary and Guide*. Forest Grove, Oreg.: International Scholastic Book Service, 1976.

———. *Data Communications Directory*. New York: VanNostrand, 1976.

McFarlan, F. Warren, and Nolan, Richard L., eds. *The Information Systems Handbook*. Homewood, Ill.: Dow Jones–Irwin, 1975.

Index